THE QUES
EXECUTIVE EFF

"This volume provides a superb integration of human emotion and motivation with a comprehensive analysis of the structure and functions of complex organizations. By following Dr. O'Roark's unique *invitational leadership approach* and model for charismatic leadership, the effectiveness of executives and managers in business, industry, and government organizations will be greatly enhanced."

Charles D. Spielberger, Ph.D., ABPP, Distinguished Research Professor; Director, Center for Research in Behavioral Medicine and Health Psychology, University of South Florida

"Ann O'Roark has distilled more than 40 years of teaching, counseling, and consulting to executives into an easily read book that aspiring executives—and even those who have made it—will find interesting and helpful. No slogans, no easy answers, but useful wisdom among lively examples from real life."

Harry Levinson, Ph.D., Founder: The Levinson Institute & Harvard Professor Emeritus

"How much would you pay for one day of consulting time with a seasoned psychologist-consultant? Here, for less than the cost of a modest lunch, Ann O'Roark's *The Quest for Executive Effectiveness* summarizes over 30 years of her experience consulting to organizations and managers. Her thoughtful examination of business needs and personal characteristics—including the rarely studied managerial psychology of curiosity, anger and anxiety—provides much food for thought for executives and psychologists alike. Skip lunch; buy the book; then read it and practice its sage advice."

Rodney L. Lowman, Ph.D., Systemwide Dean, College of Organizational Studies, Alliant University — CSPP

"Most comprehensive and scholarly, yet eminently readable. Any student of leadership—from beginner to the seasoned CEO—will find this book to be invaluable. I am impressed with [Dr. O'Roark's] insistence that organizational change starts on a very personal level— with self-motivation. An excellent contribution to the field."

Betty L. Siegel, President, Kennesaw State University, University System of Georgia

"With considerable experience earlier in public service and later in assessment, training, and counseling of business executives, Ann O'Roark provides a model of executive excellence with pithy illustrations and evidence. She lays out the leader's need to be both transformational and transactional in providing vision, direction and organization, to be emulated and trusted, and to use 'invitational power' to bring about honest and realistic participation. It is a fresh and refreshing point of view."

Bernard M. Bass, Ph.D., Co-Director of the Center for
Leadership Studies, Distinguished Professor Emeritus of
Management, State University of New York at Binghamton

". . . a unique way of communicat[ing] sophisticated concepts in an understandable manner for everyone to grasp and apply."

Willa Hertwig, Northwest Florida Realtor & Developer

"It is such a gem . . . it will contribute in my Leadership Course and in our other courses here in De La Salle University."

Nativada Dayan, Ph.D., The Philippines, Private Practice
Psychologist, Gov. Advisor and Court Expert Witness

". . . it is excellent, a very valuable teaching document. . . . some of your anecdotes are just so spot-on."

Francis Macnab, Ph.D., Australia, Director of Counseling &
Consulting Center, Church and Government Leader

"In *The Quest for Executive Effectiveness,* Dr. Ann O'Roark offers a comprehensive model of management and delineates a process by which executives can develop and hone their skills so as to become more capable leaders. This text, which provides relevant and useful suggestions for anyone who has to coordinate the efforts of a group, is a valuable resource for enabling one to be a more capable administrator.

". . . Ann M. O'Roark, . . . using psychological principles as a guide, composes a mix of theoretical and academic disciplines to produce an outstanding resource for anyone who aspires to positions of command in the workplace. O'Roark's text provides insights into workforce psychology and executive practices in order to aid those who are in and who plan to be in positions of leadership to fine tune their strengths and to become aware of their weaknesses."

Florence L. Denmark, Ph.D., Robert Scott Pace
Distinguished Professor and Chair, Psychology Department,
Pace University, New York City

THE QUEST
FOR
EXECUTIVE
EFFECTIVENESS

Turning Vision Inside-Out
Charismatic-Participatory Leadership

ANN M. O'ROARK PH.D.

Symposium

Published by Symposium Publishing
an imprint of Blue Dolphin Publishing, Inc.

For inquiries or orders, address
Blue Dolphin Publishing, Inc.
P.O. Box 8, Nevada City, CA 95959
Orders: 1-800-643-0765
Web: www.bluedolphinpublishing.com

ISBN: 1-57733-058-7

Library of Congress Cataloging-in-Publication Data

O'Roark, Ann M.
    The quest for executive effectiveness : turning vision inside-out
    charismatic-participatory leadership / Ann M. O'Roark.
        p. cm.
    Includes bibliographical references and index.
    ISBN 1-57733-058-7
        1. Executive ability. 2. Leadership. 3. Management. I. Title.

HD38.2.O76 2000
658.4'092–dc21   00-039756

Cover layout: Jeff Case

Printed in the United States of America

10   9   8   7   6   5   4   3   2

Table of Contents

EXECUQUEST

Preface

"Rich man, poor man, beggar man, thief. Doctor, lawyer, *executive* chief." What was your childhood dream? What did you want be when you grew up? You probably did not shift your gaze to the distant horizon and say, "I want to be the chief executive officer of NBC or IBM or, maybe, AT&T." Dreams of far-reaching achievement more frequently spring into young-adult minds. This is the time when we stand eager for a challenging quest. We feel like adventurers and explorers searching for a fountain of youth, a lost ark, a holy grail.

And, later, more mature and experienced, we realize that, like fountains, arks, and grails, executive success remains elusive and mysterious. Like the seeker of the rainbow's end and the legendary pot of gold, the seeker of a lofty corner office is spurred onward by reports of astronomical executive salaries and payouts, even to the non-performing CEOs. The story of Apple computer's $6.7 million severance to Gilbert F. Amelio, on top of $2 million salary and bonus, sweetens the allure of a management-career from junior high school on through graduate school.

An executive gambit is as tempting as a lottery ticket, especially as the prize builds to hundreds of millions of dollars. As with a lottery ticket, the odds are against winning first place. Dozens win smaller prizes, becoming senior executives and CEOs of companies that are less affluent than the multiple-merged giants. Fortunately, many who dream of becoming head of a business or service enterprise are compelled by motives that lie deeper than a desire for bigger paychecks. In fact, most of the management-career people whom I have met across forty years were there because they wanted to *make a difference* in the corporate success.

Margaret Wheatley, a best-management-book-of-the-year author, and Warren Bennis, long-time promoter of productive-potentials in work groups, began their recent books stating their concerns about present corporate life. As in earlier writings, their indefatigable optimism prevails. In *Why Leaders Can't Lead*, Bennis soon admits, ". . . I do think change is possible—even change for the better. . . ."

Wheatley, in *Leadership and the New Science*, writes, "I am not alone in wondering why organizations aren't working well . . . why does change, which we're all supposed to be 'managing,' keep drowning us, relentlessly reducing any sense of mastery we might possess?" In answer to her own question, she concludes that we are over-managing and under-trusting.

Executive effectiveness and leadership success appear at times to be phantoms-of-the-theater of organizational life. As Shakespeare would warn, kingly pretenders strut about on corporate stages giving brief executive performances, paying dearly for fleeting moments of glory.

Historians, the playwrights of real-time drama, tend to portray non-survivors as authority figures who stood rigidly in place, like Custer at the Little Big Horn, and like zealot Jim Jones with his self-serving, self-destructive encampment. Both the general and the minister exhibited unusual initiative and effort to realize their particular vision, just like leaders who survive crisis episodes. Even admired, tenured executives are found to be full of paradox and contradiction. Sometimes the flaws directly relate to their adaptive flexibility strength. Win, lose, or draw, executives move others beyond seemingly insurmountable barriers toward an image of achievement.

Many phantoms of the executive suite are unmasked in this book. You are invited to look each phantom in the eye and see what part of yourself might be reflected there. Warren Bennis, popular expert on executive leadership, described struggles he faced during his own executive experience in order to point us in the direction of success. After confronting the hazards of rapid change, he observes that the most important change "begins slowly . . . as, one by one, individuals make the conscious choice to live up to their potential." He firmly asserts that the cornerstone of executive effectiveness is, always, a matter of trust. This book centers us on taking time to build that trust in oneself, in and among co-workers, and as a corporate asset.

Part One of *The Quest for Executive Effectiveness* is about priorities. First priority is a look within the self that produces the executive vision. Next is attention to beliefs about others who give the vision its life and form. The executive's beliefs about the work itself and an ability to establish workplace values wrap up this picture of putting things in order for beginning the execuquest. *Part Two* is about what happens along the way toward achieving the vision. It is a close look at the dynamics of curiosity, anxiety, and anger. These emotional resources shift the weight of surprise toward constructive change. *Part Three* recognizes organizations as fields-of-potentials for leadership impact—positive *and* negative. Executive power is manifested through expectations, controls, attitudes, and productivity drive. Authoritative power can foster or inhibit individual and collective achievement. We foster productivity as we become quick to realize *what's important.* With clear and compelling visions, we who chose to be executives are able to seize-the-moment. We can work wholeheartedly, effectively, and successfully at being an *executive.*

Webster's New World Dictionary, 2nd Ed.

Middle English and Latin > executus

As a noun, executive means:

1. **a person, group of people, or branch of government empowered and required to administer the laws and affairs of a nation.**
2. **any person whose function is to administer or manage affairs, as of a corporation, school, etc.**

As an adjective, executive means:

1. **of, capable of, or concerned with, carrying out duties, functions, etc. or managing affairs, as in a business organization.**
2. **empowered and required to administer (laws, government affairs, etc.,); administrative; distinguished from legislative, judicial.**
3. **of administrative or managerial personnel or functions.**

The *executive* word comes from two Latin words—ex + sequi—which literally mean *to follow-up, to pursue.* It refers to a person who gets something done or produced. In addition, there are legal connotations as associated with the obligation to carry out the provisions of a last will and testament. Other legal responsibilities include the assignment to put someone to death in accord with a legally imposed sentence. Other times, the legal assignment is less violent and merely requires one to complete or make valid a deed or contract by signing. A vocational twist on applications of the term "to execute" is found in artistic connotations, where the use of the word refers to playing a musical instrument, performing a role in a play, or completing a complex dance movement.

An executive, or senior manager, is someone who is hired-and-paid to be a leader. In *Learning to Lead,* Jay Congers reviews ways to transform managers into leaders that were popular during the 1980s and 1990s. He writes, "I brainstormed about vision statements with the most imaginative of participants; I leapt from ropes in trees with the most courageous; . . . and I learned the new models of leadership with the most curious. . . ." He found no one program that provided a complete definition or perfect guide to what is required to be an executive.

I work with one of the programs that Conger describes in detail—the Leadership Development Program (LDP). This five-day course, initially designed by the Center for Creative Leadership, Greensboro, NC, has been franchised and up-and-running in Florida since the early 1980s. I was on the start-up faculty team and and also served as staff psychologist. I continue to provide feedback consultation to course participants about their results from a battery of psychological tests and multi-rater evaluation surveys.

My many faceted career introduced me to both experiential and cognitive development programs (journalism, education, parenting, business office management, therapist, organizational consultant) and includes fifteen years of conducting executive effectiveness courses sponsored by the American Management Association, certification as a human-relations laboratory-trainer, as well as first-hand experience working in the executive suite as the Assistant State Treasurer and as a Deputy Secretary on the Governor's cabinet in the Commonwealth of Kentucky.

Over the years, clients, course participants and employees asked me to put together a summary that covered the topics included in my courses and management philosophy. This book combines those messages. My thinking is drawn from three streams of knowledge. Part One is grounded in perceptual psychology. Part Two comes from personality theory and behavioral medicine. Part Three builds on organizational psychology, referencing both psychodynamic and system concepts. The section titles map the territory to be covered.

Part One.

eXecuquest   Quest Priorities: Putting Things In Order

Every Success Has a Beginning; The Truth Begins With Two; Enterprise and Investment; The Critical Core. Like the knights in heroic myths of old, executive strength lies in personal integrity and attributes. What's the condition within the executive who is responsible for the visioning, the setting in motion and the achieving? The business of turning an individual vision into a collective success takes shape over time and through trust. Due diligence begins with checking first things first. The basic equipment is the self.

Part Two

eXecuquest

Zest and Vitality from *Curiosity, Anxiety, and Anger.*

Curiosity: A Taste For Adventure; Anxiety: The Executive Challenger; Anger: The Hero Emotion; The Vital Signs of Wholeheartedness. Motivational astuteness is critical in executive quests. Trust recurs at the center of the critical path. For risk-taking adventurers in the era of armored knights, confrontations with unfamiliar dragons and unfriendly cultures tested how well questors had tempered their innermost nature. Today, demonstrated valor and accurate perception continues to engender trust. Trust is a filter point through which surprise encounters must travel. The executive's application of emotional wisdom and vigor heralds productive change.

Part Three.

eXecuquest

Charismatic-Participatory Leadership

Great Expectations; Who's The Boss? Pathfinders and Mapmakers; Making A Difference. Here are deeper looks at the effects of power in an organization. Knights carried their shields and lances, and an executive carries the trappings of the leadership role. The argument here is that the contemporary venturer, a corporate executive, is most successful with invitational power. Autocratic and coercive approaches to organizational productivity may reap immediate gains, but executives who take the long view learn that lasting success is earned through a disciplined process of trust building.

Background Reading

Three popular writers who address both the hazards and the joys of executive work approach the issues from different directions. Appealing to the need to ventilate about the road blocks and turmoils associated with leadership positions, Warren Bennis provides two useful case-books, one, *The Unconscious Conspiracy: Why Leaders Can't Lead* (1976), New York:

AMACOM; and a sequel, *Why Leaders Can't Lead: The Conspiracy Continues* (1991).

Margaret Wheatley's 1992 book, *Leadership and the New Science: Learning About Organization from an Orderly Universe,* San Francisco: Berrett-Koehler Publishers, moves quickly from a pessimistic recollection of wasteful over-management to an optimistic plunge into new ways to work in open systems.

Jay Congers takes the here and now intermediary path. His 1992 book, *Learning to Lead,* San Francisco: Jossey Bass, is written in an optimistic tone and takes a practical, systematic approach to identifying what can be done to do better work in the businesses as they exist in most places in these times.

Acknowledgments

The writing of *The Quest for Executive Effectiveness* leaves me both humble and grateful. The fast-change world of free enterprise organizations is mind-spinning, as slight shifts in economies and markets confuse and reignite issues as quickly as a Turkish earthquake. To write about this volatile human domain is humbling. I am increasingly grateful for the stabilizing reassurance of accumulated knowledge—with its solid ground of recurring messages. I chose to work as a consultant in the fast-lane realms, but could not have made contributions to the well-being of the individuals or the organizations without the assurance that the academic scholars were, slowly and steadily, refining our wisdom about how things can work together for productive, healthy consequences. My appreciation goes to many colleagues, mentors, friends, relatives and titans-in-psychological-history who enabled me to envision and complete this undertaking.

Formal acknowledgment to those who have been quoted and whose theories are discussed is given in the Background Readings, References, and Index. These instructive predecessors represent a small portion of those gifted teachers and associates who educated me, inspired me, stimulated my curiosity, and provided the scientific and conceptual foundations for all that is written here. I consider this reference group to be my professional heroes.

Those who became personal heroes are the educators, colleagues and family members who encouraged me to never give up this quest. They helped me sort out, then spell out the ideas that were *most important* in my mind and heart. Moreover, they contributed their own talent and spark to the shaping of this handbook for executive coaching.

I thank you for steeling my courage and reviving my determination through periods of personal loss and discouragement. Without you, I would not have persevered to complete the *execuquest* message.

xiii

Particular contributions to the substantive thoughts were offered by my doctoral chairman *Arthur Combs* and were offered through professional associations—especially the Society of Psychologists in Management and APA's Division of Consulting Psychology—by the sage and incisive *Harry Levinson.* There is no way to overstate the importance of the instruction, wordsmithing and opportunities/challenges offered by neighbor-colleague *Charles Spielberger.* Legal, ethical, and impeccable executive thinking were role-modeled by someone who is both a Professional and a Personal Hero, *Dulaney O'Roark, Jr.* From the table of contents onward, his essay-writer's eye helped me say things in "plain vanilla" and to be alert to possible "falling fire."

Information about the necessary practical parts of publishing proved as challenging as the thinking, composing, and editing work. Thanks to *Robert Wesner, Lawrence Erlbaum, Frances and Clifton Dowell* for taking time to advise and steer me in doing the packaging and marketing work required to get a book out the front door.

Friendly Editing with an experienced readers'-eye made a difference in how I proofread. I thank *Jean Reed* and *Cathy Brown.*

Professional Editing by *Paul Clemens,* Blue Dolphin's CEO-publisher, gave a finishing polish and lift to the manuscript. This extra effort made a great difference in the clarity and cohesiveness of the message. *Linda Maxwell's* considerate transfer of the manuscript into book format took the sting out of recognizing more editing work needed to be done.

Artwork made a difference in how I visioned the whole and its parts. The sketches from *Elizabeth Croley O'Roark Scheben,* and the photography work of *Scott Scheben* and *Laura Krieger* added "flavor" to my tasks and captured the essence of important messages. Another artwork medium is communication of a **Belief in the Value of the Project.** For their supportive contributions—beyond the call of duty—I thank *Naty Dayan, Aileen Pollock, Jane Fowley O'Roark, Warren Robbins* and *Ken Bradt.*

Most importantly, I was uniquely fortunate to have had, during most of the composition season, a constant reality check. Besides a gift of supportively honest feedback about what was easy to read and what was puzzling, I received a gift of *evidence that genuine invitational leaders exist* and can hold-the-course for more than ninety years, until final taps are played: *Dulaney L. O'Roark, Sr. 1908-1998.*

Ann M. O'Roark, Ph.D.
St. Petersburg, Florida
September 1999

PART ONE
What's Important?
Vision, Motivation, and Action

A Responsible Thinker
Photograph by S. Scheben

*"A Vision with a task is
the hope of the world"*
Sussex, England church wall inscription
Photograph by S. Scheben

The Truth Begins with Two
Photograph by L. Krieger

I

PART ONE

What's Important? Vision, Motivation, Action

Introduction. Quest Priorities: Putting Things in Order

The bright, energetic person who steps onto an executive track soon discovers that there are no time-outs. When competitive hormones surge, there are few safe houses and a scarcity of impartial referees. Anyone, who stops to smell the roses, misses the airplane. If your head is nodding in agreement, this book is for you.

INDIVIDUAL VISION

eXECUQUEST

TRUST

COLLECTIVE SUCCESS

Do not expect to find magical formulas promising abracadabra charisma or ten-steps to sure-fire success; instead be prepared to be introduced to the now-known components of transformational behavior along with essentials involved when setting the stage for realizing success. Most of the following anecdotes and quotes come from the people in executive effectiveness courses I taught and from organization consultation clients. Their heroic tales, wry humors, and career-threatening struggles were invaluable for my on-the-job education and optimism.

No, the quest for executive effectiveness, summed up by a long-time colleague as the *execuquest,* is not understood in one book. Nor is it comprehended in a short course on all-you-ever-need-to-know-to-succeed-in-business. Yes, the challenge of thinking deeper and clearer about what you are doing is worth the effort.

3

What you will find in this book is an executive "time-out." You are invited to fine-tune your personal impact and to cultivate the strength and power of invitational leadership. Pre-quest equipment-check begins by looking inside, by getting beyond accumulated rust that limits contact with your personal core and vision, in order to understand the value of disciplined application of emotional resources. The pre-flight check concludes with a review of the complexities of combining multiple talents and knowledges to "drive" a collective venture and to do the work necessary for achieving the mission.

The agenda for this executive-coaching huddle begins with *what's important* when putting priorities in place—*self, others, and task.* Part Two reviews recent understanding of the vital-sign emotions that are essential guides for navigating the turbulence of surprise and change. Part Three rehearses alternative scenarios—worst case, nothing-new case, and the benefits of a merger of participatory management practices with an enterprising vision. Inspirational, charismatic executive behavior makes the collective difference.

Part One in *The Quest for Executive Effectiveness* is about seeing what's important for success in the short run and for the long haul. Scanning an environment and selecting the priority focus is a matter of competent perception. The interpretive drive that co-exists with perception is *apperception,* a less familiar word, but one that pinpoints the important executive function here. Perception and apperception both come from the word *percept,* which is defined as an internal image that your sense organs generate. Executive focus is a process which engages your physical equipment, including your eyes, ears, skin, and brain, in determining what to pay attention to first. Assuring top performance from this physical gear requires time and thought.

Perception, the start-up phase of recognizing what's important, requires fusing bits of information gathered by sense organs into a coherent mental alignment. Apperception, which occurs automatically, is the *value-added* activity. As a prelude to focus it is more than taking an upside-down image on the back of the eye and turning it right-side-up in the brain. Interpreting the meaning of percepts depends on how you integrate sights, sounds, smells, contact sensations and, then, finally, evaluate meaningfulness and goodness in what you are seeing with the help of past experiences. Apperception culminates in a decision about importance. And actions reflect that inner judgment.

Champions in business ventures, like their athletic contestant counterparts, can cultivate a time-out habit. They learn to value the lessons learned from post-event replays of perception-apperception processes.

They intently review scenarios, calibrating on-the-spot judgment-calls against consequences and alternative actions used by winners. To illustrate the apperception process in an everyday context, imagine a street in front of a downtown office building. A traffic light sets in motion a simple perception-apperception sequence that is critical to survival, executives and others alike.

Step one: *The color of the street light is red.* This is a visual sensing event, which becomes information when external data bytes are received and organized by the optical system. Step two: *Red means stop the car.* This interpretive event depends on selection from past experiences associated with the color red. For U.S. motorists the interpretation and action are instantaneous: *Put your foot on the brake and come to a full stop ahead of the white line on the street pavement.* Step three: Past history with local traffic rules extends the interpretation and leads to subsequent action. *It's OK to turn onto the right-hand lane if no car is moving toward that lane from the left-hand lane.* Countless similar, often unconscious, apperceptions get us to work every day. When the inner judgments lead to a collision with another car or pedestrian, the driver missed important perceptions or was deliberately defiant. Reviewing the sequences behind decisions that end in accidents may prevent future crashes.

From *Webster's New World Dictionary* (p. 66)

apperceive vt [Latin *ad,* to + *percipere,* perceive] 1. Psychol. to assimilate and interpret (new ideas, impressions, etc.) by the help of experience.

apperception n. 2. the state or fact of the mind in being conscious of its own consciousness.

Definitions of APPERCEPTION from the Experts:

G.W. Liebniz (1646-1716): a final clear phase of perception where there is recognition, identification or comprehension of what has been perceived.

J. H. Herbart (1776-1841): the fundamental process of acquiring knowledge, recognizing relationships between new ideas and existing knowledge.

W. Wundt (1832-1920): the active mental process of selecting and structuring internal experience, *the focus of attention within the field of consciousness.*

Linking directly to the purpose of Part One, increasing competence in picking-out what's important, is a conscious awareness that our apperceptions are determining the way we problem-solve and behave. What I think, or believe, about the meaning of my percepts, will determine how I go about establishing and influencing relationships and activities. Essentially, apperception serves as an inner-executive, taking care of organizing and planning my behavior.

Apperception, if likened to genetic codes, can be described as the primary determinant of leadership style. In addition, it can be studied as a fossil of personality. In fact, Rorschach inkblots capitalize on that phenomenon. The images and thoughts that a person reports to the therapist while looking at standardized, ambiguous blots, called Klexa by their originator, Herman Rorschach, are data points. When repeated themes and good-bad evaluations are organized by a trained interpreter they reveal recurring patterns which, in turn, fossilize generic apperceptions that serve to structure and organize personality and behavior.

Apperceptions are also at work—and observable—in leadership training activities and simulations. A popular leadership "exercise" involves asking a group of five to eight persons to each create an ideal individual to take on leadership of an imaginary New Planet. Later, as members of a leaderless decision group, they are asked to state to the rest of the group the reasons that their ideal leader is the person best suited to fill the leadership role on this new planet. After all the ideal leaders are described, the group is instructed to select the one individual most qualified to become leader of a new world. The "catch" is that the final instructions to the group stipulate that the group is to rank in order the remaining candidates for succession planning.

Many managers participating in the exercise have come to the course looking for ways to speed up their progress along the executive track. Many interpret the instructions as a competitive challenge and strive to "sell" their nominee to the bitter end. Others hear the shift in the final instruction and realize that selecting a leader who is *best suited to do the job* is a collaborative task. The group needs to forget "selling" and agree to establish mutually acceptable criteria. Then they can rate the several ideal leader-candidates in light of job requirements. How that assignment is handled boils down to a matter of apperceptions—the interpretations, values, and experiences each person brings to the discussion table.

Chapter 1. The first three chapters focus on basic priorities. Greatest short-term and long-range payoffs stem from giving attention to the condition of self-apperceptions. *Every Success Has a Beginning* is about affirming who-and-what I am. Case records of dropouts, in schools, in prisons, of street people, and of those exiting the executive ranks, are filled with examples of the painful consequences of harboring negative self-apperceptions.

A clear illustration comes from interviews with young women who dropped out of Olympic gymnastic programs after being in intensive training since pre-adolescence. They described severe personal trauma suffered after constantly hearing coaches motivate/chastise them by saying they were clumsy, fat cows, or stupid, retarded learners. Anorexia, depression, and suicide are not uncommon experiences for petite gymnasts who enter the competitive quest for gold, silver, and bronze medals.

While many sports trainers have long used positive visualizing to enable athletes to focus in spite of pre-contest jitters, the power-of-positive-thinking slogan carries a buyer-beware caveat: Abundant self-confidence that leads to rating one's self higher on performance scales than others do is considered a telltale indicator of future failure. Researchers find overestimation of self to be a red-flag marker on the selection field, saying that such overly confident managers often prove difficult to "bring aboard." Selection specialists say to search out individuals who demonstrate an *openness* to new experience, and look for those who have a history of participating in innovative or start-up activities. A willingness to learn new tricks, even in old dogs, is considered a better sign of future success than self-reported high levels of self-esteem on questionnaires or multi-rater appraisals. Wholeheartedness is not the same thing as bravado.

Chapter 2. *The Truth Begins with Two* is about the importance of apperceptions about others—who and what "they" are. Unappealing as it is to scrutinize ourselves for prejudices and biases, these self-defeating expectations that can linger inside the brain's storehouse of percepts are dangerous. It is only by, with, for, and through others that executive vision converts from a solo fantasy into a here-and-now product, service, or process. Failure to incorporate others into the business-process equation is what derailed countless reengineering ventures. Re-inventing and reengineering stand credited with more damage than intended because enthusiasts failed to factor in the violations to relationships among people who were being uprooted or discarded—and those who were kept on. In the aftermath of radical rightsizing efforts that failed to produce intended improvements, a loss of trust became palpable. It is difficult for downsized workgroups to feel surprised by violence in the workplace, corporation hopping, or executive attrition rates.

Chapter 3. Completing a basic priorities triangle is the work itself. *Enterprise and Investment* puts a focus on "Why is it that we are together in this place at this time? What are we doing? Is it worth doing?" "Do we push the elevator button up or down?" Successful enterprise emerges from the mind of the executive or manager with a vision and an ability to gather a cadre of committed fellow workers. Others must agree that a vision is do-able, has merit, and is something our pooled talents can bring off—with a reasonable reward, return-on-investment (ROI). The successful executive creates a field of visions where others can come and work on an enterprise-dream. An open-to-all field of visions undergirds a considerable portion of democratic society's durability and achievement. Citizens are guaranteed access to participation in economic endeavors and government-by-the people. All workers are invited to have a voice and to be productive. When not driven by greed, open fields of visions are creative, fertile grounds for demonstrating our talents and our problem solving ingenuity.

Chapter 4. Is the work worth doing? That's a matter of values, yours and others. This is the topic of the fourth chapter, "The Critical Core." An executive cannot turn any vision inside out without the help of others who have come to trust the leader and value the vision. Trust springs from common values. Would-be leaders who fail to highlight and heed shared values are headed into abandonment and insurrection. On a national level, when executives neglect valued collective issues, the opposition political party is voted into office. The British and the French can quickly oust a political leader with a vote of "no confidence," which says they no longer trust that person to be representing the best interests of those they serve.

Similarly, in a far less complex network of issues and sentiments, six sub-contracted, licensed hairdressers walked out on the owner-manager of a new, flourishing, and very up-scale women's beauty salon. Why? Because the rather affluent, up-and-coming hometown businesswoman instituted a new policy to keep a percentage of each contractors' tips. In no way did the businesswoman understand and respect the importance attached by the beauticians to the gratuities given to them in appreciation for good work. Executive greed broke the employer-employee trust-bond.

In *The Critical Core* values are shown to be the unifying percepts. Trust is an ambiance-product that facilitates individual productivity and corporate progress. Ironically, recent attempts to isolate the essence of trust suggest that trust is not the same thing as distrust. Furthermore, trust is not found to be a global characteristic. It shows itself to be a contextual variable. Trust of self, interpersonal trust, and trust of institutions are distinct and independent. The converging of shared values and high trust emerges as a strategic and priority objective in executive work.

Chapter 1

Every Success Has a Beginning

Executive success begins with an inquiring mind, a curious heart, and a brave spirit. Keen interest motivates the executive questions: What should we be doing? Is it worth doing? How should we do it? How well are we doing?

Executive or not, from birth to death each of us strives for maximum organization and integration of experience and information, always directed toward four goals: Survival, Adequacy, Growth, and Meaningfulness.

First: Who *Am I?* Can I Be . . .
> **A Responsible Thinker**
> **Non-stop Doing-and-Undergoing**
> **Wearer of Many Hats and Multiple Faces**
> **Necessary, But Not Sufficient**

"... *[we] behave according to the facts as we see them. What governs behavior ...
are unique perceptions of self and the world—the meanings things have. . . .*"
Arthur W. Combs, *Individual Behavior*. p. 17.

"... *the means to and the realization of one's ultimate value . . . are: Reason,
Purpose, Self Esteem, with their corresponding virtues:
Rationality, Productiveness, Pride.*"
Ayn Rand, *The Virtue of Selfishness*. p. 25.

A Responsible Thinker

How do you think your staff and direct reports would respond to these questions about you?

(1) My CEO is inconsistent. Associates never know what to expect. Arbitrary in applying rules and policies.

My CEO is consistent. Associates know what to expect. Fair and realistic in applying policies and rules.

1	2	3	4	5	6	7

(2) My CEO is unclear about beliefs and values. Is willing to take a stand on issues. Perceives self in defensive or helpless ways.

My CEO is confident. Takes a stand for beliefs. Sees self as competent and worthwhile. Secure enough to ask for feedback and criticism.

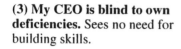

| 1 | 2 | 3 | 4 | 5 | 6 | 7 |

(3) My CEO is blind to own deficiencies. Sees no need for building skills.

My CEO is always looking for ways to improve self and skills. Realizes deficiencies and acts to remedy.

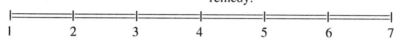

| 1 | 2 | 3 | 4 | 5 | 6 | 7 |

High profile or low key, every success has a beginning. Abraham Lincoln began in a log cabin in Kentucky. His larger than life statue sits in Washington, D.C. as a symbol of greatness in the nation's executive office. His birthplace, a log cabin in Kentucky, preserves a message for later generations that from the most humble beginnings can come heroic achievement. Persistent in the acquisition of knowledge, dedicated to personal integrity, and champion of human rights, Abe Lincoln began with little more than the shirt on his back and an unflagging perception of meaningfulness inherent in himself, in the people about him, and in the work to which he chose to give his life. This value carried him through periods of serious public and personal tribulation.

Executive success stories do not always have log cabin beginnings, or grand and tragic endings. Take the case of a twentieth century man who also began his days in Kentucky. Now a multi-millionaire retired bank president, William E., Jr., grew up in a comfortable, well-appointed but not ostentatious home some 100 miles north of the Lincoln log cabin. He is the only child of the founder of a community oriented bank. The high school gymnasium in the moderate sized town is named for his civic-minded father. William, better known as Bill, went to the state university, doing well enough in courses and taking time to establish friendships that have lasted a lifetime. One of those college friends became his wife. After a brief tour of duty with the U.S. Navy, they returned to Kentucky where Bill took on a leadership role in the bank with his father. Since that time, Bill and Betty have devoted time to charitable organizations, such as the crippled children's foundation. They have also invested in community revitalization projects, restoring historic office buildings and an old, abandoned railroad station.

Nothing in this executive success story is likely to fill pages in the *Britannica* or the *Guinness Book of Records*. Since Bill retired from the bank, he has started at least seven business ventures which he is actively managing or financing. Although one of those ventures may catapult him into the headlines, because "It's not over until the fat lady sings," the odds are he will continue his remarkable success trajectory without fanfare. He has established and maintained a balanced life—success at work and success at home. Following in his footsteps, one of his two sons is determined to reestablish a community-focused, personalized service bank in the image of the business his grandfather founded. Bill's older son and his teacher-wife hold a vision of overcoming the loss of humanness in financial services that resulted after a megabank bought up and restructured the family bank. Bill's younger son, trained as a professional photographer, captures leadership presences on film.

One of Bill's most noticeable characteristics, as his son's photograph shows, is a steady, calm, natural assuredness. He likes who he is and capitalizes on what he knows to be his competencies. He is genuinely interested in, and enjoys, others. He cares about their well-being and fair treatment. He relishes his work—especially start-up ventures that can benefit the community he knows and loves.

If this were not an example of executive success that I followed closely for over forty years, I might be ready to say it sounds too good to be true. Indeed, life was not easy or perfect. Some investments and business decisions didn't go as planned. Personal and family health threats caused disruptions and alarms. Maturing children voiced contrary opinions and unexpected interests. Nevertheless, a solid set of apperceptions and a clear vision of balanced life-achievements brought Bill to the top of an unpublished-but-known-to-all list of successful executives in the community.

Success does not need to begin with poverty or affluence. It begins where you are today. W. Clement Stone, a CEO who writes glibly about guaranteed success, says that "any miserable failure can be successful"—provided that person will set goals and dedicate thirty minutes each day to creative thinking. He urges people to direct their thoughts, control their emotions, and achieve their goals. His can-do formula appeared in an early issue of a magazine called *Success.*

Stone's assertion comes across as somewhat arrogant, yet gets our attention and confronts us with a critical first-focus when beginning on a quest for executive effectiveness: *You* must assume responsibility for your *own* success. Even so, his confident conclusion that *anyone can be successful* is questionable. Many persons who are honest, industrious, educated, and goal setters find that executive success eludes them. In some cases, it was the organization that failed. Other times, a family system took an unexpected twist. And, sometimes, the pathways were blocked by hostile fellow workers who diverted constructive efforts.

As the twentieth century folds into the next millennium, managers across the country may start their quest in a less optimistic climate than those who set out in the mid 1950s. American Management Association (AMA) *Management Review* reporters forecast that the new century brings "a monumental lack of executive talent [that] will last for decades and cripple companies." Stuart Crainer and Des Dearlove predict that the single most critical issue for companies will not be the impact of the internet, technology, or nanosecond change, but a shortage of executive leadership talent (*MR*, July-Aug. 1999. pp. 16 & 17). The road to executive effectiveness begins wherever you are —discouraged or enthusiastic, younger or older. Our lifespans lengthen, adding years and decades to survival expectancies. Statistics now indicate that most people experience three major job changes. Many transitions are forced by technology shifts and corporate shake-ups. At the same time, numerous achievement-oriented workers are already out looking for fresh challenges in new venues.

"What should I be when I grow up?" That question pops-up regularly during consultations with executives from leading US and multinational companies. Asking half in jest, and spoken more like a statement than a question, corporate fast-trackers are reassessing their potentials and directions. They are looking to me for short-term and long-range "how-to's" for navigating mid-career, or later career decisions and choices.

Whether set in motion by a production goal, an unexpected opportunity, or a right-sizing mandate, senior level managers confront change at every turn. The tempo of change, the radical nature of changes, and the fall-out range of the change event, like a category four hurricane, leaves managers feeling out-of-control and hope-depleted. A typical post-change reassessment pilgrimage was described by a marketing vice-president in a technology company that is doubling in size. During an executive development program, looking more like an all-American business hero than a troubled manager, he asked his coursemates to discuss how their companies handled loss.

He requested that they concentrate on two organizational scenarios and two interpersonal issues. In scenario 1 a co-worker leaves of his own accord. In scenario 2, the person leaves by organizational desire. First, he wanted to hear each coursemate's views on what changes in corporate operations would likely result from each of the two scenarios. Then, he wanted to learn what types of conflict others experienced when they had been in similar situations.

After listening to the experiences of other executives-in-training, this "high six-figure-income" executive talked at length about his own dilemma and why he asked about how others handled loss of co-workers. In his company, there are no farewell parties when someone leaves, not even a clue as to whether a departure followed from a scenario 1 or scenario 2 situation. The staff is told that they are now expected to take on the duties and tasks of the former co-worker. A gag rule is enforced which states that any background on the departure is provided only on a need-to-know basis and must be directly linked to getting-the-job-done.

The V-P, an unusually quick-minded, rational thinker who knows he is favored to be the next CEO, was openly concerned about the corporate directive not to acknowledge the departure or to allow any farewells or grieving. Not only was he struggling with the loss of a valued co-worker, and an impending need to promote or reject prevailing corporate phi-losophy, but he was at the same time in the process of adjusting to a recent divorce. His wife left him saying that she did not enjoy being a distant second-fiddle to his job. He acknowledged that his fascination with work challenges left him little time to get to know her very well before or during the marriage.

Why does a strongly motivated achiever look inward? Frequently, because their underpinnings are kicked away. Prolonged emphasis on process-efficiency can sabotage three conditions that maintain work motivation—security, growth, and relatedness. Terminations of com-rades can intensify anxiety. Wondering "Will I be next?" in the wake of an unexplained departure can abort any sense of relatedness.

The wondering continues. Is this what being an executive requires? Here today, gone tomorrow: A profits-and-growth soldier of fortune, not only finding it lonely at the top but also accepting the notion of disposable relationships.

Without a doubt security and staying alive will command the first order of business. This basic motivation born out of a sense of threat will compel and drive individuals and work groups. All attention quickly goes to how to go about surviving. In workplace circumstances, organi-zational-survival choices have implications for long-range security for employees, vendors, and contractors. Healthy corporate decisions are informed and deliberate, fortified by plans that cover likely consequences in the years and decades ahead. At the same time, short-term pain and on-going relationships are neither neglected nor over-dramatized. The tunnel-vision apprehensions that follow threats to security, growth and relatedness are addressed by intentional expansion of options.

Expanding a field of options is not as simple as going back to school and taking another course or degree. Do not be lulled by sincere reports from persons lending their names for use in advertisements to proclaim this or that course is "the best training program I ever attended. It changed my whole outlook on how to manage people." Countless seminars, workshops, and in-house learning events were spawned by human resources specialists, inspired by *the learning corporation* philosophy. These enthusiasms make it easy to forget that as recently as the mid-twentieth century, business administration courses did not isolate management as a career track. Business schooling involved accounting, finance, and record keeping, along with the dreaded theory of economics course. Actually, very few senior executives formally studied business management, let alone executive effectiveness.

The 1950s and 60s gave rise to the first generation of Masters of Business Administration (MBA). Toward the end of the 1900s, the great corporate rush to hire super-educated management specialists waned. Business leaders and assembly line workers finally found a point of agreement: academic training—even an Ivy League MBA—too often failed to connect with workday realities. Illustrating this phenomena is the story of a man who was in executive training with the marketing V-P. The neatly groomed and intensely attentive man, self-proclaimed as a top-of-the-graduating-class MBA, surprised everyone when he reported that he was only attending the program at the insistence of his superiors. His boss advised him that if he did not become aware of what was not clicking between himself and his co-workers, he would, for the second time in his MBA career, loose out on becoming a senior officer in a company. Will he be able to listen to the people about him? Will he, then, be able to simplify his storehouse of theoretical models into everyday workables? Will he allow his academic self to be re-educated by colleagues who have been on-the-job educated? As long as he is searching and questioning, he remains on the path.

Over 2500 years ago, *listen to the people* was the chief admonition to leaders in the Chinese government. This wisdom comes from a student of Confucius, Mencius. Confucius, a magistrate who went on to become assistant minister of public works, and later minister of justice in the Chinese state of Lu, began his own government career by managing stables and keeping books for granaries. After he fell out of favor with political power holders, at the age of 56, he turned his attention to the teaching for which he is still respected. He was the first in that culture to concentrate on teaching as a means of improving society. He established teaching as a vocation in China, promoted education for all the people, and initiated a humanities training program for potential leaders (*Encyclopaedia Britannica*, Vol. 16, p. 654).

Historians who reviewed the several streams of cultural evolution for examples of management practices credit the Egyptians with being the first in the recorded history of Western civilizations to evidence management excellence. Evidence of technical achievement circa 2,550 BC, over 4,500 years ago, remain visible today, proudly weathering storm and time. Constructing the great pyramids and sphinx required artistic and engineering vision, complex coordination of materials and work forces, and profound drive to manifest their belief in the meaning of human life. Debates about apparent worker-abuse and human sacrifice are on-going as excavations of these mausoleums continue to reveal detailed aspects of that early civilization. Their unparalleled products humble and amaze the most sophisticated of today's architects and builders.

An equally famous, but minimally verifiable, management tale is best known as the hero-legend of the Trojan horse. A wooden horse brought about a colossal management failure. Oral history tells us of a ten-year war between the cities of Troy and Sparta that took place about 3200 years ago. After years of extended warfare, the Trojans experienced economic strains to the point that they were forced to budget carefully. Their efforts to implement cutbacks and to become more efficient were organized by the earliest reported official planning board. Although this board is thought to have prepared thoroughly, to have proposed logical defense strategies, and to have collaborated harmoniously, the Trojans were soundly defeated. The Spartan warriors who were encamped outside the walls of Troy, following advice from their clever tacticians, built a giant wooden horse which they offered as a gift to their enemies. The flattered citizens of Troy came out from behind their walls to accept the gift horse. They moved it into their city square. Later that night, Spartan invaders hidden inside the horse sprang from their compartment and opened the city gates for their comrades. That was the end of the Trojan Planning Board.

Success comes in diverse patterns. What is your pattern? Intense and dramatic? Easy-going and calmly assured? Which would you prefer—becoming an executive in public welfare and education, supervising the construction of enduring monuments, plotting innovative plans for the defense or for the offense? Where are you willing to dedicate your efforts?

Historically and geographically, from ancient China and Egypt to ivy league MBAs, any way you define executive or codify leadership training, the name of the game is accepting responsibility for your own success by listening to others, by setting goals, by coping with loss, and by simplifying questions and answers. For those called to become an executive, who accept the job to work as visionary, as planner, and as motivator, and who are able to present a credible executive presence, Harry Truman sums it up, "The buck stops here." As CEO of Local No. 1, your first job is to organize your own inner resources so that they serve to maximize your probabilities for success. No one else can do it for you.

GW expected to become company president. He had long wanted to be president of the moderate-sized warehousing firm. He was a final candidate but lost out to an outsider. Eighteen months later, GW continued "steaming" about his disappointment. GW described the new president as lacking knowledge about the industry, making poor business decisions—and even then the decisions were made very slowly—which GW explained is especially hard on a business with a low profit margin situation. Besides, the CEO proved to be a self-serving "chore and bore" to try to work with.

GW considered his failure to be chosen as president to be a direct consequence of his scores on a psychological test battery. GW described how some headhunter "shrink" said test scores showed GW to be argumentative, insensitive and not a team player. This surprising information continued to haunt GW. How could this be true? He got nowhere trying to challenge the results with the psychologist, and could not get free of a sense of self-doubt. Nor his anger: anger that the tests could be so obviously wrong and still be believed by those who worked with him.

GW is presently serving as Vice President in charge of sales and marketing. He is proud of his evaluations from students in the local community college MBA class that he teaches. His ratings are all outstanding with effusive compliments. He believes his early educational background, a liberal arts with a degree in theater, helps his effectiveness in both teaching and sales. An advanced degree with CPA certification came later, after his military career. GW is openly proud of his war record. He was recognized as a hero. He describes how he learned well the lessons of "search and destroy."

He is sure, as a result, that he is a powerful and competent leader. He is sure he is better suited for the role of company president than the quiet mouse the shrink selected. Surely any shrink who knew their business would not schedule a psychological selection assessment so soon after GW's major open-heart surgery. Such post-operation results had to be biased, or flat wrong.

GW came to the executive effectiveness course to get over this anger and lack of trust for the boss. His wife, the only one he has talked with about these feelings, suggested the course as an opportunity to get opinions from real people rather than tests, and to see what peers know based on their experiences with similar situations.

At the end of the course, GW thanked the members of the class for clearing up in a few hours what he had stewed about for months. Direct, but supportive feedback about his frequently dramatic, sometimes confronting and almost always persistent interaction allowed GW to see the two consequences of his talent—one effect allows him to be an excellent instructor and salesperson, and a second effect makes it difficult to get him to listen to new ideas or individual problems, needs or preferences. The second effect did lead, even in the group's short exposure to each other, to perceptions that GW has, indeed—at times—been argumentative, insensitive, and not a team player!

GW told one of his favorite stories: He recalled having a hunting knife when he was a young man which became dull. He took his birthday money to buy a new knife. The storekeeper in the small town where he grew up said to him, "GW, you don't need a new knife. You just need to sharpen the old one, regularly. This knife you have is a lifetime investment, if you take care of it." GW explains his insight as one of realizing he lost confidence in himself, got mixed up in his thinking about himself because of the psychological report, and that he had concluded he needed to become a new knife, when he actually needed to not be so personally wrapped up in corporate issues, to do some professional listening and problem solving—rather than resorting to his tactics of the 1960s when he learned to "rush in and neutralize the enemy."

GW's Question: How can I stop putting myself down, stop being so self-centered, give up being so rigid, quick and set in opinion, not talk so long at a time, losing the point in the wake of extended background briefings, humorous asides and knife stories. How can I focus on the strengths I bring to constructive leadership: tenacious perseverance toward a goal; ability to take an objective, logical problem-solving perspective; and independent initiative leading to discovery of new and better ways to do business?

The talent for objective problem solving is a good prognosis of success for GW in his quest. He is likely to be able to move beyond overpersonalized, overemotional worrying. GW heard from his peers that it is important to accept the dark side of self and others, giving up a need to be godlike, or perfect, or all responsible. This freedom is a beginning of realism about the strengths in the self: proud of and trusting in what's possible without being consumed by or afraid of what's missing or imperfect.

GW's peers recommended he put his own internal executive function to work, taking charge of organizing, administering and managing his strengths. They advised that cultivating the executive ability to manage himself would keep him from becoming overstressed and resorting to obnoxious, overbearing cockiness. From a bottom-line psychological perspective, in order for GW to learn how to trust his boss, he must regain trust in himself.

Non-stop Doing-and-Undergoing

Not everyone is inclined toward a management career. Regardless of career choices, each self, like an energizer bunny, keeps on going. Each self has an executive component, which may be used a lot, a little, or now-and-then. As an obvious demarcation between living and inanimate objects, human growth and development experts elaborate on the capability to maintain oneself by renewal. This scientific tenet allowed John Dewey, an early twentieth-century philosopher-scientist-educator, to insist that humans survive, attain self-renewal, and learn better ways *by doing and undergoing the consequences of that doing.* He mapped the relationship between democracy and education on the basis of his pivotal assumption.

Dewey's logical mind valued the potentials of directed energy. Dewey recognized that transmission of experience and information in an orderly fashion is essential to improving quality of life. He considered focused communication, formal and informal, and directed problem solving to be the essential elements of education and training.

Dewey's specialized environment important to successful transmission of quality is a place where certain aspects of the environment are simplified and ordered. Schools and corporations both qualify as specialized environments. How successful they are depends on leadership direction. Dewey prefers the word "direction" to "control" for describing an executive organizing function: "In short, direction is both simultaneous and successive. At a given time, it requires that, from all the tendencies that are partially called out, those be selected which center energy upon the point of need. Successively, it requires that each act be balanced with those that precede and come after, so that order of activity is achieved. The key words are focusing and ordering . . . one spatial, the other temporal."

Psychologist-educator Dewey considers geography (spatial; *focus*) and history (temporal; *order*) the fundamental contents of knowledge. A similar message comes from Mexican tradition, from a Yaqui Indian educator, Don Juan, who was made famous by anthropologist Carlos Castaneda. Don Juan teaches that one must first be a warrior, i.e., a trapper, a hunter, a person who knows the land and the plants and the animals that inhabit the land. Only with a keen sensing knowledge of the geography and customs of local inhabitants can a person become competent and then innovative.

The key to achieving the highest levels of wisdom, according to the Yaqui teacher Don Juan, is controlled folly: manage thyself first. His idea of executive behavior is controlling the environment by cultivating appropriate habits. Don Juan, master of peyote-mystique whose final examinations were pass-fail wilderness encounters, is in agreement with John Dewey. Classic academician Dewey also advocated habituation. He recommended that a balance-and-flow of activities be used routinely in order to be efficient. Dewey also encouraged habits active at higher levels of thinking and consciousness. These were the habits of flexibility that readjust activity to meet new conditions. In Dewey's language, the follies Don Juan said needed to be controlled are any habits that distract from focusing and ordering, whatever reduces one's efficiency.

Rekindling of a faded interest in habits, Steven Covey details seven self-management how-to's in *The Seven Habits of Highly Effective People.* These apply directly to executive functioning: [1] be proactive, [2] start with the end in mind, [3] put first things first—"things which matter most must never be at the mercy of things which matter least"—Goethe, [4] think win-win, [5] seek first to understand then to be understood, [6] synergize—value differences, [7] sharpen the saw.

Dewey would interpret the sharpening of the saw as practicing thinking in a classroom setting. That classroom setting, or learning environment, needs to be like a simulator where the problems one practices solving are those with which there is already a genuine interest and a continuous aspect; or a problem develops within the ongoing interesting activity. The instructor asks that the individual then make observations and process information needed to deal with the problem. Practicing these higher order thinking habits allows for the emergence of solutions which can be developed in an orderly way. It is then important for that individual to have an opportunity to test solution ideas and discover their practicality. Covey's seventh habit, and Castaneda's warrior training are consistent with Dewey's principle of Doing-and-undergoing-the-consequences of that doing.

Wearer of Many Hats and Multiple Faces

Responsible Thinker, William. (Will)

Will has adopted the US as his home base. A genuine international-age manager, with experience on three continents and in four countries, this younger generation fast-tracker is hyper-bright, quick-witted and bitingly humorous, verging on the super-critical. Will's question to the executive discussion group is: How to neutralize the impact of a mentor-boss who sweeps in from overseas "making an ass of himself and ashes of the project staff."

The enormously successful boss has wealth, has status, and has power—and has a drinking problem that leads to insulting behavior. Overindulging in alcohol during recent site visits to the US checking progress on a new venture, was followed by the UK-based boss making racial and homosexual slurs to US operations employees. Disregard of others' feelings or beliefs extended to the boss's personal life. Abusive behavior toward wife and children, negligence in straightforward reporting of work-related facts and exhibition of several varieties of self-indulgences began to be more typical than occasional.

Will's mind stays in a quandary because of a loyalty toward the person who had given him his fast-track opportunities, and admiration for the early corporate achievements made possible by this boss-mentor's once-keen thinking. The relationship with the boss was more puzzling to Will than his previous assignment ever was: directly supervising 30 keen-minded, highly competitive-aggressive "direct reports" at the company's office in Paris. Will agreed with the executive coursemate who suggested that Will was allowing this boss to "live rent free in his mind."

Another coursemate compared Will's situation with that of co-dependency. Several members of the group reported experiences with Alcoholics Anonymous, for themselves, or as family members of an alcoholic. Based on the group's collective wisdom and on Will's reports of prior efforts to talk to his boss about the drinking and unpleasant social exchanges, everyone agreed that confronting the boss with the work problems stemming from his excessive use of alcohol was unlikely to be productive.

A few months after the course, Will telephoned to let me know his new plans. He has decided to look for a job with another young, progressive company in the U.S. city where he is living with his American wife and young child. Two factors led to his decision: 1. The company is about to pull his venture project back into the corporate offices in Europe, and 2. the mentor-boss has now become quite hostile toward him. [His boss discovered that the most recent of his wives has discussed with Will and Will's wife her distress about her husband's affair with a woman in one of the company's foreign offices.] Apparently, for Will, this was the final straw: Will's gift for enjoying business complexity and fast-paced sharp logic could no longer stomach the personal complexities and illogic inherent in his mentor's current lifestyle.

Will's favorite solution analogy: Here are two pairs of chopsticks. What's the difference between the two? There's the simple answer, and the complex answer. The simple answer is that one pair is shorter and blunter than the other pair. The complex answer is that one pair is Japanese and the other is Chinese—each pair is representative of vast cultural differences, which can also be seen in the simpler lettering of Japanese writing and the more complex symbolism of the Chinese letters and word pictures. Do we need the simple answer or the complex one?

Will's simple solution is to move his considerable talents to a new business. Will's complex solution is to end his co-dependency with his mentor, his boss, his homeland contact. It is, indeed, cultural. It is also personal: trust in self—without a safety net.

Will's story involves three important relationships that are part of every manager's work life. There are times when a manager is the boss, times when that manager is a direct report, and times when the manager works among peers. The shift between (a) acting as the legitimate leader of the group, (b) carrying out duties with or for higher ranking executives or owners, and (c) collaborating on a project as a colleague-expertise specialist, is sometimes referred to as changing hats. Will had little trouble wearing the hat of boss to high energy direct reports, he had minimal trouble leaping nationality gaps between himself and the North American peer-coursemates, but he had great trouble with the direct report hat when the boss's feet of clay tracked mud on Will's office floors. Was the demise of working rapport a result of a Western civilization cultural- custom? Social drinking of alcoholic beverages—to excess.

Social drinking, a subset of cultural practices, inhibited Will's executive quest—in that particular organization. More often, broader, generic cultural differences impact executive effectiveness. Today's executive meets cultural issues in: international business arenas; organizational policies, practices, and norms; individual diversities among employees. One way executives can analyze culture is as costumes, customs, and rituals reflect it. How do we dress to go to work? Suits, overalls? How do we address each other? Mr. Jones, Mary Jane? How do we celebrate major events, transitions? Merger [wedding] parties, Termination [funeral] processions? These are ritual ways people devise in order to help each other hold it together, and keep their focus—the original support groups.

The culture of management behavior, as described in management training courses and popular publications, does not contain a protocol for a literal "changing of the hats" when shifting from one relationship-role to another, but the literature does have protocols for managers' behavioral flexibility which is always anchored by rules. Popularized as situational leadership by Kenneth Blanchard and Paul Hersey, the manager's flexibility is far from free-form. Blanchard and Hersey, in partnership and in solo practice, provide page-upon-page of constraints and conditions associated with prescribed managerial behavioral shiftings. Growing out of research conducted at Ohio State in the 1940s and 1950s, variable effective tactics for managing others are articulated as functions of the subordinate's ability and willingness e.g., knowledge + experience and motivation.

Managers who use situational leadership strategies are trained to assess the nature of the task, and the employee. A manager improves supervisory effectiveness by changing hats through four styles: directive, coaching, encouraging, and delegating. These changes can come across as inconsistency if the direct report is not alerted to the rationale for the different hats. This means a collaborative approach to assessing direct reports' status on a continuum of ability + willingness, a procedure which is closely akin to critical pathway approaches to decision making.

Critical pathways are branching charts of Yes or *No* responses to a set of generic work-conditions in persons and situations that serve as templates for managers' thinking and deciding process. These behavior protocols illustrate when it is appropriate, even working smarter, to behave in ways that are not necessarily natural or habitual. It's the published decision rules and core values that maintain continuity and cohesiveness.

Without a unifying factor, shifts in leadership style could seem more like the multiple personality than an intentional effort to behave in more effective ways. Consistency and continuity within the changes of behavior associated with the different role-relationships, whether these are due to working in different authority configurations or to working differently according to individual differences among those being supervised, depend upon congruity with the inner-executive: That core of beliefs about the self which maintain dynamic integrity—dynamic in that it is open to new experience and learning, and integrity in that it is sound and complete, of a conscious whole piece.

The reflection of integrity is believed to show in expressions on the face. The face, capable of multiple variances and subtleties, can reveal unspoken thoughts. Who does not recall mother's raised eyebrows or the teacher's slight expansion of the nose? In a reverse example, card players are noted for poker-faces that give no expression, no clue as to how good the cards they are betting on really are. Professional actors and con-artists project they are something they are not, and convincingly express feelings not a part of their inner self. Faking who and what you are takes a toll on even those who do so for beneficial purposes. Actors have identity issues to work through after particularly demanding roles; those taken into witness protection programs have whole new lives to undertake.

Even without unusual and irregular circumstances to cope with, undertaking responsibility for one's integrity and congruity while at the same time incorporating new information, adjusting to life-cycle developments, and compensating for unforeseen changes, is a major endeavor. Executives and managers are not alone in being alert to every clue about how to maintain an effectiveness edge. In an effort to use scientific methods for identifying the innermost components of healthy, achieving persons, studies conducted at the University of Florida generated a set of distinguishing perceptual characteristics. The following apperceptual variables describe individuals rated as more effective by supervisors and peers: They consider themselves to be more adequate than inadequate; more able than unable; more dependable than undependable; more worthy than unworthy; more wanted than unwanted; more willing to engage in new experiences than closed to engaging in new experiences; more focused on the big picture and long range than on lesser details and short-term rewards; more interested in standing in someone else's shoes to understand their perspective than in remaining distant and critical of other's behaviors.

W.W. Purkey, a self-concept specialist, is convinced that we are never finished products. Our growth is never completed. That inner executive, the self, is continuously busy assimilating new ideas and expelling old ideas. As these beliefs and attitudes about Who-I-am change, behavior changes. Adaptation is considered by behavioral scientists and anthropologists as conducive, even necessary, to survival. Why is it, then, that consistency and integrity are most frequently at the top of surveys asking for employee opinions about the most important executive characteristics.

Opinions can be interpreted in terms of a simple or a complex implication. In this case, Will's complex answer is necessary: Consistency must reside in the innermost self, in the core of integrity and reason. Executive consistency is not demonstrated through trivial routines. A leader's consistency is not intended to overpower flexibility, adaptability, spontaneity, or innovation. The consistency that promotes survival and stimulates growth is, in the final analysis, perseverance in the pursuit of better ways while remembering who-I-am, where-I'm-going, and what-Time-it-is.

Necessary but not Sufficient

The executive keeper-of-the hourglass never forgets that management is not a solo act. That simple and obvious understatement serves as a membership recruitment slogan for the New York based world-wide American Management Association. AMA's four-week basic training course, *The Management Course,* is for early career managers and can be spread out over eighteen months. The focus sequence is management, finance, marketing, and leadership. Each section emphasizes the joint-venture, collective enterprise nature of management. In contrast, this chapter and the other three chapters in Part One emphasize the person-as-manager. The focus is on ordering the inner-executive, and carries an ironic component. In the self-apperception constellation, a bright, northstar-like characteristic is humility. Humility, in an old-fashioned sense, is not a matter of being self-depreciating, but a matter of appreciating others. It is recognition of one's personal incompleteness and individual handicaps. It is an acknowledgment that in life there are few if any solo acts. Without others to learn from and work with, each individual would need to reinvent the wheel and discover fire.

Each person has less of some abilities and talents than are sufficient to do a competent job. An executive who is aware of personal handicaps is more likely to succeed, especially if that executive is able to hire or merge forces with someone who is strong in that necessary ability. We are all handicapped in one way or another—the handicap may be physical, mental, economic, educational, or social. It's the fortunate person who is in touch with what needs to be overcome. Knowing one's handicaps and blind spots let's you go about filling in the blanks and become more effective at thinking and problem-solving.

A popular way to discover blind spots in management effectiveness is administration of a 360-degree questionnaire, using items similar to those at the beginning of this chapter. These surveys provide a safeguard against being unaware of the image one is projecting to others. Variations of these structured feedback surveys gather opinions and observations from those who work for, beside and above that individual, as well as from the person being evaluated. Getting consolidated and stratified results of these so-called benchmarking instruments became the popular improvement technique of the 1990s. Enterprising management gurus and uptown publishers outdid each other preparing freshly intriguing questionnaires with colorful, cleverly charted profiles and reports.

The challenge for the discerning executive becomes one of selecting an appropriate 360-degree tool: what should the questions be about? What's important for improvement here and now? More frequently than desirable, organizational decision-makers put cart before the horse, i.e., an executive takes a survey for a leadership development course and goes back to the organization full of enthusiasm and determined to have everyone in management discover the benefits of hearing it like it is, and find out how others really see you. Now and then, their eager motivation for plunging others into this bath of feedback contains just a touch of retaliation. Some who get less than accolade ratings may want others to know what it is to struggle through the SARAH syndrome: Shock-surprise, Anger, Resistance, and Acceptance, Help. It is not unusual that even very-senior managers feel badly when co-workers don't score them as nearly perfect on most dimensions.

Although very few executives have the time to become a renaissance thinker-philosopher, most executives periodically browse the aisles of their favorite bookstores, which are now stocked with pre-digested summaries, checklists and opinions. The booksellers even provide comfortable chairs for veteran book scanners. Some executives surf the cyberspace to keep in touch with the latest from leading management experts. Abstracts of what's currently considered important for individual success show amazing continuity with policies promoted by Confucius: management of self, continuous improvement, integrity, and honorable character. Continuous improvement is an ongoing process of intentional searching, of organizing and sequencing, of application and extension, and of keeping one's innermost spaces cleaned up.

There are genes that keep the innermost bloodways clean, an essential job that contributes to longevity. An Ides of March test with the potential to predict when one might die was a *Wall Street Journal* lead-story. A gene known as apo E is the marker for survival. Four known types of apo E work as housekeeper genes. Their job is to carry around-and-out things like cholesterol and spilled blood. Apo E2 is a good housekeeper, while apo E4 is a sloppy housekeeper. E4 is a litterbug that allows the trash to build up and shorten the life span. If a person has E2 genes, a long life is expected. Those with a lot of E4 genes are not able to maintain a healthy system so long. WSJ does not expect that many will be willing to take the Ides of March test to learn if they have a short time or a long time to continue the quest for executive effectiveness.

The bad news-good news here is that management of the innermost self as efficiently as apo E2 will not prove sufficient when taking on complex organizational challenges. The good news is that abundant natural and human resources tip the odds to favor survival. Even as apo E2 has a responsible ally in apo E3, the gene that is not quite as efficient as E2, there are co-workers to help get the work done and to slow down pollution. In Chapter 2, *The Truth Begins with Two* points out the importance of apperceptions about others and the value of humility.

Background Reading

Ira Gordon, professor at the University of Florida, published and taught about a birth-to-death human development model of striving of maximum organization and integration of experience and information toward four goals: survival, adequacy, growth and meaningfulness. See, *Human Development from Birth Through Adolescence,* 1969, NY: Harper and Row Publishers.

Success in executive roles has been prescribed by business leaders, psychologists, and mystics. For readers interested in the perspective of a successful CEO, look for articles published by W. Clement Stone, an entrepreneur who announced a formula for guaranteed success in 1985 in the magazine titled *Success,* No. 32, 4, p. 80. The last decade of the 1900s saw iterations of mid-century psychological thinking refreshed and promoted by Steven Covey. Covey details his preferred self-management how-to's in *The Seven Habits of Highly Effective People,* N.Y.: Fireside, Simon and Schuster. More fanciful, allegorical prescriptions were offered in the last half of the twentieth century by an anthropologist, Carlos Castaneda, who wrote a series of tales based on his research in Mexico and under the tutelage of a Yaqui Indian teacher called Don Juan. *The Fire Within,* 1984, was one of the later books which included *The Teaching of Don Juan: A Yaqui Way of Knowledge, A Separate Reality,* and *Tales of Power.* NY: Pocketbooks, Washington Square Press.

For materials describing the prescriptions leading to situational leadership success, read articles and see training videos prepared by Ken Blanchard and/or Paul Hershey. Before going separate ways in their consulting practices, they collaborated to publish the underpinnings for their prescriptions: "Life Cycle Theory of Leadership," *Training and Development,* 1969, No. 23,26-34; *Management of Organizational Behavior,* Englewood Cliffs, NJ: Prentice-Hall, 1977.

Earlier fundamentals of adult change and development stem from seminal work by John Dewey, the early twentieth century psychologist-philosopher-scientist-educator. His famous book, *Democracy and Education,* has been published and republished over the years: NY: The Macmillan Co., 1916, 1944, and 1964. Another, more ancient foundation, comes from the work of Mencius, a student of Confucius (*Britannica,* 16, 654).

The *Wall Street Journal* is a source of continuous insight into what is current and what is pragmatic about the executives. Hal Lancaster's columns provide informative, easy-to-comprehend illuminations and archival-worthy anecdotes. The reference section names primary source articles.

Chapter 2

The Truth Begins with Two

An ancient koan meditation can extend our thinking, as it did for Zen students, to a greater awareness of reality: *What is the sound of one hand clapping?* Effective executives applaud with both hands to show respect for others as dynamic self-systems, committed to achieving the same four goals of *survival, adequacy, growth, and meaningfulness.* Together we can seek to be:
  - Success ala Le Jazz Combo
  - Collaborators in Transformations
  - Free Agents and Strange Attractors
  - Complementary & Contrary: "Swiss-Cheese" Assets

Peter Drucker. *1994. There is a great deal of talk these days about "teams" and "teamwork" ... actually people have always worked in teams; very few people ever could work effectively by themselves ... until now the emphasis has been on the individual worker and not on the team. With knowledge work growing increasingly effective as it is increasingly specialized, teams become the work unit rather than the individual him[her]self." —The Atlantic Monthly*

Walter Tubb. *1974. If I just do my thing and you do yours, We stand in danger of losing each other—and ourselves. I am not in this world to live up to your expectations; but I am in this world to confirm you as a unique human being. And to be confirmed by you. We are fully ourselves only in relation to each other; the I detached from a Thou disintegrates. I do not find you by chance; I find you by an active life of reaching out. Rather than passively letting things happen to me, I can act intentionally to make them happen. I must begin with myself, true; but I must not end with myself; the truth begins with two.* —Saranack Lake, NY: *Land's End Newsletter*

Success ala Le Jazz Combo

Without others who follow, there can be no leaders. A paradoxical lesson from parades and organizations is that even the most brilliant individual bandmasters and CEOs who work alone seldom produce

29

much of consequence, no matter how grand their design vision. Executive vision, like a marching band formation, emerges as a successful event only when the idea is turned inside-out. An executive's mental product must be executed by others, and is in the final analysis an imprecise forecast of the end result. A photograph at the opening of this section shows a classic automobile with its image floating on a pond's surface, an image that is as non-dimensional as was the concept of that car when it floated in its inventor's mind.

Another aspect of this two-way dependency is suggested by a sculpture near a prominent point on Tampa Bay along St. Petersburg's downtown waterfront. Named simply, "Truth," the 25-foot tall abstract artwork, which is also pictured at the opening of this chapter, consists of two triangular monoliths, similar in size, in unity of structure and in unyielding quality. Closer inspection shows that they are not identical as they stand together on a raised granite platform. The apex of the sculpture is formed by the touching tips of the huge geometric forms, each tilted to stand taller along one edge of its base. The grounded bases are about 10 feet apart leaning toward each other, slightly off-point. The flat planes of the pyramid-like forms that face each other are blue. The triangular surfaces that face outward are black. These heavy, self-contained creations work together to balance each other and make a unique visual statement. This artist understood the truth of beginning with two and demonstrates that one construct alone would not be able to stand to reach its highest potentials.

Realizable ideas flourish when several individual strengths support and balance the execution of the idea. When a vision attempts to stand in space and time to do a job, each contributor changes the outcome and the centers of momentum. More and more often, success in corporations appears to be a matter of assembling counterpoint abilities in jazz-combo types of work groups, where results depend upon the combined quality of work done by persons with independently functioning talents. Peter Drucker was among the first to predict the age of transformation. Next-generation organizations will rely on workers with widely diverse accumulations of information and training.

As well as being a clever analogy, a jazz-combo image transforms our thinking about workplace diversity. "Valuing diversity," became a widely used sound-bite spin of traditional melting-pot values. The "gold" is in the perspectives and abilities available from workers with different cultures and heritages. While a far cry from painting falcon heads on human-form god-heroes, today's leaders use equally creative determination as they strive for collective success a la le jazz-combo workteams.

If a jazz combo approach is applied to management, respect for specialized knowledges and skills will be the easy part. More subtle challenges surround the cultivating of respect for others' productivity-patterns, work habits and contribution-potentials. As with most on-the-job training, it takes extra effort to make a practical, here-and-now *useful* connection for managers. Results-oriented employees see themselves as already full-time busy producing their bottom-line target, too busy to be bothered with diversity training and communications skills classes. Relevance is easier to establish by beginning with a look at daily give-and-take behaviors.

These work behaviors can be measured with a brief questionnaire. Individual scores indicate how much a person initiates and is open to actions associated with group *inclusion, control,* and *openness.* Using everyday events moves naturally into team building as discussions assess if differences affect tasks and output. Employees who feel *included* are more likely to do a better job and to support a vision. They believe that they are a wanted part of the venture.

Some workers prefer a lot of up-front information, clarification, and introduction. Others will want less. Even so, all work relationships begin with inclusion agreements and "contracts." The formal inclusion contract is a legal statement of terms and conditions of the work being offered and accepted. This is the official hiring and terminating document. Equally influential are unwritten assumptions and expectations. The mid-1990s brought far-reaching changes in the known but unwritten inclusion assumptions about how employers and employees behave toward each other. This underlying *psychological contract* is defined differently by psychoanalysts and business school theorists.

Commonplace use of the term psychological contract refers to unstated agreements and norms of behavior in the workplace. The implicit expectations are attributed to both the employees who are payroll-and-benefits entitled and to their bosses, the vision-makers and business-initiators. Such expectations typically operate on the back roads of consciousness directly impacting relationships among everyone who is charged with making a work vision a reality.

A decade of change in workplace norms became apparent in the descriptions of training to build management skills. Career planning is billed, *not* for lifelong retention and in-house advancement, but, rather, to prepare an employee for lifelong employability. In other words, the programs are geared for *outplacement readiness*. Current reshaping of unwritten expectations stems from irrevocable shifts in scope and pace of work. First, global perspectives are replacing strategies that confine operations, economic or workforce decisions to national boundaries.

At the same time, and possibly a by-product of the global community phenomena, many workplaces are undergoing a stepped-up pace of change. Plans are shifted from incremental to immediate implementation. This is found prevalent in corporate adopting of more electronic and less mechanical technology. An increasing number of companies endorse management philosophies and strategies to promote decentralized operations with workflows involving matrix cohort groups.

Furthermore, the unwritten contracts surrounding *inclusion* issues surface as co-workers talk about differences of opinions about the day-to-day events. They discuss how frequently we should get together; how much we want to talk to each other; and what amount and detail of business information needs to be provided. Yes, this is less cosmic sounding than the demise of an employee's cradle-to-grave relationship with an organization; however, it is not unusual to find that this once-upon-a-time guarantee lurks behind unproductive or counter-productive behavior.

Individual scores reflect employee preferences for a lot or a little *inclusion, control,* and *openness* on the job. Group discussions permit review of differences seldom put on the table for direct attention. Such as, Who wants to be part of that group? Who wants to be calling the shots, making the decisions, and taking on responsibilities? Who prefers for someone else to exert strong control of the situation? Who seeks close ties with workmates? Who sees candor, continuous improvement, and innovation as valued outputs?

These questions are answered by the long-popular FIRO-B questionnaire. When a person puts their own FIRO results beside the scores of fellow workers, everyone gets a picture of similarities and differences in *inclusion, control,* and *openness.* FIRO-B is an acronym for the awkward-to-say title, Fundamental Interpersonal Relations Orientation-Behavior. The scores are frequency estimates, 0 to 9(hi), and are often recorded in semi-musical notations, 3/4, or 5/8, or 1/3. Test-author, Will Schutz, introduced the FIRO-B for team building during the 1940s, 50s and 60s. His tool is one of several early methods used to enable persons who work together to come to know each other more quickly.

Because of its brevity and readily understood scales, the FIRO-B continues to be widely used. It is familiar to hospital emergency rescue teams and space exploration crews, to production groups and service providers, to workers in start-up organizations and in long-established firms. An electronic-technology specialist, assigned by the Navy as part of a specially selected, ad-hoc crew for the maiden voyage of an untested nuclear submarine, told the following story.

There we were: a thousand feet underwater.

I scowled at the sagging mattress, swaying ever-so slightly not two feet from my face. The pings of submarine soundings occasionally filled the silence. Visions of numbers on flip-chart paper, taped to the walls of the training room we worked in last week, filled my mind.

Six numbers for each crew member. Six numbers, describing how we each said we behaved when it came to matters of inclusion, control, and affection. Six numbers which supposedly held the secrets of how we could survive 180 days—and nights—underwater on this nuclear invention of defense.

Survive in close quarters. Without coming to blows. Without serious emotional outbursts.

John: 5/2 - Inclusion preferences are based on a scale of 0 to 9, where the top number tells me about John's "expressed Inclusion." The number 5 shows that he is moderate in inviting others to be involved. His "wanted inclusion" is at a lower level The number 2 suggests that he does not need or want to be into everything that is going on. John reported a 7/3 behavior preference for expressed and wanted Control. This means he expresses control fairly often (at a 7 level on the 9 point scale), and he wants others to be controlling or directing much less often (3 is in the lower range of "wanted Control"). Lastly, in reflecting on John's Affection scores, it is clear these behaviors take a back seat to expressed Control. John expresses affection at a 3 level, and wants to receive warmth from others at a 2 level. His whole chart on the wall is vivid in my mind:

	Inclusion	Control	Affection/Openness
expressed	5	7	3
wanted	2	3	2

Harry: Inclusion 3/6; Control 4/ 4; Affection 5/ 5.

Steve: 3 / 0; 9 / 7; 1 / 4.

Inclusion, Control and Affection—or Openness, which the instructor advised us is now the politically correct title for this critical zone of interpersonal relations.

How the hell they figure out—or make up—this stuff is beyond me. And it sure doesn't make this Pullman bunk feel any less like a coffin. OK. OK. They made some points.

When Steve gets off in the corner and whittles away on some stump of wood for hours on end, I recall Inclusion—3 over 0. Steve expresses inclusion, which means I can expect him to initiate conversation at a level 3, not often, but once in a while. And he very seldom wants others to include him—he prefers a lot of privacy and quiet time. So when he's whittling, I can just leave him alone and not worry about it.

When John and I work together, he's the one with that 7/3 Control score, he's for sure likely to want to call the shots, make the final decision. Hey, I don't mind so much, I'm the one with 5 over 5 on Control. I'm pretty even handed on control stuff—just so it is organized and someone is responsible. Yep, I find John's 7 over 3 tells it like it is, it fits with how he works. I don't mind so much now that I know it's hard for him to turn over the helm to *anyone* else, *not* just me.

Steve is the harder puzzle. Doesn't want to be included, so says that score of 3/0. He wants to be let alone. The Control at 9/7 says he wants everything ship shape—tightly controlled by everyone all the time. That's a pretty good idea considering we are down this deep underwater and he's the man on the radar monitor. The rub comes in knowing he's got a 1 over 4 in affection/openness. He expresses trust and camaraderie at a level 1 and wants to become trusted pals at a level 4. How does one go about being buddies and show friendship to someone who keeps you at arm length all the time? How do I know when he's down or depressed? Or angry. Or needing me to show I'm on his side, that I really do appreciate his skills at the radar?

Lesson to Myself: *"This FIRO stuff helps me know what to expect and is a good start at understanding others."*

Having an internalized map of *inclusion, control,* and *openness* behaviors of a work group allows for reality checking and self-regulating. It also fosters interpersonal respect. Adjustments in subtle behaviors sets up improvements in work conditions. Diversely skilled hi-tech strangers are better able to collaborate. In the final analysis, their productions are not all that different from musicians who work with saxophones and trombones. Both rely on coordinating subtle rhythms and interpersonal behavior. Thus, they transform expertise into sound-messages that co-workers can integrate into their efforts.

Workgroup paradoxes resolve when a vision-goal is actualized. The inside-out maneuver, transforming inner-vision and paper-plans into productive activity, seems to work best when automatic responses spring from optimistic foundations. In times of heavy-duty ups-and-downs, the fortunate executive relies on a resilient set of positive beliefs about self, others, and tasks.

Finding that subconsciously motivated thoughts impact how we judge ourselves and others was surprising to a group of ivy league professors. These researchers announced recently that nothing is safe from the scrutinizing eye of the unconscious. However, many central Europeans, especially since the days of Freud and Jung, place great value in the unconscious. They accept that an inner process evaluates incoming perceptions and influences opinions and behaviors without a person being consciously aware of it. Certain subconscious mechanisms, such as skills used by typists and pianists, are less ominous sounding and are representative of automatic behaviors guided by an internalized "supervisor."

Attention from U.S. researchers to important effects of subconscious internal processes lends strong incentive for taking inventory of our backlog of perceptions. It would be easier if we came with housekeeper genes that recycle outdated or contaminated mental products and processes, similar to the apo E2s that clean out accumulated trash and spilled blood from the circulatory system. As it is, executives with fast-paced schedules acquire a storehouse of perceptions, some of which remain accurate, relevant, and useful—some of which do not. They must schedule time to sweep out mental litter. The myriad of impressions that expedite executive analysis of new situations are automatic-pilot actions that quickly multiply and can build to a point of overflowing or imploding. Excess apperceptions contaminate and clog the free-flow of respect for self, task, and others.

Others have keen instincts for when they are being respected and when they are not. There is an instantaneous detection function in our infrastructure that picks up on negative regard in each of three critical venues: self, others, tasks. An expected generation of excellent managers failed to materialize in spite of corporate efforts to refine and train supervisors in people management competencies. It did not matter what advanced technical or administrative skills a manager could perform, and it did not matter if a manager mimicked words of high profile motivators. When acts and words did not ring true, that leader got little more than a raised eyebrow from others unless the leader resorted to coercion.

On the other hand, tough talk, which sounds at times like harassment, can come from a Bear Bryant and be heard for what was underneath, his unshakable belief in the adequacy of each team member and of the meaningfulness of each person's efforts. A banner over his office door while he coached at the University of Kentucky read: We issue everything but guts.

Winning coaches and sports teams are favorite sources for quotes and anecdotes about coping with weekly competitive struggles. Suitable analogies for executives who deal with long-term survival with multi-group complexities are not quite as easy or frequent. Instead of instant replay videotapes, organizational leaders review biographies, histories, anthropological studies, and archeological discoveries. Such wide angle views with exposure over time are more instructive as we decipher what proven leaders believed and how those beliefs were acted upon. A look at the evolution of the Egyptian civilization reveals the benefit of their belief in positive regard for others' points of view. Respect for others allowed powerful national leaders to include lesser factions without violent coercion.

Five thousand years ago, Egyptian leaders effectively managed a melting pot of cultures. The Pharaohs governed social and business activities from 3100 BC through 330 BC, resulting in one of the longest lasting government systems. Executive responsibilities were defined through descriptions of the chief god, Ra, who was considered to be the direct ancestor of the king-administrators.

Ra, the sun god, rode in a solar boat across the daytime sky and traveled at night in another boat across the underworld. Ra arose fresh each day from the ocean of chaos to administer correct world order expressed through truth, justice, and proper social behavior. Ra's son, Horus, was equated to the ruling king. Known as the Living Horus, the Pharaoh served as administrator of correct world order.

Responsibility for ecological, social, and spiritual harmony continued to be led by the Pharaohs from the time Menes united upper and lower Egypt through the extended period of integration of small cults scattered along the banks of the Nile. Their administration of truth, justice, and proper social behavior ended when invading Roman armies overwhelmed them. A paradigm that helped the Pharaohs remain chief-executives for a period of thirty-one dynasties included a concept called *syncretism*. Syncretism refers to the leaders' intentional efforts to reconcile divergent, often contradictory, features of cultures that originated in northern and southern Egypt and along the riverbanks. Evidence of syncretism is visible in pictorial representations of the Egyptian gods. This artistic compositing technique demonstrated a respect for, and an inclusion of, communities with independently developed norms and religions.

Egyptian leaders worked proactively, non-coercively toward solidarity. One national god was used to incorporate several different cult gods. Animal features used in pictures and icons to depict gods in the small cults were added to the traditional humanform gods recognized by the larger culture group. Characteristics, names, and heroic episodes from the life stories of different local gods were attributed to one national god. The enduring quality of the Pharaohs' syncretism can be seen in current-day symbolisms. Falcon representations linked to governmental authority figures, begun with the merger of Ra with falcon-headed Horus, god of the Lower Nile, can be tracked historically. These symbols, which became prevalent in German warfare, survived and are seen in a number of present day national emblems

Non-violent methods of survival, as illustrated by the Egyptians, require emphasis on synthesis. This incorporating of others' ideas and points of view is done by leaders who follow through on vision updating. The Egyptian leaders of a melting-pot society built on positive beliefs-about and respect-for others. They wove together elements of the situations at hand and transformed their initial ideas into an inclusive system by using creative innovation rather than battle swords. Success ala le jazz-combo, in the old as in new cultures, calls for adaptive skill, and artful blending of diverse ideas.

Collaborators in Transformations

Creative potential is often represented by the fertilization of the female egg by the male sperm. A new life is a prime example of the value of becoming collaborators in transformations. A French priest-archeologist, Teilhard de Chardin, wrote about being collaborators in creation. He encouraged people to think and to live so that they contributed to an ongoing evolution toward a higher state of being. He said that together with others, we are to "proceed as if limits to our abilities did not exist."

We face severe limits when we attempt to proceed without others. Even after conception and birth, we need others to get us going, to keep us on track, to surprise us with a new perspective. Studies of children who survived in the wild without human guidance show that they were constricted in learning and had considerably shorter life spans.

For the vast majority of us, experiences between birth and death will include similar physiological transformations, primarily constrained by a family's level of knowledge and nutritional habits. In infancy our dependency upon older, wiser beings is obvious. Gradually, infant dependents acquire skills. We become agile and proud in moving ourselves about, in speaking our minds, and in thinking through our actions. Throughout our years, we re-experience periods of dependence, most commonly, when we go into a new situation, when we try to learn a new skill, or as we adapt to changed procedures or relationships. Along the way there are periods of counter-dependence and rebelliousness. This growth process moves ever toward independence, and, eventually, into interdependence. The age of self-sufficiency tempered by cooperative engagement with others lasts until later years. Then, a gradual reduction of capabilities and strengths increases dependency.

Counter-dependent phases occur periodically—typically in age ranges of 2-3; 13-15; 33-35; mid 50s; mid 70s. After achieving independence, usually in the 18 to 22 age range, the trend is toward interdependence. Once a person learns how to organize and perform activities to carry out the business of daily living, that person begins to elaborate on these skills and capabilities. Many find careers providing skilled services that take care of others' daily living needs. Whether providing or receiving such services, non-abused persons mature into a sense of self-as-adequate. Most persons develop genuine interest-in and respect-for others and can acknowledge their own important-but-not-perfect status within a social group.

Inevitable person-to-person differences that are not appreciated are likely to be persecuted, especially when part of dependent-counter-dependent scenarios. At the trial of persons involved with a Texas sect that opposed social norms and authorities, the defense attorney's first act was to object to the labeling of the people on trial as Branch Davidians. The defense logic insisted that this "group name" allowed others to dehumanize and daemonize the individuals, who were the remnant of a larger extended family group. The survivors of the to-the-death shooting stand-off with federal agents faced murder charges. They were prosecuted as responsible in the deaths of other sect members who died while their fortress house burned.

Their lawyer described his clients, the defendants, as persecuted victims. The defense strategy was to influence perceptions of jury members. His evidence would sound different, more favorable, if the accused could first be presented as innocent, hapless devotees. The label Branch Davidians, so the attorney argued, would lead the jury to unconscious pre-conclusions, such as attributions of self aggrandizement, deliberate suicidal ideation, and a knowing commitment to conditions leading to others' deaths.

Under more typical life conditions, body and mind remain receptive to growth processes and new inputs. Individual storehouses of perceptions, like magnets, gather and organize new perceptions. The survival-and-growth biased infrastructure is oriented to making improvements on the past and to transforming as much as possible in the surrounding world. If we do not become rigid, as do ill-fated cult groups when they lock into behavior to protect cherished perceptions at all costs, we continue eager to become ever more effective in situations to which we are exposed.

I finally realized why I struggled for two weeks to get more effective at expressing the ideas for this chapter. Trying to write about the importance and the role of others in achieving a vision, felt like trying to re-write *War and Peace.* Day by day, others in my work and family life intervened in ways that were amazingly helpful and/or harmful to my work on the chapter. During the first week of the struggle, I was distracted by strong emotions about the cousin who got me my first professional job and gave me the most grief in my working years. I learned that while she survived a major surgery, the prognosis described a rapidly growing, terminal cancer.

A different emotion scattered my concentration the second week. I received a telephone call from the administrative head of a professional association in which I had held a position as an elected board member for eight years. This colleague, recently hired to fill the organization's part-time post, told me he decided to disregard an agreement he and I worked out that could improve organizational decision-making. He arbitrarily conducted a board voting process in a less inclusive, but quicker way that was personally convenient. I was surprised, disappointed, then angry. I find that someone who reneges on agreed ways of working together violates a deep-seated sense of fair play and ethical social behavior. I must conclude that an apperception process is making the judgment, and ask if this automatic pilot work is out-of-date or inaccurate.

During the same two weeks, I spent extra time with family and associates. I took my grandson to the dentist for his first filling. I had lunch with a man whom I love dearly and listened spellbound to his latest Harrison Ford adventures. He described, in detail, about flying into Angola and, in the process of completing environmental and ecological fact-finding for business developers, how he wound up cavorting in a speeding boat, full of intoxicated, daring-do mercenaries. His stories entertained me and reminded me why I would be signing up for days of genuine worry if I ever said "Yes" to his periodic suggestion that we establish a permanent relationship.

After lunch, I fulfilled a promise to a fellow consultant. I completed proposal details on a potential joint-venture project. While faxing the finished outline for consulting-training work in the Panama Canal Zone,

I wonder if a government agency's administrative group, even though based in the exotic tropics, could be as stimulating, diverse, and impressive as a group I worked with the previous month.

What was great about that particular group? They had the stamina for high risk ventures without abandoning all controls like the speedboating Angolan entrepreneurs did. Moreover, they left me feeling proud of American managers and executives. The fact that they are real inspires me to keep finding time and improving skills in order to write this book. They motivate me to re-concentrate, to set aside the distracting concern about terminal cancers and arrogant behaviors which were diluting focus. I returned to work with renewed clarity about these *others* and how they can be sources of great hindrance as well as of great help.

In the inspiring class that lingers in my memory, each up-and-coming executive arrived with an irrepressible openness to improvement. Although I've observed similar short-course dynamics for over fifteen years, this particular luck-of-the-draw class demonstrated that collaborative diversity, especially in full array, optimizes potentials for personal growth and creative transformations. The following section contains thumbnail synopses of salient characteristics, showing the range of gender, nationality, religious preference, knowledge base, race, status, age, health, and traumatic life events that represent an almost-too-good-to-be-true composite portrait of an All-American management group who helped each other become "even more" capable. Names, of course, are changed.

Gerry: Strong, silent, Clark Gable type. One-time professional soccer player, single again, now in investment banking and wondering how to establish better relationships with co-workers—these new peers-and-others he's starting to work with. The group's devil's advocate asked him how he met—i.e., picked-up—women. Gerry replied: I sit at a bar and wait for them to come to me. When the group's laughter died down, poker-faced Gerry smiled: Yep, it's time I invested in getting to know others. It's time I go to meet them.

Murray: Graying hair, distinguished, clean-cut, Vietnam hero. Talks of celebrating with employees; talks of integrity in the midst of cut-backs and layoffs; talks of difficulty having his agenda heard by higher-ups. Murray usually talks last—firmly, clearly, impressively, but last and with little visible affect and no direct attention to his own wants, needs, hurts, dreams—no personal exposure. He heard the others in that room, who admired and respected his dedicated contributions—in fighting the country's battles, in fighting the company's battles—and who said that if they worked for him and he was basically the same as he was with them that week, they would need to hear and to feel that he would personally fight for them. Employees want to feel a boss will do battle for their needs and rights. They prefer that he not wait until the last minute to step forward. Murray signed up to be one of the first to speak to the group the next day, and talked about his new leadership strategy, asking for comments and showing warm, sincere emotion.

Edward: Ivy league scholar with big plans and achievement dreams, disenchanted, and moving away from career to get back-to-the-earth, independent and self-sufficient. Now, talked into being re-engaged with fast paced publishing, he's an idea generator, a tough critic with clout, and a thinly disguised, razor-sharp, unforgiving cynical edge. Edward, initially interested in thinking about his current disenchantments and when to leap out into a greener pasture, provided useful yet stringent comments whenever a person would ask for his viewpoint. The group's increasing thirst for, and respect for his opinion and perspective stunned him. Edward put a muzzle on his critical, saber-toothed super-ego. He reported that when he got back to his office the next week, his secretary remarked, You seem really relaxed. Is this going to last? In his e-mail message to me he included his reply: You bet.

Aaron: A holocaust child, a whiz-kid financial genius, a Rabbi, an offensive-defensive go-getter with business-passion. Pulling no punches; leaving no stones unturned; bearding the lions; hitting below the socially acceptable belt. It was Aaron who was taken on, challenged in some way or another, by each strong-willed group member with an interest in asserting an image as a boss. Aaron was disliked and ignored by others, until the class discovered a value for his bull-in-the-china-shop behavior. Aaron's audacious intrusions, often spiced with guilt-trip projections, frequently connected to something that eventually turned out to be critical and relevant to the issue at hand. Another gradual realization dawned on the class, that Aaron willingly backed off when someone had a reasonable, or humorous but logical, counter-point. At the same time, Aaron discovered to sense curious, new pleasures—the pleasure of letting others be right sometimes, the fun of actively contributing as others lead the action, and the virtue of being a challenging, but not violent receiver of others' negative emotions. He was able to not personally hurt while putting himself forward as a target for those who needed to be able to express their angry reactions to objectionable ideas, or to feeling walked-on. For Aaron, his early life history translated into the ability to sense and to respect the tragedies and prejudices in others' walks of life.

Beverly: Beautiful and black with attitude. Dramatic non-verbals, sarcastic grins, and powerful debate rationales. Controlled, directed smarts. A keen instinct for when something is not on-top-of-the table, when hidden agendas and glass ceilings are part of the environment. Not sure if she wants to try to smash through those glass barriers with her wit and charm to "show those suckers what's possible." She wonders aloud if this impression that she's being set-up and fenced-in, that she's being taken-advantage-of and kept-in-her-place are workplace realities—or her active imagination working overtime. She's considering how to get off the corporate executive track, and to get herself back into independent creative work and counseling. She would want to provide consulting services to those, like herself, who want to break out of economic and social limitations that surround them, inhibiting their talents. Beverly heard how loudly her non-verbal behavior was interpreted by her classmates as "attitude" and "put-down." She recognized this was a detriment to building the trust so important for opening corporate executive doors. She learned how her strategy of saying, I'll get back to you later on that, could make others feel she had a hidden agenda of her own, when actually she just wanted time to get things put together in a clear, complete, compelling presentation—wanting to have things perfect.

Sonja: The executive who said she liked to have fun while working, introduced herself to the group and gave her life history in a record setting 57 seconds. Sonja's discovery that week was that she had liked meeting new people when she didn't expect to find it worthwhile or interesting. She found that she could express her differences of opinion to even those she found to be the least approachable (such as, brash, over-verbal males). And she learned that she comes across as a knowledgeable manager, a good executive, and a strong leader when she isn't talking in hit-and-run, 57-second sound bites. The others in the group called it her "I am an important busy-person language." Sonja shifted from repeating "I know I'm a good manager," to offering information and suggestions, inserting different ideas and approaches and demonstrating her strengths. She practiced and enjoyed allowing her experienced wisdom and caring to be visible, unrushed and unpushed.

Tim learned that his humorous twist on every exchange *did not* make others feel his leadership ability was less, but it did make them feel he did not take them seriously. Tim also realized that his real hopes and needs got buried beneath the funny shaggy dog tales. He wished he had been his "real self" earlier in the week and had not kept others at such a distance until so late in the game. He knew from bitter experience that drinking alone is dangerous, and now he saw that thinking alone can be equally dangerous.

Stan: The easy-to-like, quietly heroic director of 90 managers scattered around in regional agency sites. While his high stress level was hidden behind a pleasant calm affect, he struggles internally with the challenge to feel adequate while being the one sounding board for so many individuals in charge of sub-units, and each under the gun to re-organize, economize, and cut back. Stan also plays a part in illustrating the point in a later section of this chapter.

Rajo is a handsome, rash, bright, courageous, caring, witty, young Turk. His incessantly hard-working energy included an intense determination to find out what skills are needed by executives—and acquire them asap. Rajo softened his edge as he recognized his intuitive gift for seizing the moment needs to be tempered. Rajo intends to begin by not neglecting to have patience with others beside and below him in his organization. He also intends to stay alert to when others above him see his zest and to overload him, and at times, send him into harms way.

Jack, the statesman and a self-proclaimed "natural" directive leader, is determined to end his career years by learning to mentor and to encourage participative management. That week, he realized he was working too hard to come across as believable in his newly acquired style. He also heard, with great relief, that others did not want him to throw out all of his old straight-forwardness. Others saw his natural directive behaviors as helpful on several occasions during the week. His blunt approach turned the tide when someone seemed to be "doing-a-number" on him or others.

Wil is spelled with one l, please. This distinctive variation from the expected turned out to be the lesser surprise about Wil. He soon dispelled every stereotype of professional football players. Not because Wil wasn't physically big—he is huge, in fact—but because his mental powers are more impressive than his muscle powers. The biggest block to his executive impact was a combination of youthful appearance and measured, carefully worded dialogues which gave others an impression that he was working-a-play—manipulating data and ideas to his own advantage.

Ned introduced himself as an average-Joe, working his way up through the ranks without a college degree, a man of the earth who can fish and hunt with the best of them. He showed his ability to spontaneously leap to the core of a problem and to calmly insist that everyone stay on track until a solution was generated. Since Ned wants to work on becoming recognized as a leader among executives, he heard that this begins by planning how to give first impressions that fit the occasion. Those first steps included: how he introduces himself and making sure he does apologize for not having a college degree; how he dresses and taking into consideration that executives in his industry seldom wear their combat boots at the Board meeting; and, how he gives opinions, speaking for himself without frequent name-dropping or attributing an idea to a well-known author or his favorite consultant.

And **Brent**, the youngster. A quiet, playful financial specialist, Brent is a fairly late bloomer. He is just choosing to capitalize on a natural perceptiveness about people and management. He decided after spending this week with these people that he was at last motivated to become more visible in his company, vowing he would become an active, contributing member of the executive management team. He heard how the group felt disappointed and undermined by his lack of intentionality or commitment, and how valuable his knowledge and insights were in balancing perspectives.

Free Agents and Strange Attractors

The superstar class introduced above underscores the role of others in the development of executive's insight. This group of 13 acted out what it is that keeps management dynamic: active openness to advancement and improvement. This anecdotal evidence of widespread drive for growth and improvement shows that those "others" out there are, indeed, organized processes.

Proof that we are non-stop movement toward maximum organization and integration might come from content-analysis rulebooks for popular sports. We organize our leisure time activities, constantly elaborating and expanding the rules of the games each year. If that doesn't prove that organized striving is a basic life process, then consider a classic perceptual "trick."

What do you see?

```
X   O   X   O   X   X   O   X   O   O   O   X   O
X   O   X   O   X   X   O   X   O   O   O   X   O
X   O   X   O   X   X   O   X   O   O   O   X   O
X   O   X   O   X   X   O   X   O   O   O   X   O
X   O   X   O   X   X   O   X   O   O   O   X   O
X   O   X   O   X   X   O   X   O   O   O   X   O
```

Did you see Xs and Os in random order in rows; or, did you see columns of Xs and columns of Os? Most of us automatically organize the information into columns, sorting what we see on the basis of similarity.

This instinctive effort and automatic organization of what's before our eyes is a birthplace for differences of opinion. Differences of opinion pop out whenever several people look at the widely recognized black-and-white picture of a goblet, which can also be seen as two profiles facing each other. Furthermore, I can sort out the meaning of this visual information by concentrating on the dark area and its edges, then shifting to focus on the white area. I see a different picture each time I shift eye focus, but I cannot see both images at the same time.

All of us perform perceptual tricks to organize ambiguity into something that makes sense, so that the information can be understood and used. Serious disagreements stem from different "sensible" ways people can organize what they see "out there." For example, in another well-known "trick" picture, are we looking at a profile of an old woman, or a young woman? This time a solid-color sideview of a woman's face is used to show us how emphasizing different minor details in a largely ambiguous picture can lead to contrary interpretations. A feather added to the hat leaves a sense of a younger woman. Lines that suggest a heavy neck and chin will lead to an impression of great age. Who is "right" and who is wrong? Heated debates are not unusual.

Athletes who become free agents don't hesitate to speak out about how they see the *facts* about what's out there and interpret realities of their value to the success of the team. In football contract negotiations, free agents can—and often do—get a great deal more money than others playing for the same team. At other times, a free agent winds up just that—free, with no income or teammates.

Americans fight wars to protect freedoms, including the right to speak out and to see things differently. We pride ourselves on outlawing human slavery and child abuse. Still, we remain on guard, fearful that others, if left to their own devices, will resort to violent behaviors, become disorderly, and cause the opposite of sensible order—chaos.

In times of chaos it is impossible to know what will happen next. Yet, chaos-theory argues that even disorder never goes beyond certain boundaries. Scientists show that nothing is without a recurring pattern and organized movement. Computer-generated studies find that over time every moving point is drawn into a visible shape and pattern, as if contained by an invisible basin. Chaos theory calls the invisible shape a *strange attractor,* and the shape that is formed in the computer is called a *fractile:* the order in chaos.

Given time, we usually discover how others we work with are organized and their different perceptions of realities that lead to our disagreements. More often much of human behavior seems random and unpredictable. Reading behavior backwards, getting at underlying thinking and beliefs, an individual's invisible basin that gives shape to actions, requires systematic observation of that person. An extended surveillance of a new coworker is rarely possible. Job assignments move us into an active working relationship immediately. Few companies keep a consultant available to conduct on-the-spot team building interventions. Such likelihoods mean it is advisable to meet strangers with a plan in mind. One approach to building a working relationship is spelled out in an unpublished formula. Newt Fink, a human relations trainer in New York, calls the procedure he recommends, ACTAAC.

This acronym stands for Acceptance, Caring, Trust, Affection, Affirmation, and Celebration. Step one is to pay close attention to what another is doing and saying. Asking questions for clarification. Saying out loud what you think that person is intending. Listening carefully to reactions to what you question. Will that person say: *Yes, I do prefer neat dressers. No, I'd never buy stocks short.* You can soon come to a fair assessment of a person's abilities, interests, and ground rules. Your job at that point is to *accept* what a person presents. Accept does not mean you agree, like, or can go along with it yourself. You just receive what is offered. The hard work is to avoid "seeing" what you wish to see there. You actively resist organizing data to suit your inclination.

Caring means you jointly take care of getting something done. This can mean doing an assigned job, completing a task, accomplishing an objective. In the process of carrying out your shared activity, all that you hear and observe will give credibility to, or cast doubt upon, previous self-reported beliefs. This is walking-the-talk time. It's a demonstration of how much you care about doing the work well. In that sense, caring does carry the connotation of having a positive regard for what we are doing and for those doing it.

The third phase of coming to know someone is called *trust*. In this formula trust is an active verb. I *trust* you to be where we need to be, on time and in the right uniform. Or, I *trust* you will be there, fifteen minutes late, out of breath and in your red jogging shoes. I *trust* you to give honest, full disclosure. Or, I *trust* you to give me an optimistic, best scenario, the one you think I'd most like to hear. In this case, to trust means to predict. We get a probability estimate. We expect that someone will perform in a way that is similar to previous behavior. Are the odds 1 in 3, 7 in 10, 99 in 100? We keep in mind that the best predictor of success is prior success.

If we find that we have similar core values like honesty, hard work, logical argument, then, we are likely to experience mutual *affection*. Affection is more than vague respect for rights and capabilities and it is not a prelude to sexual activity. ACTAAC affection describes relationships like: Cagney and Lacy. Butch Cassidy and the Sundance Kid. Amos and Andy. Charlie's Angels. The gang at Cheers. Veterans who were wartime comrades-in-arms. A basketball team that won the NCAA. Elizabeth Taylor and Montgomery Clift.

No-strings-attached affection produces mutual *affirmation*. I affirm you and you affirm me. We are OK just as we are—with all our warts and wrinkles, and even with our imperfections in thought and deed. In fact, we are more than just OK. We are likable, lovable, because we have quirks. When we work together, I feel proud to be me, to be able to offer what I can do. And because of these positive attitudes, I can risk learning new things. I know that, if in the process of learning, I look silly or seem dependent or inept, you will still hold affection for me. You will still encourage my improvement efforts, urging without demanding, suggesting that I keep on trying. And vice versa.

Celebration caps off the ACTAAC process. We heave a sigh of relief when hard work is over. And we can celebrate that it was good to work together. Victory parties sometimes can be gala extremes, if a task was difficult or life threatening. Smaller celebrations are interim milestone time-outs for those who work together. They are relaxing moments shared by those who understand the "inside" jokes, who remember what was fun, what was done especially well, and what was goofed. Celebrations can be over tea and coffee, can be dinner, can be a long walk, or an evening at the ballpark. Now and then celebrations are a company-sponsored recognition ceremony. Any way the celebration happens, it is a culmination of relationships that formed and matured on-the-job.

Supportive and appreciative relationship is not easy to cultivate in our democratic society of free agents, each with our own invisible basin of beliefs and values, and each proud of our special cultural roots. With each wave of immigrants and multi-national enterprises it becomes more important to find ways to stand in each other's shoes. Only then do we see the sense of things according to diverse perceptions and apperceptions. Understanding and respecting the meanings others attach to what they see is complex, much in the same way that interpreting a work of art is difficult to fathom.

A 1999 exhibit in New York City, featuring a Madonna portrait made in Africa, caused outcries of blasphemy so vehement that the mayor took a critical position. He threatened to withdraw funding for the art show. Was this art at its most vile? Or is it a graphic witness to vast cultural differences in the meanings attached to what we see out-there. The African artwork used elephant dung as a prominent ingredient along with the paints. The stylized figure of the virgin mother was surrounded by diverse images of the male genitalia. An art critic explained that in Africa, elephant dung is associated with fertility. The same meaning is given to the male genitalia. For people of the culture of the artist, the earth mother and her fruitfulness were optimistic expressions of hope for the future. For others raised in a traditional Western religious belief system, this picture was an outrage. U.S. culture considers animal feces to be unclean, worthy only to be mentioned in oaths of loathing.

We in high-tech environments have come far from our agrarian lifestyle. Heated debates cannot prove who is right and who is wrong about the real meaning of the Madonna painting. Each group will see according to their organization of reality. We can hope that respect for "strange" ways of looking at things will grow, and that we can sort out the shocking exhibitions that are money-making con acts from those that are genuinely innovative and culturally honest.

Complementary and Contrary: Others As "Swiss-Cheese" Assets

The FIRO behaviors chart and the ACTAAC relationship flowchart give us different ways to think about *what's important* for people who are brought together to do a job. They are springboards for addressing behavioral diversities that enhance work-group success and contribute to a productive enterprise. Another way of describing work-groups and predicting how compatible and productive they are likely to be is a Myers-Briggs Type Table. This grid presents 16 ways people go about problem solving. In order for a group to be equipped with every coping "strength" that unit would have 16 coworkers, one of each "type." These personality types were hypothesized by Carl Jung, a Swiss physician-psychologist who lived at the turn of the 20th century.

The Myers-Briggs Type Indicator (MBTI) is a questionnaire prepared by Isabel Myers and her mother, Katherine Briggs, that concentrates on a particular portion of Jung's work. The type table grid emphasizes complimentary and contrary ways people use to gather information and arrive at conclusions. The questions were written to sort out what's happening in an individual's life at the time of responding to the MBTI items. A person's scores, reported as one of the 16 psychological types, offer a plausible framework for reading behavior backwards.

Isabel Myers and her mother were interested in discovering recurring patterns people use when engaging with others and when going about the business of problem solving. They wanted to help people connect with promising career paths and to encourage them in continuing in a lifelong process of development. Each pattern is associated with particular strengths, and certain blind spots. No one pattern is ideal or best. Therefore, MBTI team-building workshops foster positive regard for self and for the diversity provided by other types. Confusion can come about when results from one-shot MBTI assessment are assumed to reflect a lifetime preference. Another common misunderstanding occurs when workers think their less preferred options are inoperative. Locking into one pattern misses the point of lifelong improvement, and can lead to a self-fulfilling rut or cop-out. A larger issue is that of full reliance on any one questionnaire or theory. To use just one of the three approaches described above will underestimate the importance of the other characteristics, theories, and circumstances.

Clever anecdotal descriptions of the sixteen patterns predict what people who report each preference are likely to do, feel, and experience. Enthusiastic endorsement by most of those who get their MBTI results gives reassurance that the questionnaire does tap into their life experience. Two examples below from the superstar executive class show how MBTI results can help to sort out what's happening and which behaviors to "trust" that a person will repeat. The MBTI extends our ability to read behavior backwards, or, put in the vernacular, to understand *where a person is coming from.*

The first anecdote is about the compounding consequences of the most easy-to-observe MBTI dimension, an individual preference for Extraversion or Introversion. Beverly, the strategic planning executive constrained by *glass walls,* said on a noticeable number of occasions during class discussions, "I'll get back to you later." Her MBTI scores reflected a preference for Introversion over Extraversion, indicating a pattern of choosing to reflect before acting whenever possible. The young, sharp-witted Black woman was not—in that instance—exhibiting her *attitude* toward established, older White males. She was doing what most every person who prefers Introversion would do. She wanted to pause and give deeper attention to the matter at hand.

An introverted characteristic in no way establishes or negates the presence of *attitude.* Her attitude, which led to others feeling put-off or put-down, was picked up in her non-verbal grimaces, raised eyebrows, and a negative shaking of her head while others were speaking about their point of view. Many Introverts do not demonstrate any *attitude.* Also, imagine how Beverly's attitude would impact others if she had preferred Extraversion. In general, those in leadership roles can and must Extravert. Not only will an executive need to speak up and use a good amount of "air" time, an executive will need to be competent at extraverting. That requires practice, especially for the estimated 50% of managers, who are reporting preferences for the quieter, more reserved, and understated pattern.

Stan, another classmate with MBTI preference for Introversion, directs 90 managers who are scattered across a regional zone. On the first day, classmates agreed that he was the most easy to like and talk to in the group. Back on the job, Stan struggles to be fair to each of his 90 managers as their organization prepares for massive staffing cutbacks.

High stress levels lay underneath his pleasant, calm *first-impression.* His MBTI preferences, Introversion, Sensing, Feeling, and Perception (ISFP), are rarely reported by executives. One descriptive hypothesis for the ISFPs predicts typical behavior will be: *Retiring, quietly friendly, sensitive, kind, modest about their abilities. Shun disagreements, do not force their opinions or values on others. Usually do not care to lead . . . do not want to spoil the present moment by undue haste or exertion* (see MBTI Manual, page 20).

Stan is a leader who likes being a leader and wants to continue to lead. Some ISFP predictions, like the ones just above, did not fit Stan's estimations of himself. He found, however, that other ISFP predictions were right on target. They were capsule reflections of behaviors and emotions he experiences in his day-to-day struggles (see MBTI Manual, page 25). These MBTI hypotheses allowed Stan to organize his thinking about what he was doing. He was able to get clearer about what he wanted to do differently and the particular skills he needed to improve. In order to fulfill his leadership role well and remain as fair as possible, he decided to enroll in negotiation-skills training. In the interim, he believes a coursemate's suggestion will prove practical and do-able. His ESTJ classmate explained one of his favorite lessons-of-experience as practicing Solomon's wisdom: let your managers decide if or how to cut up certain of the programs.

The full MBTI grid-portrait of this outstanding class does not represent thirteen of the MBTI strengths. In fact, they represented only half of the complete team, 8 of 16 possibilities. They were, nevertheless, exceptionally productive. Our world is populated with people like Stan who do not fit neatly or completely into any one of the sixteen patterns.

The "Superstar" Executives

MBTI TYPE TABLE

ISTJ Sonja	ISFF	INFJ	INTJ Will
1	**0**	**0**	**1**
ISTP Tim; Ned	**ISFP** Stan	**INFP**	**INTP** Beverly; Gerry
2	**1**	**0**	**4** Edward; Murray
ESTP Rajo	**ESFP**	**ENFP**	**ENTP**
1	**0**	**0**	**0**
ESTJ Aaron; Jack	**ESFJ**	**ENFJ**	**ENTJ** Brent
2	**0**	**0**	**1**

The overriding benefit of MBTI training for executives is the recognition of the need to become competent with each MBTI characteristic. Not until we reach late mid-life are we expected to achieve Jung's vision of a mandala-circle of skill-on-all-scales. Before that stage of life, a type table can guide employees, hourly wage earner and salaried alike, to clarity about how co-workers can be complementary. Recognizing who can fill in our skill gaps reinforces how diversity can strengthen our productivity.

Yes, it is easier to talk with someone similar to ourselves, someone with the same MBTI preferences, of the same gender, and the same cultural heritage. And, yes, we can learn most from others who have different ways of gathering information and reaching conclusions. These others can be role-model teachers. We can learn from them new ways to gather data and arrive at decisions, ways that can lead to the full development of our own problem-solving competency. Reviewing a type table together lets workgroups defuse difficult-to-discuss problems and concentrate on how to merge their diverse strengths.

Structured instructional approaches, such as offered by the MBTI and FIRO, are proven aids for working well with others. Just as often, folk wisdom brings home the value of complementary and contrary human assets. The following paradigm for down-to-earth respect for others was learned on a rainy night in Georgia. A small group of us sat on bar stools unwinding, and dissecting the long day spent in intensive team building. The workgroup's leader eased others' left-over tensions as she spun out the story of her Swiss Cheese Philosophy.

The altruistic executive director of a regional mental health center launched into her homey analogy with a twinkle in her eye, and genuineness in her voice. She said she concocted the Swiss cheese theory so she could talk about her work without using threatening "clinical" terms. She learned how to present a credible argument, one which gained community support for the agency's social and psychological services. Her on going challenge was to make the work of the mental health center comprehensible while generating positive regard for and among patients, clients, staff members, board members, elected officials, and local citizens. The Swiss cheese image established a common ground among the disparate groups.

She began her public speeches talking about her Swiss cheese view of the communities served by the mental health center. She described how she discovered that each individual has a contribution to make to a community. She learned as she met with different families and groups throughout the catchment area, that, collectively the community is able to fill in holes and gaps in each other's lives. She presses on with rationales for funding particular services, such as education, counseling, medical resources. In her final community project, she spoke to the leaders of the community about the need to fund assisted-care residential facilities.

She was convincing as she pointed out how each of us needs others to cover "empty spaces" at times. No matter who we are or how much we have achieved and produced, when taken as a single slice of humanity, we are as full of blank spots as an ordinary slice of Swiss cheese. She advocated that it was only when we put ourselves together with other selves than any semblance of completeness or solidness is possible. She fills her argument with stories about area people who prove her point, sometimes in poignant ways, sometimes in funny incidents, and always described with respectful caring.

As I reflect on this executive's years of work during a time when mental health funds and public interest waned, I grow sad. This earnest champion of others' needs has made a major career shift. She now sells real estate, has a high six-figure income, and owns her own impressive beach property. Yet, I am sad—more for others than for her.

After several years of success, and about ten months before she changed career tracks, a number of community leaders organized to block approval of an assisted-living home for retarded adults which would be built in an established residential area. Residents became fearful of a negative impact on surrounding property values and derailed the project by criticizing, not the director's proposal, but the director's personal life. Newspapers picked up on vague allegations, dwelt on rumors, and ran a feature story about acceptable sexual orientations.

Familiar with the power of the Southern-bred community culture, and recognizing the "handwriting on the wall" that she would no longer be productive in her work, she rechanneled her keen thinking abilities. The Swiss cheese executive directed her energies toward filling holes for people in more profitable work venues. She is happy and successful in business and private life. Even so, I remember her talent and vision as an advocate of needed social reforms in the community and an investor in training for her staff, promoting their progress toward management excellence. I remember the exceptional leader who fell victim to others' perceptions, fears, and anxieties. And, I wonder if she remembers the Swiss cheese philosophy.

Tom Peters, the promoter of excellence in corporate ventures, claims that perception is all there is. High profile stories of corporate gossip make the point painfully clear. Two high performing Bendix executives lost their jobs because of rumors of an office romance, which, in spite of their protestations that there was no romance, the company determined as an unacceptable perception. Apple Computer stock prices dropped because it appeared that management had become disorganized. Suggestions that there might be mad cows among the grazing herds causes humans to stampede.

Executives work to prevent perceptual stampedes, their own and others. They take time to review and sort inputs. They clear out the litter and spilled blood. They organize information to resource jazz combo work groups, to encourage collaborative transformations, to respect the free agent and strange attractor-nature of others, and they value their complementary, sometimes contrary, assets in the work arena. Executives are busy, actively protecting diverse points of view as the beginning of truth, managing to stay humble and generous no matter how large the corporation grows, and no matter how widely known the company name may one day become.

Background Reading

Tom Peters, the promoter of excellence in corporate ventures, is frequently quoted as saying "Perception is all there is." His book with Robert Waterman, *In Search of Excellence,* the 1982 "must read" book published by Harper & Row, now serves as a guide to understanding which excellent companies did not survive the decades. A stronger, scientific support for the paramount function of perception is provided by Arthur W. Combs in his republication of *Perceptual Psychology,* Springer, 1999.

While many jumped on the bandwagon of popularity experienced by the Myers-Briggs Type Indicator, Isabel Myers and her mother, Katherine Briggs, intended their questionnaire to be used to apply to a particular portion of Jung's work. They wanted to look at constructive uses of differences that arose as a consequence of preferences related to perception modes and decision-making modes. The best source of information about the way the MBTI questionnaire approaches Jung's complex and diversely understood theory of personality development is *Gifts Differing,* written by Isabell Briggs Myers and her son Peter B. Myers, published in 1980 by Consulting Psychologists Press. The history of the development of the questionnaire and guidelines to appropriate interpretations of the scores are found in the *Manual: A Guide to the Development and Use of the Myers-Briggs Type Indicator,* updated by Mary H. McCaulley in 1989 and, again in 1998 (Myers, I.B., McCaulley, M. H., Quenk, N. L., & Hammer, A. L.), published by the Consulting Psychologists Press of Palo Alto, CA.

Newt Fink, the director and facilitator for adult education and training programs based on methods and theories introduced by Kurt Lewin and like-minded social scientists, developed the ACTAAC acronym to describe the course of events he found to be associated with building lasting and productive relationships. Acceptance, Caring, Trust, Affection, Affirmation, Celebration. The center is no longer operating and Newt Fink retired without publishing his numerous teaching rubrics. He could be contacted through the Synod Office of the Presbyterian Church in Saranac Lake, NY.

The Encyclopaedia Britannica, 15th Edition, provided background for quotes from Teilhard de Chardin and historical data about the early Egyptian civilization and cultures along the Nile River.

To read more about Peter Drucker's prediction about the dawning of a new age of transformation, see his book, *Managing the Future,* or his article in the *Atlantic Monthly,* Vol. 274, No. 5, Nov. 1994, pp. 53-94.

"Truth" is a 25-foot tall sculpture in the Vinoy Park, St. Petersburg, FL. The abstract work was completed in 1982 by St. Petersburg artist, Rolf Brommelsick. The photograph of the Tampa Bay waterfront sculpture is by Laura Krieger, staff for the Leadership Development Program conducted by the Management Development Institute based at Eckerd College.

Chapter 3

Enterprise and Collective Investment

An enterprise is organized, dynamic, and directed toward survival, adequacy, growth, and meaningfulness. An enterprise thrives with people who are committed to working together on a vision expressed as goals requiring multiple talents.

- Goals are Start-up Signals and Finish Line Markers
- Ethical Work and Critical Paths
- Resilience and Giant Steps for Mankind
- Direction Flows Across Change and Challenge

A task without a vision is drudgery
A vision without a task is but a dream
But a vision with a task is the hope of the world
An inscription on a church wall in the county of Sussex, England
Jim Harris. *Getting Employees To Fall In Love with Your Company*

Webster's New World Dictionary.
enterprise. *(French: to undertake) 1. an undertaking; project; [A] a bold, difficult, dangerous, or important undertaking [B] a business venture or company.*
enterprising. *1. showing enterprise; full of energy and initiative; willing to undertake new projects. syn. ambitious.*

Goals Are Start-up Signals and Finish Line Markers

Some of us work to live, while others live to work. Executives tend to be among the latter, workaholics and Type-A persons who put in long hours with few, if any, days off. They find their work absorbing. The busy executive has a vision to turn inside out, and becomes fascinated with making it happen. The free enterprise crusade is conceived as bold, difficult, dangerous, and above all, a good investment of time, talent, and resources.

A decision to become an executive is a watershed choice, yet only the first among decisions that format the future of the quest. Priorities will *out,* spawned by that ever-active perception and apperception process, and will guide the selection of the kind of work to pursue, the management philosophy, and the ethical conduct of internal and external business relationships. Thus, an executive's beliefs impact organizational outcomes. Each enterprise will require investment of time and effort to clarify the way the company will work together, the means-to-an-end, as well as agreement on the destination and outcome, the end-in-itself.

Across the history of mankind, since the discovery of uses for controlled fire and the construction of the wheel, meaningful activity is associated with good health. Individuals and groups that radiate vitality and success are applauded for what they do and for the zestful way they go about it. Energy and activity are considered to be signs that all is well.

For most of our adult lives, that meaningful activity is called work. *What is your job? What kind of business are you in?* Curiosity about worklife is quick to follow introductory exchanges of names, home towns, yesterday's sports results, or local weather. Work is considered, by many counselors and therapists, to be the second most influential factor in one's life, a close second to family. In certain cases, work becomes *the* most influential factor for most of a person's life. Not surprisingly, the latter group includes a considerable number of executives.

Some of us work to escape family problems or controls, others work to be eligible for affordable health care. The reasons people work are endless. Most often people say they are working to get money to buy a house, to buy a car, to get a boat, to afford a diamond. . . . Some dream of retiring young and well-off so that they can enjoy many golden years. Artists, professionals, technical specialists and lucky career-satisfied workers claim that they work because of an enjoyment of the work itself. For most of us, it's a combination of reasons. We can even notice that our main reason to work shifts with maturity, and in response to unexpected trauma or disaster.

Visionary executives are compelled by a goal that turns their work into a grand adventure, filled with purpose and unknowns that are as challenging as were the vigorous expeditions of the twelfth century that Crusaders undertook for a grand cause or idea, or against some suspected abuse. Such dedicated self-investment inspires others to enthusiasm when they hear about the mission. Followers glow with admiration for someone with clear goals and the willingness to do *whatever it takes* to move in the direction of progress toward that intention. Inspired employees and peers work eagerly with redoubled energy on their assigned tasks.

Inspirational leaders are found working inside and outside of ready-made business or government structures. How long such a person remains with a venture after the start-up phase depends on what the entrepreneur values about the work. What's important? The end, the means, or both? When money-and-personal status are foremost, leadership with that workgroup is likely to be as brief and distant as possible.

Most of the executives that I have met work for more than the dollars. They work for the challenge and stimulation inherent in the activity. They find pleasure in the process and the products of their worklife.

Why Work?

		Short Term	Lifelong
1. As a means to an end	Objective	**Money** Fly-By-Nite Dilettante Possessions	**Lifestyle** Retirement Perks Family Obligations Bequests
2. As an end in itself	Objective	**Excitement** Start-up Fun Opportunists Stock Marketeers	**Fulfillment** Achieving a Vision Absorbed, Fascinated Enjoying Work

What makes an executive's work different from play? One distinction is that results of a complex and evolving vision are remote in time. Ideas that stimulate executive behavior are, in many ways, advanced versions of childhood play. A child skipping stones across a pond behind grandfather's house had great fun. That fun was in counting the hops before the stone's final plunge underwater, seeing how far ripples traveled from that final drop-point, searching for flatter stones that might skip farther toward the center of the pond. Then, there is the analyzing of the best throw, practicing to perfect the tossing of the stones, and the wondering if it's possible to make an island in the middle of the pond this way. A vision of a new product makes an activity more meaningful. Such impromptu and systematic playing on a muggy summer afternoon is a forerunner of future corporate planning. It's a thinking through of possibilities and factors to make something work well or to produce something new. Later, a full-blown executive spends afternoons gearing up for long-range business success.

Playtime experiments guide a child's selection and adaptation of materials and processes (the means) to make the idea come true (the desired end). What we call work, at any age, is when completion of the idea takes a long of time of concerted effort or when we are given a job without a clue as to what the activity produces in the end. Just knowing about expected outcomes and purposes will give meaning to actions that would otherwise turn into drudgery. Business administration specialists picked up on the motivational appeal of goals. They built management procedures for how to prepare mission-goal statements and mapped participatory planning down through each work unit. Management-by-objectives (MBO) became the rigor *du jour,* reaching a zenith in the 1970s and 1980s. Managers' spent time with their subordinates drafting goals and objectives to be included in a corporate strategic plan. Senior managers and executives fleshed-out the business plan by analyzing strengths-weaknesses-opportunities-&-threats. It became possible to direct and control activities in ever-larger businesses. At the same time, workers at all levels in an organization were included in a piece-of-the-action. Each employee could see where his or her work fit into the big picture.

MBO swept through workplaces like a seasonal flu virus. Business leaders and educators were convinced that fame and fortune awaited those who could reduce their work to clear and measurable statements of expected outcomes. Best-of-all MBO-worlds included objectives with action plans detailed into time and task charts, preferably PERT (Program Evaluation and Review Technique) or Gantt (a tracking of concurrent and interdependent subprojects). Output had to be foreseen and reported in quantifiable terms. The more detailed and specific, the better. Ideally, everyone knows when a goal is satisfied and can join in celebrating the achievement. A requisite debriefing, often reminiscent of Monday Morning Quarterbacking, would point out flaws and failures. Specific numbers that pinpointed imperfections were to show the workgroup how to do better next time.

I overdosed on MBOs. To this day, I cringe at the idea of goals, objectives, and action plans. Each class of executives that I taught concluded with a goal setting session. As each class worked on their own development plans, I set a good example and worked on goals for myself. During that same time, during the early 1980s, I contracted with a regional, acute-care, medical center to pull together their comprehensive package of annual-goals-and-objectives. I soon lost track of how many hours I spent collating, cross-referencing, and editing. My work area was stacked knee-deep in papers. There was plenty of workspace since I was given free run of an out-of service nursing station on the seventh floor of the hospital. My only distraction was emergency fire alarms going off in the deserted wing. I trekked down a dank, cement-enclosed stairway each time the old electrical system was tested. In all of those stacks of papers, nobody had an objective to notify de-activated stations when the alarms were simply system tests and could be ignored.

More distressing than paper shuffling and false alarms were discouraged, feet shuffling managers. Their resistance to the MBO project gave me a caution that was not a false alarm. As I met with bright medical professionals holding positions as health-care managers, sooner or later those with more than one year's tenure would point to a bookshelf lined with three-ring notebooks emblazoned with the corporate logo. Binders layered with dust held previous years' hopes. They marked a manager's years with the company. These managers resented using their time to plot out new objectives which they were convinced would be irrelevant before the coming year was half-finished. All enthusiasm lay buried in black-and-white-print, the ghosts of objectives-past and other unfinished plans. Unit objectives were overpowered by industry-wide changes. The fastest thinking, most up-to-speed department head struggled to cope with advances in computerized technology and in patient treatment modalities; at the same time they were confronted with constraints in government-regulated cost containment, in widespread restructuring of insurance company coverages, and in financially floundering consolidated hospital coalitions.

During the late 1980s and early 1990s, work stress emerged as more important to organizational productivity than detailed forecasting of non-durable objectives. In the case of the regional hospital, my consultation assignment shifted when the chief executive became aware of a pressing need to address employee distress and morale. I administered a job stress survey to organize the managers' grumblings into information about work overloads and excessive pressures. I needed to find common ground, to get evidence of the stressors that bothered many managers.

To get a stress calibration, survey reports were collected from each work unit and corporate level. Stressors that managers perceived to cause more than an average amount of stress were identified. Then, recommendations were drafted, suggesting ways to alleviate or remedy the conditions or procedures causing most managers distress. Two years later managers reported a reduction in stress overloads from the initial distressors. Consequently, different stressors rose to the top of the list of sources of stress for the acute care center.

Initially the top stressors for a majority of the 52 managers were: *deadlines* (70%); *fellow workers* (67%), *paperwork* (64%); *crisis* (64%); and *insufficient personnel* (56%). A close runner-up was *interruptions* (46%). Follow-up activities began with assigning each leading stressor to a task group for validation and clarification.

Each member of a task group came from a different department. Together, they prepared recommendations for solutions. Senior management authorized most of the suggestions proposed by the cross-department committees. In a subsequent assessment, deadlines, fellow workers, and paperwork dropped out of the top stressor spots. Deadlines went from being the top ranked stressor to sixth. Stress caused by fellow workers, which was one rationale behind setting up cross-department task groups so fellow workers could get better acquainted, dropped from second place to eighth. Excessive paperwork—linked in the managers' minds with goals-and-objectives busywork—went from third ranked to fifth. Dealing with crisis situations dropped from fourth spot to eleventh, which was especially noteworthy in an acute-care center.

What new stressors came to the top? Insufficient personnel, salary, and equipment. Not one of these impacted as much as 50% of the management group. Interruptions also moved up—from sixth place to fourth, yet was impacting only 36% rather than 46% of the group. In a structured survey, when one item moves down in importance, by necessity another moves higher on the list. Interestingly, in this case, a slight reduction in overall stress level was overshadowed by the variety in sources of distress. Less than half of the individuals were reporting overloads of stress from any one source.

Stress overloads and department improvements are both manageable when management applies systematic thinking to the puzzle of what's limiting productivity. Then, a target can be set. Managers can specify a desired change, a goal. Overdosed or not, we know setting goals will remain important. Goals get us out of the starting gate and into the race—moving forward, turning a vision inside-out. Common goals lift workers above immediate differences, and allow them to concentrate on contributing to the shared vision. A common goal provides workers with both a start-up and a finish line—and with a built-in dissatisfier. A time of let-down, like a post-partum, can follow the completion of a project. Especially for those whose work is more than a means to an end, and who thrive on the action of the hunt, an emptiness reaction is not unexpected. A new goal is often the quickest antidote.

Ethical Work and Critical Paths

Post-project blues seldom last long. New trouble spots will need attention as long as an organization operates. Endless problems to solve and few quick-fixes will dissipate any illusions that being given a natural talent for having an enterprising vision — even for the hyper-bright — is a one goal, one path undertaking. Survey analyses of management careers predict that professional workers can expect seven job changes and three career changes. Most likely, managers will stay longer with work where there is a personal fit with the substance and the demands of the work itself. How many executives do you know who could have made the statement similar to this one allegedly spoken by a vegetarian who oversees the promotion of beef for a state agriculture department: "It [being a vegetarian] has nothing to do with my work. It's a personal preference."

Those who work to promote or produce something that they personally eschew may find themselves working between the proverbial rock and a hard place. Fortunately for the vegetarian alluded to above, public sentiment has not soured toward the beef industry as it has toward cigarette producers. Managers who work for tobacco corporations and attended executive training classes that I conducted faced aggressive challenges from their counterparts from other industries. "How does it feel to work for a company responsible for millions of deaths each year?" This abrupt question was addressed to the young, non-smoking, planning executive of a nationally known cigarette manufacturing firm on the first morning of a week-long program. A ready smile accompanied her cogent, logical, data-filled and positive response. Her neatly articulated reply suggests that her company was very aware of the strength and tenor of prevailing social opinion. Her field of work, in a once-respected and profitable industry, is now quickly criticized as a public pariah.

Corporations, no longer able to guarantee lasting respect for the business activity any more than they can guarantee career-long job security, reframe recruiting appeals to offer training for employees in skills that will carry them across inevitable changes in their worklife. Portable skills needed by executives are more than technological know-how and competence in intellectual property development. For an executive, it's the skill to attune inner judgment-filters to be sensitive to social trends and to the ethical implications of the nature of the work. They need a quick sense of what's important about the work per se, substance and processes. Executives must see the heart of the issues that impact the immediate, the big picture, the long-run, and the vision.

In the late 1800s work was sorted into six or seven categories. These were translated into English under the labels of realistic, investigative, artistic, social, enterprising, and conventional. Common sense job-distinctions were based on the nature of the work as follows:

> *realistic* - hands on work with things, i.e., skilled crafts,
>   engineers, plumbers;
> *investigative* - mental activity working with ideas, i.e., biologist,
>   mathematician, scientists;
> *artistic* - creating ideas and things, i.e., musicians, painters,
>   librarian, reporter;
> *social* - helping people, i.e., priest, teachers, therapists;
> *enterprising* - managing people and ideas, i.e., managers,
>   executives, lawyers; and,
> *conventional* - fitting into established structures and standards,
>   i.e., secretary, accountants.

Most occupations call for blends of generic classifications, as in the case of bankers, who usually report a combination of interests that sort-out under *conventional* and *enterprising*. Newer classification formats attempt to keep pace with changes in processes, activities and functional emphases associated with an expanding lexicon of jobs. One popular codification employs a set of seven generic classifications: Producing, analyzing, creating, helping, influencing, organizing, and adventuring. Connections between the two classification systems are, in most instances, easy to see. For example, farming and forestry are placed under the *producing* label, which is quite similar to the realistic category.

An interest in leadership is grouped with politics, sales, and advertising under the title, *influencing*. Insurance specialists, retail store managers, and hospital administrators report interests that fall under the *organizing* category. An all-new *adventuring* category captures the interests of those who are emergency medical technicians and test pilots, along with persons engaged in military service and athletic careers. Three other terms complete David Campbell's modernization of the original vocational interests: *analyzing* which is like investigative, *creating* which is similar to artistic, and *helping* which parallels social.

Each classification, by any label, includes jobs and types of work that range from highly regarded to outcast or illegal. The job title CEO is typically held by people who report vocational interests that mix *influencing, organizing,* and *adventuring,* most often with that priority order. The prevalence of these interests is not surprising. CEOs and visionary executives are reported to be individuals who, on occasion, are willing to take risks and to "push the envelope" of social norms and ethical parameters, although to a different degree and in a qualitatively different way than will jewel thieves and scam-artists. In the vocational records, *influencing* jobs are found to be filled by those who are generally confident in their ability to persuade others, and who are outgoing and relish verbal jousting. CEOs and executives are often hired to be resourceful at doing whatever-it-takes to turn the vision inside out. They first influence others to entertain the vision and, then, they motivate others to work enthusiastically to make it happen.

Typically, individuals in the *adventuring* jobs like to confront competitive situations, and have the stamina to enjoy intense physical activity. Much as they are interested in winning, they are also resilient in defeat. These characteristics contribute to an ability to survive the heat of demanding, stressful choices inherent in corporate leadership. What lends stability and, I suspect, inclination toward socially sanctioned work activity, is the interest called *organizing.*

People who are attracted to jobs and vocations falling in the organizing domain are usually good with details, budgets, and cash flow. They like managing projects, supervising people, solving the day-to-day problems that inevitably crop up in organizations, and assuring the quality, quantity, efficiency, effectiveness, and meaningfulness of the work. An I-O-A order of vocational-interests among CEOs lends evidence for a common-sense conclusion that executive-leaders *thrive when influencing others and are stimulated by opportunities to take calculated risks for escalating the success trajectory for the enterprise, when those risks are supported by comprehensive "homework."*

In Sydney, Australia, I learned that a majority of Australian CEO's have an *artistic/creating* interest among their top three categories. I wonder if some future comparison of U.S. and Australian CEO's top vocational interests will show that the Australian *artistic* interest replaces *organizing* in the top-three profile more often than it does the *adventuring* interest. Yes, it could replace the *influencing* interest, an option that seems unlikely to me, a U.S. American. But then, I hesitate to predict. I recall frequent surprises in cultural variations that I encountered on that trip. While in Sydney, I heard that Australians expect everyone to queue-up with an egalitarianism that is symbolized by an oft-repeated Aussie insight-tale. Caesar sent a runner to remind his too timid son that the best way to keep order in the region that he was assigned to govern was similar to cutting off the heads of the tall poppies in his castle garden. As the ruler of the kingdom, the son was expected to eliminate any local person who stood taller, stronger or ahead of the others.

It is not unusual to find that work assignments, personal inclinations and family demands are incompatible. Job satisfaction is rarer than desirable. Moreover, survival necessities and social practices shape individual abilities and beliefs. In Pacific Rim countries, the oldest-profession-in-the-world is included in their entertainment industry and is a source of livelihood for people whose most marketable skill is an ability to perform sexual activities. Ethical, legal, and health ramifications are raised by affluent societies and religious groups in protest against this type of work. Multinational objections to the lucrative international child prostitution business are vigorous and unified.

Yet, in most nations and in all recorded historical periods, visible minorities of citizens "make a living" doing work that is illegal or considered to be destructive to the well-being of the customers and, or, the workers. James Michner's books, such as *The Source* and *The Caribbean,* suggest that this was true even in pre-recorded history.

Declaration of a job as evil is far from being a simple issue. For example, selling drugs can be legal or criminal. Pharmacists sell approved and medically prescribed drugs. Small-time "pushers" as well as Mafioso-type drug-lords sell millions of dollars worth of non-approved drugs. Questions surround the determination of beneficial vs harmful effects of drugs. Some addictive substances are criminalized, like marijuana. Other addictive things are legalized, like alcohol. Hotly debated ethical and moral issues remain unanswered. In the meanwhile, a majority of people voluntarily pick work that is consistent with personal views, and that will contribute to the collective well-being. Less fortunate others do whatever work they can that will pay, even if that means filling out forms and standing in lines for welfare checks or food stamps, or even prostituting themselves.

In addition, group survival needs give rise to another realm of vocational options, such as the armed forces, state and local law enforcement agencies, and federal agencies including CIA, Alcohol, Tobacco and Firearms, FBI, Secret Service. Much of this socially sanctioned work is increasingly scrutinized and criticized. William Egan Colby, former director of the U.S. Central Intelligence Agency and a career intelligence-gatherer, commonly called a "spy," explained the virtue of his occupation by quoting Nathan Hale in an interview with *Time* magazine. Hale, a colonial soldier who was hanged by the British during the American Revolution for being a spy, said, "Every kind of service, necessary to the public good, becomes honorable by being necessary." Acceptance of Hale's philosophical view as a way to differentiate between good and bad work relies on the definition of *the public good,* and on an initial agreement about which public constituencies are included.

Accepting that the critical path of work, however virtuous, will never be trouble-free can be hard to stomach until one is faced with the prospect of not having any work to do. A whimsical commentary attributed to heroics in another troubled time in American history comes from the great depression of the 1930s. A man is said to have come home from work one day and told his family that the good news was that he didn't have to go to work the day after tomorrow—and that the bad news was that he didn't have to go to work the following days either. Such wry humor is intended to convey an underlying conviction that whatever life dishes out can be handled. Self-sufficient, determined, and rugged individualism is a long admired virtue inherited from America's new-world settlers, regardless of their point of origin.

Late in the twentieth century, free enterprise and service organizations suffered a memorable, but less widespread period of depression. Whole scale layoffs or riffs of mid-level managers followed in the wake of quick-fix efforts to maintain competitive production and pricing as U.S. markets were flooded with low price-tagged imports from less affluent societies. Management turned to statistical controls, touted as Total Quality Management (TQM), and promoted cost-cutting by introducing efficiencies for managing-the-process. The upshot was a decimation of management employees.

Analysis of the organizational downsizings that took place during the 1990s by the American Management Association showed that 18% of the cuts were middle manager jobs, a group that accounted for only 5% to 8% of the workforce. Repercussions proved more far-reaching than expected. A workworld side effect was widespread change in inner mind-sets among white-collar professional workers.

These buffer zone management workers served on the organization's front lines justifying decisions and behavior of senior managers.

Corporate pruning of workers previously charged with communicating corporate goals and achieving executive visions boomeranged. This rift within the private sector ranks put in motion a revision of attitude and trust that is reminiscent of stateside reactions to the 1970s Vietnam conflict. In that era, decisions by government executives to send American military personnel on a cross-cultural crusade precipitated widespread alteration of public sentiment about loyalty to federal decisions, especially those that irrationally wasted lives. Corporate victim or not, mid-career management specialists adopted an amended set of unwritten rules-of-work as they envisioned future critical-pathways in worklife with less corporate loyalty and more ethical questioning.

The initial aftermath to management job cuts was predominantly anxiety-filled. Depressive-reactions were experienced by both *the-fired* and *the-not-fired.* Adding to the bad-guy image of corporations, journalists began featuring stories about executive-track employees who suffered flash-backs to early-life parental or peer abandonment. Corporate downsizing behavior was judged as precipitating serious health problems and acts of violence in workers who found mid-life abandonment to be one straw too many. It was during the peak of the business world's pell-mell rush to efficiency by focus on task and neglect of relationships that one of my executive development classes, a group of ten, had two participants who were in the midst of coping with the recent suicide of a mid-manager. Their subordinates attributed these deaths directly to management cutback decisions. In one instance, the employee shot himself in the office where he had worked, after shooting and killing three of his former co-workers.

The end of the anxiety reaction to downsizing came when the public's cry of outrage made headlines. Nationwide expressions of anger followed an announcement of a planned reduction of 40,000 employees by the grand old parent-figure corporation, AT&T, familiarly known as "Ma-Bell." Cutbacks in staffing were revealed in conjunction with the news release about a further subdividing of this remnant of an American-enterprise icon. Spontaneous and broad-based expressions of disgust for the corporate behavior rallied the disenfranchised middle-managers. These workers had no unions. They had grown up believing that studying hard and remaining loyal would assure them of jobs. Termination packages were refused by a considerable portion of that 40,000 affected by the AT&T cutback plan. In their own ways, they said, fire me, if you dare, and become a proven self-serving corporate bully.

Like recovering from a death in the family, work-related traumatic loss will be followed by the commonly expected emotional pattern of shock: denial, anger, bargaining, depression, and, finally, acceptance. The depressive symptoms can begin early, during the denial experience. These down-times are predicted to continue in varying degrees of intensity and to be experienced even in the phases of anger and bargaining. It's the presence of hope that permits eventual acceptance and positive reengagement.

Resilience and Giant Steps for Mankind

Resuscitating employee enthusiasm becomes a critical executive skill in the wake of structural changes, whether these are internal shutdowns and staffing reductions, or involve corporate mergers and acquisitions. The abandoned-manager syndrome has variations, each of which produces ripple effects. Those who hold onto a job post, while senior executives, company names, and corporate logos are replaced, feel battered and suffer multiple bruises. Articles in the American Management Association's *Management Review,* the source for downsizing figures used here, indicate that half of these survivors have job stress symptoms, that corporate morale and commitment goes down, and that 60% wind up with higher work loads. Moreover, AMA's survey of subsequent corporate actions show that managers' lingering anxieties were not projections without substance. It turns out that companies that downsized once were more likely to downsize again.

Management that aspires to continuous improvement takes on a continuous motivational challenge. Innovative responsiveness to in-flight conditions and durable beliefs about the meaningfulness of the work replace old-time executive paternalism. Fresh approaches establish a basis for employees to regain sufficient security to become interested in the business and to experience camaraderie in their workday. The way to find out how intensive a resuscitation needs to be is to get out and about, asking questions: *How are things going? What do you need? What's the biggest recent screw up? How did management help? Who was most put out by this? What can I do to help?*

Executives who perform corporate-CPR after transitions and other "little deaths" like firings and re-locations, let workers know that the boss is interested in the employees and that they can have their say. This is a significant move toward restoring positive attitudes about tasks at hand. CPR is especially important when goals are mandated. Attention from the person in charge ameliorates the severity of predictable responses to experiences of loss or abandonment.

The U.S. government and citizen-legislators began taking responsibility for, and giving resuscitation attention to, the acute loss experienced by the North American Indian nations. Recent government efforts to support resilience and provide opportunity for advancement, even at this very late stage of the chain-of-consequences, are accompanied by a revitalization of energy and activity among the Native American populations. Shawnee, Apache, Sioux, Hopi, Iroquois, Dakota, Cherokee, Mohawk, Seminole and other industrious Indian nations once prospered on the North American continent. At the turn of the twenty-first century, 300 years after Indian tribes confronted overwhelming numbers of European invaders with superior weaponry, a few of the remaining proud and complex cultures are becoming entrepreneurial. Some Indian nations started "gaming" in new fields and without bows and arrows. Full-range gambling casinos are being established on impoverished Indian reservations with government authorized operating licenses.

Big time capital-gain dollars, all without taxation, enabled a N.Y. tribal council to pay off a loan of millions within six months for construction and start-up expenses of a Las Vegas style casino. Profitable as this new business is, ethical issues about the nature of the work inhibit other long struggling communities from taking advantage of the gaming licenses envied by other U.S. ethnic groups. One tribe steadfastly refuses to jump into the gambling business opportunity, insisting on maintaining the sovereignty of their own nation. They vow to engage in enterprises that do not capitalize on human weaknesses or frivolities, but that will contribute to the quality of human living.

Lower-income mainstream workers complain that the U.S. is the only nation in the world to win wars, and then have the former enemy come out ahead. Examples include colorful recollections of tales from wilderness-pioneers and wild-west wagoneers that describe inter-tribal wars, scalpings and brutalities that took place long before some original residents of North America engaged in wars and burned out, pillaged, and ambushed foreign newcomers. Arguments against what is seen as giving an unfair advantage to a former enemy stray to talk about how after WWII Japanese manufacturers took American know-how and captured the automobile manufacturing market, putting hundreds of laborers out of work.

These protesters describe tribal mentality as so rigid and stubbornly resistant to science and industrialization that they preferred alcoholism and madness above education and technology. The dissatisfied workers conclude that Indians did not self-destruct to the point of extinction only because the American government allocates taxpayer dollars for their housing, education, and sustenance. They consider it a great insult to victims of Indian violence that this new special dispensation from taxation and restrictions on once-illegal gambling is accumulating new tribal wealth, while the blue collar laborer stays poor. What the argument fails to notice is the re-emergence of a Native Indian spirit of can-do, will-do, and their willingness to manage a contemporary business. What is also missing in this view is any realization of how similar their identification with their victimized ancestors is to the argument given by Bosnian Serbs in 1999 for why they had a right to exterminate Bosnian Albanians, whose ancestors slaughtered Serbs four centuries ago.

Enterprising casino operators see their new work quite different from the way their critics judge it to be. Native American enclaves are re-motivated by an enterprise that provides work and affords self-sustained survival, adequacy, growth and meaningfulness. Nathan Hale says that a service necessary to the public good becomes honorable. If *public good* refers to the good of the Native Indian public, then, according to Nathan Hale these services are honorable, and the casino business ventures are making a giant step forward for a notable portion of that public. At the same time, other Native Councils are considering and addressing the "good" of the customer-public, especially those that are or might become addicted to gambling.

Discussions about work that is fair, legal, or healthy are important for long-term success. They sometimes mask important clues about the nature of resilience and the making of giant steps for the survival of humankind. An advance planning capability and a willingness to move to where-the-action-is is believed by anthropologists Allison Brooks and John Yellen, to be a major reason that very early humans survived and the less mobile Neanderthals became extinct. Moreover, the work of establishing relationships, building a society, forming a network of exchanges and communications is credited as being the most important factor in the survival of humans 250,000 years ago. This sort of creative thinking is suggested as more significant than the development of tools or cave-wall sketches.

There is evidence that humans used long-distance trading networks in Africa at least 100,000 years ago. Why else are seashells found far from the ocean? Apparently humans were trading "quality" stones even in prehistoric days. Evidence also suggests that the garment industry may be one of the oldest forms of work. This same archaeological discovery, ancient needles and beadwork, indicate that the earliest people who discovered the benefits of traveling and of maintaining a networking community, soon began to live in larger groups and to have increased interest in expressing both group identity and individuality. It appears that descendants now living in the latitudes of the earth considered as the East and the West emphasized different aspects. The East highlighted the group identity in communality values and the West highlighted individuality in personal identity.

Health benefits of group life are seen in comparisons of same era human remains with Neanderthal teeth and fractured bones. Multiple survival advantages came to early humans who stayed in extended family groups, did more collective hunting, and developed more strategic methods of working—harpoons that could be thrown, multiple work sites (remember the first rule of business success? location, location, location). Actually, our ancestors only settled down to live in one place some 8,000 years ago when community numbers increased and the climate changed. They had long known how to domesticate plants, but they apparently liked to travel to warmer climates. Some things change, and some things don't.

The Native Indian's decision to engage in a venture where profits swim in is quite reminiscent of choices made by the earliest of human survivors. Some 80 to 100 thousand years ago, according to anthropologists who organized the evidence reported here, ancient humans not only made harpoons to spear giant catfish, they studied the habits of the fish, and timed their visits to the fishing areas when the fish were plentiful and easy to catch. These clever hunters were also able to figure which water holes would not dry up and would travel to that site to hunt for animals that came searching for a drink.

> *If you are to be a leader . . . you must listen in silence to the mystery, the spirit.*
> Leaf Dweller (Kapoisa Sioux).
> *You cannot harm me, you cannot harm one who has dreamed a dream like mine.*
> Dakota Prayer Song.
> *Time is more a proving factor than a controlling factor to the Indian way of living.*
> Herbert Blatchford, Navajo.
> The Native Indian American Educational Foundation (NIAEF) 1999 Calendar.

Direction Continues Across Change and Challenge

> *"I rush forward with arms outstretched toward the goal. . . ."* Philippians: 13:3
> *"The power in organizations is . . . generated by relationships."* Margaret Wheatley

A starship named Enterprise and its space-trek quest came to symbolize a courageous, enthusiastic work group with a captain who never lost a sense of direction. An executive's inner gyroscope and compass does more to sustain the corporate work than goals, more than career ladders, more than organizational regrouping and retooling. It's the executive who assimilates and interprets new ideas and impressions and is the keeper-of-the-direction. The Japanese call this *hoshin kanri* according to Michele Bechtell in her book, *The Management Compass. Hoshin* is the combination of two Chinese characters. *Ho* means "method" and *shin* means "shiny metal showing direction." *Kanri* means "planning." The chief executive is the planning captain of the enterprise, the "shiny metal showing direction."

Business leaders who function in a society with freedom of occupational choice will need to show direction by addressing work mismatches and preparing for mid-course corrections, as did mythical Starfleet venturers. Those willing to take on executive leadership roles inherit the task of weaving the fabric of the organizational culture. Work cultures can be more, or less, concerned about blending talents and matching assignments. Work operations can be structured as tightly knit, or loosely connected. Personalities can be vibrant and bright, or muted and subtle. But, in all circumstances, the adaptive difference is the creative thinking and advance planning of the humans whom we fantasized as existing on spaceships in the future and those who did live in caves and trees 100,000-200,000 years ago. The innovative minds of twenty-first century executives will also need to cope with mid-venture changes and challenges. It's a keen sense of direction that guides executives through adjustment decisions and career and life transitions.

Elizabeth is an amber-haired, high energy manager-in-charge of a banking center. She steadily advanced from teller through the operations ranks to accept the leadership position in an important, but trouble-spot office that turned-over and burned out a series of managers. In fact headhunters tracked her down for this job because of her reputation as someone who shaped up the most difficult branches in the organization where she worked for fifteen years. The talent hunters convinced Elizabeth to accept a large salary increase, a position of authority, and fresh challenge.

Known as a spunky lady, she maintained her direction in the wake of two corporate mergers. Her vision is of an executive position in a banking firm that genuinely cares for customers and employees as individuals. Elizabeth began her career in a well respected statewide bank which underwent radical restructuring. During that time, she was one of the operations managers who reached stringent financial goals on schedule. Suddenly, as far as employees knew, the bank was acquired by a larger regional bank. Senior officers of the original statewide firm made hefty profits while little information or reward filtered down to the business offices and the employees who achieved the goals that earned millions for corporate leaders.

Offices were shut down, new procedures and computer systems were introduced. Elizabeth was sent to close out deactivated offices, to turn over branch operations that were sold to another bank, and to give the bad news to employees who were not retained. During that time she was operations manager in the largest office in the region, also known as a trouble spot. Teaming with her Branch Manager, the two got their staff up and going. Morale was back in gear within four months. That office went from the bottom to the top of the list of achievers.

Not many months later, the regional coalition was acquired by a nationwide banking firm. Elizabeth's branch manager was terminated. No one replaced her for many months, then a temporary person came in for a few weeks. Eventually another Branch Manager was assigned full-time to the office. That manager, pleasant enough, knew nothing about operations and had little banking experience. In spite of running the office on her own in the interim, and being given public recognition and award certificates, Elizabeth's promised raises failed to come through for a year. The reason given was that there was no Branch Manager to conduct the regular review and sign off on her increase. She was ready to listen to the headhunters.

Here is a woman who knows her business and industry, who motivates her subordinates, and who handles with aplomb the sensitive, the threatening, the curious situations that happen in everyday branch offices. Shortly after she became a head teller, a man with a strange appearance came into the bank at closing time and aroused her concern. She stepped to the open service window and asked the pregnant teller on duty to let her handle the customer. The customer carried a paper bag and wore a stocking over his face. As he reached the desk window, he pulled a gun from his pocket and pointed it at Elizabeth, touching her temple with the barrel. He told her to put the money from the cash drawer in the paper bag. She did. She also put "bait" money in the bag, a special pack of false bills. The pack is actually a dye pack that explodes within a short time after removal from the drawer, marking the individual holding the money. That stain remains visible for a long time.

The man, fortunately, left the bank immediately. The bag exploded. The police arrived, responding to the alarm alert sent when the bait money was removed. Elizabeth later testified in court to identify the robber who threatened revenge. After she overcame post-traumatic-reaction, she served on a special bank support team that was called out periodically for emergency duty. They were sent to calm and reassure robbery victims when other offices experienced hostile or violent incidents.

Some years later, she confronted a customer who told a teller that he would blow up the bank if she wouldn't cash his $10,000 check. The teller refused because he had no identification, and called in an officer, Elizabeth, to verify bank regulations. That episode was handled without the police, but law enforcement officials were needed on other occasions. Police were called to settle a loud and heated family feud that erupted in the lobby, and in another incident they stood escort for a man in camouflage pants who was threatening to "do some damage" if he couldn't have his car title in his hands immediately. The missing title was an aftermath of the first merger of computer data. It needed concentrated research and time to locate the records, something that was achieved once the menacing man was subdued by police presence. The necessary background information was then obtained and the title was soon located.

Another time, the police called Elizabeth in the middle of the night to come to her branch office. They received a "911" report that an elderly man was kicking the ATM. She drove over and recognized the man as a regular customer. He had ridden his bicycle over from his nearby apartment to get cash and forgot how to work the ATM. A different comical-appearing emergency was more reminiscent of a Keystone Cops scene that occurred one afternoon after Brinks pick-up agents secured the collection for that day and were locked back into their armored delivery van. Smoke was pouring out from under the vehicle. Flames shot out. Elizabeth and the tellers ran to stand in front of the van, waving their arms to keep the driver from trying to start moving. Other bank employees phoned for assistance and rushed with fire extinguishers to help as the fire department and police arrived quickly to rescue the Brinks employees. Regulations require that these security guards not dismount once they have completed a collection.

This is only a sampling of the weekly episodes Elizabeth can report. Some are not as dramatic, but nevertheless, are uncomfortable, such as having to tell an employee that she has head lice or firing an employee suspected of stealing from cash drawers. Her personal life challenges and changes have also been complex, requiring spontaneous courage and long-term fortitude. She fought a field fire that threatened her first home; she had a serious melanoma; her spouse left her for an 18-year-old with red-red hair and tried devious methods to get custody of their two sons; her best friend died of lung cancer; her older son died in an accident with unexplainable circumstance while at his father's house. Even before her tears stopped flowing on a daily basis, she plunged into planting trees and flowers in her garden and re-decorating her home top to bottom.

Elizabeth expresses zest for her work responsibilities and great compassion for others around her. She is able to stand tall in confronting angry, irrational customers. She will work until she has a job done. She has maintained a direction toward her goals across more changes and challenges than many people face in a lifetime. And she is mid-career. The talent hunters got lucky while she got to advance in the direction of her vision. A fresh challenge arrived the first day of her new executive job. An irate business owner and bank customer came to her to present his lawsuit against the bank. He was missing small amounts of money from drive-through deposits made by his employees and accused the tellers. The greater likelihood is that one of his own employees tampered with deposits or business books. Not wanting to get into detective work, a settlement offer was developed and proposed. He got some reimbursement and was asked to close out his accounts. Of course, Elizabeth was able to convince him to settle out of court and was able to turn her attention to her executive agenda, the re-motivating of over-stressed employees. She is happily busy and is proving that the talent hunters made a good recommendation.

Leaders find that executive "direction" cannot be delegated to a group process. Direction provided through MBO, TQM and similar management techniques was intended to increase productivity. Moreover, collaborative methods of establishing goals and standards allow employees to be involved in the quest for productivity improvements. Executives sought to conduct more of their business in the sunshine, to become union-friendly or immune, by involving all workers in writing objectives. While the management approach was more democratic and a far cry from the sweat-mill indifference to employees' ideas and well-being in the early twentieth century, these task-oriented methods also fell short. Instead of easy solutions, the executives found that the cultural fabric the methods wove was shot through with stressors. Burnout experiences of employees of this era were analyzed by Christina Maslach and Susan Jackson to consist of emotional exhaustion, disengagement, and reduced sense of personal accomplishment.

Strategies to counteract burnout and to revitalize a work culture are suggested by two scales found within the stressor survey mentioned earlier in the chapter. This Job Stress Survey consists of thirty commonly experienced work stressors, most of which sort out, statistically, as *work pressure* and *support*. Work pressure distressors are relieved by attention to organizational tasks and mechanics. *Support* distressors require attention to the relationships and leadership styles. These differences stood out in survey results from a technical agency that conducted operations at three separate sites. All units experienced frequent work pressure. Each work group received unexpected assignments with fast turn-around demands. They worked for customers with immediate needs for solutions to compatibility problems with communications equipment. In spite of short lead-times and no margin-of-error, the group reported lower levels of work stress than many companies. Their secret?

Support from superiors was especially strong. The specialists recognized that their bosses were doing everything possible to see that they had what they needed to do their work. They felt appreciated, respected, and valued by the executives.

Their chief executive went the extra mile to sort out which distressors were prevalent at each work site and attended to each group differently. One subgroup's distressors were related to *interruptions, job descriptions,* and *disagreeable duties.* The first two are *work pressure* items, addressed by changes in descriptions of work assignments and management policy. A second worksite experience related stress to *advancement, insufficient personnel,* and *fellow workers.* This work-group need support from the leadership, attention to individuals and career tracks. An executive like this one can be thought of as the organization's housekeeper-gene, clearing out organizational pollutions and promoting optimism.

David Campbell is the author of an organizational survey that is also used to identify stress overloads in a workgroups. Campbell finds that higher ranking executives in organizations he surveyed are "the most satisfied, are more motivated, happier with their lot, and, in short, appear more optimistic than others in the company or firm." Campbell further notices that optimism appears to be on a continuum, steadily increasing as a worker rises through an organization's hierarchy. Much of his evidence comes from a questionnaire with 14 pre-selected scales to collect employee ratings of [1] the work itself, [2] the working conditions, [3] freedom from stress, [4] co-workers, [5] supervision, [6] top leadership, [7] pay, [8] benefits, [9] job security, [10] promotional opportunities, [11] communications, [12] planning, and [13] innovation. The 14th scale obtains an average of the previous scales.

One set of Campbell's survey results are summarized briefly to illustrate his point. Group average results on a percentile scale of positive responses show that Executives are seven percentile points more satisfied than other management and 16 percentile points "happier" than the non-management group.

Items [as Listed above]	1	2	3	4	5	6	7	8	9	10	11	12	13	Overall avg. 14
A Utility Organization														
Corp. Executives	57	58	58	50	57	52	58	58	53	48	61	59	54	58
Other Management	53	49	53	51	52	52	47	52	48	50	53	54	53	51
Non-Management	49	46	52	48	44	42	34	48	34	47	40	49	49	42

David Campbell draws several conclusions from results found in his surveys. He suggests that while it is common sense that there are reasons for someone to be happier and happier the higher they rise in the organization, because they get more pay and benefits, it may also be that the happier or more optimistic you are, the higher you will go. He states that it seems clear to him that leaders are more optimistic than their followers, that optimism improves performance, and that optimism can be learned. Therefore, he suggests that in order to improve the performance of an organization, leaders should create and teach optimism.

An Alabama governor gave an unusual demonstration of an executive determined to maintain direction and to promote the optimistic attitude. According to the National Public Radio Morning Edition newscast, this governor campaigned for office saying he would get approval for a state lottery that would bring large sums of money to use to improve the state education system. On October 13, 1999, after the vote went against allowing a state lottery, NPR reported that the governor smiled and said, "We will try something else tomorrow." An enterprise, whatever its purpose, keeps moving forward when the leader can inspire others to continue making a collective investment of energy and talent in the direction that the Shiny-Metal is pointing.

Background Reading

The *Management Review (MR)*, published by the American Management Association (AMA), presents numerous reports of surveys sent to AMA membership. AMA reports that the 9,500 organizations that are members account for one-fourth of the U.S. workforce. Information can be obtained by calling the AMA library in their NYC offices, from the APA website and through email inquiry. MR editor (1999) is Barbara Ettorre. bettorre@amanet.org http://www.amanet.org

MR survey articles published in 1998 and 1999 were: The AMA Research Report prepared with the participation of the Business and Professional Women's Foundation, "Senior Management Teams: Profiles and Performance," appears in *MR*, September 1998, p. 37; The "AMA Global Survey on Key Business Issues," appears in *MR*, December 1998, pp. 27-37. "Making Knowledge Stick," by Louisa Wah, May 1999, pp. 24-29. Data on management cutbacks is from articles published in 1996 and 1997.

Other *MR* source articles include: "Reengineering Tales from the Front," January 1995, pp. 13-18, and "Empty Promises," July 1996, by Barbara Ettorre. The first describes reengineering as different from TQM or performance improvement and gives examples of war stories; the second article discusses the broken contracts between employees and management and rules governing the workplace. Reengineering is also discussed by Oren Harari in 1995 and 1996 whose articles are listed in the Reference section. Michele Bechtell's book, *The Management Compass,* is available from AMA, 1995.

Abandonment and downsizing are reviewed by Nathan Seppa in his article," Downsizing: A new form of abandonment," which appeared in *the American Psychological Association Monitor,* May 1996, pp. 1-38. Burnout as defined and studied by the *Maslach Burnout Inventory* is explained in *The Manual, Second Edition,* published in 1986 by Consulting Psychology Press, Palo Alto, CA.

The wave of interest in casino gambling and issues surrounding the government licensing of taxfree enterprises for Indian Reservations is summarized in J. P. Shapiro's cover article "Gambling Fever," for *U.S. News and World Report,* Jan. 1996, pp. 52-59.

For those who step into executive careers without management preliminaries, the *Hip Pocket Guide to Planning and Evaluation* is easy to use and understand. This handbook by Dorothy P. Craig, published by University Associates, San Diego, CA (1978) shows handy details for using project management tools mentioned here: PERT (Program Evaluation and Review Technique) and Gantt.

Occupational stress background information can be located in the References section, esp., Lazarus, 1991. For reports of top three stressors for a majority of managers in different types of businesses and service organizations, see *Stress and Emotion,* Vol. 15 and 17. Taylor & Francis Publishers, 1995, 1999 (in process). and *Optimal Challenge, Job Stress Survey Applications,* 1999 (in process), Odessa, FL: P.A.R Publisher, A.M. O'Roark.

For more information on the seven categories of types of work and David Campbell's surveys contact the Center for Creative Leadership (CCL), 5000 Laurinda Ave., Greensboro, NC, 27438-6300. Campbell's review of results from his client organizations was reported at the annual convention of the American Psychological Association, August 16, 1998. The presentation outline is titled "Optimism: The Leadership Edge." The quote is from page one of that handout. David P. Campbell is senior research fellow for CCL. His articles and monographs are available through the CCL offices. For details contact David Campbell at the CCL offices in Colorado Springs, CO 80906.

Other information on the importance of optimism is found in research and publications of Martin Seligman of the University of Pennsylvania. Albert Bandura of Stanford University and Lewis Curry of the University of Montana. Seligman's "Message from the [APA] President," 1998, Convention Program Book, states that a set of human strengths exist that are the most likely buffers against mental illness: courage, optimism, interpersonal skill, work ethic, hope, honesty, and perseverance.

Type-A persons who put-in long hours, rush about busily, and are prone to experience anger were found at risk for heart diseases when stress was first focused as a major threat to executives. Holmes and Rahe developed the first measure of stress in 1967, The Social Readjustment Rating Scale, after Hans Seyle published the *Stress of Life* in 1956, NY, McGraw Hill. Selye's *Stress without Distress* came out in 1974, Lippincott Publishers, Philadelphia. In 1979 Charles Spielberger wrote about *Understanding Stress and Anxiety,* London, Multimedia, Harper & Row. His basic research has since indicated a key to stress is connected to anger, providing foundation for books by other research and popular writers. In 1993 Redford Williams, M.D., and Virginia Williams, Ph.D. updated the public awareness of the Type-A person in their book, *Anger Kills,* First Harper Perennial publication.

The abbreviations MBO and TQM have become ubiquitous in management circles. The earliest references credit Peter Drucker with the "MbO" insight. MbO as Robert Blake and Jane Mouton labeled it in their 1976 classic, *Consultation,* Addison Wesley Publishing Company, soon became MBO. By 1980, Janic Day included it as a basic and generic concept in *A Working Approach to Human Relations in Organizations,* Brooks/Cole Publishing Co., Monterey, CA. In *Stogdill's Handbook of Leadership: A survey of theory and research. Revised and expanded edition,* 1981, The Free Press, Publishers. Bernard Bass traces the history of research on goal setting beginning with R. G. Davis, 1942, Knickerbocker, 1948, Bellows in 1959, and Cattell, 1951. R. G. Davis is quoted as considering the executive leader to be "the principal dynamic force that stimulates, motivates, and coordinates the organization in the accomplishment of its objectives (p. 12). TQM is attributed to the work of W. Edwards Demming and J. M. Juran. *Management Review,* January 1998, pp. 17 and 18 includes them in a timeline of the century's most influential forces in management thinking. Tom Stevens published one of the last interviews with Deming, "Management today does not know what its job is," *Industry Week,* January 17, 1994, pp. 21-22 & 24-25.

Chapter 4

The Critical Core: Trust and Values

> Values are priorities with emotional energy. As we order, organize, and integrate our activities for survival, adequacy, growth, and meaningfulness, we reveal what's important to us in ways all the world can see and come to trust.
> - Clarity of Commitment: A Critical Core in Survival
> - A Universal Language: Search for Adequacy
> - Chains-of-Succession: The Path of Growth and Development
> - Meaningful Passages: An Unfinished Journey

The door to motivation has but one handle. It is on the inside. Anonymous

Number 1 = Work should be fun. Enjoy it.
Number 2 = Work is important. Don't spoil it . . . .
Number 3 = People are important . . . each one makes a difference.
What it takes is humor, altruism, old-fashioned straight talk.
Herb Hand, President SW Airlines,
Southwest Airlines Values

Trust is the expectation by one person, group, or firm of ethically justifiable behavior
. . . on the part of the other person, group, or firm in a joint endeavor
or economic exchange.
LaRue Tone Hosmer, Ph.D., Academy of Management Review, 1995, p. 399

Clarity of Commitment: A Critical Core in Survival

A uranium rod deep inside a nuclear power plant is the critical core that generates energy for electric current distribution. Deep inside each human is a critical core of values that works to fuel our living, our doing, our thinking. Given good health, that values-core supplies appropriate wattage to activate our laughter, our tears, and our love life with results as powerful as those produced by plutonium, or fossil ores, or hydroponics. Core values give us our sense of commitment and purpose. This nature-nurture current of apperceptions is the inspiration behind our actions that reveal what we consider important. Moreover, values are the basis for bonds of trust among individuals.

What about core *executive values?* What values power the success of an executive? The case argued here is that each executive answers this question periodically, consciously and individually, refining and refueling their values-core by searching the depths of their thinking with an eye on maintaining productive priorities. It takes vigilante attention to eliminate ideas and attitudes that may be out of date or mean-spirited, and to make militant compensation for the motes that sit in one's own eye.

Great success begins inside, and will reflect the values that are attached to one's self, to others, and to one's work. Such is the story of an obscure 18th-century inventor, a man who valued his own thinking, who valued seafaring sailors, and who valued working long and hard. He is the subject of a surprising literary sensation of spring 1996, a slender volume titled *Longitude,* written by Dava Sobel, and is subtitled: *The True Story of a Lone Genius Who Solved the Greatest Scientific Problem of His Time.*

The Truth About Diamonds: They are Pieces of Coal That Stood up Under Pressure and Stayed on the Job. One translation of this folk-wisdom to humans is found in the book, *Longitude,* a hero-tale about John Harrison, the reclusive rural clockmaker and inventor of the chronometer. He worked for four decades to turn his vision inside-out. He succeeded and produced a tool that made it possible for others to travel far and wide safely because they could navigate accurately while at sea. Although his name is not familiar to many of us, he did collect the equivalent of $20 million from the British government for his enterprising effort. Had he lived in the 20th century, he would likely be hailed as a successful nerd and compared to computer masterminds like Bill Gates. *New York Times* critics suggest that *Longitude* became popular because it celebrates individual genius.

In general, the belief that some are born to be great has gone out of fashion, a victim of anti-heroic advocacy that claims all are equal, and none to be considered more valuable or gifted than others. Nevertheless, many of us paused in sadness at the loss of an exceptionally able sailor-Admiral who committed suicide rather than submit to protracted public embarrassment. Media harassment regarding the legitimacy of Admiral Boorda's medals and the accuracy of details in his military records would have disgraced him and his organization. This U.S. Chief of Naval

Operations had dedicated decades of his life to protecting the honor and dignity of his country and its naval corps. His competence was so outstanding that he rose to the highest executive position.

As a sailor who became the number one Admiral of the Navy, he navigated across the gamut of oceans, seas, and military ranks, but chose not to navigate the tempest of professional dishonor. Boorda knew his individual behavior could be used to reactivate negative impressions of the Navy which were lingering in public memory after the embarrassing "Tailhook" episode of abusive sexual harassment of women in the corps.

Mike Boorda's co-worker, Lawrence Korb, a former Assistant Defense Secretary, understood the significance of the media's accusation that the Admiral himself added a bronze "V" to his Naval medals. This prized symbol of valor is awarded for exposure to personal hazard due to direct hostile action. Korb was quoted in Time magazine in May of 1996 as saying: "Since a military officer can ask you to lay your life on the line, you have to trust that person 100%. . . . You can understand why he'd [Boorda] take it so seriously—it goes right to the core, particularly now, when the Navy is trying to restore a sense of honor."

Today's executives find little relief from the duty to embody the best that their group can be, no matter how vigorously extreme egalitarians hammer down on the heads of any tall "nails" that dare to stand up higher than any other worker nails. The executive is de facto a totem, a symbol for the entire organization, regardless of industry or tribe. Trust is a central determinant of organizational success—whether the hero is a solo inventor of navigational tools who trusted in himself completely, or the commander of an armed naval organization, who had to be completely trusted by others. Stamina and resilience are required in order to survive exposure to personal hazards whether they come from the immediately hostile actions of military, civilian, or media groups—or from longitudinal slow-motion, as in the single-minded perseverance of a John Harrison determined to turn a vision inside out.

Under pressure, our automatic pilot makes immediate judgment calls about what's important. On-the-spot selection of priorities will put first things first. Decisions pop out that reveal core values and show others what's going on inside. If Admiral Boorda had lived to see how President Clinton responded under fire from hostile public opinion, he might have considered a different strategy for demonstrating valor under media attack, one that permits survival and continued productive service in spite of diminished admiration.

A Universal Language: The Search for Adequacy

Pressure and spontaneous response clears away window dressing to expose core value. The critical core holds the unedited answers to pertinent questions: what's important to me, what do I want to get out of life, and how do I want to go about getting what I value. Angry behavior is a good indication that something of great value is present. One attempt to examine values and to compare differences in priorities begins with 18 lifetime goals: *a comfortable life, equality, an exciting life, family security, freedom, health, inner harmony, mature love, national security, pleasure, salvation, self respect, a sense of accomplishment, social recognition, true friendship, wisdom, a world at peace, a world of beauty.*

The order of the 18 preferences indicates which values are most likely to energize the person responding. We could make a convincing case that, in the language of the 18 lifetime goals, Admiral Boorda attached importance to national security, self-respect and social recognition—as revealed through others' respect and admiration.

Values governing the way we go about obtaining our prized lifetime goals arae on "the other side of the coin." What kind of behavior do we value most? Is it: *ambitious, broad-minded, capable, clean, courageous, forgiving, helpful, honest, imaginative, independent, intellectual, logical, loving, loyal, obedient, polite, responsible, or self-controlled?*

Returning to the Boorda example, we could surmise that the Admiral valued reaching his lifetime goals by being honest, responsible, obedient, and loyal. Boorda's sense of success in his lifetime goal, *national security,* was annihilated by his value for how to achieve his lifetime goal. Betrayal of his priority value, *honesty,* dominated and imploded the sense of self and remaining values.

It is possible to link this set of dual-track values with workplace activity. The connections show up in a management team's self-description of collective aspirations. During a period of expansion, senior employees of a weekly newspaper used the values they selected from the sets of values listed above when they crafted priorities for their soon-to-be-daily publication.

Comparison of individual rankings showed that common goal-values were *health, family security, freedom* and *self-respect.* The management group's top how-to values showed strong agreement that they wanted to reach these objectives by being *honest, ambitious, independent, intellectual,* and *capable.* Their final declaration was journalistically crisp and reflected four of their shared values: *ambition, intellectual* [activity], *family security,* and *capable.*

We will be the leading newspaper [ambition], *keenly aware of the changing needs of the community* [intellectual activity] *with emphasis on publishing information relevant to the lives of the people we serve* [family]. *We value our fellow employees, both personally and professionally, recognizing them as proficient craftsmen* [capable] *and responsible team members.*

A different but equally value-laden mission statement was seen posted on the cafeteria wall in a small hospital:

Above all else, we are committed to the care and improvement of human life.
In recognition of this commitment, we strive to deliver high quality, cost effective healthcare in the communities we serve.
In pursuit of our mission, we believe the following value statements are essentials and timeless:
We recognize and affirm the unique and intrinsic worth of each individual.
We treat all those we serve with compassion and kindness.
We act with absolute honesty, integrity, and fairness in the way we conduct our business and the way we live our lives.
We trust our colleagues as valuable members of our healthcare team and pledge to treat one another with loyalty, respect, and dignity.

A link between personal and organizational values is considered to be a key to effectiveness that executives may be overlooking. This conclusion was drawn from results of a survey of 1,460 managers and chief executives that was conducted by Schmidt and Posner for the American Management Association. Responses showed that managers who had a value compatibility with their company's expressed values were the same ones who had greater confidence in fulfilling lifetime ambitions, who had less stress spilling over into their home lives, and who held more positive opinions about organizational stakeholders—owners, board of directors, executives, employees, customers.

In conducting this survey, a special list was prepared that would gather values and opinions about desired organizational goals and strengths, requisite managerial competencies and abilities, and the relative importance of the several groups of corporate stakeholders. Survey items are provided at the end of the chapter. Both men and women named *effectiveness* as the top organizational goal. Women selected *organizational leadership* and *organizational stability* as next in importance.

Men ranked *organizational reputation* and *efficiency* as second and third in goal importance. The managerial attributes most valued by women were *ability, ambition, skill, cooperation,* and *flexibility*. The men gave highest priority to a*chievement [drive], job satisfaction, ability,* and *creativity*.

Managers' strong positive self-regard was revealed when both men and women gave first stakeholder priority to *myself*. Last place stakeholder position went to *government bureaucrats*. Male managers placed higher value for owners and customers than did the women, whose priorities were managers, employees, and co-workers.

Groups of managers who reviewed these survey results during the next decade disagreed with the above opinions. Most post-survey group discussions concluded that the targeted organizational outcomes and goals in their companies were *growth, profit optimization,* and *high morale,* not effectiveness, leadership, stability, reputation, and efficiency. These opinion-givers, mixed groups of women and men, selected as priority managerial attributes *cooperation, skill,* and *creativity,* and put at the top of their stakeholders lists those who are *customers* and *employees*.

Getting clear about values in one's own mind, and clarifying values that serve as bonds between a company's stakeholder groups contribute to effectiveness. The caveat is not to give absolute authority to one preempting value. Premature deaths of gifted leaders, from Joan of Arc to Admiral Boorda, are messages that survival means avoiding rigid propositions. This includes not getting into situations that are self-defined as everything-or-nothing, my-way or no-way. The adequate, long-term leader values the importance of values. They recognize that commonly held priorities speak in a universal language, one that is understood cross-department, cross-levels, cross-cultures, cross-oceans. They see that values cultivate trust. This executive does not lock into overdrive on any one concept to the detriment of continued growth, development, and meaningfulness.

Chains of Succession: The Path of Growth and Development

TORI-TORI is not a World War II battle cry. It's a post-war acronym for Trust, Openness, Realization, and Interdependence. TORI was once proposed as a grand solution, a way to bring about peace for everyone, everywhere. And it all began and ended with trust.

While trust is widely declared as essential for stable social relationships, few scholars or scientists attempt precise definitions. Ironically, a universal agreement on the importance of trust in human activity is countered by an equally widespread lack of agreement about what trust is other than a vague, implicit moral duty. An extended avoidance of the trust-word became explicit when the senior research fellow at the Center for Creative Leadership declared he found it to be impossible to address trust as a leadership variable. David Campbell's 8 tasks of leadership with 22 sub-scales, described in Chapter 10, do not make mention of the words trust or control. Campbell's work and books selected for promotion by publishers are mirrors for a shift in work place zeitgeist.

For example, just after mid-twentieth century, bookstore shelves were lined with volumes detailing management methods built on grand aspirations for attaining trusting cooperation among workers. Then for a decade, writers of books on tough tactics and quantifiable objectives treated trust as a wimpy word. As the statistical grand solution fell short, the never entirely-silenced advocates of participative management and quality of worklife, like Bennis and Wheatley, began to be heard again. Once again trust advocates command bookshelf footage, gather nonfiction awards, and gain best-seller market status.

Moreover, an unexpected urgency for understanding trust arose from a fresh direction. Medical researchers linked trust and control to cynical distrust, hypertension, and cardiovascular disease. Heart disease remains a leading cause of death in the United States according to the Center for Health Statistics. Coronary disease is frequently associated with executive stress and considered a major cause of loss of executive talent at the peak of a career. Studies of Type-A workaholics suggest that hostility, as expressed by cynical distrust and aggression, is the most lethal component in the coronary-prone behavior pattern.

Motivated by health-risk implications, medical doctor Redford Williams of Duke University prescribes trust as an antidote to heart disease. In his book that recommends learning to trust others more, he assumes trust to be the opposite of cynical hostility. Williams concludes that if we learn to reduce hostility and anger in our daily lives, we will limit their harmful biological effects on our bodies. Although the admonition to cultivate a trusting heart is turning out to be an oversimplification, it rekindled interest in trust as a key concept in a universal language. Heart disease factors are of concern to executives around the globe. Executives are ever alert to connections between factors predictive of life and death, especially when they are linked to both personal and corporate survival and adequacy.

Ongoing chains-of-investigations are challenging the early assumption that trust is a single, all encompassing attitude. Far from being unidimensional, trust and distrust are showing up as independent factors, and coexistent. Trust, as it turns out, shows that it is not monolithic nor an undifferentiated attitude. Dimensions of distrust can coexist with beliefs that people are typically trustworthy. A case is made at the University of South Florida Center for Research in Behavioral Medicine and Health Psychology for three separate, unrelated trust contexts. Self-trust is not the same as interpersonal trust. They are both different from trusting an organization. All three are expected to be independent from distrust. This means that there are independent characteristics of trust and of distrust that are attached to the self, others, and institutions.

The medical chain-of-diagnosis that shows trust is important in healthy etiologies introduces a compelling reason for understanding how each kind of trust comes to be. Healthy hearts are the added-value for the presence of trust in the workplace. If trust is, indeed, a healthy sign, and distrust is an indicator of early onset of heart disease, then cultivation of high levels of trust in a workgroup is an investment in employee well-being and long-term productivity.

Texas Instruments was taken by surprise when their 58-year-old president, free-trade advocate Jerry Junkins, died of a heart attack while in Munich on a business trip. Similar realizations that executives are prone to sudden death renewed interest in corporate succession planning. Developing the business plan for chain of leadership is a project that is never finished or comfortable to work on. It puts fast-trackers face-to-face with where they stand in the corporate line of command, and can leave them with personal questions: Is this what I really want to be doing? Am I doing what I like and liking what I do? Is this job worth dying for?

Similar self-discovery questions are posed in TORI programs. These workshops reify a theory built around progressive levels of interpersonal trust. Jack Gibb's Trust-Level Theory places trust within a developmental model, progressing through five phases represented by the TORI acronym: [T] Trusting me and being who I am; [O] showing myself as an Open person; [R] Realizing my natural potentials; and [I] living Interdependently with others who are encouraged to realize their own unique abilities. TORI workshops explored issues like executive vision and management of others. They initially proposed unrealizable ideals. In 1978, Gibb wrote that he believed he would demonstrate that leadership, reward, discipline, value, supervision, role, responsibility, and authority are superfluous and, in fact, counter-productive. However, unequivocal advocacy of leaderless groups gave way to promotion of self-directed teams, led and controlled by statistical measurements. And today management continues to search for more effective ways to foster productivity.

What proves durable about the trust level concept is that high level achievers do work at discovering and nurturing their own unique set of talents. They work interdependently with others whom they encourage to realize their own talents. Senior executives have genuine humility. They know that "I-am-unfinished," a work-in-progress, and always in a state of "becoming." Growth and development is associated with respect for one's own potentials and respect for others as role models. As Gibb explains, the TORI model calls for behaving with dignity, congruity, and personal sincerity. The interdependent phase, or highest trust level, is a time when I am what I seem to be, and I can concentrate on the moment at hand, discovering what you and I can achieve by working together.

This invitational approach to success builds on a belief that when I trust myself, and when I am trusted by others, I am more apt to experience internal peace. I will, then, have little need to compare myself with others. I am not compelled to expend energy or time defending or hiding my vision, my values, or my perceptions. I am free to express my enthusiasms, my frustrations, my appreciations, my disappointments. The presence of trust is considered a catalyst that promotes collective success.

Others who write with more temperate tones, describe trust as "vital for the maintenance of cooperation in society and necessary as grounds for even the most routine, everyday interaction." This opinion written by L. G. Zucker was reframed in 1991 by J. K. Butler to fit a corporate context. After conducting a series of studies, Butler concludes that trust is essential to the development of managerial careers. Furthermore, a number of those who limit their research to investigating trust in the workplace see distrust as a prominent management consideration. Distrust is primarily discussed by those in what is commonly referred to as a pessimistic side of business administration known as economic-exchange theory.

Opportunism in business transactions is a cause of pessimism in finance departments that suffered high-risk losses where *agent* relationships were established between individuals, groups or firms. An agent relationship exists when someone in a group is representing another department or the whole organization. In the widely publicized situation of Nick Leeson who was the agent representing England's Baring Bank in Singapore, Leeson acted as the dealmaker for his principles in derivatives trading and was also head of the settlement department, the group that processes all the bank's financial transactions. The bank measured Leeson's work in terms of his outputs, his trading activity, and not his management methods. He ambitiously increased his derivatives trading activity that led to corporate disaster while he managed the processing of these transactions in ways that enabled him to secretly take personal profits.

Opportunism, such as exhibited by Leeson while acting as agent for senior bank officials, is defined as self-interest seeking with guile. Guile includes cheating, misleading, distorting, disguising, and confusing. In this economic context, trust gets discussed as the absence of distrust. Trust is a matter of doing business in "good faith" that there will be no one taking excessive advantage of others. Violations of good faith gave financial specialists like those at Barrons Bank memorable reason to believe in distrust as an imposing reality.

The medical and legal-economic discussions mentioned above are not as complex as philosophical dialogues about where trust fits within broader social and moral ethics. Getting at a definition of trust, as a consequence of good and bad behavior associated with self-interest, covers two millennia in Western thought. Students of Eastern civilizations can trace similar ethical discourses on good behavior back as far as the 6th to 3rd century BC when thinkers such as Confucius, Mengzi, and Laozi emphasized principles of moral autonomy, universalism, and altruism, similar to recent U.S. interest in the growth and transformation of the self through a series of TORI stages. These efforts to examine Eastern moral development as a universal human process primarily look at role-taking and the strategies and value hierarchies people use to solve moral dilemmas. Both moral stages and value hierarchies are also inherent in the Gibb trust-level model.

As hypotheses in cross-cultural investigation, moral development models are not intended to establish the comparative moral worth of persons or societies. Assumptions being checked out by means of scientific data-collection projects are generic topics. Selected to represent global aspects of the human experience, the evidence of group sanctions and rulings about good and bad are being considered without value bias, as objectively as is humanly achievable. These universal objects of group concern and regulation are classified under labels such as *life, property, affiliation, authority, contract, punishment, conscience, erotic love, civil rights,* and *religious* or *metaphysical* areas. Some codification topics relate to the Confucian cardinal virtue of *jen,* or humanity, as reflected in universal human features: goals, fears, desires, intentions, thoughts.

LaRue Tone Hosmer traces the Western stream of thinking about trustworthiness providing a series of brief, edited versions of maxims, quoted below, that capture the central point of commonly held beliefs about trust along a time-line sequence. He begins his tightly woven, insightful historical chain-of-definitions of trust with a summation of ideas espoused by Protagoras, who speaks directly to today's enterprising executives: *Never take any action that is not in the long-term self-interests of yourself and the organization to which you belong.*

The shift of emphasis by Plato and Aristotle is a move to include others along with self and organizations. At this point, trust means the fair and courteous treatment of others such that distrust is eliminated and there is an avoidance of inciting envy. Hosmer's updated maxim says: *Never take any action that is not honest, open, and truthful, and which you would not be proud to see reported widely in national newspapers and on network television.* To these definitions of good and trustworthy behavior, St. Augustine added compassion and reciprocity: *Never take any action that is not kind, and that does not build a sense of community, a sense of all of us working together for a commonly accepted goal.*

Problems caused by the fact that not all people act with compassion were addressed by Hobbes and Locke, saying competition needs to be restrained by law. Hosmer's cogent translation is: Never *take any action that violates the law, for the law represents the minimal moral standards of our society.* Other precautionary trust-principles are attributed to Bentham and Mill: Never *take any action that does not result in greater good than harm for the society of which you are a part.* Kant moved into the realm of universal trust-laws*: Never take any action that you would not be willing to see others, faced with the same or closely similar situation, also be encouraged to take.* And, Jefferson and Rousseau reminded definers of trust about individual rights: Never *take any action that abridges the agreed upon rights of others.*

Pragmatic economist Adam Smith noted that protecting individual rights will not take care of basics like food and shelter and productivity*: Always act to maximize profits subject to legal and market constraints with full recognition of external costs, for maximum profits under those* *conditions are the sign of the most efficient production.* A concern for those who are disadvantaged comes from Tawls: *Never take any action in which the least among us are harmed in some way.* Then Nozick advocated for the individual's choice about being included, or not being included, in an overall distribution of goods and services: Never *take any action that will interfere with the rights of others for self-development and self-fulfillment.*

These swings between trust as a business fairness contract and trust as a human-rights moral-obligation are elaborated and summed up by Hosmer in the Academy of Management Review, 1995. He concludes that: Trust is the expectation by one person, group, or firm of ethically justifiable behavior—that is, morally correct decisions and actions based upon ethical principles of analysis—on the part of the other person, group, or firm in a joint endeavor or economic exchange.

While historically respected definitions shifted in emphasis of what trust means, there is continuity in an implicit contract-promise to not take advantage of others for personal gain. Interestingly, this interpretation of trust can be translated into values that Rokeach listed as lifetime goals and how-to behaviors. Hosmer's definition suggests that the trustworthy person is one who is *loyal, obedient, responsible, honest, self-controlled,* and whose primary goals are sense of *accomplishment* and *social recognition.*

Meaningful Passages: An Unfinished Journey

The purpose of detailing connections between values and trust in a book about successful leadership in the workplace is not to provide a *prescription* for executive effectiveness. Refreshing our awareness of historical views makes explicit that there exists a direct path between our active values and the persons and ideas that we decide to trust or to distrust. It is important to be able to understand that values we cherish impact who and what we currently trust or distrust. Trusts and distrusts may or may not be similar to those that were active when we were six or sixteen years old but need to be based on updated mental processes.

Life *passages* are more numerous than once thought and maturing is seen as ongoing across the full lifespan. Genetically coded rhythms and cycles for the ripening of cells and bodily capabilities are found to operate with a wide "normal" range, varying considerably from one person to another. An additional consideration is that meaningfulness for one phase of living is not automatically or appropriately transferable to the next phase. Values and trust must be adapted and acclimated to new conditions.

Furthermore, in making predictions of future behavior, both positive trust and non-biased distrust are useful, as when we can "trust" that someone's behavior will be an exaggerated, over-reaction to a situation. Positively trusted coworkers are most likely to be those whose values prompt them to use strategies that are similar to our own. We build fruitful, enjoyable alliances with those whose goals and methods are similar to our own, whether or not we actually become members of a famous rat-pack like Sinatra, Sammy Davis, Jr., Dean Martin, and Peter Lawford, or a famous basketball team like my college mates, Alex Groza, Ralph Beard, Frank Ramsey, Cliff Hagan, and Lou Tschiropolis, or a yet unknown entrepreneurial group going for their Initial Public Offering of stock shares.

Congruency between work behaviors and goals, or between work activity and how-to values, allows people and their organizations to reach beyond survival struggles. Progress toward growth, development and meaningfulness relies on reordering our out-of-date perceptions and maintaining our on ongoing exposure to alternatives and contingencies. It is pointless to internalize the 1970s grid-management command-ments, where one style of management is promoted as "best" and something that can be memorized, rehearsed and followed forever. The argument presented here is that the odds for success will increase when executives adopt an invitational approach, one that favors situational, contextual contingency thinking. Such executives cultivate value priori-ties for flexibility, adaptability, and "exaptability" [a recently coined word that means novel ways to use changes that came into being to serve another purpose].

Part One of *The Quest for Executive Effectiveness* concentrates on the executive job of organizing one's own inner resources to maximize probabilities for success, and emphasizes understanding the role of core beliefs in regulating effective functioning. Part Two looks at the execu-tive job of working with and inspiring human emotions that motivate action. The chapters present the foundations for emotional wisdom. Part Three explores the executive as a "significant other" role-holder in the corporate culture and life, one who is granted legitimate power to influence and change that organization in constructive or destructive ways. Part Three details the invitational leadership model that I based on several historically productive chains-of-insight. This is my recommendation for executives who are interested in building an organization with a future.

The following questionnaires recapitulate chapters in Part One. They are for a time-out reflection. They can facilitate sorting out and focusing of values and apperceptions.

Chapter 1, *Every Success Has a Beginning,* shows that self-importance is different from the importance-of-the-self. An inner core of trust in self is not an overabundance of generalized confidence. It means honest self-appraisal of what's important and what's excellent. Senior management positions with broader spans of responsibilities require more frequent on-the-spot judgment-calls and become increasingly dependent upon apperceptions, our inner automatic pilots.

A dialogue with yourself is easy to initiate, although sometimes difficult to complete. For example: *Knowing that I am an organized, dynamic process directed toward four goals: survival, adequacy, growth, and meaningfulness, I take this time-out to update my unique goals, and preferred methods. At this point in time, I am . . .*

A Values and Priorities Worksheet

Roles I am filling at this phase of life. "I am . . . "		Attitudes and feelings I experience most often. "I feel . . ."	
List & then rank order:		List & then rank order:	
1. Executive	6.	1.	6.
2. Spouse	7.	2.	7.
3.	8.	3.	8.
4.	9.	4.	9.
5.	10.	5.	10.
The Goals I value most.		How I want to Reach My Goals.	
List & then rank order:		List & then rank order:	
1.	6.	1.	6.
2.	7.	2.	7.
3.	8.	3.	8.
4.	9.	4.	9.
5.	10.	5.	10.

Chapter 2 is about others, diversity and prejudices. Intended or not, a leader's prejudices and biases are revealed in amazing ways. This happened in the early stages of jockeying for the 2000 presidential nominations, one third party campaigner denied that he was prejudiced against ethnic or racial groups. On TV's *Face the Nation,* a panel member commented that if the candidate wasn't anti-Semitic, then he was doing a good imitation of someone who is.

In a context that is more business oriented, evidence for our ability to sense another person's underlying values is provided by Thomas Mahoney and John Dekop who made a comparison of successful and unsuccessful plants in two industries. They concluded that the values and beliefs of the managers provided the fundamental basis for rejuvenating plants. Their case study example came from two automobile production centers in California. A New United Motors Manufacturing, Inc. (NUMMI) plant under Toyota management was producing the Nova, Prism, and Toyota trucks, and the Van Nuys plant producing Firebirds and Cameros was under General Motors (GM) management. In 1984 the NUMMI plant was closed and a plant in Van Nuys was scheduled to be closed. In 1992, the NUMMI was producing a full line of vehicles and the Van Nuys plant was closed.

At the Van Nuys center, trust was low, time orientations were short-term, expectations were unclear, and production focus was on quantity. At NUMMI commitment from corporate leaders went deeper than lip-service to investment in keeping the plant going. The executives informed and involved workers. Moreover, they were willing to share the pain of salary cuts and layoffs. Union representatives were included in decisions about hiring and selections. Problem solving was entrusted to direct contact, hands-on workers. A core respect for others and a commitment to quality work was communicated by what executives did and how they did it.

If you are interested in checking what you are likely to be communicating to others, you can start your inspection by working through "The Executive Effectiveness Profile" (EEP) which is presented below in full. The EEP is a 1986 adaptation of a multi-rater survey developed by Del Poling and Barbara Mink. Arthur Worth and I revised the wording for use in management development programs for municipal utility companies. The original version is found in *Developing and Managing Open Organizations,* written by Oscar Mink, Barbara Mink, & James Shultz. Recently updated, the book was first published by Learning Concepts in 1979.

A. The effective executive has a positive self-regard and sense of purpose, which remain open to feedback and self improvement. Is consistent on the basis of a set of qualities, values, and beliefs that are visible in actions.

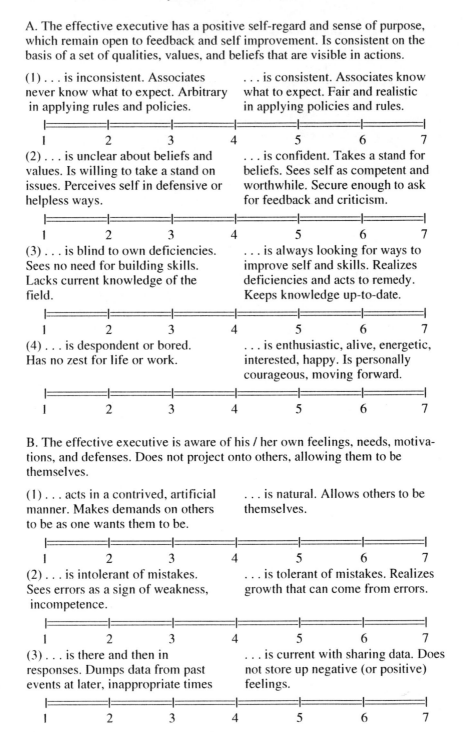

(1) . . . is inconsistent. Associates never know what to expect. Arbitrary in applying rules and policies.

. . . is consistent. Associates know what to expect. Fair and realistic in applying policies and rules.

|═══════|═══════|═══════|═══════|═══════|═══════|
1   2   3   4   5   6   7

(2) . . . is unclear about beliefs and values. Is willing to take a stand on issues. Perceives self in defensive or helpless ways.

. . . is confident. Takes a stand for beliefs. Sees self as competent and worthwhile. Secure enough to ask for feedback and criticism.

|═══════|═══════|═══════|═══════|═══════|═══════|
1   2   3   4   5   6   7

(3) . . . is blind to own deficiencies. Sees no need for building skills. Lacks current knowledge of the field.

. . . is always looking for ways to improve self and skills. Realizes deficiencies and acts to remedy. Keeps knowledge up-to-date.

|═══════|═══════|═══════|═══════|═══════|═══════|
1   2   3   4   5   6   7

(4) . . . is despondent or bored. Has no zest for life or work.

. . . is enthusiastic, alive, energetic, interested, happy. Is personally courageous, moving forward.

|═══════|═══════|═══════|═══════|═══════|═══════|
1   2   3   4   5   6   7

B. The effective executive is aware of his / her own feelings, needs, motivations, and defenses. Does not project onto others, allowing them to be themselves.

(1) . . . acts in a contrived, artificial manner. Makes demands on others to be as one wants them to be.

. . . is natural. Allows others to be themselves.

|═══════|═══════|═══════|═══════|═══════|═══════|
1   2   3   4   5   6   7

(2) . . . is intolerant of mistakes. Sees errors as a sign of weakness, incompetence.

. . . is tolerant of mistakes. Realizes growth that can come from errors.

|═══════|═══════|═══════|═══════|═══════|═══════|
1   2   3   4   5   6   7

(3) . . . is there and then in responses. Dumps data from past events at later, inappropriate times

. . . is current with sharing data. Does not store up negative (or positive) feelings.

|═══════|═══════|═══════|═══════|═══════|═══════|
1   2   3   4   5   6   7

C. The effective executive responds to others in a direct and timely manner. Open to different ideas, persons, and experiences. Constantly interacting with environment and learning.

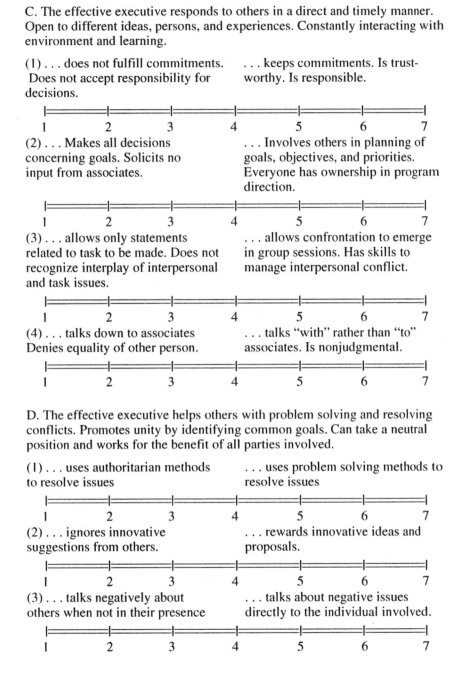

(1) . . . does not fulfill commitments. Does not accept responsibility for decisions.

. . . keeps commitments. Is trustworthy. Is responsible.

|—————|—————|—————|—————|—————|—————|
1　　　　2　　　　3　　　　4　　　　5　　　　6　　　　7

(2) . . . Makes all decisions concerning goals. Solicits no input from associates.

. . . Involves others in planning of goals, objectives, and priorities. Everyone has ownership in program direction.

|—————|—————|—————|—————|—————|—————|
1　　　　2　　　　3　　　　4　　　　5　　　　6　　　　7

(3) . . . allows only statements related to task to be made. Does not recognize interplay of interpersonal and task issues.

. . . allows confrontation to emerge in group sessions. Has skills to manage interpersonal conflict.

|—————|—————|—————|—————|—————|—————|
1　　　　2　　　　3　　　　4　　　　5　　　　6　　　　7

(4) . . . talks down to associates Denies equality of other person.

. . . talks "with" rather than "to" associates. Is nonjudgmental.

|—————|—————|—————|—————|—————|—————|
1　　　　2　　　　3　　　　4　　　　5　　　　6　　　　7

D. The effective executive helps others with problem solving and resolving conflicts. Promotes unity by identifying common goals. Can take a neutral position and works for the benefit of all parties involved.

(1) . . . uses authoritarian methods to resolve issues

. . . uses problem solving methods to resolve issues

|—————|—————|—————|—————|—————|—————|
1　　　　2　　　　3　　　　4　　　　5　　　　6　　　　7

(2) . . . ignores innovative suggestions from others.

. . . rewards innovative ideas and proposals.

|—————|—————|—————|—————|—————|—————|
1　　　　2　　　　3　　　　4　　　　5　　　　6　　　　7

(3) . . . talks negatively about others when not in their presence

. . . talks about negative issues directly to the individual involved.

|—————|—————|—————|—————|—————|—————|
1　　　　2　　　　3　　　　4　　　　5　　　　6　　　　7

E. The effective executive communicates with others in a timely manner, sharing relevant information. Allows individuals to perform different functions based on expertise. Balances concern for individual with task achievement. Encourages professional growth among group members.

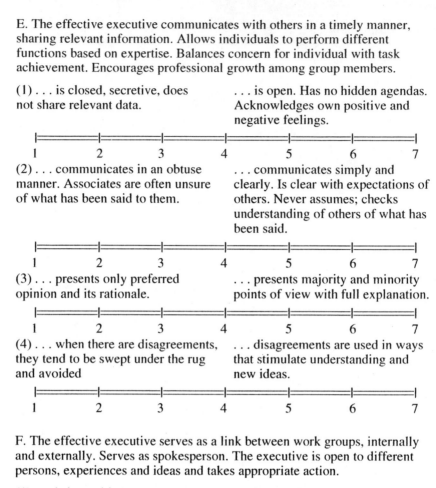

(1) . . . is closed, secretive, does not share relevant data.

. . . is open. Has no hidden agendas. Acknowledges own positive and negative feelings.

```
|=======|=======|=======|=======|=======|=======|
1       2       3       4       5       6       7
```

(2) . . . communicates in an obtuse manner. Associates are often unsure of what has been said to them.

. . . communicates simply and clearly. Is clear with expectations of others. Never assumes; checks understanding of others of what has been said.

```
|=======|=======|=======|=======|=======|=======|
1       2       3       4       5       6       7
```

(3) . . . presents only preferred opinion and its rationale.

. . . presents majority and minority points of view with full explanation.

```
|=======|=======|=======|=======|=======|=======|
1       2       3       4       5       6       7
```

(4) . . . when there are disagreements, they tend to be swept under the rug and avoided

. . . disagreements are used in ways that stimulate understanding and new ideas.

```
|=======|=======|=======|=======|=======|=======|
1       2       3       4       5       6       7
```

F. The effective executive serves as a link between work groups, internally and externally. Serves as spokesperson. The executive is open to different persons, experiences and ideas and takes appropriate action.

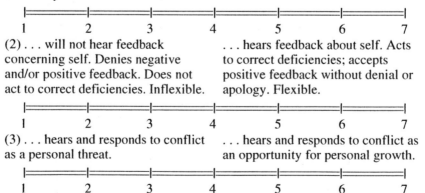

(1) . . . is insensitive to statements by others. Gives responses which do not reflect understanding of what others say or feel.

. . . is an active listener. Takes time to hear associates and respond in a relevant manner.

```
|=======|=======|=======|=======|=======|=======|
1       2       3       4       5       6       7
```

(2) . . . will not hear feedback concerning self. Denies negative and/or positive feedback. Does not act to correct deficiencies. Inflexible.

. . . hears feedback about self. Acts to correct deficiencies; accepts positive feedback without denial or apology. Flexible.

```
|=======|=======|=======|=======|=======|=======|
1       2       3       4       5       6       7
```

(3) . . . hears and responds to conflict as a personal threat.

. . . hears and responds to conflict as an opportunity for personal growth.

```
|=======|=======|=======|=======|=======|=======|
1       2       3       4       5       6       7
```

G. The effective executive remains clear about essentials of the vision and responds to potentially conflicting situations in effective and appropriate ways. Realizes the importance of a cohesive organizational identity. Is aware of various approaches and uses them at the right time and place.

(1) . . . openly criticizes others. Fosters fragmentation within the organization.

. . . recognizes areas of fragmentation within the organization and promotes cooperation to unify total organizational effort

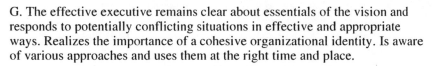

| 1 | 2 | 3 | 4 | 5 | 6 | 7 |

(2) . . . works on a day-to-day basis. Does not look up to see where the group is going. Responds to crisis and is reactive.

. . . constantly works with group on long range goals—one to three years 5 to 10 years. Looks to outside sources for trends and is proactive.

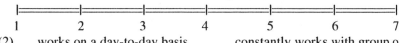

| 1 | 2 | 3 | 4 | 5 | 6 | 7 |

(3) . . . denies need for change.

. . . promotes change in positive terms.

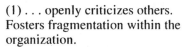

| 1 | 2 | 3 | 4 | 5 | 6 | 7 |

H. The effective executive is able to see how all stakeholders and collaborators function and affect each other. Has a grasp of the total input-throughput-output process and can suggest ways to improve efficiency.

(1) . . . does not know how the various suppliers, consumers, and production units are organized and work together.

. . . knows how groups think and work and how they affect each other.

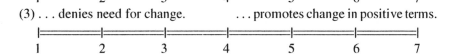

| 1 | 2 | 3 | 4 | 5 | 6 | 7 |

(2) . . . operates from a win-lose stance. Sees groups competing rather than cooperating.

. . . operates from a win-win stance. Fosters cooperation among work groups

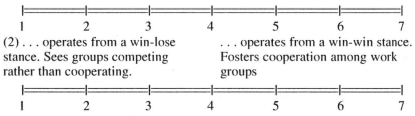

| 1 | 2 | 3 | 4 | 5 | 6 | 7 |

I. The effective executive is part of the world beyond the organization and its network of collaborators. Is able to gather and use information on the impact of the organization on the social system and the industry.

(1) . . . is not involved in government or community activities.

. . . participates in government and community. Aware of interplay between organization and community

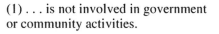
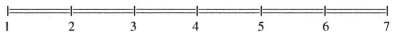

| 1 | 2 | 3 | 4 | 5 | 6 | 7 |

(2) . . . is closed to data from outside the system. Does not see larger societal trends. Caught unaware by changes in consumer demand.   . . . relates from larger economic and social system to goals and objectives. Products and services are timely and wanted.

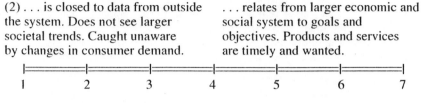

Nine Dimensions of the Effective Executive: How did you rate yourself?

1. Sense of Self-Worth   A. _____
2. Awareness of Knowledge, Skill, and Values   B. _____
3. Hears and Responds to Others   C. _____
4. Promotes Unity   D. _____
5. Facilitates Interaction   E. _____
6. Represents the Group in the Exchanges of Information F. _____
7. Clear about Essentials of the Vision   G. _____
8. See How All Fits together in the Achievement
   of the Vision   H. _____
9. Sees How the Enterprise Fits into the World   I. _____

Chapter 3 is about work itself and the importance of goals, ethical considerations, resilience and maintaining direction. The trends for the future are clear: Workplace stressors will continue to multiply and workplaces will become even more complex networks. Fortunately, management expert Margaret Wheatley's books suggest five points that can be monitored by executives who want to keep in touch with the workplaces they influence.

New Science Calls for Leaders to Pay Attention to these Items. How often do you think about these issues?	Self-Rating 1 Frequently 2 Occasionally 3 Seldom

1. Feedback.   The need for positive and disquieting feedback keeps a system moving forward. It is the resiliency rather than the stability of the individuals and the visions that keep systems alive.
DO YOU SEEK POSITIVE AND NEGATIVE FEEDBACK?

2. Participative Management. Leadership is seen as dependent upon the relationships that are valued. All we can legitimately expect from others is new and interesting information. Solutions are viewed as temporary events.
DO YOU EXCHANGE INFORMATION WITH A WIDE RANGE OF OTHERS?

3. Information.   Information freely generated and freely
exchanged is the natural control mechanism in a group.
DO YOU ENCOURAGE PEOPLE TO MEET AND
DISCUSS HOW THEY ARE SEEING THINGS AND
WHAT'S NEW?

4. Autonomy.   The belief is that autonomy can exist only at
the local level and that individual changes are absorbed by the
group and a new stability is produced by others adapting to
changes in direction.
DO YOU OVERCONTROL, PRESCRIBING HOW ALL
ARE TO ADAPT TO CHANGE?

5. Self-Referencing.   It is necessary to sort out the living
from the dead and to treat these aspects of our worlds differently. The dead are objects that thrive on routines and stan-
dardization. The living are ideas based on information and
flourish when clear about their identity, goal, and values,
when kept in motion by contact with other ideas.
DO YOU ARTICULATE A CLEAR CORE OF VALUES
AND VISION?

Chapter 4 is one of three linchpin chapters. The role of trust and
values as a key to motivation comes in Chapter 8, at the end of Part Two.
Chapter 12 gives an organizational perspective of trust and values and
concludes Part Three. Here the focus is the person who is the executive
and the one who will be responsible for building a trusting climate.
Warren Bennis includes the management of trust as one of four competencies he found prevalent when he interviewed 60 corporate leaders. He
sought to understand what was important in executive success and
concluded that the critical factor is reliability. One Bennis interviewee
who admired his boss said, "Whether you like it or not, you always know
where he is coming from, what he stands for."

In contrast, Ronald Reagan was considered by many as popular and
inspirational until the Iran-Contra incident. Whether trustworthiness
became a problem because he lacked information or because he participated in deliberate disinformation, Reagan remained beloved by some,
but no longer believed. Trust as a function of executive reliability calls
for constancy of commitment to stated values. Voters and workers alike
know the necessity of changing short-term objectives. They must trust
that the direction remains anchored by bedrock values and up-to-date
competence, with a belief that there will be no intentional lies.

This last worksheet contains lists used in the management survey
described earlier in this chapter. Social issues and concerns were added

to the three survey lists for post-survey discussions to explore corporate social responsibilities.

What should be listed among the top three in each column?

Organizational Values	Organizational Stakeholders	Manager Characteristics	Social Concerns*
1.	1.	1.	1.
2.	2.	2.	2.
3.	3.	3.	3.
growth	boss	skill	hunger
efficiency	customers	success	education
productivity	myself	ambition	drug abuse
stability	managers	competitiveness	aids
service to the public	employees	creativity	the homeless
effectiveness	general public	ability	human rights
organlizat'l lead'shp	gov't bureaucrats	job satisfaction	crime/violence
reputation	owners	achievement	marriage/divorce
profit	elected public	cooperation	the jobless rate
high morale	officials	flexibility	child abuse

*If a company or group decided to dedicate funds and/or require managers to contribute time to some community project: what would be most beneficial for the best interests of the organization and the community.

Background Reading

Values assessment information discussed here comes from Milton Rokeach. His *Rokeach Values Survey* is published by Consulting Psychologists Press, 577 College Ave., Palo Alto, CA 94306. Copyright 1983, Form G, 1988. He wrote about values as an enduring belief, a mode of conduct, an end-state of existence, and social preferences in *The American Psychologist,* 1971: "Long Range experimental modification of values, attitudes and behavior." Vol. 26, p. 453-459.

The second survey instrument discussed was prepared by Barry Z. Posner and W.H. Schmidt during the 1970s for the American Management Association. Posner later published *The Leadership Challenge* with J. M. Kouzes, 1987, SF: Jossey Bass.

Other sources for *values* references are:

Sid Simon who directed a training center in central N.Y. state's Adirondack mountains for many years.

Charles L. Hughes whose *Value Systems Analysis* culminated with placement of an organization in a hierarchy of organizational cultures patterned after stages of human evolutionary development.

1. *Reactive,* physiological needs, survival;
2. *Tribalistic,* safety and security needs in a threatening world of clans, rituals, superstitions;
3. *Egocentric,* self-centered aggressiveness;
4. *Conformist,* structure and the right-way with clear social roles;
5. *Manipulative,* achievement oriented and self-serving aggressive;
6. *Sociocentric,* concern for self-discovery, acceptance, human dignity and uniqueness of the individual;
7. *Existential,* a personal activist who lives within the society's constraints while enjoying maximum individual freedom, self-motivating, tolerant, expects high levels of performance, responds to reasons and competence, not status or position driven.

Florence Kluckhohn and Fred Strodtbeck were anthropologists who did initial studies of values as the essential core of a culture.

Sociologists Talcott Parsons and Edward Shils' considered values as basic normative principles within a society.

Psychologists Robert E. Quinn and Michael R. McGrath developed a competing values paradigm that assumes all knowledge is organized around a person's consistent set of perceptual values.

Widely regarded books addressing the management of shared values and corporate culture are written by Ralph Kilmann and Edgar Schein.

Other *trust* references:

Atlas, James. (Sunday May 26, 1996). An ongoing love affair with the lone genius. *St. Petersburg Times.* 5D. First appeared in *NY Times©.*

McDonald, P. & Gandz, J. (1992). Getting value from shared values. An organization can turn shared values into competitive advantage. But we need to develop values-measurement profiles relevant to the modern corporation. *Organizational Dynamics,* Winter 1992, 64-77.

Schmidt, W. H. & Posner, B. Z. (1970). *Managerial Values in Perspective: An AMA Survey Report.* NY: AMA Membership Publications Division, AMACOM.

Schmidt, W. H. & Posner, B. Z. (1982). *Managerial Values and Expectations: The Silent Power in Personal and Organizational Life. An AMA Report.* NY: AMA Membership Publications Division, MACOM.

Zoglin, R. (May 27, 1996). A question of honor. The Navy's top admiral takes his own life rather than face queries about his right to a coveted award. For a "sailor's sailor," it seemed the only way out. *Time Magazine,* pp. 30-32.

The medical connections between trust and coronary heart disease are reported by Redford Williams, M.D., of Duke University. The research supporting *trust* and distrust as separate characteristics and differentiated into trust and distrust for self, others, and organizations is reported by C. D. Spielberger, Ph.D. and Karen L. Pellegrin, Ph.D. of the University of South Florida.

Warren Bennis continues to be a prolific author of books about leadership and healthy work groups. For example, *The Unconscious Conspiracy: Why Leaders Can't Lead, 1976; Leaders, the Strategies for Taking Charge, 1985; Why Leaders Can't Lead, 1991.* This latter book is the one which includes his list of four things leaders need to manage: attention, meaning, self and trust. The quote is from the 1991 book.

Butler, J. K. (1991). Toward understanding and measuring conditions of trust: Evolution of a conditions of trust inventory. *Journal of Management,* 17, 643-663.

Thomas Mahoney and John Dekop published the interesting tale of two companies in *Organizational Dynamics,* 1993, NY: American Management Association, "Y'Gotta Believe: Lessons from American vs Japanese-run U.S. Companies."

Zucker, L. G. (1986). Production of trust: Institutional sources of economic structure. 1840-1920. In B.M. Straw & L.L. Cummings (Eds.), *Research in organizational behavior.* Vol. 8:53-111. Greenwish, CT: JAI Press. [The quote used here is found on page 56.]

Trust, A New View Of Personal And Organizational Development by Jack R. Gibb, 1978, Los Angeles, Guild of Tutors Press, International College. The interdependent phase is discussed on p. 87.

The history of definitions of *trust* by LaRue Tone Hosmer, University of Michigan School of Business Administration, appeared in the *Academy of Management Review, 20,* 2, 379-403, 1995. LaRue Hosmer quote is found on p. 339.

PART TWO

SURPRISE & CHANGE
Emotion & Motivation

THE EXPLORER

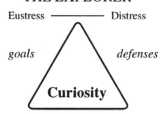

Eustress ———— Distress

goals   *defenses*

Curiosity

Survival Value & Distress Potential

Feelings
Wonder
Attraction
Possibility
Mystery

If I investigate new ideas and information, the good things of life will be discovered.

GOALS: adventure, creative innovation
ACTIONS: Willing to test, experiment, flexible, optimistic

THE PROTECTOR

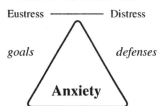

Eustress ———— Distress

goals   *defenses*

Anxiety

Survival Value & Distress Potential

Feelings
Worry
Tension
Apprehension

If I am alert to possible dangers, I can assure success.

GOALS: security safety
ACTIONS: double-checking; slowing down or stopping movement; withholding and challenging or withdrawing

THE HERO

Eustress ———— Distress

goals   *defenses*

Anger

Survival Value & Distress Potential

Feelings
Injustice
Irritation
Impeded
Frustration

If I point out flaws and react to insults directly, the good things of life will be achieved.

GOALS: competence, justice, success
ACTIONS: loyalty, seeking excellence, action

CURIOSITY ANXIETY *ANGER*
EMOTIONAL WISDOM

II

PART TWO

Surprise & Change: *Emotion and Motivation*

Introduction: Zestful Living with

Curiosity, Anxiety, and Anger

". . . the reasons a gull's life is so short are boredom, fear, and anger."
Jonathan Livingston Seagull by Richard Bach

Part Two is about spirit. You can feel the spirit of the group when you walk into a place of business. Spirit is a pervasive energy field produced by persons and relationships. It's the pitch-blend of organizational life. This dynamic of corporate life is a product of emotional vitality that exerts a power in a way analogous to the radioactive substance in certain metallic minerals. Neurochemically-active emotions generate internal and interpersonal tenor and tension that shape organizational climates.

The three emotions discussed in the following chapters are known to stimulate the autonomic nervous system, indicative of their special value-added role in the survival of the species. Survival of the executives of the species depends on strategic integration of vital-sign emotions. Each emotion exerts a distinct yet not independent influence on behaviors. Key to executive success is leadership activity between corporate experiences of surprise and adaptive change. At these critical points in time, an executive's will-to-survive reflects the character and mix of inner emotional strengths.

Organizational nuclear-fission comes from the heat produced by a trio of stress-related emotions, curiosity, anxiety, and anger

Part One argues that *cognito-ergo-sum* is the beginning of executive effectiveness. We can thank René Descartes for underscoring the importance of "I think, therefore, I am" as early as 1649. Part Two introduces a second dimension: *I am not alone, therefore, I feel*. Chapters in Part Two build on the observation that surprise-and-change is a natural process that aids in survival, challenges adequacy, stimulates growth, and reaffirms meaningfulness. The goal of this natural process is emotional balance and interpersonal trust. Part Two's argument proposes that these primary-color emotions are manageable influences on behavior, health and personality. Moreover, they serve as relationship mediators and can be regulated in order to stimulate beneficial surprise-change outcomes: balance, trust, and productivity.

Part Two is concerned with spirit as an élan and esprit de corps that mobilizes talent. It is my observation that quality-of-worklife and daily enthusiasm emerge from relationships among co-workers. Where does the animating force come from? What causes vivacity and ardor? Emotions drive characterizing dispositions. Those dispositions generate a felt, but invisible energy, that is often called *attitude*. It's a difference you sense when you go from one work group to another.

Differences in mixes of vital-sign emotions, curiosity, anxiety, and anger, conspire to promote survival. In everyday activities the three emotions blend into more complex conditions. Combinations of these emotions can result in prevailing attitudes such as optimistic, depressive, opportunistic, entrepreneuristic, defensive, evangelistic, fatalistic. Repeated patterns of emotional activation form a residue that lingers beyond surprise-and-response experiences to color incoming information.

This emotional trio will determine how we handle stress. Since they are seldom experienced in an isolated form, managing and coordinating emotional vital signs is an exquisite challenge. Even the most versatile and experienced leaders are fascinated and frustrated by the effort to achieve productive levels of trust and motivation in themselves, in their managers, and in their workforce cadre. The task is daunting, requiring an ever-sensitive attention to the shifting of balances in the group's emotional mix. Why bother? Because emotional over-activation speeds-up and heats-up destructive processes within our bodies and within our organizations. Equally dysfunctional is underactivation or the engagement of one mode to the exclusion of the others.

Without guidance, primary-color survival emotions like curiosity, anxiety and anger can become counter-productive in persons and in corporations. Executives with depth of emotional wisdom assert leadership over the blend of psychological vital signs. Intentional modulation of emotional intensities influences employees' sense of stability, progress, and involvement. Understanding built-in emotional response patterns allows executives to invite appropriate thinking and coping behaviors.

Most of us cling to souvenirs and rituals, to mantras and songs. Such talismans are relics of past emotions and bolster our sense of continuity, of identity, of immortality. It takes a jolt to pry us away from our security blankets, no matter how frayed and irrelevant they become. Surprise is a natural jolt. No amount of strategic planning or intensive thinking can eliminate surprise. The unexpected pops up in each day. Maybe good. Maybe bad. We have three choices: to *move toward* the surprise, to *move against* the surprise, to *move away* from the surprise.

A Wise, Old & Unsung Hero

An older man, stooped by years of working the fields, was questioned about his life by a neighbor's grandchildren who were eager to learn from his wealth of experience. He recalled a time he went to a farmers auction to get a sturdy plowhorse. He smiles as he tells how proud he was, as a young man, to be able to bargain for a handsome, prancing horse at a much lower price.

The youths exclaim, admiringly, "How clever of you. How fortunate."

With a shake of his head, the white haired man said, "Maybe Yes. Maybe No. That fine horse was high spirited and one day threw my older son into a ditch and broke his leg."

"How dreadful," the grandchildren cried.

"Maybe Yes. Maybe No. That was just before the big war when all young men were sent off to fight in defense of the country and our freedoms. Many were killed. But because of my son's injured leg, he did not get sent to war."

"What good luck," declared the youngsters.

"Maybe so. Maybe not. That older son stayed home, took charge of the farm. When his younger brother came back to help, they quarreled bitterly about how things should be done on the farm and how best to take care of me. They have never spoken since."

"Awful!" said the children.

"Maybe Yes. Maybe No. Since that day I live in peace and quiet, and I do whatever I want each day."

Adapted from Thomas Crum, *The Magic of Conflict*

As the old man learned by watching what happens after a surprise, whether it's a bargain horse or a broken leg, the long-term good or bad effects of a surprise are not fully apparent at first. Much depends on the kind, and the intensity, of your emotional response and your ability to move beyond surprise, wholeheartedly.

Chapter 5.   *Curiosity: A Taste for Adventure* highlights an emotion reported to have a gene of its own. Whether or not the gene theory proves to be true, common sense connects this emotion with lively interest in figuring out how a better mouse trap can be produced faster, or more economically, or with fewer rejects. Curiosity motivates us to reach out toward life's surprises. It's behind the appeal of what's new. Curiosity moves us toward novelties in our environment with eager anticipation. It can even overcome our apprehension, suspicion, and reluctance in the presence of strangeness.

The novel, the ambiguous, the complex will stimulate an executive's curiosity. It's what motivates the pushing, and expanding, and stretching of the envelope. Curiosity gives the courage to adventure beyond the known and proven. Embracing adventure and working with untested components can lead to disaster as well as to innovation. This produces an elegant purpose behind the call for a leader's attention to emotional integration and modulation. Hardy executives are able to balance high curiosity with appropriate cautions, better known as anxiety. Curiosity that gives the leadership advantage is not the same thing as Evel Knievil, daredevil behavior. The curiosity that becomes helpful and healthful for corporate executives is an intellectual interest as opposed to sensation-seeking interest in physical thrills, highs, and indulgences, even though some adventurers are known for both attributes. Sky-diving a la former President George Bush at age 80+ and tales of Asian executives enjoying a taste of poisonous fish are not part of the definition of curiosity presented in Chapter 5, although researchers find sensation-seeking useful in separating depression from anxiety.

Chapter 6.   *Anxiety,* the *Executive Challenger,* points out that worry and emotionality, two aspects of anxiety, can be beneficial. Anxiety serves as an executive challenger, a devil's advocate. Worry brings an executive face-to-face with conflict. The chief executive makes the judgment calls on business activities: *Is this good or is this bad for productivity and quality, in the short-term and in the long-range?* First, the executive searches for clarification of the situation, then comes a *fight-or-flight* decision moment.

As far back as the 1920s, Walter B. Cannon noted the changes brought on in living creatures when they are confronted with stressful stimuli. The adrenal glands and the sympathetic nervous system in both animals and humans were noticed to activate changes in internal biological processes that attempted to bring about an equilibrium or balance. When danger cues persist, an individual's muscles tense and tighten in readiness for rapid and vigorous action and the heart works faster to provide more blood to the brain and muscles. Just as the body's reserves are called out to aid in responding to personal threats, executive anxiety serves to pump up the organization, heightening corporate alertness and mobilizing collective energy. When converted into a motivational call for targeted activity, executive anxiety boosts productivity.

Chapter 7.   *Anger: Heroic Idealism in Action* puts a fresh spin on what has been labeled the killer-emotion. Anger is a normal experience that varies from mild frustration to rage and hostility. When translated into appropriate behavior, anger provides the motivation and courage to initiate needed changes. Anger is present in those who are idealistic and have a genuine concern for quality of life, work and product. Anger is the defender of what is loved, whether it is self, family, work, products, possessions, environment, or beliefs. Noble as anger can be, anger is well known as the killer emotion because it is a salient feature in the behavior of many victims of heart diseases and stress disorders. While social correctness calls for putting-a-lid-on-it, neither good health nor social justice benefit from denying the message delivered by the emotion. Without anger, we put ourselves at risk for being walked on, ignored, mistreated, or abused by others who drive toward their own goals without a strong ethical value for how-to achieve the goal. The hard-wired anger emotion serves a survival and growth purpose, especially when it is understood, appreciated and appropriately applied. Executives who capitalize on the information they can obtain from moments of anger are potentially dedicated and heroic problem solvers.

Chapter 8.   *Wholeheartedness and a Passion for Life sorts* out what's involved in a giving-it-all-you've-got attitude. The spirit of wholeheartedness comes from applying your mix of curiosity, anxiety, and anger in concert with your pattern of problem solving. Emotions set the stage for interpreting what you see. Seeing friends, or seeing foes sets in motion very different attitudes and actions. Someone savvy about our inner workings is able to promote equilibrium among the vital-sign emotions that will benefit self, others, and task. An organization where workers exhibit an enduring dedication to that undertaking is likely to have a leader who can emphasize curiosity, or anxiety, or anger at strategically appropriate points. Skilled management of emotions allows interpersonal trust to emerge.

Emotional energy that activates the autonomic nervous system will nurture or abort trust between persons. It's the failure of individuals to manage their emotions that led Karen Horney, a mid-twentieth century therapist and theorist, to write eloquently that we must eliminate our Dr. Jekyll and Mr. Hyde attitudes toward other persons. Her private practice dealt with helping persons addicted to a single coping strategy to learn how to recover and integrate a full range of coping options. She advised that the three types of action options for responding to life's experiences, toward, away from, or against, do not become mutually exclusive in mature, normal adults. Horney observed in her clinical practice that when one coping pattern is allowed to take over to the exclusion of the other two, an individual becomes dominated by one of three undesirable attitudes: helplessness, hostility, or isolation.

Based on Horney's observations, it appears that trust can stay-the-course across a lifetime, even through surprise-and-change events, when a full compliment of responses is available. Healthy adult coping patterns evolve as we are able to let go of early childhood fears, even those that are justifiable, of being left alone and helpless in a potentially hostile world. Letting go of fears does not mean loss of reaction ability. Loud noises and the sensation of falling produce spontaneous reactions in infants. Startle sensations are important signals that something is out of balance. Even adults need these early warnings that something's amiss. These are signals of dangers, some external and some internal. When trust in others is lacking, "startle" or "falling" sensations result in more intense experiences of anxiety or anger. As state anxiety and anger move to higher levels, it becomes harder to direct them toward constructive coping. If trust in others is strong, surprises that evoke adult variations of early responses to loud commotions and falling sensations are not likely to interfere with coping behaviors that are effective and admirable.

The following chapters speak about emotional infrastructures typically avoided by management architects. Ignored or not, curiosity, anxiety, and anger, will be experienced by executives, professionals, and employees. Each will express emotional vital-sign intensities in keeping with their unique patterns. Throughout life, constructive relationships continue to be a matter of learning to understand, direct, and maximize the power of the emotions and the coping abilities available in self and others.

Background Reading

Emotions are thoroughly described by scientists Hans Eysenck, Charles Spielberger, and M. Zuckerman. Spielberger and Eysenck studied three basic emotional factors. Zuckerman addresses the DNA, psychophysiological, hormonal, and other biological links to emotion and behavior, which is beginning to fill in many gaps in understanding the way people act and react.

Elkman & Fiesen found evidence of six universal emotions that cross cultural and national boundaries: happiness, surprise, fear, sadness, anger, and disgust.

Spielberger, director of the Center for Research in Behavioral Medicine and Health Psychology, University of South Florida, primarily studies three basic emotions: curiosity, anxiety, and anger. He links these inherent, neurochemically active human characteristics with heart diseases, cancers, and more complex emotional affects such as depression. His research provides the basis for the "spirit" paradigm presented here.

Eysenck's emotional basics are labeled as continuums: *extraversion-introversion, neuroticism-stability, and psychoticism-normality.* Eysenck defined his terms in order to look at similarities between animal behavior and human behavior. He hoped to contribute to our knowledge of human behavior by distinguishing between behaviors that are influenced by genetic givens and behaviors that are influenced by social influences. Eysenck, a British psychologist, who died in 1997, found the animal world to also have three primary emotional behaviors: affiliative and socially positive (which he equates to the extraversion factor); aggressive (which he equates to the Psychoticism-normality factor); and submissive (which he equates to the Neuroticism-stability factor).

Eysenck was able to make arguments supporting similarities that cover everything but play, grooming, and enthusiasm. He overcame translation problems encountered when he compared different human cultures and different types of living creatures. He observed that both animals and people interact with others in three similar ways: seeking each other out for socializing; being fearful and avoiding others; and with hostility that leads to attack. In this instance, Eysenck agrees with psychoanalyst Karen Horney that we can move toward, away from, or against others as we cope with life's challenges. Even so, Eysenck, always a person of strong convictions, considers psychoanalysis as a pseudoscience that needs to be eliminated as an accepted scientific methodology.

CURIOSITY ANXIETY *ANGER*

Chapter 5

Curiosity and the Executive Edge

Curiosity as a motivator is a "hungry" emotion. It's a hunger to find, to explore and to feel good. Curiosity begins in infancy with our quest to satisfy the need to test out everything at hand as a potential source of food and it quickly diversifies. Curiosity motivates our thirst for information and our fascination with physical well-being and pleasure. Curiosity supplies a "go-for-it" enthusiasm that sets us off on adventures in pursuit of *survival, adequacy, growth and meaningfulness.*

- Strategic Thinking Is Executive Adventure
- Is Curiosity the "Prime Mover"?
- Intelligence, Curiosity and Quantum Science
- Executive Risk Taking: Gambling in Corporate Suites
- Curiosity Sparks a Leadership Advantage

It was a dark and stormy night and the man in the trench coat turned up his collar against the chilling wind. He glanced quickly sideways at the rainswept cemetery, his eyes lingering on a small eerily white stone marker near the back wall. He tucked the small black box more securely under his arm, hunched his shoulders and tightened his grip on the object deep in his coat pocket.

Why did the man look at a particular stone marker in the cemetery?
What is in the black box?
Is the object in his coat pocket important?
All is revealed at the end of the chapter in Mystery Footnote 1.

Strategic Thinking Is Executive Adventure

Mystery-story fans are eager to know "who done it," how-and-why. Who among us mid-lifers didn't speculate about *Who-killed-J.R.?* when America's most popular nighttime TV serial-of-the-decade left that question unanswered from May to October? It proved to be such an effective marketing tactic that it was replicated into triteness by competitors. Our search for answers, our drive for closure to unfinished business, and our thirst for novelty and adventure are all associated with the emotion we call curiosity. Curiosity is also a major contributor to the most complex corporate activity: the work of building an organization with a future.

Workplace fascination with the mystery of and curiosity about how to create a competitive advantage is well worth an executive time-out, especially when it sharpens important capabilities. In management-lingo, the Return-On-Investment and Assets (ROI / ROA) will be high if a thinking-and-learning workout strengthens *core competencies,* such as curiosity and thinking, that are necessary to *core capabilities* such as determining effective long-range objectives. However, curiosity is not your typical agenda item at your typical company retreat. 'Typical' get-aways for corporate leadership will schedule time for evaluation by-the-numbers-for-the-year, short-term goal-setting, and golfing. Curiosity is easier to associate with adventurers on an Australian walkabout in the outback doing a periodic sorting-out of life's purpose and meaning. Actually, both groups are adventuresome, peering into the mists of the future in order to get a better fix on a vision of success for the long run. What are they looking for?—ways to be stronger contenders in achieving desired rewards.

Competitive advantage, a perennial business objective, was traditionally spelled out by an organization's planning staff during closed-door, high-level meetings. Strategic long-range and big-picture work took a back seat in the era of radical reengineering and of corporate revamping by wonder-worker executives. These same CEOs racked-up turnover speed records that look like those set by athletic coaches who fail to win enough ball games fast enough to satisfy alumni and owners. Nevertheless, executive new-hires are moving into the corporate fields with vigorous confidence in their winning game plan, frequently called a *strategic vision.*

Many of these executives use *visioning* as their tool-of-choice to select prime business targets and to pick out makeover sites with high visibility. Some new chiefs impose their vision in ways that become *a trip* on others. Others see the process of visioning as a way to create shared meaning and direction while verifying where to set up productive turnarounds. For this latter group, *strategic visioning* begins a process of turning a vision inside-out. Thus, strategic visioning can be a corporate-wide, full-court press activity.

The new corporate leader faces a publicized 100-day-window for making-a-difference and gets busy asking questions, pinpointing talents and vitalities, and gathering critical-mass energy to implement valued changes. This brand of strategic visioning depends upon a competency Henry Minzberg called *strategic thinking,* a competency that includes a large portion of curiosity. Initially, in 1983, Minzberg advised executives that they needed keen thinking plus intuition, the ability to quickly construct possibilities. Culling mental collections for best alternatives and combinations of information and processes needs to be executed by executives while in action. Like agile legal prosecutors, they must excel at "on-their-feet thinking." Minzberg observed that no time is allowed in the real world for using neat, classical problem-solving models that are included in typical strategic planning exercises. Furthermore, reality prohibits use of the step-by-step flow charts from management school designs of logical *decision-trees.* Ten years later, in 1993, the veteran iconoclast solidified his argument for the demise of strategic planning. Since then, he decided that he was premature, or a rebirth has occurred.

Strategic planning, as reframed, is no longer assigned to an isolated staff group or conducted as an annual paperwork chore. Upgraded to strategic visioning, planning emerges as an all-hands search-and-acquire activity. Everyone is given a vested interest in (1) identifying and learning or bringing on-board the necessary *core competencies* with which (2) individuals strengthen the company's *core capabilities* to provide (3) *value-added* services and products. In other words, the question is: (1) what can you learn to do well (2) that the company can offer (3) that someone wants or needs? Putting those answers together is strategic finesse, a complex challenge described by Carl Long and Mary Vickers-Koch in *Organization Dynamics,* 24 (1), 1995.

Strategic thinking is hardly a recent invention. Historically, the word strategy comes from a Greek word, *strategia,* which means generalship. During the 1800s it was used to refer to the science and art of pulling together economic, military, and political resources to achieve the objectives of a country or group of countries. When Peter Drucker applied the word in 1954 to the business context, he translated it into two questions: *What is our business, and what should it be?* His direct, parsimonious approach stimulated others to prepare formal statements like: Strategic planning is . . .

the determination of the basic long-term goals and objectives of an enterprise, and the adoption of courses of action and the allocation of resources necessary for carrying out these goals.
    —Alfred Chandler, 1962. Quoted in Long & Vicker-Koch, p. 9, 1995.

Talk about business strategy soon included discussions about company capabilities to cope with competitors and environmental turbulence. Sets of managerial competencies were selected as necessary under three types of conditions so that the company could cope with stable, or reactive, or anticipatory conditions as they might arise in the organization or in the larger community. Assessment of in-house competencies became necessary to assure the presence or absence of skills and talents needed to perform standard business functions, such as marketing, production and procurement under conditions of changing technologies and markets.

As planning activities shifted from attention to *how to become successful* to *what are the key indicators* of success, managers adopted a bottom-line focus and a drive for short-term profitability. Executives learned this ends-over-means approach was like trying to win a tennis match by watching the scoreboard rather than the ball. Next, business excellence began to be attributed to *corporate culture,* placing emphasis on a big picture of the corporate environment, norms and values. Excellence criteria from 1970s' work of Tom Peters and Robert Waterman were reformulated during the 1980s by John Kotter and James Heskitt who studied companies that worked on managing the organization's culture, climate, and attitudes. They saw that firms with an emphasis on performing better had a decided advantage. The companies in these comparisons that worked to become more productive showed a 700% net-income increase as compared to an average 1% increase in firms that did not promote cultures where performance improvement was emphasized and supported.

Higher performing companies focused on shared values, individual competencies, corporate capabilities, and adaptive functioning. Long and Vickers-Koch report that executives in high-performing companies were ready and able to recognize what gives a special advantage at specific points in the organization's *value-chain,* which begins and ends with the key stakeholders. These groups include the board of directors, stockholders, employees and customers. Executives take action to *align* competitive advantage competencies to improve functional processes that will enhance the company's core capabilities. Corporate outputs that provide tomorrow's competitive advantage are called cutting-edge core capabilities. The shift of planning attention to address topics such as alignment of assets, interpreting market demands, and capitalizing on adaptable processes introduces a whole realm of management jargon and flow charts.

Long and Vicker-Koch provide examples in their 1995 article about how organizations strategize around core capabilities that range from Wal-Mart's cross-docking strategy to decisions by the Williams Companies, makers of steel pipe lines, to diversify their business and use their abandoned gas pipe lines for fiber optics cables. The Williams Co. made the front page, lead paragraph, of the Wall Street Journal, November 9, 1999, in Bernard Wysocki, Jr.'s article, "Defining challenge: corporate American confronts the Meaning of a 'Core' Business." Williams Co. is credited with sticking with a formula of success based on the drop in costs as transport volume increases. It meant sticking with big pipeline projects and big customers, users of steel pipes and fiberglass pipes. Wysocki summarizes corporate strategic thinking in 1999: "Focus is in these days, both on Wall Street and in boardrooms across America, and this raises a surprisingly complex question: what constitutes core business? Is it a product? A cache of intellectual property? Or, is it a business design, such as the one used by online retailer Amazon.com, Inc. that can be deployed across multiple industries?"

Executives who recognize what makes for a core business advantage in the minds of the various levels of corporate stakeholders are comfortable and skillful when promoting performance improvement, learning, inventing or adapting, and risk-taking adventures. Even in the midst of corporate fragmenting and regrouping or while riding waves of technological renovations, such executives are able to call forth the emotional energies necessary to align competencies, processes, and capabilities. They rely on disciplined curiosity for exploring and pioneering—for a resilient "Go for it!" Re-stated in Peter-Drucker style, a business design for executive behavior could be as succinct as: Q. What is the work of the executive and what should be the focus of that work? A. The executive's core capability is strategic visioning and the leading-edge of strategic visioning has a core emotional competency—curiosity.

Executives who cultivate and manage curiosity as a core competency introduce a charismatic spirit into their 100-day window of opportunity that can extend into a record-breaking tenure. The curiosity advantage can prepare an executive to be ready to act within a short time frame, to implement value-added products and services, and to be timely in responding to emerging business fields. A well-honed curiosity leads to calculated risk-taking adventures that succeed by virtue of their solid information bases. Curiosity as the lead emotional motivator holds the reigns on anxiety and anger and provides stamina and enthusiasm for rigorous thinking and strategic focus.

Is Curiosity the "Prime Mover"?

Detective story fan or not, executives quickly come to see how opportunity and motive play leading roles in problem solving for workplace ventures, dysfunctions and mysteries. The curiosity tickler at the beginning of this chapter is designed to arouse interest in hearing answers, filling gaps and reaching closure. This is a paragraph of mystery-writer clichés that are deliberately misleading. The story behind the tickler paragraph is not an Agatha Christie puzzle because no crime is involved. It is about a wise and mature man who is a senior manager, who lives in a small town. He is on his way to his son's house on a rainy December night wearing an all-weather coat to protect himself from the wind and chill. Have you already skipped to the end of the chapter to see what Mystery Footnote 1 reveals? Some readers do, some readers don't.

Curiosity as a motive is stronger in some executives than in others. A curiosity that leads to the accumulation of a breadth and depth of information gives the executive an edge in discovering and creating opportunities for innovation. If you put together this naturally occurring storehouse of information with naturally occurring health-maintenance neurochemicals and T-cells that are produced in conjunctions with experiences of curiosity, you have one Very Important Emotion, a VIE. The following sections elaborate on curiosity's role in survival, intelligence, creativity, and well-being.

Curiosity can do a lot more than kill the cat. When not indulged excessively, curiosity activates initiatives, enhances the auto-immune system and sustains speed of mental functioning. It's an emotion associated primarily with pleasant feelings and happy anticipation, the effects of powerful endorphins and enkephalins that are our internally produced chemicals with opium-like high feelings. Psychics, casino *le croupiers,* and stand-up comics as well as entrepreneurs would be out of business if curiosity were not a powerful motivator of behavior. Universities, research institutions and kindergartens would shut down if people lost their thirst for knowing how, why, when, and what if.

Curiosity separated from anxiety and anger is as hard to look at as a magic-eye illusion picture. Refocusing the eyes to sort patterns from a unidimensional surface into three-dimensional scenes is a learned skill. For those who persevere, an unexpected scene emerges from a tangle of color and lines. A complexly composited reality transforms into a recognizable picture with hologram depth.

Taking a deep look at an emotion requires a similar perseverance. The pay-off is also an insightful experience, an understanding of feelings that are frequently avoided or denied, especially on the job. In the work world, feelings are eschewed as unimportant distractions, irrelevant sensations to be denied, shunned, ignored as much as possible. Executives and clerks alike pay an equally high price for using the avoidance tactic. It cuts off potentials for high energy, causing them to miss out on meaningfully exciting work, and on the benefits of self-produced healthy good feelings. Without contact with our emotional motivators, we can quickly dissipate enthusiasm, commitment, loyalty, and high hopes, reducing job assignments to here-and-now busy work. We feel like we are bogged down in mazes of management-by-endless-and-pointless objectives, paperwork, and deadlines. Work becomes a tangle of tasks with no depth.

Curiosity is given first place in this magic eye picture of three vital emotions because it is considered to be the start-up emotion. While bushes, flowers, and trees can stay rooted in one spot and use the air and soil to grow to maturity, people must find food. During the early months, babies put everything into their mouths. "What does *this* taste like*?*" Babies are indefatigable explorers. Unsupervised trial-and-error application of curiosity gets infants and toddlers into a lot of trouble.

Accidental death records include numerous autopsies of infants and young children who tried to eat plastic bags, parts of toys, or unsecured poisonous materials. Many of us recall more than one frightening, anxiety laden, incident in our own childhood—or from our children's early years, or from stories told about neighbors' children. I have a particularly vivid recollection of a time when my sister choked on a penny I gave her as a gift. She was almost a year old and I was six. Fortunately, Mother was close at hand and quickly dislodged my "gift" from the baby's throat. [Ironically, that baby grew up to become the wealthiest member of the family.]

Historians and anthropologists provide the evolutionary twist to this understanding of how emotions contributed to survival of the species. Scholars agree about what was important in the lives of cave dwellers and wandering tribes: it was critical to find food, to avoid dangers, and to overcome obstacles. Humans with the best adaptive capabilities lived the longest. In one long-view perspective, the human story is a survival-of-the-fittest scenario. Civilized living progressed because curiosity motivated humans to explore, and exploring led to finding more food, better shelters, and improved quality of life. Not only did these earliest ancestors find food, they also found predators and hazards. Empirical and biblical reports agree: along with apples and knowledge, humans found "snakes in the grass."

A potential hypothesis takes shape: Basic to survival are competencies and processes for locating food, for detecting dangers, and for strong action to remove obstacles. We come equipped with a number of autonomic nervous system functions that facilitate this work. Three are the neurochemically produced emotions, curiosity, anxiety, and anger.

Rutger's Clayton Aldefer, a group dynamics and work motivation specialist and self-styled devil's advocate, contends that there are three primary motivators for workers: *growth, security, and relatedness*. Each of these complex motivators can be related to the three basic emotions that power an executive's work. *Growth* and improvement begin with *curiosity*. *Anxiety* comes with recognition that in executive jobs there is no safety-net of *security* for corporate success. Problems with coworkers, colleagues, and competitors are *relationship* issues that arouse *anger*. Interpersonal difficulties create obstacles to success. "People" issues produce barriers to goals and generate aspersions on others' abilities or ethics.

A further insight into the important roles of curiosity, anxiety, and anger is seeing how it's possible to experience emotions in both positive and negative ways. For example, the negative side of curiosity can be boredom. The positive side of anxiety can be optimism. Rather than experience anger, we can feel appreciation.

Students of prehistoric life hypothesize that early-on in the history of the species, exploring fields and forests for food and outsmarting dangerous animals and elements also became enjoyable in a fundamental way. These scholars surmise this is why, although these survival procedures are no longer relevant food-gathering techniques in industrialized communities, to this day hunting and fishing remain popular sports, hobbies, and vacations.

Even with all the benefits that curiosity brings to survival, adequacy, growth and meaningfulness, without balance and limits curiosity is dangerous.

Busy-Body or Inquiring Mind?

A woman executive, 45 years old, returned from annual vacation, was summoned to the office of the CEO, and was fired. She was instructed to clear her desk and leave that day. This senior Vice-President had held a top-level position in the organization for over ten years. For the last two years she spent much of her time serving as an elected officer in community associations, working as a lobbyist in the state capitol, and cultivating joint-venture projects between her company and other similar corporations. During that time period she hired a skilled individual with plenty of initiative to take care of the internal details of her division. This deputy became frustrated with the Vice-President's frequent absences, and especially irritated by her pressing curiosity about everything that happened while she was away. He began to undermine her credibility with her peers and employees by wondering out loud if her insatiable inquisitiveness about plans and activities in other production divisions was motivated by self-serving rather than corporate-serving interests. Then, during her annual vacation, when a competitor with whom she was known to be collaborating was awarded a coveted contract from the state, she abruptly lost organizational support.

The Inside Story:

State Curiosity 98th%. Trait Curiosity 85th%

These results are taken from her management assessment scores.

Was she a busy-body with insatiable curiosity or
a corporate traitor selling secrets to the 'enemy'?

My money is on the insatiable curiosity.

She later started up two innovative health organizations and
was very successful

When people roam new territories, as in days of old, they risk exposure to life-threatening or career-terminating encounters. Anxiety serves as our early warning system, motivating us to take precaution. It is important to keep in mind that concrete jungle predators and techno-logical inventions can and do kill us as dead as can lions and tigers and bears, or tornadoes and hurricanes and lightning storms.

Even forewarned and realistic about the way things work in the world, we become frustrated when we are slowed down or limited in our progress toward a goal. It doesn't make much difference if our quest is to reach a favorite berry patch or a well-stocked supermarket. That inner reaction is similar to what happens when administrative red-tape stands in the way of certifications and academic degrees. The angry emotion is also aroused if we are passed-over for a well-deserved promotion. We dislike being unable to make progress toward our goals.

Any irritation can become intense, even to the point of feeling furious. Hard as anger is on the functioning of heart structures, it is not all bad. Anger has its opposite *action* and *reaction,* a law of nature learned by first-year physics students. Anger means we care, we appre-ciate, we hold firm values. If we don't care, if we don't have a liking or affection for something or someone, we don't experience anger. Anger brings us face-to-face with our sense of justice and our idealism.

. . . It's *not fair* that a less dedicated, less skilled person got that raise and position that I applied for! . . . It's *not right* to allow some people to go hungry while others horde enough food for a small city. . . . We *should* all be working overtime to do our assignments perfectly, to achieve unblemished competence records. . . .

Curiosity, anxiety, and anger emotions, like other motives, are seldom, if ever, pure and uncontaminated by other motives. They are not singular in experience or expression. In my organizational consulting practice, I notice that curiosity prevails in successful executives, yet is tempered by the back-up cautions provided by anxiety. Typically, anger is the second back-up contributor, motivating the drive for excellence and quality of work. For executives, anger usually had the lowest level of intensity and frequency of the three vital emotions.

In several organizations where I conducted assessments for the entire management group, mid-managers' experiences of anger were stronger and more frequent than their levels of anxiety and were more often their primary emotional motivator. Those higher on the management ladder apparently maintain a realistic proportion in their anger experiences. An illustration of how anger's motivational energy overcame promotional obstacles comes from Doug Bray's report of studies done by AT&T's Bell Laboratories. Higher levels of "spontaneity" and impulsive energy were more characteristic of managers without college degrees who advanced farther than other managers without degrees. The moral of this story is that there are times to speak out, to tell it like it looks to you, to leverage the emotion for engaging in logical problem solving. Chapter 6 describes the motivational effects of anxiety and Chapter 7 discusses the virtues and dangers of the anger emotion.

Emotional motivators are now better understood and publicly discussed. They are called psychological "vital signs" and described as indicators of a person's Emotional Quotient, an EQ. Some writers like Daniel Goleman go so far as to say that EQ is more important than IQ, the Intellectual Quotient. The following sections review the vitality curiosity brings to IQ, EQ, and wisdom.

Smartest Man in the World

A humorous story made the rounds about the President scheduling a trip to Rome using Air Force 1, an airplane dedicated to the President's use for carrying out his work related to the business of running the country. Since elections were coming up the next year and budget cutting was making headlines, the President decided to give the trip added value. He needed to attend an important meeting and would be taking Henry Kissinger along to give advice, but there was room for other passengers. The President invited one of his major competitors in the up-coming election. He also invited an older priest who had been too poor all his life to visit the Vatican or to meet the Pope, and a struggling but promising NYC art student who had never seen the great paintings in Rome. All in all there were six persons making the trip on Air Force 1. About midway across the Atlantic, the pilot came into the cabin and announced that there was a mechanical failure that could not be repaired and the plane would soon crash into the ocean. He said that by some misfortune there were only five parachutes stowed on board for the trip. He took one parachute out of the storage space, demonstrated how to put it on and how to activate it once outside the aircraft. He then said, "I am the most talented pilot in the Air Force and I must live to train others. Happy Landings to the rest of you." With that he opened the cabin door, and jumped out.

The President said, "Since I am the President of the country, I must live to serve the people." And he took a parachute and jumped out the door.

Then the politician took a parachute and said, "I am the most likely candidate to oppose the President in the next election and I must live to protect the people from him. Good-by."

Whereupon, Mr. K. took a parachute, saying, "I am the world's smartest man and I must protect the world from the thinking of politicians."

When they were alone, the Priest and the Student looked at each other for a few moments. The Priest spoke first. "My son, I have lived a long and satisfying life. I am ready for the next life. You are a young person with much ahead of you and a great talent to develop. You must take the last parachute and jump."

The Student smiled and patted the Priest on the shoulder. "Thank you, Father. But, not to worry. The smartest man in the world just jumped out of here with my backpack on his shoulders."

The moral of the story? Even the smartest man in the world can get into trouble without an active curiosity checking out what's here-and-now.

Intelligence, Curiosity and Quantum Science

Intelligence is arguably an essential competency for an executive. A leading proponent of this position is Fred Fiedler whose insightful work linked leadership effectiveness with quick thinking and situational variables in the work setting. Fiedler told a conference group in Jerusalem that when selecting an ideal executive that he recommended an old, bright one. The mature leader who maintains speed with new learning has the advantage of making on-the-spot decisions seasoned by experience. Fiedler, widely-known for his work identifying good leaders by the strength of their ratings of their least preferred co-workers, continues to award priority status to an executive's intelligence.

Other reported secrets of leadership success fill volumes and libraries, but do not add up to one formula for all. Those who tried to do meta-analysis of the literature say that all that can be said, for sure, is that leadership success depends on the combination of task, place, and mix of persons present. Reviewers grudgingly admit that, in general, leaders are somewhat brighter than the average of the group they are leading.

What makes one individual somewhat brighter than the average of a cohort group? That person is a more actively curious person. Active curiosity means gathering information for the fun of it, being on the look-out for what's new or interesting, and wondering how things work or how they could be made to work better. For the curious person, information collecting is a hobby, one that increases in value over time, especially as that information becomes organized and displayed.

Curiosity gives a competitive advantage to an executive, or to a street gang leader, because it nurtures and enhances IQ. An active curiosity gains value as it becomes obvious that IQ scores vary significantly within an individual over time. Scores decrease if a person is not engaged in new learning and experiences. Estimated potentials, obtained both in early years and in later years, are known to be influenced by nutrition and environment. Head Start, a pre-school program for children of poor families, produced dramatic leaps in IQ scores of children who were given enriched diets and exposed to large amounts of information and appreciation. This variability showed that heredity is far from the whole answer. It suggests that attributing differences in intelligence to matters of gender, nationality, race, or culture is a spurious distraction. Such arguments are political, not scientific.

Recovery-of-function programs for stroke and head injury victims are showing IQ score gains in more and more patients that are similar to those that Head Start found in children from poor neighborhoods. It appears that when an older or a younger person receives nourishing food, interesting new information, and encouraging support, intelligence indicators improve.

Curiosity that motivates a person to gather information was first noticed as a type of exploratory interest. William James, who is considered the father of U.S. psychology, referred to this type of curiosity as *scientific curiosity*. James realized intellectual curiosity was more than attraction to something novel with a hope that it could aid survival. He noticed how curiosity drives us to resolve inconsistencies and to fill in our gaps in information or understanding.

Seeing Is Believing. Or Is It Wishful Curiosity at Work?

12

A   13   C

14

Interpreting inconsistencies and closing gaps can be automatic perceptual events, as illustrated in the example of letters and numbers above and in the earlier discussion of differences in opinion in Chapter 2. Thinking can be tutored to take advantage of techniques associated with investigative research, logical or legal opinions, and mechanical trouble-shooting. Subconscious or intentional, the result is a wealth of information that gives a competitive advantage to business managers, to scholastic aptitude test-takers, to detective agents and to national defense planners. To grasp the fullest implication of the curiosity-edge, we only need go as far as the introduction to a physics textbook or Fritjof Capra's 1975 book, *The Tao of Physics.*

In quantum physics, information is considered to be the building block of the universe. From Hubbell pictures of a less-than-1-degree slice of the universe which show 50 billion galaxies, or five times greater than predictions—to subnuclear discoveries of three basic sub-molecular ingredients, everything is in constant motion, informing and changing whatever it contacts. Closer to home, bits of information work together to form human bodies. Genes order the initial structure of each body. In each of us continuous activity, such as growth, development, maturation and productivity, is supervised by information from our genes plus *information* from the contact with the environment, which changes and replaces our initial cycles and genes.

The regenerative concept of information in larger living systems was proposed as early as 1980. Jantsch described an ecosystem as an "information system which manifests itself in the organization of matter," evolving as it accumulates information. Margaret Wheatley, management consultant and leadership theorist, author of *Leadership and the*

New Science, extrapolates Jantsch's thinking to the way humans work and the new job of leadership:

> *The fuel of life is new information—novelty—ordered into new structures. We need to have information coursing through our systems, disturbing the peace, imbuing everything it touches with new life. We need, therefore, to develop new approaches to information . . .(p. 105).*

Wheatley boldly declares that information that is freely generated and freely exchanged will be the secret power in organizations in the future (p. 145). She advises executives to encourage rather than manage information. She recommends that they apply genius and not control to information. She makes her case by transferring insights from the way the universe achieves order and is self-perpetuating, to how executives will best manage complex, proactive organizations.

The scientific observation is that information has a capacity to produce new information. One conclusion is that as long as information is given opportunity to travel, productivity and long-term survival are assured. It is curiosity that provides the motivation to explore, to find pleasure in novel information. An individual's curiosity-edge assures opportunities for information to travel about at a local (individual) level. Executives with a core curiosity-competency generate opportunities for information to travel at global (organizational) levels

Wheatley comments that heavy-handed control frequently interferes with natural flows of information at global levels. Control is used as a protection by leaders who see little relevance in natural-science laws. Impatient executives reap no insight from hearing a principle that *information is self-organizing and will put itself into a life-sustaining pattern.* Wheatley, nevertheless, suggests that executives can learn to rely on two complimentary processes for achieving well-ordered work groups: tasks that create new information and tasks that feed information back on itself. She urges initiatives such as matrix structures, professional networking, 360-degree surveys, cross-functional training, task groups that involve members from a variety of departments and work levels, rewards for continuous improvement of technical processes, as well as numerous similar open organization procedures.

Wheatley describes leaders of the future as working to create opportunities for receiving information, and publicly rewarding those who are courageous enough to gather both affirming and disconfirming information. Scientific, or intellectual, curiosity requires bravery and risk-taking.

Mystery Story Fans, Here's more of the dark and stormy night story.
Tally Ho! The Hunt Begins

A professor gazed out across a classroom full of well-dressed, well-fed, sleepy-eyed students on the third day of this least-preferred, last segment of a required logic course: rational thinking. The professor posed the reluctant scholars with a hard question: "Which is worse: Ignorance or Apathy?"

An expected answer came from the back of the room, " I don't know and I don't care."

The professor raised high over his head a small black box. He shook the box vigorously. The contents clunked back and forth. "What do your think is in this mysterious black box?"

Silence.

He slowly opened the box and took out a book he had received the night before from his father. He walked through the rows of desk-chairs, holding up the book so everyone could see its title: *The Precious Present,* a slender and small book written by Spencer Johnson (1994, NY, Doubleday Publishers).

When he returned to the podium at the front of the room, he announced, "You will find a stack of these books in the back of the room. Please pick one up, read it tonight, and tomorrow I will ask you the question: 'Which is worse: Ignorance or Apathy.' Class dismissed."

F.Y.I. The professor got his idea for "motivating" the bored students from his father, an experienced manager in a local company. The previous evening, a typical cold and windy New England December night, his father walked from his home some five blocks away. He made an early delivery of a holiday gift he had carefully chosen after hearing his son's description of this group of particularly disinterested, less-than-eager students. The simple message about the value of staying interested in the here-and-now that is described in *The Precious Present* helped re-motivate the father following the recent death of his wife, the professor's mother.

Executive Risk Taking: Gambling in Corporate Suites

A lead paragraph in a 1996 *Time Magazine* article asked readers, "Do you get a kick out of dangerous sports like skydiving and whitewater rafting? Do you jump eagerly from job to job or even get a thrill from rearranging the furniture? If so, you are probably what psychologists call a "novelty seeker." The report goes on to describe the discovery of the first gene considered to be linked to a *normal* personality trait. The January 15 report was one of many announcements of gene discoveries. Gene research went into slow motion when pharmaceutical companies reduced funding to such projects. The complexities of genes did not provide quick solutions or marketables. Interactions and effects of a gene proved to be even more complex than the composition of that gene.

The so-called "thrill seeker" discovery was based on a genetic analysis of blood taken from persons whose answers to personality questionnaires showed them to be explorers and excitable. *Time* reports these as two hallmarks of novelty seeking as defined by medical scholars. It is a very different approach than that of the personality theorist discussed above. Blood samples from individuals identified as explorers and excitable showed these persons to have one longer-than-average gene. That gene's name is D4DR and it is found on chromosome 11. A confounding point in this medical lab information is that it lumps together: excitability, people who crave thrills, and a normal personality trait that psychologists call a "novelty seeker."

Non-medical scientific measurements, commonly called psychological tests, have been used to investigate curiosity beginning with William James. Many of these studies show the distinctions between interest in exciting physiological sensations and interest in intriguing cognitive perceptions. Cognitive, intellectual curiosity is not necessarily present with sensory, experiential curiosity, and vice versa. The "Eureka!" of the mathematician and the "Geronimo!" of the sky diver are accompanied by a rush of adrenaline, but the triggers for the neurochemical firing seem to be different. Both exclamations are indicative of risk-taking, a trying-out of something innovative, and both are adventuresome. However, Eureka and Geronimo are typically spoken by very different people motivated by very different kinds of curiosities.

Cognitive curiosity is believed to be aroused by discrepancies between incoming bits of information. The resolution of the accompanying sense of conflict is pleasurable and encourages more cognitive exploration. Sensation-seeking curiosity is associated with higher thresholds of anxiety, such as tension, conflict and discomfort. Sensation seekers are not as quickly aware of apprehensions or discomforts. These are persons who push the limits of body sensations to get extra rushes of emotions. They like action-risks such as wild roller-coaster rides, extreme sports like hang-gliding, dangerous foods and intoxicants, or sexual activities that mix a higher percentage of discomfort or pain with the pleasure.

Genetic researchers and the news magazine reporters state that the long D4DR gene alone does not compel people to take up bungee jumping or air surfing. They recognize that there are another four or five dopamine-related genes that contribute to what they consider to be an innate curiosity temperament. Perhaps collaboration between genetic and personality specialists will uncover evidence that this long gene on chromosome 11 is included in two or more independent clusters of genes. And, perhaps they will conclude that excitability is unrelated to intellectual curiosity and cognitive exploratory behavior. Such gaps and inconsistencies in our current information will keep researchers curious about curiosity for a long time to come.

In the meantime, executives can continue to capitalize on the curiosity emotion for new learning, for information gathering, and for business venture courage. Armed with integrated data, and open to incoming news, the executive adventurer moves confidently into un-tested domains without being foolhardy or brazen. Those who pioneer corporate frontiers are forging into the white waters of innovation and creativity. This core curiosity competence contributes to an individual's adventuring and risk-taking capability and varies in intensity and frequency from person to person. The good news is that adventuring, risk-taking and corporate-suite gambling savvy can be adapted to fit the job circumstances. It can be cultivated or tamed, increased or subdued.

Creativity and innovation emerge from information as we introduce twists, combinations, refinements and extrapolations while remaining willing to look several directions at once. Janus, the Roman god of doorways, is usually portrayed with two faces, one looking each direction, right and left. Sometimes Janus is shown with multiple faces, looking in all directions. Janus has come to represent the creative process because of his ability to look at things from different angles. The advantages of acquiring a wide range of information is both old and new, classic and quantum wisdom.

Creative people who have longer and more productive careers than others have benefited from two important social influences. The influences are labeled as [1] *developmental* influence and [2] *productive* influence. Developmental refers to conditions that are conducive to the identification and training of a talent. Productive refers to factors that support or inhibit creative outputs after a talent has been cultivated.

Mentors and opportunities to practice are especially important in the development phase, which is traditionally associated with childhood and adolescence. Productive use of a developed ability flourishes best when individuals are associating with other creative people who come from a variety of specialties and workgroups. A second influential factor is that the innovator is not subjected to creativity killers, i.e., working under close scrutiny, given external constraints or reasons to be creative. This information contributes to life-span research and stands opposed to limiting the identification and development of creativity to any one age-period. Post-retirement creativity is flourishing in later years as products of increased vitality and longevity. Numerous retirement programs stimulate health and curiosity in all areas of life: mental, physical, social, and spiritual.

Talent and creative ability discovered in post-retirement is seldom able to strengthen corporate capabilities or competitive advantages. Academies of senior professionals are springing up near colleges and universities with resources that allow the elders to conduct research, engage in debates, and to test new engineering or construction designs. They may soon be able to directly contribute to business and corporate ventures.

Non-retired executives who employ strategic visioning approaches are more interested in addressing untapped competencies among current employees. Executives who are skilled at broadening and elevating the interests of employees deliver outstanding leadership. These five-star executives are called transformational leaders by Bernard Bass, who was identified by *Fortune Magazine* as America's foremost expert on leadership. Five-star leaders inspire employees to exert extra effort and to exceptional levels of performance in three ways. First they have an ability to be inspirational and to make a charismatic impression. They give individual consideration to employees. They provide intellectual stimulation by challenging others to think, to develop, and to expand their abilities.

These three behaviors separate transformational from transactional leadership in the model proposed by Bass. Charisma is considered central because transformation depends upon a leader's ability to evoke emotion. Followers develop intense feelings about charismatic executives. The employees and coworkers have trust and confidence in these leaders, believing that they can overcome any obstacle. This non-grandiose type of charisma is found to some degree throughout organizations of every sort. Such individuals inspire loyalty to the organization, command respect, and have a special gift of seeing what's "really" important. These executives become symbols of success and accomplishment. Whether the relationships are positive or negative, there is likely to be more turbulence because of the executive's ability to inspire, to enliven, and to heighten motivation. It is an arousal of emotions and a demonstration of EQ.

Gambling in corporate suites is both necessary and legitimate. This executive "business" is a form of innovative risk-taking in core work activity and in talent identification and training. Executive gambit work is not done in an isolated skunk works, but in corporate headquarters where an executive with transformational capability has an optimal level of the curiosity competency.

Curiosity Sparks the Leadership Advantage

The successful executive will keep focusing and refocusing on what's important. Disciplined curiosity works as the leading edge in individual and corporate capabilities. The application of curiosity in strategic visioning, in quantum and transformational management practices, and in courageous innovation is the leadership-edge that produces an executive advantage.

Transformational leaders who evoke emotion become charismatic. Emotional intelligence is proposed by *USA Today*, *Time Magazine*, and Bantam Press publications as the true measure of human intelligence. Oversimplifying to an IQ vs EQ debate is not likely to result in much more than sales of magazines and books. This is a both-and situation where emotional wisdom increases cognitive capability. Executives with high IQ speed of new learning, whose curiosity inspires well-founded *Go-For-It* work, will, indeed, have a leadership-edge. These are the ones who will be out front, far ahead, and shaking-the-trees while others are raking-the-leaves.

Interest in "emotional intelligence" is credited to Peter Salovey and John Mayer, and to Daniel Goleman who published a book by that title. These New England professors are interested in the regulation of emotion, the use of emotion to enhance living, and a redefinition of what it means to be smart. Human development specialists like Jerome Kagan quickly point out that it will never help to get an "average" score of anyone's emotions.

Neuroscientists are pinpointing where the chemical actions take place in the brain. Rather than discussing emotions directly, they talk more and more about connections between limbic systems and the neocortex, and the brain's adaptive, versatile, fail-safe interconnectedness. Neurochemistry gives us another example of the value of information flow and connection. They provide bio-technical explanations that move us beyond right brain/left brain dichotomies.

The foundation of emotional intelligence is considered to be self-awareness, an ability to know what emotion is being experienced. That ability will be triggered by a curiosity about what's happening, and will influence decisions and choices about behavior. The emotions being studied as major contributors to "emotional intelligence" are identified as anxiety, anger, and optimism. I suspect that optimism, by their definition, is the positive side of anxiety; and, that curiosity will turn out to be an independent factor. The EQ advocates look at what they call emotional skills: empathy, graciousness; and converse behaviors: over-ambitiousness, authoritarian, conflicts with upper management. Their mixed bag of emotional and behavioral factors takes them quickly into discussions that confound social values, moral codes, and individual virtues.

I submit that *emotional wisdom* as provided by curiosity, anxiety, and anger proves a more straightforward, elegantly simple understanding of executive quests and effectiveness. The motivating power of the three emotions is firmly rooted in neurochemical activity. The inspiring, charismatic executive capitalizes on an understanding of the universality of emotions to maintain personal and corporate motivational balance. Emotional wisdom calls on curiosity, first and foremost, in order to promote intelligence, to stimulate creativity, and to point the direction for productive risk taking.

Mystery Footnote 1
1. **Q. Why did the man look at a particular stone marker in the cemetery?**
   A. His **PAST:** The man looked at the grave of his wife, recently deceased, age 65. A victim of breast cancer.
2. **Q. What is in the black box?**
   A. His **PRESENT:** The black box contains a "present" the man is taking to his son. This gift for the holiday is a book titled, **The Precious Present.** A *carpe diem* parable, urging the reader to seize the day, fits right into his son-the-professor's strategy. The professor uses curiosity to encourage his students to debate ignorance and apathy. Possibly the students will conclude that ignorance leads to apathy and is, therefore, the most detrimental to productive living in the present.

3. Q. Is the object in his coat pocket important?
A. His **FUTURE:** In his pocket, the man keeps a calendar book where he records appointments and goals for the future.

Questions and Answers. Footnote 2

1. **Q.** *Who thinks curiosity is the first motivator?* **A.** Anthropologists, historians, and psychologists.
2. **Q.** *What do curiosity, intelligence, and quantum science have in common?* **A.** An interest in collecting as much **information** as possible.
3. **Q.** *How is curiosity involved in executive risk taking?* **A.** Curiosity stimulates learning and information gathering as well as a taste for problem-solving adventure which equips an executive with extra confidence and courage for risk-taking.
4. **Q.** *Why call curiosity the leadership-edge?* **A. When an executive has cultivated curiosity as a core competency, it informs strategic visioning, guides transformational leadership, and gives competitive advantage.**

Background Reading

For more details about strategic visioning refer to the critical overview of strategy by Henry Mintzberg, *The Rise and Fall of Strategic Planning*, NY: The Free Press, 1994. He elaborates on problems with the traditional planning process and outlines the future emphasis on strategic thinking. He advocates that the manager-planner should stick to implementation tactics for management's strategic thinking—the visioning work. Taking a broader view, Gary Hamel and C. K. Prahalad discuss "Strategy as Stretch and Leverage," in the *Harvard Business Review*, March-April 1993. Other contributors to this area of thinking are Peter Drucker, Michael E. Porter, John Kotter, and James Heskett. The quote from Alfred Chandler is from 1962, *Strategy and Structure: Chapters in the History of American Industrial Enterprise*. Cambridge, MA: MIT Press. The Chandler quote is found on page 9 of Using core capabilities to create competitive advantage, *Organizational Dynamics*, Summer 1995, pp. 7-22, by Carl Long & Mary Vicker-Koch.

Curiosity has been linked to physical health, productivity and longevity since the 1970s. An early report of beneficial effect on the functioning of the brain and body is found in the November 1984 issue of *Psychology Today*, pp. 62-72. An interview with Marian Diamond, "A Love Affair With the Brain," describes 30 years of research that confirms the lifelong plasticity of the brain. From page 70: [Interviewer] *Hopson: What would enrichment be for an older person? Diamond: That depends on the individual, since no two human brains are alike. Some people do crossword puzzles. Some go back to school. Some like to visit neighbors. The main factor is stimulation. The nerve cells are designed to receive stimulation. And I think curiosity is a key factor. If one remains curious for a lifetime, that will surely stimulate neural tissue and the cortex may in turn respond.*

Diamond and a team of colleagues at University of California at Berkeley drew a straightforward conclusion: "Use it or lose it" (p. 64).

Connections between curiosity and T-cell production is also reported in the research of Norman Cousins. One of his popular books is *Anatomy of an Illness as Perceived by a Patient*, 1979, NY: Norton. *U.S. News and World Report* asked on their front cover, "Are you losing your mind?" The article titled, "Brain Power," debunked myths about how the brain ages and lists do's and don'ts for keeping sharp. For example, the November 28, 1994 article by Joannie M. Schrof reviews and extends the "use it or lose it" belief about our brains. The advanced word on this maxim is, Yes, but don't engage in boring or repetitive mental activity: "Pursue eclectic interests" (p. 91).

Research on curiosity as a measurable emotion is being conducted at a number of universities, among them the Center for Research in Behavioral Medicine and Health Psychology, the University of South Florida. Most historians consider that the concept of curiosity was introduced as early as 1890 by William James, who considered it to be one of the primary instincts. William McDougal, 1921, suggested that curiosity and fear were antagonistic. Exploratory behavior and arousal are linked to curiosity in research literatures. The arguments continue about it being a basic or a secondary learned response. Daniel Berlyne is considered an early productive contributor to experimentation on human curiosity and exploratory behavior. Optimal stimulation theories include attention to cognitive reactions to physiological stimulations and the mixes of basic emotions, e.g., anxiety with curiosity. Zuckerman noted individual differences in sensation seeking, and Spielberger has refined the state-trait measurements of intellectual curiosity. See reference section for publications by these authors.

Transformational and charismatic leadership is described in depth in the writings of Bernard M. Bass. Although *charisma* is a frequent topic in anthropological literature and political science studies of great leaders, it is popularly associated with religious and entertainment world figures, occasionally with a public, elected official. The words "transformational leader" was better received by U.S. employees in business and industry settings. The word "charismatic" in conjunction with leadership is viable in international discussions.

For information about emotional intelligence read Daniel Goleman, 1995, *Emotional Intelligence: Why It Can Matter More than IQ.* New York: Bantam Books. *Time Magazine* featured EQ on its cover and ran a feature article by Nancy Gibbs with Alice Park, Jessie Birnbaum, Sharon Epperson, Lawrence Mondi, James Graff, and Lisa Towle, October 2, 1995. The story reports on scholarly interpretations of what it means to be smart, reporting that "new brain research suggests that emotions, not IQ, may be the true measure of human intelligence" (p. 60).

Connections between curiosity and creativity are found in R. J. Sternberg and T. I. Lubart, 1995, *Defying the Crowd: Cultivating Creativity in a Culture of Conformity.* NY: Free Press; and, in Lubart & Sternberg, 1995, "An investment approach to creativity: Theory and data. In S. M. Smith, T. B. Ward & R. A. Finke (Eds.), *The Creative Cognition Approach,* (pp. 269-302). Cambridge, MA: MIT Press. Extensions of curiosity and creativity into executive power were reported by A. M. O'Roark (1992). Assessing hardy, creative professionals and leaders: Curiosity with an edge, *Transactualization as Creativity: The Will to Power.* Basic research in this topic is done by I. A. Taylor. A reference can be found in *The Journal of Creative Behavior,* 8(2), pp. 114-115. Taylor, Sutton & Haworth, 1974, "The measurement of creative transactualization: A scale to measure behavioral dispositions to creativity."

CURIOSITY   ANXIETY   *ANGER*

Chapter 6

Anxiety: The Executive Challenger

Anxiety is a heads-up alert. This sweaty-palm, shaky knees, cold feet emotion, called fear, is hard-wired to keep us out of harm's way. Our natural worrier skill, it motivates us to be cautious in the search for survival, adequacy, growth, and meaningfulness.

- **Fear Is Natural: Effective Response Is Learned**
- ***High Anxiety* is Working Without a Safety Net**
- **The Art of Anxiety Management**
- **Mobilizing Resources For Action**

"We have nothing to fear but fear itself."
F.D.R. circa 1933

Gulf War Battalion Commander. *"I want to talk to you about fear. You will be afraid. If you're not afraid, there's something wrong with you. . . . It's OK to be frightened. It's natural. You're going to be scared. And fear is not a bad thing. It can be used as an advantage. Let me tell you some of the physiological things that occur when you're afraid—when you're really afraid. I'm talking you-believe-you're-going-to-die afraid. It's only happened to me a couple of times. . . .*

"Now I would not have done that [He pulled the driver out of a tank that was on fire, an early career deed for which the commander received a medal for bravery]—*not even at that age, and I was 25 or 26 — if I hadn't been afraid. Gentlemen, I had the strength of ten men—because I was sorely afraid. . . .*

"Physiologically, what fear does to you is, it pumps adrenaline into your system. It does a couple of other things: it drains the capillaries of the extremities of the body—the arms, the legs. And what that does for you is, if you get shot in the arms or legs, you won't bleed as much. You'll know when you're afraid, guys. You'll have this need to urinate. You will taste a metal taste in your mouth like you had maybe a half dozen nails, No. 10-sized nails [in your mouth].

"It is going to happen. Understand it. Cope with it. Talk to each other about it. Understand with each other that all of you are afraid. Men don't like to admit stuff like that. . . . But it's OK to be afraid. Do not let it dominate your mind. If you become frozen with fear . . . that's not good. And the best way to get over that, in the presence of the enemy, is to fire one round. As soon as you do that, it's like a release. It will come to you in a moment—you will know what to do."

St. Petersburg Times, p. 1, February 19, 1991. St. Petersburg, Florida

Fear Is Natural: Effective Response Is Learned

Warriors acknowledge how fear tastes and feels on battlefields, and they learn how to overwhelm their anxiety with a more powerful motivator—*the cause*. Anxiety is laid aside in response to a call to honorable duty. Firing a round of bullets is like a teenager's shout of *Yesssss*, or the Civil War *rebel yell*. This burst of energy declares *this I do-or-die*. I learn that I can defy fear for a cause that is worth my sweat, tears, and blood. I learn how to ignore anxiety and to break free of my immobilized, frozen state.

Non-military executives are equally well-acquainted with fear. They wake at 4 a.m. flooded with images of all that must be accomplished during the day ahead. They have nightmares about financial statements covered with red ink. They carry briefcases stuffed with unfinished work home each night. These responsible workers worry each vacation day about what's not getting done in the office and make plans for what to do as soon as they get to their desk. It's a natural gearing up of the body's strengths to wage the battles of business and commerce, a condition endemic to a leadership position.

It may be obvious that executives who hate living with ambiguities and surprises are likely candidates for physical illness and for career-path derailment, or both. It is not so obvious that constructive consequences can follow anxiety episodes, such as those that became familiar experiences in corporations during the last decade. For example, experts on what to do after-the-downsizing or after the merge-and-streamlining tell us that it is healthy for workers to acknowledge feelings of anxiety as a survivor of a major corporate layoff, sell-off, or dismemberment. A period of apprehensiveness, accompanied by guilt and/or grief, is considered a necessary, positive step toward accepting the new circumstance and moving forward toward recovery and change. Specialists who deal with aftermaths of death, loss and post-traumatic stress reactions now apply their insights to radical change in work settings. Most are variations of Elizabeth Kubler-Ross' writings that introduced a general public awareness of widely experienced emotional patterns. She advocated the healing effects of open discussion of fears and pains subsequent to traumatic life events.

However, it remains unacceptable for a company CEO to do a lot of wringing of hands and shaking of the head while saying, *I'm afraid that we are going into debt so deeply that we'll never get out*. Corporate managers are expected to demonstrate optimism, to keep morale up, and to be buffers. They are to assure that harsh business probabilities do not undermine the conduct of routine work and doing today's job well. Across the years a number of organizations invested in my services as they planned for cut-back and outplacement support. I faced uniform resistance from executives to any suggestion of open discussion of the bad news. Nor would they acknowledge the presence or effects of emotions churning in themselves or coworkers. When business is difficult, executives *keep a stiff upper lip,* working hard to buffer their employees and themselves. They put on a happy face and bite the bullet.

Looking behind appearances, psychological assessments of management groups show that persons working in higher level positions, in general, report higher levels of trait anxiety. A stronger intensity and frequency of worry and tension is found to be present in executives with or without pending layoffs, restructurings, or budget reductions. The fact that executives must work under the pressure of knowing that they have no right answer in the bottom left hand drawer of their desk may have partially prompted W. Edwards Deming's recommendation that management needs to drive fear out of the workplace. Deming argued that only then can everyone work effectively for the company. This maxim is one of Deming's fourteen Total Quality Management (TQM) principles used as guides for management of team effectiveness and cost-reduction programs.

Two TQM consultants, Kathleen Ryan and Daniel Oestreich, propose to eliminate fear in the workplace by unearthing the *undiscussibles* in an organization. In consultant-facilitated disclosure of undiscussables, fears are stated publicly. The purpose is to engender openness and respect within workgroups. These TQM consultants found that *management practices* proved to be the primary *undiscussible.* In order to qualify as an indiscussible, a topic had to represent a problem or issue that employees hesitated to talk about with those who are essential to its resolution. A second qualifying criteria is that failure to discuss the matter poses a potential barrier to quality work or effective work relationships. In this instance, *management practices* referred to such things as manager's behavior, technical competence, assignments, terminations, favoritism, and dissemination of information about corporate motives and politics. The largest subset associated with causing fear was *the boss's interpersonal style.*

Employees were concerned about repercussions from speaking-up to their supervisors. They worried about immediate abrasive behavior. They suspected there would also be delayed, subtle threats and ambiguous retaliation. Other topics in the undiscussible category were loss of credibility or reputation, lack of career or financial advancement, or loss of employment. Techniques suggested by Ryan and Oestreich for training managers how to drive fear from the workplace include giving leaders explicit descriptions of ways that bosses strike fear in the hearts of the workgroup—i.e., tone of voice, silent stares, blaming.

Strong reinforcement for addressing management's *fear-power*, comes from a seasoned consultant, Lester Tobias, who draws on his consulting experience to identify perennial organizational issues. Tobias concluded that all bosses always *intimidate* all subordinates all of the time. He writes that he uses the word *intimidate* intentionally, to imply a generating of fear. The negative consequences he associates with employees' fears include the setting in motion of a host of defenses. The defenses range from ingratiating behavior to counter-dependency. Tobias finds that each defensive response takes away from genuine discussion of interests and issues, and thereby prevents employees from working effectively for the company. Tobias' dramatic statement strikes a sharp point to get the full attention of those in authority.

One key limitation to TQM techniques for eliminating fear is that nothing is geared for the executive who sees the debt rising and the market share plunging. Inviting open dialogue about what is causing fear in a worker's day, does not bring relief to an executive attempting to buffer self and employees from sharp-edged choices that call for termination of employment, of ways of doing business, of chapter 11 bankruptcy declarations. What do executives say when put on the spot about cut-backs, imminent but unannounced? Some advise *white lies*. Some say *talk straight*. All say, *whatever you do, there will be unpleasantness to deal with.* There is no way around pain-producing decisions, and no way an executive can avoid the responsibility for making the tough necessary business choices.

High Anxiety Is Working Without a Safety Net

A first step in moving beyond fearing fear is learning to live with anxiety. To coexist with anxiety means understanding how it works. Anxiety is an unpleasant emotional state or condition that includes experiential, physiological, and behavioral components. Most authorities agree that fear is experienced by all humans and animals and that it is a product of a psychobiological process that consists of three major elements: an encounter with a stressor, which is perceived by an individual as dangerous or threatening, and culminates in an emotional state of tension, apprehension and worry which is called anxiety.

Sigmund Freud equated fear with objective anxiety, which is proportional to a real danger in the external world. Freud made a distinction between objective anxiety and *neurotic anxiety*. Neurotic anxiety was used to refer to emotional reactions that are greater in intensity than would be expected on the basis of the objective danger.

More recently, statistical techniques applied to anxiety survey data have detected relatively independent factors for *state* and *trait* anxiety. These characteristics are positively related to each other, but logically different. State anxiety refers to an unpleasant emotional state that consists of unpleasant thoughts, insecurities, and uncomfortable tensions, and is accompanied by the arousal of the autonomic nervous system. State anxiety varies in intensity and fluctuates over time as a function of perceived physical or psychological danger.

Trait anxiety is considered to be relatively stable and a measure of differences between individual tendencies to perceive a wide range of situations as dangerous or threatening. It follows that people high in trait anxiety are likely to experience higher levels of State anxiety more frequently. Considering the tendency of executives to wake at early hours thinking about the demands of the day ahead, it did not come as a surprise when I found that many executives in leadership training courses reported above-average levels of trait anxiety. Questionnaires, given as part of a stress assessment component in a week-long course for senior managers and executives, reflected not only above-average levels on measures of trait anxiety, but also on at least one of the other two emotions assessed—anger and curiosity.

When assessing a company's total management group, comparison of senior and mid-level management scores showed higher trait anxiety scores in many senior managers' profiles, while many mid-level managers reported higher scores on anger scales. Common sense suggests that those with a broad range of responsibility, and accountability for large budgets, are constantly scanning the big picture for signs of trouble. Numerous sources of anxiety are inherent in the assignments given, for example, to a department head, a division chief, or a regional director. Their job requires them to spot the danger signals early enough to take corrective action. Those willing to accept management duties are persons similar to stock market investors and racetrack gamblers. They thrive on pouring over many factors and predictors, as they have much to win—or lose. Those who have a taste for adrenaline rushes seek out anxiety-producing situations. It usually takes stronger risk factors to make veteran adventure-lovers uncomfortable.

Objective anxiety earns the title of Executive Challenger because it frequently shows up in psychological assessments as an executive's strongest emotional motivator, and because it is an emotion executives, frequently, if not all the time, stir up in employees. The argument here is that the Challenger is not all bad. Coming to recognize the benefits accompanying anxiety is a step toward managing its intensity and learning to collect side-effect dividends.

Turning fears into productive objectives, such as determined efforts to insure that work sites are clean and safe, to insist that equipment be kept in working order, and to expect workers be ready and able to do jobs competently, would hardly be judged as a bad motivation. Such fears do not result in a freezing of behavior. In optimal conditions, it is anxiety's influence that causes the adrenals to pump extra neurochemicals into the bloodstream, firing-up a worker's *peak performance potentials.*

You know anxiety is standing in the challenger's corner of the corporate sparring-ring whenever you see executive flurries to exert control in a situation. As early as 1936 Freud published "A Danger Signal Theory," noting this role of anxiety in personality dynamics. Ambiguous supervision and disorganized operations alert managers that it's time to engage in planning activities—scheduling, programming, flow-charting. This urge to get things in order so they can confidently "head 'em up, and move 'em out" and "get the show on the road" is filled with strong elements of anxiety, and a lot of anger. These emotions combine to generate the initiative and responsibility that is how and why many executives made it past the other brown suits or through the glass ceiling into the senior management cadre.

Frustration with chaotic, uncoordinated activity and a determination to survive inspires leaders to make a plan and execute it. Anxiety in the face of ambiguity and erratic activity prompted incredible feats of collective achievement. Executive masterminds overwhelm and manage yellow-bellied anxiety again and again in corporate America. It's commonly called *strategic planning.* I have spent hours in conference rooms filling chart paper sheets with goals, objectives, task assignments, measurable dimensions . . . all so a CEO or senior Vice-President could relax. Detailing all assignments reassures upper-level management that non-productive activity and wasteful redundancies will be few and far between.

Anxiety, seen as a naturally occurring signal that something needs to be clarified and corralled, becomes an ally pressing an executive to pay attention to something important and potentially destructive. When unacknowledged, denied or misunderstood, anxiety becomes a source of distraction and subversion. Like an untamed horse, it can rear up and unseat the most solidly positioned executive.

Unfortunately, all anxiety has been stigmatized as the mark of a *neurotic* personality. We can thank, or curse, Sigmund Freud, again. This turn-of-the-20th-century mastermind stood toe to toe with the Challenger. Concerned about the non-objective anxiety in the minds and behavior of his patients, Freud gave it a name: *Neurosis*. His treatment method used with upper-and middle-class Austrian patients is called *psychoanalysis*. This technique of recalling and uprooting *early life traumas* proves useful in treating anxiety emotions, especially those that become intense and uncomfortable enough to inhibit productive emotions and behaviors in the current day. Psychoanalysis is the long way around the block, and can prove to be a "snipe" hunt with no early traumas to blame. Management of anxiety by couch-confessional methods is too time-consuming with too uncertain an outcome for business leaders who need to cope, today, with a myriad of close encounters with objective fear.

Turn-of-the-21st-century masterminds are extending early definitions and explanations of fear and anxiety by subjecting the emotion to rigorous investigations. Controlled studies were sparked during the mid-century recognition that executives were especially at-risk for major stress disorders, such as heart disease, hypertension, ulcers, arterial dysfunction, burnout. Once physiological patterns were linked to emotional characteristics and tracked, anxiety's role in the high incidence of executive hypertension became measurable and manageable. As a consequence of greater understanding of the connections between disease, autonomic nervous system functioning, and individual emotional traits, the 50% likelihood for executives to experience stress-related disabilities at the peak of their career has been significantly reduced.

Although it turned out that anxiety did not have the leading role in heart disease, it clearly has a leading role in other stress illness and is a significant compounding factor in hypertension. Even when anxiety is not the dominant cause of a terminal illness, it is unpleasant like a common cold or flu. Knowing what anxiety is does not eliminate its detrimental impact on performance. I have consulted with a number of managers who were held back by fear of making public speeches. This fear placed as the number one worry among managers in a survey conducted in 1993.

In a recent consultation session with an experienced senior level manager from a Canadian telecommunications mega-corporation, fear of making speeches turned out to be the pivotal factor limiting his advancement within the organization. A series of personality tests and multi-rater assessment questionnaires indicated above average strength in most of the characteristics generally considered essential for executive effectiveness. But he would not stand up and talk; it made him too uncomfortable. A similar block to success held back one of my earliest clients. His solution was to hold a tack in his hand and squeeze on it while making required presentations to business groups. Physical pain overwhelmed the emotional pain of speech anxiety. He carried a handkerchief in his pocket to absorb the blood drawn by squeezing the tack. He was relieved to learn that he was not the only muscular, healthy man to be challenged by speech anxiety discomfort. Adopting a humorous "Get Smart" view of his *old tack-in-the-pocket routine* enabled him to take a first step toward less masochistic solutions.

In addition to fear of public speaking, seven other worries surfaced in a survey of managers conducted by *The Wall Street Journal*. Those fears are *heights, deep water, financial problems, insects, flying, death, and cancer.* Two of the eight, public speaking and financial problems, are work related and inhibit job performance. Managers must speak if only to give instructions and information to others, and they must deal with budgets and payroll decisions. They cannot avoid giving speeches any more than they can avoid working out financial problems. Managers can avoid looking down from high places and they do not have to scuba dive into deep waters. They can get physical check-ups for cancer. They can buy cannisters of insect repellant. It will be harder and harder for executives to avoid airline travel as business globalization reaches to the most remote areas. None of us can avoid death. Some anxieties are worth minimizing, others require harnessing.

Although investigating peoples' fears does not involve a literal *collaring* like wildlife managers do with Florida's panthers, anxiety researchers are taking a page from the environmentalists' manual. They collar subspecies of anxiety, tracking the paths of Test Anxiety, and Repercussion Anxiety. Much can be gleaned from available therapies, especially desensitization which can minimize personal phobias. Countless reports of treating phobias show success across the range of specified aversions, such as acrophobia (fear of heights); claustrophobia (fear of closed places); fear of flying, fear of water, and even for acute panic attacks.

Work-related anxieties, however, are usually responses to concrete threats to productivity or job status. They fall into objective fear category rather than any chronic distrust of specific places, creatures, or things. Several anxiety management approaches are useful for managers who cope with objective anxiety in an age of high-tech, high-information organizations. These executives come to consider anxiety as valuable as an office alarm system. Anxiety detects the smoke of something amiss before it turns into a full-blown threat. Anxiety can work as a distant early-warning that keeps the fire from going out of control. Anxiety proves itself to be a worthy executive *challenger*, sounding the call to battle stations.

The Art of Anxiety Management

Overwhelming anxiety with a loud sensory event is a direct-attack approach advocated by the Gulf War battalion commander. Unfreezing comes with bold action, such as triggering a round of gunfire or whooping war chants while beating on war drums. In less combative settings, there is a less dramatic parallel tactic. A manager in one of my executive courses explained how he kept working in spite of deep suspicions that he was inadequate for the task. "I call it fake-it till you make-it."

This strategy is a personal favorite. What one does to whistle in the dark and carry on in spite of self-doubt will vary according to the audience and the situations. I covered up my stage-fright anxiety by lecturing in clown suit and painted face. The method was rationalized to fit neatly with the topic of my presentation: Feedback Skills, giving and receiving information about one's impact on others' behavior. I doubt that I will need or want to use my Gestalt clown routine again, and I doubt that I will suffer speaking anxiety as I did during college days. Today I enjoy the opportunity to have my say. My way of faking it until I got rid of my anxiety freeze-ups, costumed clowning, beats tacks in the palm of the hand. Fortunately, I have discovered that there are even better ways to manage anxiety states: (1) Concentrating on the task at hand, using my skills to their best advantage. (2) Focusing interest and concern on those who are listening, delivering information that will add to their effectiveness.

Three approaches to anxiety management presented below are advanced executive tools. Each can be applied by those who come in frequent contact with stressors, and those who present others with stressors. Two are for management of one's own internal experiences, and the third approach is to be used to help others reduce their anxiety levels. (1) Taming the anxiety emotion. (2) Fear Relay techniques that increase and decrease anxiety as needed. (3) Matching one's communications to another's preferred modes. Each approach has merit, as well as limitation. All are unfinished prescriptions and are still being refined by specialists who train people to cope with anxiety.

I side with the sports psychologists who consider it unrealistic and ill-advised to strive to eliminate fear. Executives need to smell danger. For example, anxiety can prompt quick action when a co-worker fails to return from a business trip. Anxiety motivates the call to the airline, to the hotel, and to the client company to find out if an emergency came up or if an accident has occurred. Keeping the reigns on anxiety begins with holding the momentum well below the hysterical point. It's a matter of taming anxiety by becoming acquainted with what anxiety is saying and learning to turn the intensity up or down to achieve optimal performance. The danger signal generates energy that increases potentials for success. Diffuse-and-mysterious anxieties become knowable natural phenomena once they are named and described.

For example, giving the name Adventure to experiences that are accompanied by vague, apprehensive feelings introduces positive hopes and detracts from negative imagery. The name you give to anxiety can be whatever works to unfreeze your thinking processes. A risky task has been called a Crap Shoot, and an unknown opponent has been named Mr. Nobody Monster. Humorous, innocuous labels are used frequently when beginning a *taming* process. But, if one is to establish a working relationship with anxiety, information about anxiety must move beyond a handshaking acquaintance. A working alliance is a process that takes time. Those executives who have experienced a full-blown panic or anxiety attack are likely to be already aware that a coach or a trainer can speed up the process of managing emotional overloads. When the anxiety load is not acute, the executive trainer is more likely to be an organizational or sports psychologist, rather than a consulting or clinical specialist.

Doing your homework on anxiety includes a background check that's as thorough as those done on employee candidates, business competitors, or zero-defect statistical tools. We began our background check on anxiety with Sigmund Freud's contribution to our understanding. The genealogy of anxiety includes Hans Selye's highly publicized Type-A experiments of effects of stress on physiological and neuroendocrine processes. Selye's work was a continuation of Cannon's work on animal reaction to painful experiences. Cannon's now famous *fight or flight* summation of fear responses was publicized during the 1950s. This post World War II era was proclaimed by many as *the age of anxiety*. During that time, poet W. H. Auden wrote a famous poem entitled "The Age of Anxiety," and Leonard Bernstein composed music for a ballet by Jerome Robbins which was also called "The Age of Anxiety."

By the 1970s the emphasis shifted away from anxiety as a solo phenomena, to "the Age of Stress." The interplay between anxiety, other emotions, and environmental conditions is reflected in news magazine feature stories and in the broadening scope of health research. Anxiety is studied in terms of its symbiotic and compounding effects, such as its role in depression and in abuse rituals.

Anxiety as a concept was dissected, exposing two major component elements. The two components of anxiety, *emotionality and worry*, were first introduced in 1967 by Liebert and Morris. *Emotionality* refers to autonomic reactions—blood pressure, heart rate, galvanic skin resistance—evoked by situations in which the stressors included an evaluation of the person. *Worry* refers to concern about the consequences of failure. *Emotionality* sparks task-irrelevant thoughts and behaviors that interfere with attention and concentration. *Worry* stimulates self-derogatory thoughts that reduce both efficiency of new learning and recall of past information.

Test Anxiety studies conducted at the University of South Florida show that the most effective improvements for students came when they were given instruction in ways to eliminate or minimize thoughts that interfered with task concentration, thoughts that were self-critical, and thoughts that incorrectly assessed the significance of the pending event. Information about study habits and skills also reduced test anxiety levels, especially when provided in a two-stage program. The first stage reduces negative thinking and expectations, while the second stage provides instruction on competencies related to learning and test-taking. The first phase is equated to giving someone who is drowning in deep waters a life preserver, while the second phase is more like teaching that person to swim.

The goals of the various techniques used in managing test anxiety are to get (a) an increase in responses that are task relevant and (b) a reduction in task irrelevant behaviors. If the anxiety management training is *emotionality*-focused, preferred techniques are biofeedback, desensitization, relaxation training. When training is *worry*-focused, the techniques can be taken from rational-emotional re-education, behavior-modification or reality therapy. Each technique promotes self-appraisals that signal self-systems are in GO condition and introduces a relevant knowledge base. For example, this review of how anxiety functions is pertinent knowledge for taming work-related anxiety, such as test anxiety or repercussion anxiety, subsets of school and work-related anxiety.

Sports psychologists are breaking new ground in managing anxiety. Their work with top athletes is directly applicable for top executives. Training programs include information from achievement motivation research as well as physiological reactions noted in stress research. Executives, like athletes, are subject to extreme levels of *fear of social consequences* because of their work that places them in highly visible performance arenas and because of the potential for public censure or praise. Training programs that integrated *test anxiety* treatments with *achievement motivation training* help athletes achieve performance in harmony with their real abilities. Leaders of these programs, which last ten weeks with one weekly session of an hour's duration, draw five practical conclusions:

1. A reduction in the *fear-of-social-consequences* takes place when emphasis is on task-oriented achievement behavior, and athletes concentrate not on outcome, but on the action itself.

2. Group training is valuable but needs to be supplemented by individual sessions since persons have very different histories and experiences of anxiety and fear.

3. *Motivation* stages need to be separated from the *doing* stages. Motivation requires an accurate view of reality in order to evaluate incentives and probability of success and failure. Action, or implementation, needs to focus on how to act to bring success into existence.

4. Assessing the level of anxiety is advantageous as a diagnostic tool. This includes assessment of its two components, emotionality and worry, and its two manifestations, temporary state and characteristic trait. Combined with a structured interview, the diagnostic approach permits targeted training.

5. Coaches and managers who supervise others for performance improvements are advised to use training methods that stress task-oriented achievement behavior and concentration towards the action itself.

Specialists in management of anxiety deal with hierarchies of expectations: such as probabilities of success and probabilities of failure; worry; and appropriateness of aspirational and action goals. Regulation of aspiration levels and an ability to design stages of action leading to success are keys to performance improvement. Sufficient lead-time practice in regulation of anxiety avoids emotional eruptiveness and increased irritability that are typically experienced during pre-start periods leading up to important events. Hyperactivity or premature activity is the most typical psycho-regulatory problem of top athletes when a major competition is approaching. The early management of pre-start activity includes maintaining ability to rest, saving one's strength, and ability to implement one's performance potential at the right moment, as reported on page 232 in *Anxiety in Sports*.

Taking their work a step further, this school of European sports psychologists promotes anxiety's *adaptational significance*, i.e., anxiety as a factor which increases total activity and work motivation. Machac and Machacova, writing in *Anxiety in Sports*, page 216, say anxiety poses the challenge to do something for improving emotional balance, for achieving a sense of security and well-being. If we are not worried about the future, thinking everything is O.K. as-is, we do not feel any motivation for training, for improvement of skills, for self-awareness that leads to self-control. With poor habits of systematic and hard training, there will be no achievement advance.

Some athletes learned to overcome this handicap by deliberately calling up the feelings of fear or insecurity to prevent self-indulgences that take time away from task concentration. Professionals use this so-called "technique of the fear relay" to increase anxiety levels as a way of overcoming training drudgery, an opposite challenge to the one posed in pre-start time frames, when the athlete needs a suitable harness to tame or reduce anxiety.

Immediately before initiation of the competition an athlete must not be completely calm. Warm-ups and the ambiance of the event arena heighten anxiety. At this point, anxiety needs to be at an optimal level, which is unique to each individual and which only the athlete knows. What often is achieved is an emotionally ambivalent situation. Anxiety alternates with pleasant, hopeful anticipation.

A training method, the Relaxation-Activation Method (RAM), has been used in Europe since the 1960s. RAM builds its program around the shifting of anxiety states in keeping with lead-time phases prior to competition in order to produce outstanding performances. Skill development takes 3-5 months and consists of 2 or 3 sessions a week of approximately 30 minutes duration each. It is possible for trainees to work at home. They are mailed instructions that guide them through three cycles of relaxation and activation in each session.

Most of the athletes trained with RAM methods suffered from excessive or premature pre-start stress. A main practical problem is inconsistent self-assuredness. Many of the athletes invited to participate in the training program put off beginning the anxiety management training until the last minute. Their ability to dissimulate difficulty, to be less critical and sober in evaluation of emotional preparation for performance, causes them to get a late start in autoregulatory programs. When they underestimate their anxiety experience and start the RAM training late, the equilibrium developed by the training, which disintegrates sooner at the time of the big contest than under normal conditions, will not remain effective as long as needed in the milieu of the big contest. It's an extreme case of "exercise it or lose it."

Sports psychologists capitalize on visualization to enhance performance and to reduce anxiety. A popular visualization training concept that works to reduce counterproductive high anxiety in high stress experiences begins with drills in relaxation techniques. Once these routines are practiced and ingrained, the instructor guides the individuals through recalling and visualizing or imaging a time of high anxiety. It is important to get the details of that experience clearly in mind. Once a person can visualize easily, and is skilled with relaxation, the relaxation techniques are used to reduce the high anxiety experience. Soon anxiety can be reduced, both in the training session and in day-to-day situations that evoke anxiety.

Training for peak performance goes another step: the performer is guided in visualizing a performance event when all went exceptionally well. Again it is important to recall all the details of how that experience felt and how it came about. This image is then cultivated and called up just before going into situations that typically arouse distracting levels of anxiety. These methods for managing anxiety are learned, and prove useful at one time or another to even those who seldom experience high anxiety.

Ryan and Oestreich addressed anxiety in business and workgroups as a barrier to continuous-quality-improvement. They found that managers didn't tell the truth about blocks to quality improvement because they feared reprisals from the boss. Their survey of undiscussables showed *management practices* to be far ahead of other topics. Employees feared that they would personally insult those with power to reward and punish. Worry about lost security, money and friendly support made telling the truth about problems with their supervisors a frozen, taboo subject.

Since Deming made it clear he did not believe management could achieve quality when people were afraid to tell the truth, trainers Ryan and Oestreich developed a process for getting to truth in ways that reduced fear of repercussion. They then sorted out the 20% of the management concerns that drove 80% of the barriers to quality and plotted these on a *Pareto chart,* a bar graph.

These TQM methods recommended for anxiety management incorporate and extend traditional organization development (OD) methods. The consultants champion a *vision* of an ideal workplace that emerged from the managers' responses to the survey. Their vision described a work environment characterized by mutual helpfulness, wide-spread respect, and frequent feedback exchanges. Those feedback exchanges would include specifics about work performance and candid statements of management-related concerns, especially the undiscussible.

Ryan and Oestreich consider the undiscussables as flags on the workplace field that mark spots where fear occurs. They use that as evidence to move executives and workers beyond denial that fear exists in the workplace. Working with a systems approach, discussion groups are scheduled with "third party" moderators who assure confidentiality of information. Following the discussions that include representatives from all levels and divisions of the corporation, summarized information is relayed to management. During all meetings, consultants model openness, respect, and willingness to be told "bad news."

A course of training for managers includes teaching them to use coaching methods, to work one-on-one with resistant direct reports, to terminate those who fail to respond to direct attention, to value criticism, to seek feedback, to follow-up on suggestions and complaints. In the process of the training, managers are given information about those behaviors and mannerisms that strike fear in the hearts of employees. Managers learn to recognize when they have been too ambiguous for other's comfort, and when they are giving double-messages that confuse or mislead others.

A second anxiety management training program, Neurolinguistic Programming (NLP) has been more popular in Europe than in the U.S. NLP develops competence in working with employees in ways that reduce anxiety. NLP's American originators, Richard Bandler and John

Grinder, introduced their technology in the 1970s. A 1990 book, *The Warrior's Edge*, reviews NLP as an influence technology. This slim volume contains instructions for anxiety management skills. The book is unfortunately littered with outdated terminologies and attitudes, but is a rare look at training found effective by military professionals.

Key components of these techniques involve simple things you can do to put another at ease, such as: assuming a *posture* similar to that of the other person; *move* in similar ways but not exactly like a "Simon Says" routine. Breathing in the same pattern as the other person relieves anxiety in that individual. When the person is comfortable and appears at ease, the time is ripe to plant an *anchor* which can be used later to reduce anxiety levels in that person. This anchor is a special *touch* or *word*. It can be a gentle hand on the forearm, or a "high five." It might be a phrase, "way-to-go," "keep 'em flying." Another suggestion for how to put someone at ease is to *listen* for how the person processes information (auditory, visual, kinesthetic) and, then, make your contribution to the conversation accordingly. If the person is visual, show *pictures* or graphs. If they are kinesthetic processors, sensory oriented, ask how they would *feel* about the change in office assignments. *Talk* a lot with auditory processors.

Mobilizing Resources for Action

Two distinct groups face fear in a workplace: those who work there and those who come there as clients or customers. Health care professionals and staff employees in the dentist's office know they can expect the waiting room to be full of anxious people. Even with today's safe anesthetics and quieter drilling equipment, people recall or hear about painful experiences. Repairing cavities and root canals have after effects like headaches and sore jaws that linger in long-term memory banks. The appointment with the dentist is a dreaded event.

Fortunately, small changes in the environment can help reduce anxiety states. For example, a recent change of pictures on the walls of my dental center lightened the waiting room mood. Where there once were full-color illustrations of decayed teeth, diseased gums, and before and after examples of dental enhancements, now there are pictures of the dentists, laboratory technicians, and dental assistants, professionally dressed and pleasant in demeanor. Other walls display pictures of picturesque and peaceful sites around the community. Moreover, reception area staff are trained in ways to reassure clients. Their personal warmth gives a final touch, which introduces a more dynamic influence than decorative, cosmetic furnishings. Both strategies reduce levels of state anxiety,

Being good at driving fear out of the workplace becomes an explicit goal in employee training for those who work in dental offices. These same employees are not exempt from chronic or acute levels of anxiety within themselves. Their anxiety is associated with job security in a period when care delivery is changing and when busy office managers and professionals can be critical, demanding and aloof.

While dental practices provide evidence of recent success in reducing levels of fear for customers, examples of effective escalation of fear date back to the fourth century in the Common Era (CE=AD). An anecdote in Chapter 3 told how Crispus Caesar was instructed to go contrary to his personal leadership style and to strike fear in the hearts of reluctant followers.

As his first job, this eldest son of Constantine was sent to govern Galleia. He soon sent a message to his famous father for advice on how to get the rebellious citizens of that region to be respectful and behave as they were told. The great Constantine sent back the message-runner with instructions to go up to Crispus, salute him, say not a word, but take his sword and go out into the garden and slash off the heads of the tallest poppies. Today, less ruthless ways of stirring up anxiety are practiced in most parts of the world. However, it is not unusual for executives to announce that there will be no Christmas or year-end bonus if goals are not completed. Threats of punishments or withholding of money remain effective ways to get the lead out of underachieving workers.

Management course instructors seldom support tough, Machiavellian practices. Some classroom lectures include evidence that scare tactics do nothing to change the numbers of drug-users. Other statistical reports are presented that indicate that the death penalty does not reduce incidents of murders or other heinous crimes. These objective appeals fail to convince many in the general public or in the ranks of corporate managers. Survivors of business and political coups know up-close-and-personal that fear is a powerful motivator.

Point a gun at a person's belly and that person is no longer a slow learner or doer. Those who experienced traumatic fear in their own lives remain convinced that a death penalty will worry potential killers. A problem with this belief is that it makes a grand assumption. They believe that killers will experience state anxiety and fear of death the same as the general, non-killer population. The dangers of grand assumptions are that they are seldom connected to reality. Anxiety and fear will vary widely from person to person. While a majority of the people will be characterized by average levels of state and trait anxiety, smaller percentages will experience overloads to the point of becoming catatonic. Another percentage experience little or inconsequential emotional fear.

A rare place of agreement between anti-capital punishment activists and subway station vigilantes is about the usefulness of the emotion fear. The two components of anxiety, emotionality and worry stimulate action and extraordinary application of the resources at hand. Besides temporarily empowering an ordinary person the strength of ten heroes, *emotionality* associated with immediate and dramatic danger, when controlled, inspires the McGuyver's and the A-Teams of TV fame to amazing engineering innovations. *Worry* about illegal substance trading has led to helpful discoveries. A major learning is that dogs can sniff out drugs in secret compartments and that they can smell bodies of missing persons trapped under the water.

Anxiety also offers assistance to handicapped populations. Blind persons use their hyperalertness to compensate for the missing sense of sight. The danger for those who cannot see and those who cannot hear is overcompensation. They can overdevelop the anxiety emotion. Paranoid-like suspicion of what others are doing and saying can produce episodes of complicated depression.

Anxiety is recognized as a powerful influence on behavior, well-being and happiness. A touch of anxiety is useful, challenging us to be better. Strong balancing emotions, like curiosity, serve to regulate anxiety, not allowing it to take over and reduce us to dysfunctional, frozen, or withdrawn states. Optimal anxiety shows itself to be a prominent motivator of executives in psychological assessments, yet in my collection of profiles, anxiety is not a lone rider. Curiosity is typically the top-gun emotion for executives with long-term health and career success. Those who strive to achieve goals and to lead others toward a vision learn to regulate anxiety levels. These leaders make use of anxiety's challenger energies to support risk taking and business venturing.

Background Readings

For a more comprehensive view of the nature of anxiety, publications edited and authored by C. D. Spielberger will be particularly useful. In 1995 two collections of world-wide research activities were published. Volumes 15 and 16 are part of a series Dr. Spielberger has edited, jointly and with guest editors: *The Series in Stress and Emotion: Anxiety, Anger, and Curiosity* is published by Hemisphere Publishing Corporation, a member of the Taylor & Francis Group, Washington, D.C. It was formerly a part of the Series in Clinical and Community Psychology. Most of the information cited in this chapter is found in volumes 13 and 14. Additional anxiety information is found in, Ed., C. D. Spielberger, 1994. Chapter 14. *Test Anxiety: Theory, Assessment, and Treatment,* Hemisphere, 1994.

Spielberger also edits *The Series in Health Psychology and Behavioral Medicine,* published by Hemisphere, which includes *Anxiety in Sports: An International Perspective.* 1989. Descriptions of RAM and of Richard Suinn's visualization training are reported here. The Machac and Machacova chapter begins on page 216

For more detail on repercussion anxiety interventions and putting workers at ease read: Ryan, K.D. & Oestreich, D.K. 1991. *Driving Fear Out of the Workplace.* San Francisco: Jossey-Bass Inc., Publishers. Alexander, J.B., Groller, R., & Morris, J. 1990. *The Warrior's Edge: Front Line Strategies for Victory on the Corporate Battlefield.* NY: Avon Books..

Books detailing TQM procedures are found in most larger bookstores.
Deming, W. E. 1986. *Out of the Crisis.* Cambridge, MA: MIT Press.
Gitlow, H.S. & Gitlow, S.J. 1987. *The Deming Guide to Quality and Competitive Position.* Englewood Cliffs, NJ: Prentice-Hall.
Rachman, S. J. 1978. *Fear and Courage.* San Francisco: W.H. Freeman.
Scherkenbach, W. W. 1986. *The Deming Route to Quality and Productivity: Roadmaps and Roadblocks.* Rockville, MD: Mercury Press.

CURIOSITY **ANXIETY** *ANGER*

Chapter 7

Anger: Heroic Idealism in Action

What we love and what we get the most angry about tell a tale of the hero within. Anger reveals our ideals, our goals, and our grand passions. Angers are indelible character markers. We go to war to defend beliefs and persons that we cherish. We fill with outraged determination when an obstacle interrupts progress toward our goals of survival, adequacy, growth and meaningfulness.

- Pandora's Box, the Anger Leitmotiv
- The Tyranny of Perfectionism
- AHA Revisited: Heart-Attacks and Anger-Attacks
- How Do I Love Thee? Let Me Count the Angers

"Anger, like love, is a moral emotion. . . . We are ambivalent about anger because sometimes it is effective and sometimes it is not, because sometimes it is necessary and sometimes it is destructive . . . anger is ultimately an emphatic message: Pay attention to me. I don't like what you are doing. Restore my pride. You're in my way. Danger. Give me justice."

Anger, The Misunderstood Emotion by Carol Tavris

Pandora's Box, the Anger Leitmotiv

Anger is a normal survival emotion. Yet, we treat anger as if it were Pandora's box. If we dare open it, to see what's inside, we believe we will let loose a horde of evils. That apprehension is not without reason. Overloaded court dockets testify to the negative consequences of anger. As far back as our earliest memories of elementary schooldays, we recall the troublemakers who were quick to anger and eager to pick a fight. Children, at predictable ages, are prone to take immediate action to resolve conflict or disappointment, fists flying, tears flowing, feet kicking. We are reminded daily in newspaper reports how often anger is the motive for adult criminal acts.

Ironically, and appropriately, anger is described by some as the moral, judicial emotion. Anger motivates acts of heroism as well as acts of mayhem. Especially, when love is involved. Strong attachment, as in grand passion, inspires both grand arts and folk arts. Do Greek theater, Wagnerian opera, country pickin'-music, and Western guitar ballads possibly have anything in common? Yes: Love, honor, anger, and death.

Oedipus Rex, the tragic hero of a classic Greek drama, is remembered as a model leader-king, yet one who inadvertently killed his father and married his mother. In mid-life, Oedipus learned that the menacing traveler he battled to the death when he was a youth was actually the king of Thebes, the husband of the woman he later met and married, and a man whose murder he vowed to avenge. His shock deepened when he was further told that the king and queen of Thebes were the parents he had been separated from in infancy. Honor-bound to carry out his pledge of vengeance, Oedipus gouged out his eyes and went into exile with his daughter to guide him. His wife who was also his mother committed suicide. This was a Freddie Kruger-Halloween plot of all time!

This fifth century BC story became a favorite example for psychoanalysts working some twenty-five centuries later. It was elaborated into the Oedipus Complex, which is used to diagnose and to explain a particular kind of love-anger conflict. This condition is diagnosed when a male child's attraction for the mother, innocent or not, is complicated by rivalry with, or anger toward the father.

Another classic tragedy, based on angers that took place more than a millennium later, is dramatized in the eighteenth-century opera, *Tristan and Isolde*. Wagner's love-honor-anger-and-death leitmotiv probed medieval erotic desire and death wishes of an heroic dragon slayer and a beautiful Irish princess. In the opera *Parsifal*, Wagner dares to suggest that there are emotional similarities in the love attraction that is aroused in sexual encounters and in religious experiences. In this opera, he explores the subtleties of the perversion of emotions and the consequences of denial of emotions.

Grand passions and perversions are no less traumatic among the poor and the untitled. From the stage of the Grand Ole Opry in Nashville, Tennessee and from roadhouse music-circuits, simple ballads passed down through ordinary folk are full of the tragic, the sadistic and the forbidden. Country-singer Johnny Cash made Folsom prison famous as a homeplace of love-stricken suitors. Cash also sang about anger and death wishes—homey tales of jealous rages, of murders of rivals, and of unobtainable loved ones. Even before Johnny Cash topped the hit parade, two unextraordinary but ill-fated lovers, *Frankie and Johnny,* were immortalized in song and dance by Gene Kelly. He staged the now famous bluegrass ballad as a musical spectacular for the 1951 film, *American in Paris.* Kelly's fusion of life's common passages into memorably innovative contexts earned him a place in history books, and speaks volumes about the universality of a love-anger connection.

Passionate love endures in spite of—or, perhaps, because of— hardships, separations, and anger-arousing experiences. Such passion inspires the extraordinary in science as well as operas, ballads, and paintings. A love-anger motif became the driving force behind Marie Curie's efforts to extract radium from pitchblende. Madam Curie loved her work and her teacher who, later, became her husband. Together, the Curies made discoveries that won them Nobel Prizes.

Yet, Marie's greatest work was done after her husband's tragic death. He was run over on a Paris street by a heavily loaded dray transporting commercial goods. Madam Curie's impassioned anger at this untimely loss had far-reaching consequences, inspiring her single-purposed dedication to completing their unfinished research. Her life of love, loss, sadness, anger, and purposeful work is a tale which could fit easily into Wagner's favorite plot: redemption through love. Her story equally well illustrates effective use of justified anger.

Justified anger is the unsung-hero emotion. Anger receives little praise because it is a closet emotion. Stress researchers early found anger to be a hard-wired signal occurring in animals and humans, a distinctive neurochemical survival mechanism. Cannon was the first to associate anger with a biologically determined fight-or-flight response observed in all forms of life. Across the ages since prehistoric eras, adults learned it was best to avoid the painful, often irreparable consequences of fighting. They worked to eradicate or ignore the presence of anger. Children who showed their anger were quickly, sternly punished. A noticeable side effect of generations of effort to civilize angry behavior is under-appreciation of anger, and failure to recognize anger as a built-in problem detector.

Anger sends us signals that it's time to attend to justice, or love, or integrity. Anger's normal job is to increase chances of survival by adjusting attention to matters of immediate importance, and to work in concert with the two other stress emotions—curiosity and anxiety. Curiosity gets us moving and exploring, finding nourishment for body and mind, and anxiety keeps us from being foolishly naive, reminding us, as the duty officer says on *Hill Street Blues,* to "be careful out-there on the street." Anger fires us up to be sure things are right for ourselves and our loved ones. Anger motivates us to pursue truth, beauty, and excellence.

In order to recover an appreciation for anger's intended beneficial function, it is necessary to look directly at anger, to acknowledge anger's influence on perfectionism, health, and happiness. We begin by taking a fresh look at anger. Everybody knows what anger is—even those who say that they never get angry. Everyone has experienced frustration, exasperation, and irritation. Unfortunately, anger is confused with hostility and aggression. Overlap and interchangeable use of these terms resulted in coining the term AHA to refer to fighting behavior. AHA, an acronym for anger-hostility-aggression, implies that the experience of anger is an all-or-nothing-at-all emotional event. The sequence begins with anger, produces hostility, and ends with invasive, destructive action.

Hostility, like anger, refers to an emotional condition that can vary in intensity from annoyance to rage. But hostility, unlike anger, incorporates permissive attitudes toward destroying objects and injuring others. Hostility involves disliking others and evaluating them negatively.

Aggression is behavior that results in punitive effects on persons or objects. Some aggressive acts are not predicated on anger or hostility and are carried out to achieve desirable, generative outcomes. Goal-driven aggression is called *instrumental aggression* in contrast to *hostile aggression*. Harmful or destructive side effects are unintended in goal driven initiatives. Hostile aggression is behavior that is punitive, and sometimes destructive, but proceeds out of dislike and negative evaluation of the object of the aggressive behavior. Sporting competitions can shift from competitive instrumental-aggression into hostile-aggression when rivalries include a preconditioned hatred, contempt, or disrespect for the opposing team.

The fresh look at anger, in its natural unconditioned form, shows it to be a survival emotion that motivates actions of innovators and idealists. Anger is recognized as a quality assurance emotion: *If I point out flaws when I see them, if I redress insults, then the good things of life can be won.* In this light, Anger serves as a first alert that quality of life is being threatened or obstructed, and corrective, sometimes punitive, action is required. (See charts in the Reference section at the end of the section.)

Using the AHA paradigm, anger is cast in a negative shadow, as something to be closeted away in Pandora's Box. Keeping a lid-on-it is taught to children at an early age. Expression of anger is punished often so angrily that people learn to deny personal awareness of anger. Effort to deny, hide or ignore anger emotions sets the stage for feeling bad about our natural selves. Dissatisfaction with how and what we are, along with strong angry feelings, often leads to depression.

Respect for the natural self is promoted by an A-Ha paradigm emphasis. A-Ha, an exclamation of insight, recognizes anger as a signal worth attending to. One way to respond to an experience of anger is as a stop-look-listen alert. Awareness of the emotion is followed by a pause, not to count to ten, but to get in mind what it is that we hope for. What is our goal of fairness or improvement? Then, with that hope in mind, it's time for an instrumental action plan, one that intentionally moves toward the generative goal. Anger -[pause]- Hope, action (A-Ha). We do not need to waste time gathering evidence of another's inadequacy or bad behavior that produces the heavy "AHA, caught you in the act, guilty, just like I thought " This cynical articulation of "gotcha" is known as nigysob: *"now I've got you, you SOB,"* one of numerous titles invented by counselors practicing transactional therapy.

We reclaim the natural power of the anger emotion and shift from the AHA! to the A-Ha mode, when we look anger in the eye. Our anger is not a mythological Pandora's box nor a Medusa's head. We do not turn into stone. Instead, we discover that anger comes in two related, but different types of experiences. One, the broad-band signal, is called Angry Temperament. The second, a personal protection signal, is called Angry Reaction. Individuals vary in their tendency to see a lot of situations as unfair, which is reflected by their reporting high or low levels of Angry Temperament. We also vary in the intensity of our reaction to being criticized, to not receiving recognition, or to being slowed down in pursuit of a goal. Such differences are reflected in Angry Reaction levels. Angry Reaction, while related to Angry Temperament, is triggered primarily by the perception of unfairness that strikes close to home—insults to the self.

Studies of the expression of angry emotions turned up more surprises. Anger expressed inwardly and anger expressed outwardly are not polar opposites of one trait. They are separate and independent. I could, for example, score high on one scale and not on the other, high on both scales, or low on both scales. Anger-in is when I know I am experiencing some mild to intensely angry emotion, but I do not express this directly to others. Anger-out is when I know I'm feeling angry emotion and I verbally or non-verbally let others know it. I speak-up, I strike others, I throw things.

The anger emotion impacts us in three ways—mind, body and behavior. The experience starts with a mental signal that something is wrong. The autonomic nervous systems kicks into action and neuro-chemicals flow through the body. Energized by the emotional state, we shape mental conclusions about the meaning of what we are perceiving. Finally, we select a behavioral action. That action depends on available resources, knowledge, recent experiences, and creative thinking skill.

New ways of thinking about anger began with attention to stress, Type-A behavior, workaholics, and studies of heart diseases. Surprise findings and subsequent changes in how researchers understood anger are reshaping approaches to longevity and vitality. Once anger proved to be the most salient emotional factor affecting heart disease patients, it wasn't long before scientific explorers mapped out topographic features of the emotion.

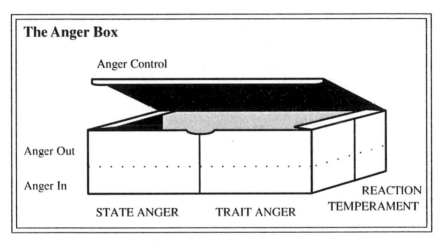

The Anger Box

Anger Control

Anger Out

Anger In

STATE ANGER   TRAIT ANGER   REACTION TEMPERAMENT

An **Anger Box** replaces Pandora's box as an overview of the experience and expression of angry emotions. First comes the clear separation of state from trait anger. State-anger describes variations of intensity of angry emotion being experienced in the present. Trait-anger looks at differences in the frequency that angry emotions are experienced in an extended time frame. State-anger may, or may not, reflect an individual's typical intensity of experience. Furthermore, state intensity does not look at source or provocations of anger. State anger reflects current circumstances. Trait-anger suggests how often and how easily the control lid on anger expression is likely to be raised.

Since one person's boiling-over point is likely to be quite different from another's, it became important to assess anger control. Measures reflect how much effort is expended to manage experiences of anger and subsequent expression of anger. Heroes who address every flaw, who always point out how things can be improved, may be acting out of love and loyalty, wanting only the best possible for others, pushing toward perfection. They are experiencing anger about the shortfalls which they see everywhere. They turn into overdemanding lovers and become unlovable.

The Mental Tyranny of Perfectionism

Few things in life attain the perfection of our first love. Few people fail to remember the first love-of-their-life. Frequently, it's a memory from high school years spiced with first kisses and first proms and first heartbreaks. Recalling first-loves may, on the other hand, bring flash-backs of hard-won baseball games, or a shiny used car, or frequently played tunes on a cherished guitar. Love at first sight may be best represented by the famous photograph showing sociologist Konrad Lorenz striding across a marshy field with a row of baby ducks following along behind him. Lorenz was the first thing these ducklings saw when they opened their eyes, so they followed him wherever he went. Other new-born ducks followed the mother duck who was sitting by their eggs as they hatched.

How long will a first impression influence where one goes? Some believe reward-and-punishment makes the difference in how long that first love lasts. Others suggest it depends on the quality of trust in early relationships. Either way, a current reading of your early imprinting is easy: What do you most admire? What are you most proud of about yourself? What makes you angry? What about others irritates you most? Angers and irritations may give the best clues to the deep roots of your own characteristics.

Externally caused surprises invoke the earliest expressions of anger, like falling and loud noises that Karen Horney would say are a reaction to internal feelings of disequilibrium. *Something is wrong. I must stop this. I must regain balance. I must not fall. I must keep out the strong sounds. I must resist invasion. Why is someone / thing causing abuse to my body. It makes me angry.*

Not everyone interprets imbalances or counter intuitive sensations as a call to aggressive behavior. Rather than instrumental or hostile acting-out, Einstein took a fresh approach to surprising external move-ment. Near the end of his life, he declared that his most happy moment came when he conceived of the man falling from the roof who dropped an object he had been holding. As the man and the object continued to fall, the man was in motion, falling from the roof—and he was in a state of rest, in relationship to the object falling beside him at the same rate of speed. As a result, Einstein formulated the theory of relativity. The startling breakthrough in the science of physics released us from Newtonian first-impression expectations. Visions of a dual state of being, without Einstein as your teacher, could cause you to question your sanity: Is something wrong inside my head?   .

Like Einstein, we can control how we respond to our physical sensations. We can decide not to deny anger signals. We can, like Einstein, edit how we behave after we get a surprising signal. Something is not moving as expected. Perhaps it needs some fixing. Or, perhaps, we need to consider relativity. Denial may bring short-term relief, but is long range trouble. Editing is goal oriented. We aim for optimizing immediate returns which pay maximum dividends in the future.

WE LIVE IN A NON-STOP STREAM OF
Experiences

Choice Point A   *Survival Minimized*
Deny: I feel no anger

Emotions

Choice Point B
Edit: I recognize that I am angry.
I edit responses:
I select a behavior   **Survival Maximized**
Likely to reach my Goals

Behaviors

When the emotion is anger,
we can focus on what we dislike out there and go to war, or
we can focus on what we'd like to see out there and
figure ways to make it a reality.

This flow chart suggests it's best to avoid denial and to work on becoming competent at behavior editing. Accept sensations for what they are. Recognize that something is falling, invading, or moving in a surprising direction. Notice how anger can be used radar-like, to show when the ship is veering off-course. Only if anger becomes king among emotions, dominating curiosity and anxiety, will the quality assurance perceptions turn ugly. Or if anger pretends to be honorable perfectionism, it will begin planting the seeds of depression.

Understanding depression and physical illness, according to Harry Levinson, arguably the senior statesman-therapist to executives, is one of the most important coping strategies for combating problems associated with recent failures in the giant corporations. He argues that understanding depression is the first step in resolving complex psychological issues inherited by second generation corporate leaders. Levinson found that talented technicians were often vulnerable to depressive rage in the aftermaths of abrupt or dramatic change.

Less than two years after the downsizing rush, numerous other contributors to popular management publications reported how re-engineering advocates were rushing to the aid of corporate human resources. The consultants were suffering from the same emotions aroused in others as a consequence of task focused, quick-fix practices built on management techniques dating back to Frederick Taylor in 1911. Hard-nosed, time-task, neo-Taylorites reported feeling pain, anger, and guilt.

What's behind the distress felt when something we advocate ardently doesn't turn out to be perfect? What's behind executive depression, burnout, heart attack, suicide? A classic example from the 1980s is Vincent Foster, the accomplished attorney who was deputy counsel to President Clinton. Psychological autopsy of his suicide suggests it was perfectionism that led to the depression that ended with a solitary gunshot. As described by Yale's Sid Blatt, this pillar of strength, portrait of poise, and person of impeccable integrity seemed outwardly successful in both his professional and personal life.

It was the intensity of his perfectionist standards and his vulnerability to personal and public criticism that allowed his inner voices to stalk him relentlessly. He lost weight, his mood was low, he spent weekends in bed with the shades pulled; he told the graduating class at the University of Arkansas Law School a few months before his death that "The reputation you develop for intellectual and ethical integrity will be your greatest asset or your worst enemy."

Suicide represents an extreme resolution of severe depression. More frequently, high achievers survive periods when they experience symptoms that would qualify them for a major depression diagnosis. Many more struggle through while experiencing several of the critical symptoms: diminished interest and pleasure; significant increase or decrease in weight; chronic fatigue; inability to sleep or over-sleeping; agitation; sense of worthlessness or guilt; reduced thinking or concentration abilities; thoughts of death.

In New Zealand, where there is the highest suicide rate in the industrialized world, it's the young men who are six times more likely to kill themselves. Analysts conclude that they are trying to conform to exaggerated standards of masculinity. Self-criticism, a key aspect of perfectionism, plays a central role in depressions and in suicide. They are expected to excel in school and in sports and to never give vent to their emotions. No wonder the families are often surprised by their suicides.

Perfectionism, according to Blatt, comes in three varieties: socially prescribed perfectionism, other-oriented perfectionism, and self-oriented perfectionism. Of the three, self-oriented perfectionism is the one closely linked to executive effectiveness. High personal standards and a need for order and organization go along with good work habits, striving, and high achievement. Executives with strong self-oriented perfectionism characteristics—an active striving to be flawless—are typically managers who have been seen as resourceful and engaged in constructive problem-solving activity.

Executives who set high expectations and standards for others, which is one of the three faces of perfectionism—if those expectations are realistic and presented in supportive ways—are identified as charismatic leaders and mentors. They inspire others to achieve even more than they ever imagined they could achieve.

Normal perfectionism, a condition found in hardy executives, is seen in executives who get a sense of pleasure from painstaking effort. These persons are flexible, adaptable leaders who seek excellence while being able to be less precise as the situation permits: Some things are worth not doing well. Milestone success leaves them with a sense of satisfaction for a job well done and a feeling of self-esteem that is grounded in acceptance of personal and environmental limitations. Reasonable expectations with periodic acknowledgment of fulfillment of objectives allow people to enjoy their strengths, to become emotionally invested—and reinvested—in their work, as they continue to strive to do their best, to get better, and to excel.

Perfectionism under the pressure of failure or in the presence of stressors that block high achievement is a prelude to a number of disorders, especially depression. Problems arise when self-oriented perfectionism is influenced by socially prescribed perfectionism, a belief that others are expecting difficult or impossible achievements, and will withhold acceptance or approval until these imposed demands are met. These external expectations are felt to be uncontrollable. They generate, like the experience of falling, feelings of anxiety, helplessness, and anger.

The debilitating perfectionism is seen in persons who have excessive concern over mistakes, who perceive high parental expectations and strong criticism, and who are doubting the quality of their actions. Some of the health problems found linked to perfectionism, in addition to depression, are eating disorders, obsessive-compulsive disorders, anxiety, panic disorder, migraine, sexual dysfunction, and Type A Behavior. These people have an intense need to avoid failure, nothing is quite good enough, and there is an endless cycle of over-striving and distress.

Depressions have two sources—either *interpersonal matters* or *self-definition* issues. Inner questioning is either about who we are, or who I am. Part One argues that answers to these questions provide foundations for individual productivity. A change or loss in self-definition is a trigger for confusions and difficulties. The first source of depression, interpersonal matters, is often related to a loss of a significant other who was greatly depended upon. This self redefinition, although often thought about when there has been a death in the family or a divorce, is also an aftermath of abandonment experiences of employees who are fired from companies after many years of employment. The second source of depression is associated with autonomy, self-criticism, and guilt. These are persons who persist in harsh self-scrutiny and evaluation. Their fear of criticism is chronic. They are often highly competitive and make many demands upon themselves.

Assessments of mid-level managers from health-care organizations and of pastors from two major Protestant denominations reflected higher-than-average levels of assessed trait anger. These data are reported in several papers I presented to the International Council of Psychologists (ICP) and the Society for Personality Assessment (SPA). Mid-level managers reported noticeably higher anger levels when contrasted with executive level staff, who reported higher levels of trait anxiety. One explanation is that senior executives know that no one has neat solutions to current industry-wide issues, while new managers, who are often selected because they are fired-up go-getters, experience impatient frustration. They assume those in front office seats-of-power are hoarding information or are incompetent to produce decisions on timely basis. *Those higher-ups are keeping me from doing perfect work.*

Pastors show higher levels of anger than curiosity or anxiety. Management theory-maker Elliot Jaques considers pastors as professionals, a career type not to be compared with those in a business management category. Nevertheless, ministers work full time to improve the quality of life for those in their care. As they go about marrying, burying, consoling and counseling in homes, hospitals, shelters, and jails, they are exposed to larger numbers of situations provoking justified anger. Consultants who help the helping professionals and business executives notice that heavy demands are placed on these individuals to assure fair, productive, satisfying experiences for others. Consultants and therapists were thinking of their associates when they coined the term "burnout." As they sought ways to slow down the drain on this talent pool, they concluded, as Levinson articulated, that one way to reduce depressive episodes is for organizational leaders to be able to recognize depression in self and others, then, to take corrective action.

AHA Revisited: Heart Attacks and Anger Attacks

Corporate leaders' concern about frequent incidents of executive illness resulted in funding for research studies that eventually mapped out the mind-body-behavior features of anger. Anger coupled with hostility proved to be the important predictor of hypertension and coronary heart disease. Investigations tracked which aspects of anger were most associated with which dysfunctions. Evidence now supports that coronary artery disease is more likely found in patients who suppressed their anger to the extent it reaches danger-zone levels on anger-in measures.

Type-A behavior patterns show that hard-driving individuals liked to gain and maintain control over their environment. Assessment of anger control shows that persons with high control scores are those who invest a great deal of energy in gaining and maintaining control over their expression of anger-out. If high control is accompanied by high angry temperament, the anger is predicted to show through as authoritarian behavior with deliberate use of expression of anger to intimidate others. On the other hand, observers and predictors also see that excessive control can at times result in passivity. High anger-out control levels and high anxiety scores are seen as conducive to depressive states.

Suppressed anger, measured by the Anger-In scale, is found associated with hypertension, especially in black males. Interpretation of Anger-In Control is underway and is expected to be correlated with elevation in hypertension measures. A tendency to work hard at control of anger expression conforms to Pandora-box beliefs about keeping anger in the closet. Excessive Anger Control is not more prevalent in either male or female populations. Gender differences on anger measures do show up in questions about particular situations. Women experience more intense anger when criticized in front of others, and males are more angry when slowed by others' mistakes. Men are much more likely to report expressing Anger Out physically or verbally, e.g. *when I get angry I say nasty things.*

While women generally seem more able to tolerate higher levels of anger without becoming ill, recurring patterns are similar in both gender groups. High Trait Anger, high Anger Control, is associated with recurrence of breast cancer in women. High scores are above 85% in a norm table developed at the University of South Florida. A high Trait Anger, high Angry Reaction, and high Anger-Out combination is an at-risk alert for possible myocardial infarcts, heart attacks, and cardiovascular accidents, strokes. These later findings will not surprise those who read the tale of Rip Van Winkle. Rip got home after a 20-year nap to learn that his ill-tempered wife, whom he avoided by sleeping as frequently and long as possible, had died of apoplexy. Internal physical disasters frequently happen in the wake of intense fury.

Specific insights into the role of anger in health have been a long time in the making. At the end of World War II the U.S. male was twice as likely to be struck down by heart failure as a Dane, a Swede or a Norwegian, and five times as likely as a Japanese man. Deaths from strokes and heart attacks had risen from 20% in 1900 to 55% in the 1950s. The federal government launched the first longitudinal study of the causes of heart attacks. With more specific information about risk factors like tobacco use and cholesterol, the general public gradually became less fatalistic about heart diseases.

Changing behaviors—stopping smoking, exercising, watching the diet—was accepted as a means to preventing heart attacks in healthy people. Next came the study of nonphysical risk factors, and close attention to the fact that many heart disease patients were ambitious, competitive, and highly stressed. The direct comparison of Type As with Type Bs showed that over a period of eight-and-one-half years the Type As were more than twice as likely to suffer heart attacks as the Type Bs, even when other risk factors like cholesterol and smoking were taken into consideration. Major components were found to be the competitive way of life, the sense of time urgency, and an excessive involvement with one's job. These factors later boiled down to hostility, irritability, impatience, and competitiveness, which gave way, under scrutiny, to the underlying anger with its power to activate the autonomic nervous system.

Anger fires up a signal that travels down the pituitary, hypothalamus, adrenal cortex pathway and puts into production excess catecholamines which in turn are what put the plaque on the inside of the blood vessels and give the heart a hard time. This is one way that perception of external irritation brings about internal actions that wear down and burn out physical beings. Other emotions collude with anger, sometimes to our detriment and sometimes to our benefit: Anxiety boosts the anger signal into a bigger whallop. Curiosity tones things down by revving up proteins in the brain and strengthening the auto-immune system.

Cynicism, an acquired attitude, is believed to stimulate production of additional fight-or-flight hormones (catecholamines, i.e., adrenalines) that accelerate buildup on artery walls—causing hardening of the arteries. Following this school of reasoning, some hostility questionnaires are measuring, primarily, mistrust. Their assertion is that those who have untrusting hearts, who believe it is safer to trust nobody, who say most people lie to get ahead, are, perhaps, not angry, just cynical. It's hard for me to believe that those who find it safer to trust nobody will not also have an emotional history dominated by anger and anxiety. They must have endured many invasive experiences, more than enough to build a cynical attitude.

Revisiting the AHA syndrome we note that hostile aggression involves a negative attitude about the object of the invasive behavior. Hostile aggression begins with a cynical attitude. Evaluating others negatively escalates the dislike, which is manifested in harmful ways as sanctioned by permissive attitudes toward destroying objects and injuring others. This recurring, destructive behavior pattern has been witnessed frequently enough and punished severely enough to produce a pervasive social norm: Deny your anger. Denial of anger proves as harmful as the dreaded AHA behavior.

If anger is, as claimed, a neurochemical process proceeding from emotion that is hard-wired for survival purposes, then the AHA is an aberrant variant of normal function. Normal processes gone haywire are examined by physicians and scientists for characterizing features and classified as disorders.

Classification of disturbances of natural processes, physical and mental, is not a new idea. Medical libraries are full of volumes describing the physical parts, their workings, their interactions, and their abnormalities. Mental workings and abnormalities are more recent targets of diagnostic and prognostic knowledge seekers. Three revisions of the original 1952 Diagnostic and Statistical Manual of Mental Disorders have been produced since 1968. While not one addresses anger directly, acute anger is frequently listed as a symptom and as a primary diagnostic criteria in a wide range of disorders — affective, organic, neurotic, psychotic.

Panic attack, an unpleasant and acute anxiety episode, offers a prototype for thinking about anger attacks. Panic attacks, described frequently in popular magazines, are DSM listed as a unique anxiety disorder.

Symptoms include difficulty breathing, palpitations of the heart, chest pains, dizziness, hot and cold flashes, sweating, fainting, trembling, fear of dying or going crazy. A panic attack brings sudden and intense apprehension, fear, or terror. These moments occur unpredictably, yet may become attached to certain situations—i.e., driving a car. The disorder often begins in late adolescence or early adult years. It may be limited to a single brief period, or become chronic. It is rarely incapacitating unless complicated by severe phobia, abuse of alcohol, or drugs and medications. Early warning clues are experiences of separation anxiety in childhood and or sudden loss of significant others. (Based on information in the *Diagnostic and Statistical Manual* and *Dictionary of Psychology.*)

Temper tantrums are recognized in children, and can continue as an adult behavior pattern. In an early consulting assignment, I learned about both the tantrum and the perfectionist. Contracted to provide organization development services, my monthly activities were periodically side-tracked to attend to special situations identified by the Vice-President. One month I talked with a computer specialist who was kicking the main-frame computer and screaming at it several times a week. Another month I spent time with a supervisor who was being heard down the hallways venting her anger at her staff. She berated them about inappropriately dressing for work and excessively wasting time.

The computer specialist was intentionally sending a message upstairs that he wanted a new computer. The woman supervisor, with no daughters of her own, was apprehensive that her young staffers were headed for personal trouble and wanted to protect them from harm. She imagined they might be attacked, or, at the very least, insulted by increased sexual attention from the large numbers of men workers.

Since those early assignments, I continue to notice that organizational consultation includes listening to a lot of anger expression.

Looking back, I see how anger attacks have a lot in common with panic attacks. In my experience, anger attacks occur more frequently than anxiety attacks in work settings.

Anger attacks include some or all of the following events: labored breathing, flaring of nostrils, narrowed eye focus, pounding of the heart, clenching of hand, arm, and leg muscles, clutching of the chest and collapsing, hot flashes, going cold, a tunnel vision awareness of circumstances and surroundings, and loss of concern for personal safety, life, or others at risk.

An anger attack brings sudden and intense sense of frustration, deprivation, or insult. These moments occur unpredictably, yet may become attached to certain situations, e.g., an umpire's ruling in a baseball game. The disorder often begins in childhood or pre-adolescent years. Anger attacks may be limited to a single brief period, or become chronic. Anger attacks are rarely incapacitating unless complicated by particularized hostility, abuse of alcohol, drugs, or medication. Early warning clues are experiences of severe punishment, falling, or deprivation in childhood. Anger expression is influenced by family and social norms, and may be affected by genetic factors or disorders such as epilepsy and certain mental or emotional retardations.

How Do I Love Thee? Let Me Count the Angers

Anger, like love, can be personal, professional, and generic—eros, filial, agape. Things that make us angry enough to take action at home, at work, or as a citizen, reveal the hero within. Angers are indelible character markers of what it is that we value and love. Martin Luther King said, "I have a dream." A legendary Mexican contemporary, Don Juan was a very different type of visionary. Made famous in the writings of Carlos Castaneda, Don Juan understood individual, separate realities and taught the importance of controlled folly. King loved his kinfolk. Don Juan loved allfolk. One advocated an instrumental, non-aggressive anger-out strategy for demonstrating ways of protecting and loving others. The second plumbed the depths of anger-in strategies, ways of controlling fascinations and frustrations that inhibit our ways of respecting and loving all life. King was angry about racial prejudice. Don Juan was angry about social norms and biases.

King, full of righteous filial anger, spoke about injustices done to people with black skin by people with white skin. He harnessed and channeled the anger of many people to move society toward the dream of equality, his goal of justice. Don Juan spoke of mastery over anger through intensive, individualized training. Don Juan's students were challenged to let go of externally imposed perspectives, and to train the powers within to extend their idiosyncratic capabilities into the world. He taught that cultivation of inner strength enables one to achieve beyond ordinary expectations and goals. He was full of agape anger about people enslaved to things, people or ideas. Both were charismatic participators in the quest for quality of life.

Most of us fall somewhere between the activist and the individualist, and all of us have at least a glimpse of what personal eros is about. Freud's love-anger-deathwish notions make sense even for those who disagree with elaborate psychoanalytic assumptions and conclusions. For the less fatalistic, living beyond first impressions and first loves is a matter of putting new spins on emotional intelligence. Anger signals that it is time for a time-out to do some planning.

Refocusing gets us to be at rest with what's beside us, here and now. Like Einstein, we shift an internal sense of falling into one of moving forward. Concentration on goals, like Marie Curie's determination to complete the research she began with her husband, gives stability as we adapt. Executives and managers who refuse to accept new goals, new technologies, new assignments are considered impossible to motivate. They are using their anger to dig their heels in, to stay right where they are for the rest of their days. Some call it being in a rut, others consider it digging an early grave.

We know, first or second-hand, the debilitating consequences of a wrong choice in a career or in a marriage partner. Struggles are inevitable either way—staying in a bad job or marriage, or divorcing and starting over. Over-estimating first impressions about jobs or people is a result of more wishful thinking than data gathering. First impressions seldom provide sufficient detail or reveal the whole story. Mistaken first loves, as well as long-lasting loves, are reflected in our angers. Too often early emotional miscalculations lead to sadness and depression. In extreme situations, regrets about affections and admirations that did not measure up to expectations are expressed in suicide or hostile aggression.

As we live out our days in the non-stop stream of experiences, emotions, and behaving, we can count on anger to be an informed ally bent on improving and perfecting things. We can tune into what our angry temperament and our angry reaction point out. We can edit our behavior, pausing the spontaneous flow of anger-out or anger-in long enough to choose wisely what to do when we lift the lid of the anger box.

Anger could be considered as the politician of the vital three emotions. Like campaigning candidates for public office, anger draws attention to what's wrong with the way things are and points out what needs to be better in the future. Once elected to office, the politician remains aware of another election in two or four years, so is a constant campaigner. Politicians and anger recognize the injustices, the obstacles, and the pains around them. This is how we discover the inadequacy of the transportation systems, the dangers in the schools, and the threats to community safety. Politicians make headlines because of their frequent expressions of righteous anger about poverty or disease or wasted tax dollars.

The citizens of Philadelphia might qualify as the best constant campaigners in the country. A survey of major U.S. cities reported that persons living in the city of brotherly love reported the highest levels of hostility, followed most closely by Cleveland, New York, Des Moines, Chicago, and Detroit. The survey found that cities with a higher hostility index were the same ones reporting more health problems and higher death rates.

Several speculations can be made about these angry residents of big cities:

1. They may have community problems identified and taken care of more quickly than other cities; or,
2. They may soon destroy their cities in great riots; or
3. Those who replied to the survey may run for public office and become the new angry voices in Washington, DC; or
4. The survey may prove as spurious as the infamous one connecting the number of stork nests with the number of births in Holland, i.e., the reanalysis of this survey will show that persons who did not die but lived the longest were the ones with the higher hostility levels.

Yes, options are still open. No, there is no final word on anger and how it contributes to our longevity or well-being. The fact that anger is a necessary and natural aspect of life makes it imperative that leaders learn how to channel this energy into constructive activity, problem solving, and quality assurance work. The wisdom of Pandora's box is hidden underneath a host of unpleasant myths and truths. Only the curious dare dig deep enough to find the useful treasures buried there.

Background Reading

Karen Horney, Harry Levinson, Charles Spielberger, Carol Tavris and Redford Williams are mentioned in earlier chapters. Specific articles and books are named in the final reference listing.

Sidney Blatt's analysis of the role of perfectionism in the incidence of suicide appeared in *The American Psychologist,* December 1995, Vol. 50, 12, 1003-1020. In this report, Blatt recommends more extensive therapy than provided by quick-cure, short-treatment modes found effective in many types of situational-reaction conditions.

CURIOSITY   ANXIETY   *ANGER*

Chapter 8

Wholeheartedness and Passion for Life

> Many executives and professionals thrive in the midst of ambiguities, complexities, and fast-paced change. They are apparently immune to Type-A stress. Their well-being is reflected in their health and commitment. Executive hardiness translates into organized momentum for survival, adequacy, growth, and meaningfulness. Hardy executives live beyond the letter-of-the-natural-law, and in the spirit of wholeheartedness.
>
> - **To Trust or Not to Trust.**
> - **Basic Skills: Giving and Receiving**
> - **Doing What Comes Naturally**
> - **Peak Performance Zone**

I have never known anyone who accomplished anything significant
who was not a monomaniac with a passion.
Tom Peters. *Passion for Excellence.* Training video

To be or not to be: That is the question.
Whether 'tis nobler in the mind to suffer
the slings and arrows of outrageous fortune,
Or to take arms against a sea of troubles,
And by opposing, end them. To die;
to sleep; no more,
And by a sleep to say we end
The heartache and the thousand
natural shocks
That flesh is heir to. . .

For who would bear the whips and scorns
of time,
The oppressor's wrong, the proud man's
stubborn refusal,
The pangs of devalued love,
the law's delays,
The insolence of office, and the spurns
That patient merit of the unworthy takes,. . .

Who would burdens bear,
To grunt and sweat under a weary life,
But that dread of something after death,
Makes us rather bear those ills we have
Than fly to others that we know not
of?. . .
And thus the native hue of resolution
Is sicklied over with the pale cast of
anxiety
And enterprise of great pith and
moment
With this regard their currents turn
away
And lose the name of action.

Hamlet speaking in Act II,
Scene 1. William Shakespeare.
circa 1602

With arms outstretched, I press on toward the goal for the prize of the upward call. . .
J. B. Philips translation of Paul's Letter to the Philippians 3:14. *The New Testament.*

To Trust or Not To Trust

"To be or not to be" is one of Shakespeare's best-known lines. These words begin a poignant soliloquy spoken by Hamlet, Prince of Denmark, a young man tormented by sorrow and anger. He became horrified when his mother married his uncle less than two months after his father's death. Hamlet was haunted by his father's ghost. This ghost insisted that Hamlet's uncle seduced Hamlet's mother and murdered Hamlet's father. The ghost urged Hamlet to avenge these crimes and assassinate the Uncle.

Hamlet abhorred the idea of killing anyone. At the same time, his outrage toward his father's brother and his own mother persisted. Unable to seek the truth wholeheartedly, Hamlet feigned madness. Under the guise of appearing to be delusional, insane and rebellious, Hamlet sought to prove his uncle's guilt and to stage an execution. Hamlet's confrontation with human lust and greed took place eight hundred years ago. Perhaps, thirteenth-century torments were not the same as those faced by today's young men and women. Or, are they?

Wholehearted, true hearted, faithful and loyal. These words are from a patriotic marching song. They tell of courage and willingness to do battle for a good cause. A different type of courage was heralded during the Vietnam conflict. Now etched in U.S. history is an awareness of passionate citizens unwilling to do battle. These youths avoided conscriptions and drafts and refused to kill or be killed for uncertain, remote causes.

In a peacetime context, passionate causes are associated with high school, early jobs, and college years. Most of us remember days when everything was immensely important. Healthy young adults are notoriously enthusiastic and hard working. They plunge full force into the mainstreams of life. First loves and first cars; first jobs and first failures; football and basketball competitions; holiday parades and fancy dress balls. Drinking too much, talking too much, driving too fast, fighting too quickly—even if we never got involved with Blood and Crips, 18th Street terrorists, or West Side Story rumbles.

Young hearts full of passion can, sometimes, be burdened by minds that are divided. Will loyalty to our patriarchal ghosts always demand blood-letting? Can we be faithful to cherished ideals of fairness, justice and dreams of great achievements and be weighted down by repugnance for violence? Hamlet decided not to express his anger straightforwardly. If he had confronted his mother and uncle with his suspicions, fewer people might have died in the play. And, we would have inherited a diluted insight into the consequences of muddled emotion and confused motivation—*when the hue of resolution is sicklied over with . . . anxiety and we hesitate to take arms against a sea of troubles.*

Most of us struggle with less cosmic passions than royal intrigue and betrayal. Yet, we all are descendants of senior adults who reminisce about their days of great hopes, great dreams, and great aspirations, about the wars they fought and the natural disasters they survived. Many of our elders openly wish to be, once again, enamored by an idea, a cause, or a person. We who are in our mid-life years take encouragement from tales of adventures and enthusiasms in later life.

The growing population of golden-agers are beginning to report experiences of wholeheartedness that are less impulsive and instantaneous than the passions of early adulthood. Seasoned later-life achievement happens if polished abilities are yoked to absorbing work. Persistence begins to balance strong emotions and environmental stressors. Optimal conditions lead to actions enriched by the lessons of youthful daring. Latent abilities emerge as older populations remain healthier longer, and as younger generations learn not to discount seasoned talent and energy. When newcomers take away problem-solving activities from tenured workers, they set in motion the dissipation of the elders' identity and sense of purpose. Thus, according to studies compiled by Neisser and Jopling, hastening the end of the person(ality).

Wholeheartedness and well-being can come about at every age if a person taps into the energy available from vital sign emotions. Managing the natural sources of motivation built into the nervous system increases potentials for meaningful, productive activity. Rich emotions can stir us to action. Emotion empowers successful leadership. Executives face the unknowns of corporate life every day. Anxiety is bound to be triggered by the ever-present need to be alert to organizational ambiguities and potentially harmful business conditions. The healthy-heart imperative is to encourage curiosity to stay in charge. Curiosity tames anxiety and anger so they can function together providing a natural leadership edge.

Wholeheartedness is a side effect of managing vital sign emotions. Adjusting the blend of curiosity, anxiety and anger lets us cope more effectively with the not-so-routine surprise-and-change episodes.

- *How can this mess be turned to an advantage?* Curiosity speaking.

- *It will take courage and smarts to figure this one out—can I do it?* Anxiety speaking.
- *It **must** be done in the best possible form. We **must** take care that it doesn't do damage to others.* Anger speaking.

Opportunities for wholeheartedness occur in every circumstance. In the productive blend, curiosity supplies the greatest amount of motivational energy. Anxiety puts a spicy challenge into the mix, while anger stands tall for quality and justice. Self-management of emotions requires the flexibility to notice the right time for more attention to anger or anxiety. Hamlet was curious and clever enough to concoct a way to establish his uncle's guilt, but failed to instruct his anger to stand aside and let curiosity look for innovative, non-violent resolutions. Rather than providing knee-jerk solutions, emotions can be harnessed in the interest of discovering constructive changes after an encounter with some surprise circumstance.

Bookshelves are full of guides on how to create change, how to cope with change, how to resist change. *Timeless Mind, Ageless Body* is Deepak Chopra's effort to advise us about how to keep changing while resisting wear and tear. The title is a good marketing sound-bite, actually too good. The title discourages those who respect solid scientific evidence, but shy away from presumptuous claims. Those readers have no way to know that Chopra gives us both types of information. Long before Chopra, countless teachers, philosophers, religious leaders, and marketing technicians actively promoted the notion that we can achieve what we set our minds to. These formulas usually involve dedication, hard work, and absolute belief that you will reach your objective. While some prefer to wish-upon-a-star, there is long-standing agreement, even among diverse instructors, that turning a vision inside-out calls for perseverance, strategic thinking, and hardiness.

Surprises force us to find ways to change. Our response to a surprise reveals our typical emotional mix at work. Our combination and proportions of emotions can generate a dilemma, much like Hamlet's, to trust or not to trust. That conclusion determines the direction of the change. If the decision is to trust, then the behavior is to move toward the surprise. If the decision is not to trust, then the behavior is to move away from the surprise, or to move against the surprise, as Hamlet did.

An informed-attitude of positive trust introduces substance and continuity to the work. Trust built on accumulated information connects the past and the future. In the face of non-stop change, what evidence do we use to decide to trust or not to trust? Five sources of information have been identified as primary determinants: *Integrity, consistency, loyalty, openness, and competence.* In other words, one's willingness to risk working with another is based on the other person's behavioral history. Hosmer's study of trust includes evidence supporting that these components underlie a decision to trust. The five determinants are essentially behaviors that demonstrate predictable honesty, benevolence, and sound judgment, each applied in conjunction with technical knowledge and a willingness to give and receive information.

Trust, defined according to these five factors, showed up in studies of executive success as an essential condition for promotion and for impact. If a manager is to move forward in the career track, superiors must consider that individual reliable and trustworthy. If a president is to initiate effective action in under-performing companies, subordinates must have trust in that appointed leader.

Conclusions drawn from these observations are that trust is a central aspect of interpersonal relationships; that trust is essential in development of management careers; and, that trust in a specific person predicts outcomes better than global attitudes of trust in general. This recent evidence strengthens Golembiewski's bold assertion, made over twenty years ago, that "There is no single variable which so thoroughly influences interpersonal and group behavior as does trust." The hourglass symbol for Part Two shows the sands of surprise passing through the narrow neck of trust. The message is that experiences across time accumulate, building the informed attitude of trust necessary-and-sufficient for effecting constructive change. The greater the number of experiences showing honesty, good will, faithfulness, reliability, and competence, the shorter the time required to come to trust and to effect successful delegating and restructuring.

SURPRISE

TRUST

CHANGE

The Basic Skills: Giving and Receiving

Informed attitudes depend upon what goes on between a person and others during many work days. It boils down to moments of giving and receiving which are the moments-of-truth for building trust. Scandinavian Air Systems (SAS) chairman, Jan Carlzon, defined moments of truth in the service industry as any episode in which a customer comes into contact with any aspect of the company, and thereby has an opportunity to form an impression. The impressions being formed are of the corporation as trustworthy.

SAS leaders conducted studies of moments-of-truth and interpersonal trustworthiness as they translate to the corporate scale. What gets high grades on service industry report cards turns out to be: care-and-concern, spontaneity, problem solving, and recovery. Management advisors Albrecht and Zemke say these four factors represent motivations imbedded in the customers' nervous system. If their intuitive connection is on-the-money, these four types of experiences leading to moments of trust are imbedded in anger [care and concern], curiosity [spontaneity], curiosity [problem solving], and anxiety [recovery]. Two of these four determinants of trustworthiness rely on an employee being motivated, primarily, by curiosity. *Did you find our service to your liking? OK? Excellent?. . . So that's the difficulty you're facing? No problem. Let me show you several ways we can work out something to meet your need.*

Two customer-priorities were expected by the SAS surveyors, and two were surprises. The expected moments-of-truth were (1) the customers' appreciation of an employee's genuine interest in the customer's satisfaction; and, (2) the customers' appreciation when an employee can discover a problem resolution around technical intricacies. A moment-of-truth surprise was how positively customers viewed (3) instantaneous decision-actions by front-line employees. Customers trust a company whose direct contact persons can alleviate their angry emotions, their push for justice—now. A second surprise was the (4) strong value for an apology when things go wrong. Employees saying they are sorry alleviates the impact of ambiguity in situations of uncertain outcome, assuaging anxiety levels.

Managers in non-service industries won't have identical exchanges that lead to trusting alliances. Nevertheless, regardless of the nature of the business, managers contribute daily to impressions that build informed trust within that organization. Trust leads to enthusiasm, élan, and esprit de corps. It mobilizes talent, speeds up collaborative processes, and gives co-workers and associates a sense of progress, involvement and stability.

It all begins with basic skills in giving and receiving information—exchanges that accumulate evidence of integrity, loyalty, consistency, competence. The following chart is based on work by John Talbot, one of my earliest instructors in the mysteries of organizational and interpersonal effectiveness.

A spirit of enthusiasm and wholeheartedness does not emerge from a narrow band of trust. Élan is rooted in a set of underlying optimistic expectations that extend beyond predictions for one single uncertain event or person. Three prerequisites for strength of optimistic trust have been identified:

- an expectation that natural cycles and social orders will persist without discontinuous change—no cataclysm;
- that persons will provide technically competent job performances—i.e., their training included appropriate and adequate education and experience for the job; and,
- that job holders will behave ethically, maintaining morally correct job performance—the rules of the game will be followed: i.e., the interests of the person who is trusting are placed before the interests of the professional who is trusted.

RELATIONSHIP BASICS

I Give and You RECEIVE	You GIVE and I Receive	Together We Build Mutual TRUST
IF YOU RECEIVE FROM ME: **I AM AFFIRMED**	IF YOU GIVE TO ME: **I CONFIRM YOU**	IF YOU COME CLOSE TO ME: **WE KNOW EACH OTHER**
If you do not receive what I offer: Then, I feel **PUT DOWN**	If you do not give your honest self: Then, I feel **PUT ON**	If you do not come closer: Then, I feel **PUT OFF**
IT MAY BE THAT Putting me down puts you up Then, I feel **ANXIETY**	IT MAY BE THAT Giving me a facade protects the real you from me: Then, I feel **DISTRUST**	IT MAY BE THAT Keeping distance keeps you from hurt and disappointment: I feel **LONELINESS**

When daily receiving-and-giving is subject to radical shifts, or if the exchanges do not reflect competence, or if there is no indication of fiduciary responsibility, then the predominant factors will be anxiety and distrust, as shown on the bottom lines of the preceding chart. At times anxiety is wise, alerting you that this is not a time to place the interests of others before your own interests, even when others are extending trust in you. There are occasions when personal duties or values bring about conflicts of interest. In such moments an impoverished mother can be caught stealing the loaf of bread for her hungry child. There are few places left in the world where her hands would be cut off; or, where she would not be trusted in the future to do whatever it takes to get an important, necessary job done adequately, with as little damage as possible.

Hamlet's struggle with trust and wholeheartedness grew out of his intense anger about his father's betrayal and death. Hamlet's suspicions were without tangible proof. He could not certify that his anger was justified. Lack of information introduces distrust in contemporary organizational life. SAS reported ways that emotions build and derail trust in their business. In Hamlet's experience of treasonous behavior in Denmark's government and in the SAS investigation of customer satisfactions, anxiety increases when there is an information void. Overblown anxiety freezes curiosity and problem-solving. Unmanaged, anxiety escalates to the point of rendering individuals and relationships dysfunctional and destructive, while depleting self-confidence. A critical factor in managing emotions and developing giving and receiving skills is the ability to gather information, compile logical informed attitudes, and apply these consistently to decision making.

Doing What Comes Naturally

The ability to step out with wholehearted confidence into high intensity situations is seen by an expert trial judge as a matter of taking time to resolve the conflicts that produce the job tensions. The Hon. John Sheperd equates stress and the challenge each judge faces in a trial case. First, information is gathered, organized, and studied. Then comes the stress for the judge. The resolution of each case requires that the judge make a decision. Judge Sheperd's opinion is that other job tension is similar to the stress of trials and that wholehearted confidence comes once conflicts are reviewed, a sentence rendered, and an action decision is handed down.

Sheperd outlined six job areas of conflict common to trial judges: certainty, e.g., probability that the judge has made an accurate analysis of the facts; the importance of a judge maintaining a positive public image; lack of awareness of the judge about personal bias; the judge's enjoyment of the power of the position; the judge's concern about sentencing, i.e., probability that the judge's sentence pronouncement will have the intended consequences and side effects; and the tension between the judge's personal needs vs. professional demands. Sheperd proposes a twofold remedy. The first part of his elegantly simple solution is to acquire maximum competence in the field. This means constant continuing education, an expanding of one's technical knowledge range—getting beyond the early specialty and learning what's happening in other jurisdictions and disciplines.

Sheperd gives equal emphasis to looking in the mirror and recognizing who is reflected there. In other words: know thyself. Sheperd notes it is absolutely essential to understand the person who acts on the basis of acquired knowledge. Objectivity and perspective about one's self is hard, if not impossible to gain alone.

Doing an in-depth check-up, such as Sheperd recommends, is now affordable and accessible. Several decades of information explosion resulted in improved personality questionnaires, many of which were developed for workshops on team building and communication skills. Assessments of major and minor characteristics are available which give us a focused look at what's reflected in our mirrors. Some of us tend to show the best side, and answer personality questions the way we would like to be more than the way we usually are. Since this is not uncommon, it's advisable to review assessment results in dialogue with an assessment specialist.

Interpretation of results also calls for recognizing biases of test authors. A questionnaire expresses authors' biases, even when it is prepared by a knowledgeable researcher. A look at oneself in the mirror will be more accurate when based on more than one questionnaire. Getting perspectives of more than one expert gives the self-image depth and dimension.

An explosion of assessment options makes it hard to select assessment tests that are easy to understand and will also address job requirements. One questionnaire with general appeal and practical value is the Myers-Briggs Type Indicator (MBTI). Easy-to-read interpretations of MBTI scores describe everyday consequences of how a person usually goes about gathering information and making judgments. An ability to make sound judgments is one of the harder-to-analyze determinants of positive trust.

The MBTI is criticized by psychometricians interested in test construction and is abused by entrepreneurs capitalizing on entertaining aspects of the theory. The intention of the questionnaire is to help people understand themselves better by understanding the theory of personality proposed by Carl Jung. The MBTI assesses two survival functions—getting data from the surrounding environment and selecting action-options. The questionnaire provides feedback about a person's current pattern of problem solving.

Each pattern is associated with particular strengths and weaknesses, likes and dislikes, goals and activities, and preferred strategies for learning and doing. The MBTI authors, as discussed in Chapter 2, agree with Jung's opinion that an individual's behavior is neither random nor arbitrary. Jung and Myers write about how people operate out of relatively stable patterns. Each of the sixteen patterns depends on alternative ways of getting information and deciding what to do about it. The MBTI asks about an individual's preferences among the characteristics that Jung reported he found in his clients and acquaintances. Based on Jung's description of innate preferences and lifelong patterns, Myers and Briggs developed their questionnaire to discover which one of the sixteen types best reflects an individual's current approach.

In the short-term, these preferences affect the kind of work we find most appealing, the skills we choose to acquire, and where we are able to shine, to be our best. When a job calls for doing things we naturally like to do, we can work with wholeheartedness. Understanding one's preferred way of getting data and taking action will not replace knowledge and skill prerequisite to competence. A fit between job and person increases the potentials for advancing in a career path, and enjoyment of work that others fail to find.

We will need to use each of the eight MBTI variables, whether or not it is a preferred process. Four of the eight characteristics provide a short-hand description of how a person uses all eight characteristics. The acronym alerts us to undervalued talents and likely blind spots, which occur when we neglect the non-preferred characteristics. Jung saw personality as a life-long development and believed that the fully developed, mature personality is able to be competent when *extraverting, introverting, sensing, intuiting, thinking, and feeling.* Myers added the *perceiving* and *judging* preferences in order to detect what characteristic a person prefers when extraverting, when working with others.

Extraversion (E) and Introversion (I) are the foundation characteristics in Carl Jung's description of personality. Jung, a physician and psychologist, observed that while all people behave in extraverting patterns sometimes and in introverting patterns at other times, none can do both at once. An obvious point, but with a consequence seldom fully recognized. It means extraverting and introverting are two separate factors, not a continuum. They are equally healthy, productive patterns, and we can function effectively in each mode. Jung saw acquiring skill with less preferred characteristics as an on-going challenge, one that can keep our days full and interesting no matter how many years we live.

The percent of E and I preferences varies according to management level in MBTI data that I collected and reported. Does a shift in the number of persons reporting a preference for E or I at the three supervisory levels in larger organizations reflect a shift in the types of people being hired, or a shift in job demands for extraversion and introversion?

Initially, the MBTI database showed three-to-one preferences in the general population for extraverting over introverting. More recently, as that database expanded dramatically, equal numbers of preferences for extraversion and introversion are reported. No differences are noted between the proportions of men and women reporting E or I preference. Negative consequences of an E or an I preference surface when one preference takes over to the exclusion of the other, or when a job demands more of the one that is less preferred.

Early life preference for extraversion or introversion results in a qualitative difference in interpersonal style and presence. That difference can be illustrated in terms of rhythm and time: Extraverting means doing, then reflecting, then doing again. Introverting is a process of reflecting first, doing, and reflecting again. Those who prefer extraverting patterns will log more time with people. Those who prefer introverting patterns will log more time with ideas.

Consistent with the demands of the roles, I found the majority of first-line managers reporting preferences for extraverting, while more mid-level managers preferred introverting, and executives predominantly selected extraverting. This finding is consistent with the demands of the role. Job analysis of management assignments by organizational level show more frequent demands for extraverting in early and later stages. Entry level management activities include a lot of direct contact supervision of workers. Top level executives represent the organization in the community and need to be persuasive with investors and board members. The mid-level group is busy making schedules, planning for the immediate future, and preparing reports. This work requires concentrated desk time.

A second shift is found in the number of managers in upper ranks who gather information in an intuitive (N) mode rather than the sensing

(S) mode. The intuitive approach to receiving information is future oriented, a collecting of options and possibilities. Intuition stands in contrast to the detail-oriented, here-and-now mode called Sensing, which is prevalent among first-line and mid-level managers.

The preference for objective decision making, *thinking*, is prevalent at all management levels. The majority of management personnel, at all ranks, prefer to be making decisions when working with others. Getting to the conclusion, using the *judging* preference, supersedes the gathering of the information. According to MBTI descriptions, management employees are action oriented and work with a calm, systematic drive to get the job done.

My ten-year collection of MBTI preferences from participants in executive development training showed no statistically significant differences between earlier groups and later groups. Those interested in management careers continue to declare the same prevailing MBTI characteristics and wide range of emotional levels. The most frequently reported type remains the introverted (I) fact-gatherer (S) with an objective decision mode. The full four-letter code for Introverted Sensing with Thinking (T) decision making is ISTJ. Due to the introverted rhythm, others notice the thinking ability first.

The greater number of ISTJ types is not surprising in executive training classes made up, predominantly, of mid-level managers moving out of an assignment that calls for a lot of reflection and desk time. Executive level work will demand more extraverting and shifting attention away from details toward big pictures.

Overall, my ten-year sample shows a slight increase in numbers reporting the values-approach to decisions *(feeling, F)*. This could be related to the 68% increase in women attendees. In general population samples, women more often report a *feeling* decision preference above the *thinking* mode. Sixty percent of the women indicate that they use the F mode, while sixty percent of the men use the T mode.

This management group trend did nothing to detract from an overwhelming consistency of characteristics across the ten years. In a time of rapid technological change, it appears that executives may find familiar behavior patterns to recognize, depend upon, and trust.

Peak Performance Zones

The stability in personality preference of those in management positions comes with a price. Patterns of functioning produce wear and tear on identifiable parts of the physical body. It is rather like frequently walked pathways on the carpet. Executives, professionals, and middle managers are reported to be at-risk for heart disease to a greater extent than other jobholders. As recently as 1991 Surgeon General reports named coronary heart disease, CHD, as the major cause of death and disability among middle-aged and older people in Western, urbanized societies. The USA was just below mid-point in an 18-country comparison of CHD mortality-risk prepared by the World Health Organization. Australia ranked 13th, right after the USA, with CHD accounting for 48% of deaths among women and men of all age groups. Finland headed the list and Japan's exceptionally low rate was the 18th place.

Studies relating occupations to stress and heart disease are difficult to interpret because they are drawn from research using a wide range of methods, sophistication and causal connections. The World Health Organization research gives results of specific comparisons, such as the contrasting of private sector bank employees and public sector bank employees. That study found higher incidence of CHD among private sector employees. An especially high incidence of CHD was found among sea officers in Norway and occupational stress was considered the major cause.

Studies of U.S.A. blue-collar workers show they have the higher incidence of cardiovascular disease when compared with engineers and scientists. Among white-collar workers, higher incidents are noted among pilots, air traffic controllers, and managers. The self-employed showed a much higher incidence of CHD than company employees.

Low job satisfaction, proposed as a likely culprit in malaise and disease, was directly linked to incidence of heart disease. Although absence of wholeheartedness about work did not predict physical problems, lack of control over excessive job stress did show as related to incidents of CHD. Shift work and monotony, factors frequently found to be contributors to physical deterioration, were found related to myocardial infarction, but not in the absence of demanding physical job activity or in the absence of debilitating personal-habits and histories—cigarette smoking, education, alcohol consumption.

Comprehensive reviews of CHD studies conclude that no single factor accounts for most incidents. Risk factors apply primarily if (a) they are connected to hard-wired characteristics, such as anger, or, if (b) they are pervasive aspects of the work environment. This translates to an executive responsibility for monitoring the work environment and its capacity for escalating Type-A behaviors into unhealthy patterns. An optimal amount of stress is stimulating and challenging, providing what Hans Selye called the "spice of life" ingredient. Crossing the optimal stress limit, which varies with individuals, results in higher risk of CHD, which means the loss of talented persons at their peak contribution potential.

Hypertensive persons respond frequently with anger when they perceive unfair treatment or blocks in their efforts to reach goals. When necessary, they may internalize their anger. High levels of anger-in are associated with very high systolic and diastolic blood pressure readings. Hypertensives prefer to cope with stress by distancing, self-control, and escape-avoidance. Non-hypertensives were more likely to confront a situation and to seek social support in anger-provoking situations. Hypertensives reported feeling more hassled in daily life than the non-hypertensives; they bumped into minor frustrations more often.

Investigations in the USA and Europe are showing that the suppression of emotions, including but not limited to anger, take their toll. Overcontrol of emotions has been connected to the cancers by researchers at the University of South Florida. Anger suppression in women who were medically treated for breast cancer predicted those who would have a recurrence of the breast cancer. Stomach cancers show strong relationship to suppression of anger. Reviews of death rates and causes of death in central Europe by Hans Eysenck and Grosarth Matticheck also found suppression of emotion to predict terminal cancers.

So far this book concentrates on the executive as a person, an individual who steps on the management ladder with a desire to be as effective as possible and to travel up that ladder as far as talent and luck allow. Enterprising executives begin with an individual vision. Culmination of that vision depends upon a host of talents in addition to vision making. They must rely on skillful perceptions, judgments, emotions, and strategies for responding to surprise-and-change. No doubt about it, first, you've got to want to be an executive. Then you've got to work hard and long to put your house in order and to develop necessary abilities.

Self-responsibility is seen in peak performers who are "in the zone." According to executive consultant Jerry Kushel, one imperative for self-responsibility is *whenever necessary, pause and think, and then choose effective thoughts.* Kushel's methods for choosing effective thoughts are easy to use in coaching sessions, or on your own. The following three activities work to maintain effective thoughts under increasing levels of self-resistance.

- Low Intensity Negative Thoughts. Overdose on non-productive thoughts, e.g., if depressed, just keep adding to the list of depressing ideas until you are tired of it. Then, shift to something that makes you feel enthusiastic, optimistic, and gets you moving on some useful activity.

- Moderate Intensity Negative Thoughts. Branding is a kind of self-hypnosis. For more persistent negative thinking, prepare a list of preferred, positive thoughts. Next, get into a relaxed state by breathing deeply, thinking of a relaxing color (green, or blue). Then squeeze your hands together. Say to yourself: "I will not be able to separate my fingers." Keep on pressing the fingers tightly, and say aloud the name of the soothing color while suggesting to yourself that the self-defeating thoughts will fade away and be replaced by the prepared, productive thoughts.

- Recurring Negative Thinking. The last method is called the closure process and is recommended when it is difficult to choose effective thoughts. One reason for persistent defeating thoughts is known as "unfinished business." This means there are topics or concerns rummaging around in the back of your mind that have not been satisfactorily decided or laid aside. Some coaches see the closure method as having four stages, similar to those experienced after a death of someone close or important to you: denial, bargaining, anger and depression. The sequence is not as important as the finding that directly addressing unfinished business allows many people to get on with wholehearted, productive thinking.

Even if a person has an inner standard to perform their best, they need sufficient reason to get going. They need to be motivated to discover what it takes to do their best. Managers can help early career supervisors and employees by mentoring, sometimes called coaching, career counseling, or competency development. A key session, according to long-time executive advisors, is the one that discusses straightforwardly: "What's in it for me." An employee does best with a personalized good reason for attaining peak performance zone. Those personalized reasons are going to have most to do with that person's values, needs, goals.

What people have in common is a value for, a need for, and a willingness to strive for security, growth, and relationship. It is possible to see an association between security and anxiety; growth and curiosity; and relationships and anger/love. Actively understood, balanced, and managed, these basics show ways through glass ceilings and into the peak performance zones.

What we know about leadership, according to recent reports is that managers demonstrate considerable competence, and, at the same time, have a dark side that is not apparent in initial discussions. That dark side can outweigh characteristics typically associated with leadership success. Experts arrive at amazingly similar notions of what's important for effectiveness:

- Dominance, assertiveness, energy, activity level, speech fluency, sociability, social participation;

- Articulate and active, independent, self-confident, emotionally balanced and hard working;

- Desire to advance, energy, readiness to make decisions, resistance to stress, tolerance for uncertainty, inner work standards, range of interests.

In the movie *Pagemaster*, Maculay Calkin played the part of a computer and math whiz-kid who became acquainted with emotions in an unusual way. He encountered an unlikely trio after taking shelter in the community library during a lightning storm. Dripping wet from the surprise downpour, Maculay slipped and fell. He hit his head on the marble floor and experienced an altered state of consciousness. Lying on the floor, he looked up at artwork figures painted on the ceiling. The images melted and dripped colorful paints that turned into animated books. The contents of each book became apparent in their behaviors and their titles: Adventure, Horror, and Fantasy.

In this 1994 family-rated Hollywood film, Maculay Calkin built on his early career success as the nine-year old star of the box-office hit *Home Alone*. In *Pagemaster* Maculay plays a 12-year-old intellectual with a reputation as a scaredy-cat. He becomes obsessed by statistical probabilities. He quotes the odds that catastrophic, dire events will happen, stats about serious injury accidents in the home, and annual rates of infection transmission in public schools. He also predicts low success potentials for schoolmates who are attempting to propel their bicycles up a ramp and over a row of barrels at a neighborhood construction site. Quantities of negative prediction data are reported from the whiz-kid, but never baseball batting averages.

The pre-adolescent genius became an expert at safety precautions. He always wore the latest in protective clothing—helmets, goggles, life-jackets; he used top-of-the-line protective gear—bicycle shields, safety belts, blinking lights, bright flags on top of tall, white sticks; and, he practiced protective behavior—not climbing ladders to high spots, not mixing it up with the kids on the street, not staying outdoors in a storm.

None of this probability knowledge or defensive behavior proved useful when he ran into emotions. From the moment he hit his head on the library floor, Maculay was dependent upon his alliance with non-statistical emotions to make a successful exit from his frightening psychedelic state. His ticket to escape was an agreement with the books, Adventure, Horror, and Fantasy, to check-them-out of the library. Before the animated journey ended, the probability whiz kid learned that these books and the emotions they represented were trustworthy, and would be lifelong friends. On the bicycle ride home, after the storm and the psychedelic concussion were ended, he gunned his bicycle speed as he pedaled up the construction site ramp and zoomed over the row of barrels.

Some translate the moral of this cinema-fable into: *Do not become a nerd or computer freak. Take a break from the internet. Get a library card. Read books, not screens.* Arguably, there is a better lesson to take away from the movie. Be proud of your emotions. Use your *courage, heart, and intelligence* wisely.

Pagemaster is unlikely to challenge *The Wizard of Oz* as the nation's beloved parable of enduring folk wisdom. The lion, the tin man, and the scarecrow reflected early twentieth-century psychology and insights about the power of positive thinking and the importance of self-esteem. Adventure, horror and fantasy captured insights for another generation.

The yellow-brick path into the twenty-first century Oz is paved with an emotion-motivation-health chain of survival. Curiosity, anxiety, and anger are seen in the *Pagemaster* animations named Fantasy, Adventure, and Horror.

- Fantasy is surely a cousin to Curiosity. *What if I were king of the world? . . . Where would I go if I won the lottery?*

- Adventure is the sunny-side of Anxiety. *Perhaps I will lose my way when I get into New York and never find the place where they sell the theater tickets at reduced rates. But if I do find it, I can see three plays rather then one.*

- Horror is the ancestor of Anger. *How could anyone let a child stay in a dark closet all day? . . .What kind of monster would order mass killing of people because of their religious or ethnic background?*

Curiosity, anxiety, and anger animate us as they provide us with a flow of information for building trust, clarifying our visions, and selecting our actions. Emotions provide the spirit" that determine much of our success. Emotion infrastructures are valuable resources available to management architects. It will not ever become a matter of do I have curiosity, anxiety, anger and a set of fairly stable personality preferences, but a matter of *will I learn to understand, manage, and maximize the power available in myself and others. Will I discover the way of wholeheartedness?*

Background Reading

Karl Albrecht and Ron Zemke's book about how to inspire a company to become customer-driven and service oriented, *Service America.* NY: Warner Books Edition, 1985, tells the story of Scandanavian Air Systems (SAS) and its chairman, Jan Carlzon's moments of truth.

Timeless Mind, Ageless Body is Deepak Chopra's book that encourages readers to get in touch with the creative core of life. He writes about the forces pervading all life from the perspective of a highly educated man, born and raised in New Delhi, who polishes his Eastern insights with American trained science, learned at Boston University. He was appointed in 1992 to the National Institute of Health ad hoc panel on alternative medicine.

Golembiewski's bold assertion is reported in the article by LaRue Tone Hosmer, 1995. "Trust: The connecting link between organizational theory and philosophical ethics. *Academy of Management Review. 20*(2), 379-403.

Myers-Briggs Type Indicator (MBTI) Questionnaires can be administered by persons qualified to purchase the test and feedback materials. Many who use MBTI results do not agree with the theory and assumptions proposed by Carl G. Jung. The assessment tool was developed by Isabel Myers and her mother, Katherine Briggs, as "straws in the wind" indicators of an individual's preferences as defined by Carl Jung. The MBTI is a state measure. Early applications were with clients interested in career planning and life development. The most accurate reporting of MBTI history and interpretation is found in the writings by Isabel B. Myers and Mary H. McCaulley. Interpreters of continuous rather than dichotomous scores are using results to discuss MBTI characteristics as traits, which is a contrary theoretical approach to personality.

Mary McCaulley. 1990. *The Power of An Idea. "The entire world is stretching out toward the intoxicating idea of democracy. . . . Changes always mean letting go of old ways to find the new. We know there will be struggle and disillusionment when people face the day-to-day realities, which are still far from ideal. There will be a tendency to blame democracy for its imperfections, instead of accepting responsibility and acknowledging we are imperfect in making democracy work . . . the idea of [personality] type [was] has a power that lets us bridge differences of nationality, of generations, of religious belief . . . each of us journeys toward living our idea of the constructive use of differences, we can make a positive difference in our world." Bulletin of Psychological Type, 13, 1, p. 1.*

Neisser, U. & Fivush, R. (Eds.) (1994). *The Remembering Self: Construction and Accuracy in Self-Narrative.* NY: Cambridge University Press.

Neisser, U. & Jopling, D. A. (1997). *The Conceptual Self in Context: Culture, Experience, Self-Understanding.* NY: Cambridge University Press

The Hon. John H. Sheperd and Jerome Frank compared job tensions to the stress a judge experiences in handing down the final judgment in a trial in *Colleague,* 2(2), 1989, and were reprinted with permission of the Michigan Judicial Institute.

CURIOSITY ANXIETY *ANGER*

Motivation: The Roles of the Vital Emotions

1. THE EXPLORER

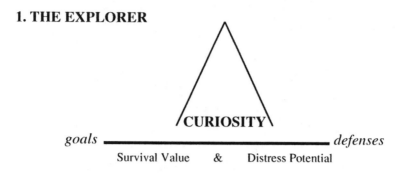

goals ——————————————— *defenses*

Survival Value   &   Distress Potential

Feelings associated with curiosity are: **wonder, attraction, possibility, mystery**
Productive logic associated with curiosity is: **"If I investigate new ideas and information, the good things of life will be discovered."**
Goals associated with curiosity are: **adventure, creative innovation**
Dangers and risks for professionals and executives include:

- Preoccupation with testing, experimenting at the expense of maintaining current productivity levels.
- Immediate change sought via manipulative, insensitive "politics" or edicts.
- Reduced ability to be seen as steady, trustworthy, realistic because of highly visible, flexible, optimistic behaviors.

2. THE PROTECTOR

goals ——————————————— *defenses*

Survival Value   &   Distress Potential

Feelings associated with anxiety are: **worry, tensions, apprehension**
Productive logic associated with anxiety is: **"If I remain alert to possible dangers, I can assure success."**
Goals associated with anxiety are: **security, safety.**
Dangers and risks for professionals and executives include:

- Preoccupation with work at the expense of attention to self and relationships
- Immediate relief sought via alcohol, drugs, sex
- Reduced ability to adapt to change

3. THE HERO

ANGER

goals ———————————————— *defenses*

Survival Value   &   Distress Potential

Feelings associated with anger are: **injustice, irritation, impeded, frustration**
Productive logic associated with anger is: **"If I point out flaws and react to insults directly, the good things of life will be achieved."**
Goals associated with anger are: **competence, justice, success.**
Dangers and risks for professionals and executives include:

- Preoccupation with fairness to those to whom one is loyal prevents seeing other points of view.
- Immediate action impulses can demonstrate less competence and result in less success
- Reduced ability to complement anything that is less than full excellence can discourage fledgling efforts and underestimate the importance of milestone progress.

Experience of anger   Expression of anger

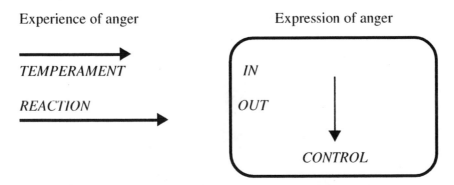

TEMPERAMENT   *IN*

REACTION   *OUT*

                                                CONTROL

OPTIMAL STRESS

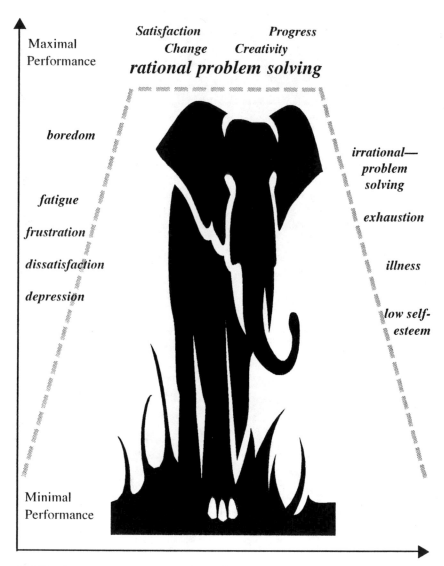

LOW Stress   **Hardiness**   **HIGH Stress**

Performance impaired by   **Performance impaired by**
Lack of Stress   **Excessive Stress**

PART THREE

INVITATIONAL POWER
Organizations with a Future

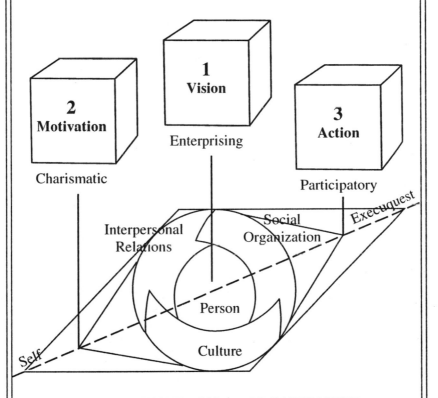

The EXECUTIVE within an ORGANIZATION
within an ENVIRONMENT

III

PART THREE

Invitational Power: Organizations with a Future

Introduction.
Charismatic-Participatory Leadership

The only constant is change. Almost twenty-five hundred years ago, Heraclitus said: "There is nothing permanent except change." The good

news is that the two-hundred-year-old voices of scientific research reassure us of continuity. Each of us observes that some things never change: we recognize many classmates at reunions, and we count on the recurring change of seasons. We see stable, predictable patterns and characteristics in the natural environment and in ourselves. Organizational theorists believe that management has a leading role in the change-and-continuity drama. They are asking managers to rethink their boundaries—those they are given to work within and those they impose upon themselves. Management consultant Tom

Brown minces no words, "Anyone foolish enough to draw up a neat-and-tidy strategic plan, using 1950s techniques, and then execute it without regard to what's happening *right now* deserves a dismal fate."

We forecast that organizations of the future will have been inspired by leaders who kept ahead of the change curve while maintaining a recognizable identity. The failure of organizations to be cohesive as well as progressive lengthens the list of companies that are dropping off the

Fortune 500 list. During a recent five-year period, 143 companies were reported to have been eliminated. How much failure is due to merger and acquisition, how much is due to asset stripping, how much is due to changed technology and environment?

An early analysis of merger outcomes found that 30 percent realized their pre-merger vision of creating value for shareholders three years later, as defined to mean, outperforming the relevant industry average. The potential value of the alliance was forgotten in 55 percent of the M&As and 15 percent were declared ill-conceived, failed or abandoned. Those that succeeded made fast and focused transitions. They maintained full awareness of their re-visioned and ambitious strategic objective. Furthermore, they charted a clear approach for aligning and integrating the merged organizations.

Even under the best of circumstances, organizations, like executives, do not live forever. An estimated average-life for a majority of organizations is 25 years. A second opinion suggests 40 years. In the blizzard of millennium hype, one long-view prognosticator risked naming five companies he expected to be around in the year 2100: DuPont, Ford, Boeing, Coca-Cola, and Procter & Gamble. Why? Because they make things that are a part of everyday living, they have strong brand-name recognition, and they are able to re-invent themselves as global leaders in their industry. These corporations are viewed as eager to adapt to the times and willing to creatively correct mistakes of the past.

Leadership is an accepted factor in determining which organizations will enjoy longer-than-average futures. A lot depends on corporate managers who have the leadership ability to turn a vision inside-out. They inspire others to contribute maximal efforts that can extend the lifecycle of the organization. The CEO leader-hero is described by Debra Benton as one who has a vision, puts a stake in the ground and leads from that point. She commends executive champions whose integrity is obvious and who can be an emotional and moral inspiration to others.

Part III "quantum-shifts" from considering an executive as person in relationship with others for a purpose and the regulator of surprise and change motivations, to looking at the executive as one who performs a legitimate power function. Without human power, organizational production and operations cease. Science fiction films give us previews of lifeless landscapes in industrialized civilizations after nuclear mega-wars or panoramic scans showing skyscraper-cities after citizens are decimated by bacterial attack. Dissonant background music emphasizes that factories and offices are frighteningly vacant and motionless. When script writers strive to depict worst-case scenarios, human-power is eliminated.

Without people, organizations become like rocks. Chicago sky-scrapers, New York's Rockefeller Center, and Detroit's auto assembly plants become twenty-first century versions of sixteenth-century Aztec pyramids, desolate relics of lost civilizations. In contrast, organizations enlivened by people are prototypes for mighty morphins, those comic-strip and television caricatures of villains and heroes made of machinery. Even physicists struggle to maintain essential distinctions between living beings and their creations. They redefine and adjust criteria between open and closed systems in an age of chess-playing computers. The last month of 1999 CBS newscasters reported that researchers at the frontier of the human-machine boundaries announced that they have developed a *nanobot*, a computer chip connected to and communicating with a human neural cell.

Until the nanobots are replicated and commonplace, executives and managers will serve as the organizational agents who distribute human power. They are the men and women who activate operations—who exert energy, who provide controls. Because managers are people, they already have open-system natures that are able to grow, change and exchange. This human capability to adjust, our plasticity, flexibility and adaptability, is what gives momentum and rhythm to closed-system, lifeless objects.

An organization can be considered to be an artifact, a creation of living beings. As such it can be studied and examined aside from the people who provide it the power to produce. The bones and relics of an organization are policies, procedures, position descriptions, awards, work spaces, tools, rituals. These by-products reflect characteristics of workers who propagate the organization. They bequeath continuity, introducing the standards and regulations that serve as a genetic coding. This is not as precise as a cloning process, or even as a nanobot might become, but it does contribute to the programming of a group's future.

Part III is qualitatively different from the first two parts of *The Quest for Executive Effectiveness.* The sum of the personalities in an organization will not add up to be the same thing as the personality of the group, nor do within-group and among-group capabilities explain the productivity of the whole. A similar fallacy occurs if we make direct conclusions about human reactions from studies of rat reactions. Scientists tell many horror stories about applying information from one species to another. Seymore Adler of the Stevens Institute of Technology, Hoboken, NJ, takes a less dogmatic approach. He expresses disappointment that the linking of personality to work behavior continues to suffer because of a lack of theoretical and methodological discipline. At the same time, he commends macro-organizational approaches to the study of organizations that use individual *state* and *trait* characteristics as explanations of collective behaviors. Adler expresses renewed respect for evidence that links individual level personality traits to organizational level criteria. The most impressive are the data showing that the dispositions of powerful founders, visible leaders, and entrepreneurs are reflected in standards for selecting new members. Characteristics of dominant executives are shown to correlate with macro-level behavior and performance of the organization as a whole.

The personality quirks of executives and managers are often, correctly or incorrectly, endowed with cause-and-effect connections to organizational activities. Analogies, while they can stretch the boundaries of scientific rigor, are easy ways to talk about complex, dynamic events. Clearly, the executive's personality exerts a powerful influence in organizational survival. Differences in wielding executive power effect both group synergy and syntality, the group's energy and personality. The chapters in Part III highlight patterns associated with executive power.

Chapter 9. Great Expectations. Assumptions and expectations grow in direct ratio to the number of persons in the organization. With so many variations of what's-in-it-for-me, it's hard to collate individual wishes except under broad expectations such as survival, growth, and meaningfulness. One or all three of these generic goals are addressed in many official mission statements, giving reassurances to employees and customers.

Threats to personal well-being are so compelling that the dark side of power is the first issue considered in this section. Abuses of executive power that can contaminate organizations are profiled as variations of the *Jackass Syndrome*, and are called Pygmalion Effects; Genesis Complex; and Houdini Magic. Expectations and assumptions of an executive are like a magnetic field. Others who have similar hopes are attracted to join the workgroup and, soon, attitudinal and behavioral patterns become as visible as metal filings pointing out the direction inherent in a magnet.

Ideally, that direction is an inspiration for healthy productivity; however, the leader may attract reflections of less noble characteristics, such as are found in individuals with grandiose or narcissistic tendencies. Executives on hubris-highs become intoxicated with power, sometimes to obliterate a sense of real or imagined inadequacy. Others become arrogantly self-serving when they recognize that their brains problem-solve faster and more accurately than many of their peers. They maneuver situations and persons so outcomes favor their own profit or amusement. Those are executives who see employees as jackasses to be managed with a carrot or a stick.

Chapter 10. "Who's The Boss?" The Issue is Control. As leadership moves into a next generation, getting a handle on the control factors and the work of bossing, is made easier by the *competitive market* theories. These are descriptive models that compare and contrast corporate cultures and can serve as a practical way to think about best-fit leadership styles at the helm of the organization. Control is considered from both sides: the webs of internal connections, and the external alliances that seriously complicate an executive's dependency network. As the once popular advertising icon, Joe Camel, discovered, it's commercial suicide not to respect the power outside the company. It is fatal to be blindsided by the symbiotic-competitive business community, by prevailing and countervailing political constituencies, or by unexpected threats in the eco-social community. The boss of tomorrow will need to climb the wind, just as young sailboaters do when they learn how to maintain the boat's momentum. Captains of organizational fortunes will come to rely on participatory command, control, and communications; will learn to offer charismatic agenda-setting and rainmaking; and will practice extending powerful, benchmarking invitations.

Chapter 11. Pathfinders and Mapmakers. Charismatic, participatory executives find hopefulness to be an asset that requires being more than being a Pollyanna town crier. Post-Oz science says successful executives do more than click their heels together three times, wishing to reach a desired destination. Those who achieve what they hope for are busy pathfinding and mapmaking—working out alternatives for moving toward the objective, then stepping briskly forward.

When the going gets tough, the hopeful rethink the goals, go out and learn something new, and bring in fresh players. Fortunately, the executive inherits a legacy of management-maps, such as Alec MacKenzie's classic, *The Management Process in 3-D,* and can pull together a traveler's guide to pathways from the how-to books of future forecasters. With hope, executives maintain their focus on pragmatism, realistic optimism, and calculated risk-taking.

Chapter 12. Making a Difference. Positive executive power flows through trust. Like sands flowing from the top to the bottom of the executive's hourglass, time filters experiences that demonstrate the truth of an executive's vision and fortitude. Navigating the white-waters of surprise and change, an effective leader moves beyond self-serving into standing tall as a pivotal component in an organization.

As the executive's vision assumes a life of its own, it shapes a culture in-and-of itself, more-than and different-from the original ideas. Together, executives, managers and workers transmit the corporate message, work to position the organization within the industry, educate and motivate co-workers, hire and empower new employees. Together, they ensure that their company is an organization with a future.

Public attention often goes to those who make un-spendable amounts of money, or who make colossal mistakes. However, those who generate the sparks that ignite the future will be those who are able to quickly access massive data sources. They will correctly identify what's important. They will find the time to teach others both substance and process.

A next generation renaissance person, the executive hero, will need to filter computerloads of knowledge and come up with an integrated perspective. Management leaders will weave threads of control and of hopefulness. The heroic executive will partner technical production with emotional inspiration, without neglecting work goals and ethics. This power to achieve a vision through motivation and action is a combination of :

- the power to survive—to be alive and well,
- the power to be adequate—to be efficient and satisficing,
- the power to grow—to become, to change, and
- the power to be meaningful—to be charismatic.

Executive effectiveness will be a product of the leader within the organization, within the environment, who is prepared for calibrating situations and inviting continuous development and effectiveness in others.

Background Reading

M&A successes and predictions about companies that will have long lifecycles are reported in Management Review articles published in January and February 1998. "The Art of the Post-Deal" (Feb., p. 17-20) is written by Ken Hodge, vice-president of Mercer Management Consulting, Inc., Boston. "The Long View" (Jan., 11-15) is written by Nancy Chambers, a writer based in Pawcatuck, Conn.

Future forecaster Faith Popcorn's techniques are discussed in Popcorn, F. (1992). *The Popcorn Report: Faith Popcorn on the Future of Your Company, Your World, Your Life.* New York: HarperCollins Publishers.

The Art of the Long View, by Peter Schwartz. The book details *scenario building,* the innovative method of fleshing out alternative futures, and selecting strategies for adaptive business planning.

Frankl, V.E. (1962). *Man's Search for Meaning: An Introduction to Logotherapy.* Boston: Beacon Press.

Frankl, V.E. (1978). *The Unheard Cry for Meaning.* New York: Touchstone, Simon and Schuster Publishers.

Chapter 9

Great Expectations
and Grand Assumptions

Expectation and anticipation are powerful contributors to goal attainment. Grand assumptions distort executives and organizations, limiting their survival, adequacy, growth, and meaningfulness. Great expectations are not grand assumptions. They are powerful invitations.

- Forecasting Success: Powerful Invitations
- A Walk on the Dark Side of Power
- Assumptions and the Jackass Syndrome: *Pygmalion Effects, Genesis Complex, Houdini Magic*
- The Right Person, the Right Place, at the Right Time

Sophocles. *Antigone.*
It's hard to know the mind of any mortal, or the heart,
till he[she] be tried in chief authority.
Power shows the [person].

Manfred F. R. Kets de Vries. *Neurotic Organizations*
". . . There are striking similarities between the neurotic behavior of individuals and the practices of failing or borderline businesses. In such neurotic companies, strategy, structure and organizational climate often reflect the neurotic styles and fantasies of the top echelon of managers."

Forecasting Success: Powerful Invitations

A quest of consequence resonates with anticipation. Adventurers are brimming with curiosity, anxiety, and attraction. Each venture begins with a time of expectation and a rush to readiness. The mission is envisioned as filled with challenging-but-achievable risks. Executives gamble on their power to invite others to join the quest. They solicit strong contributors, seeking to sign on those who have initiative and are willing to commit to the vision and goals.

Finding and motivating achievers calls for a special kind of invitational power with a management approach that is more-than participative and different-from autocratic. Applying methods similar to those recommended for *invitational teaching*, executives align stated expectations and goals with leadership practices. An early indication that a leader is relying on invitational power is when doing-whatever-it-takes resonates with ethical clarity.

Invitational expectations are viewed as genuine when the leader supports announced standards and goals through adequate budgets, staffing, space and equipment. Invitational executives are busy dedicating dollars, people, and tools that promote their intentions, using their executive power without apology and without neglecting fairness and integrity. An internal sense-of-direction is embedded in an unwavering willingness to work as hard and long as necessary, and to continuously remain open to improvement. They come across as different from dictatorial, yet with convincing authority.

Executives, like this, who are able in and of themselves to be a compelling institutional presence, became highly valued in the wake of noticeable reductions in trust, security, and loyalty among survivors of corporate re-formations. Similar executive icon effects are featured in autobiographies of American walk-the-talk leaders. Jefferson, Thoreau, Eleanor Roosevelt and Martin Luther King remind us that persons whose great expectations were achieved by inviting, inspiring, and enlisting others have been admired in every age.

An Uncommon Hero: An Invitational Approach

De was a military hero of unusual ethical competence who had a talent for finding unusual McGuyver/A-Team-ways to get the job done, whether it was setting up communications centers for command posts or serving as the base commanding officer. When WWII shooting ended and the years of supervisory rehabilitation began, this practical leader found that invitational power worked best. He chose methods natural to him, with inherent appeal to higher motivations.

During the decade following the end of World War II, De served as military governor and war trials judge in a remote Bavarian county. Later, he was assigned to be commandant of a military base and training center in a neighboring region. Each Sunday he, his wife and their three children sat together on the front pew of the base chapel. Afterward they ate noonday dinner in the mess hall with an extended family—the several hundred young soldiers assigned to that hilltop communications school.

During the winter months, De and his children sat among the ardent fans at the post gymnasium to enjoy fast-paced basketball games. Together, they cheered for the home team, the two-time league champions, a team that became the orange-corps pride of the European Theater. On-duty hours were filled with communications training coursework. Classroom instructional methods were enlivened with innovative technology, such as televised magnifications that showed big screen details of making radio repairs. The then-new methods were the ideas of the commandant. He also advised the instructors to provide frequent recognition to individual achievement. The cadre and the students were proud to demonstrate their drill skills and coordinated collective excellence for touring VPIs.

A home town atmosphere prevailed more than 6,000 miles from the USA home soil. De's willingness to be fully present and genuinely engaged with his troops as a wholesome role model was reinforced because of his allocation of resources to support and reward healthy activities. De's earlier post-war role as a judge of war crimes led him to stand resolute that no one in his family would buy-up and carry-off cultural treasures of the rebuilding country. He encouraged the people in his command to receive foodstuffs and clothing from the U.S. to be distributed to the local poor. He discouraged the men from taking weekend trips with attractive local women who were eager to trade personal favors for gifts from the commissary or post exchange.

De believed it was important to practice American democracy whole-heartedly in that foreign place, and to show trust and respect for his fellow Americans in everyday routines. To the last day. De was a hero who used invitational power to influence his family and the workers he supervised. What I noticed most is that those he led wanted to do and become their best.

This example from the post-World War II era is a reminder of the Nazi quest which gave the word *power* unforgettable negative over-tones. The dark side of nationally organized power is starkly docu-mented in histories of civilizations in both the West and the East. By addressing the negative potentials of executive power directly, we can move beyond reluctance to use the word "power" with the word "invita-tional." A place to begin is with advice that comes from management researchers and executive search firms: be sure to assess the dark side of your candidates.

It's not uncommon for an executive candidate to have attributes that are identified as *musts,* and even most of the *desirable* indicators of success, and also have co-existing flaws. Certain negative characteris-tics undermine effective use of exceptional talents and inhibit corporate progress. Some initially and temporarily hidden flaws qualify as flagrant defects. For example, alcoholism, which destroys the person. And mendacity, which is cancerous for the organization. More subtle but destructive flaws are like ordinary garden weeds that simply take over the yard. Some of these flaws emerge under extended pressure when a virtue is applied to excess. Other times unsuspicious minor flaws conceal a perennial naiveté leading to recurring failures of predictive judgment.

Many flaws that render executive strengths impotent are products of grand assumptions masquerading as a positive expectation. *I can resolve this situation by asserting my strengths harder.* Or, *I am an optimist and must trust this time to be different.* Great expectations also turn counterproductive when a superstar candidate harbors power assumptions colored by greed and aggrandizement. When a talented leader abuses power, it leaves a bad taste of power at its worst, one that can be remembered for a lifetime.

One of my most disconcerting work experiences came about while working as a consultant to a corporate planning unit. The head of the unit, an organizational effectiveness specialist, captivated the imaginations of executives and board members with a vision of creating the largest and most profitable medical center in the southeastern U.S. The scope and promise of the colorfully illustrated plan was seductively logical and commendable, and, unfortunately, without a solid foundation of accurate data and support. Within a year the scheme collapsed, the in-house specialists were dismissed, and I was left to pull local pieces of the dream back together into a coherent packet of short-term objectives.

Negative experiences, like negative connotations of the word power, will, at times, overwhelm all other recollections. The tendency is to see a snake-in-the-grass first and fail to notice spectacular flowers in the hanging gardens where that poisonous creature is traveling. I return to a positive view by thinking about my work with senior managers from every state in the country. I have met a few snakes, but I find the huge majority of organizational leaders to be well intentioned, imaginatively resourceful, and with a genuine sense of humility. They stay on guard against major-league flaws. What they forget to address is work-a-day attributes and actions that can stall a career.

Stories about how blind-spot flaws derail managers from the promotion path are popular dark-side conversations. The good news is that most blind spots may be avoided or remedied. Interviews with 800 executives in 13 organizations by staff of the Center for Creative

Leadership suggested that the fatal flaws of derailment are typically traceable to one of six sources: interpersonal problems; inability to mold a staff; overdependency on a mentor; difficulty with transitions; lack of follow-through; and/or, differences with senior management on matters of policy and strategy. The 360-degree survey evaluations of managers' behaviors are recommended for weeding out garden-variety, personal-flaws and blind spots.

Clinging to an assumption that I am without consequential blemish—*(after all, I'm a jogger and have no problems with stealing, drugs, or spouse or child abuse)*—takes second place to another innocent assumption. *When I am promoted into an executive position, I am in the driver's seat. I call the shots. Except for those few decisions I must run by the big boss, I wield the power.*

It is not necessary to be surprised by the amount of dependence inherent in managerial work. Consider the dependencies handed to a hospital manager who is hired to provide leadership to a patient services department. They rely on suppliers of medications and paraphernalia to administer the medications; repair specialists for oxygen delivery tubes, for hospital bed cranks, for toilet flushers; sanitation and sterilization technicians and inspectors; patients and their families and friends; hospital Board members and their opinions; city, county, state, and federal government regulators. . . . The complete list fills several pages, giving managers in other industries reason to be thankful they do not work in health care. The good news is that dependent relationships can be named and mapped.

Whether a manager's diagram of the department's support network includes 15 or 150 co-dependencies that do not appear on the organization chart, much of a department's achievement relies on work done by persons over whom a manager has no direct authority, supervision, or control. The manager who starts out with a dependency blind spot finds the honeymoon-phase is over and no blindspots remain after a year's experience. Laboriously developed plans are delayed and confounded by external constraints like construction-worker strikes or new enterprises offering similar local services.

In cyberspaced networks of co-workers and globalized production operations, *multiple co-dependency stress reaction (MCSR)* could well become diagnosable as "a manager who feels helplessly overwhelmed by here-and-now job complexities." *MCSR* might be listed in a next dictionary of debilitating mental-afflictions, alphabetically ahead of, and noted as more prevalent than, *multiple-personality disorder*, a diagnosis arising from repression of overwhelming early-life experiences. Tongue-in-cheek ironies aside, shattering an illusion about powerful leverage vested in a manager's job is less likely to bring on a dysfunctional condition than it is to prompt the achievement-oriented manager to learn more about power. "*What can I do to get some action? How can I motivate movement?*" In discovering answers to those questions, managers soon learn about manipulation, another loaded word that is endowed with negative connotations.

A Walk on the Dark Side of Power

If you want to see a highly indignant executive, accuse one of *manipulating* things to suit their own purposes. A brave author proposed that everyone manipulates. He wrote that it's a waste of energy to deny interest in influencing others, or to virtuously declare no desire to have the power to influence outcomes. Everett Shostrom's popular management guide of the 1960s promoted recognizing and admitting one's pattern of manipulations as the first step in learning to apply positive manipulative strategies. He proposed eight manipulation styles, called the *judge,* the *protector,* the *bully,* the *nice guy,* the *calculator,* the *clinging vine,* the *dictator,* and the *weakling.*

A chart of the Shostrom styles, included at the end of this chapter, illustrates how he envisioned a dark-side and a sunny-side for manipulative methods. For example, the *judge* is the name of the style used to denote a person who holds some form of sanctioned authority in a relationship. When wielding power, a *judge* style is used to manipulate in a negative way by being sharply critical of others. The style can shift to a positive tone while continuing to do the work of expressing one's own opinion. The *protector* is the style used by one whose manipulations emanate from a position of no assigned, recognized power, a polar opposite to the power position of a *judge.* A *protector* can, nevertheless, exert dark-side manipulations such as being over-protective. The *protector* shows a sunnyside when acting as an encouraging guide.

It is not hard to understand why Shostrom's slender volume, *Man, the Manipulator* went through 12 printings in 10 years. Readers readily identify themselves and their associates with manipulations described. Moreover, they relish identifying with historical figures who are selected to exemplify each style, i.e., the *weakling* = Eleanor Roosevelt; the *dictator* = Winston Churchill; the *clinging vine* = Pope John; the *judge* = Thomas Jefferson. Fascination with the manipulator concept faded when research did not validate this clever analog.

A more objective, and now classic, observation and codification of ways people influence others proposed five "bases of power" that were successfully linked to formal investigations of leadership and management practices. Seven bases are currently endorsed as ways that power is exerted over others. In this paradigm, *invitational* power as proposed here would be classified as a form of *legitimate power*, which is defined as an economic and legally-based right to call-the-shots. It is power that is accorded to position. The other bases of power are: [2] expert; [3] referent; [4] reward; [5] coercive; [6] information, and [7] connection.

Both "manipulative styles" and "power bases" were proposed by social scientists who began with a belief that influencing another's behavior is inherently neither good nor bad. Power exerted over others may be experienced as coercive or consentive; and, it may appeal to higher or lower values and motivations. Problems are likely to arise as the use of power is contaminated by a leader engrossed with grand assumptions. Whether from a sense of inadequacy, or in the aftermath of organizational confusion, these leaders can shift to dark-side strategies. Heroes become anti-heroes, and act more from self-serving assumptions than in the interests of collective benefits and productive expectations.

Anti-Hero

An example of self-serving power comes from leadership in a fifty-five-year-old professional association. Professionals are pledged to a code of ethics and practice standards and, therefore, generally believed to be a locus of Platonic and democratic ideals. This story about a president of a small group of practitioners and academics is as stereotype breaking as finding an invitational hero in a military setting.

Instead of finding open-minded, mutual respect, the situation reveals a self-aggrandizing mind-set, where authoritarianism overwhelms a naïve change-agent. This leader's Dr. Jekyll-Mr. Hyde transition from a low profile, buddy-buddy colleague to a gloating, throttle-the-opposition chief officer shows the truth behind Sophocles' lines in *Antigone:* "It is hard to know the mind, or the heart, of any mortal till he [she] be tried in chief authority. Power shows the [person]."

During a lengthy period as secretary of the association, the not-yet-elected-president's conversation sparkled with elaborate anecdotes of his unparalleled dedication to family, to colleagues, and to all-American football. Once finished with conference planning tasks as president-elect, he suddenly underwent a metamorphosis, becoming an unabashed autocrat, bristling with hubris and self-satisfaction. Passionate in his top-dog role, he ostracized and de-powered the treasurer, the administrative officer, and an influential past-president.

He began directly supervising the work of office staffpersons who were subordinates of the administrative officer. His micromanaging involved withholding information and introducing dis-information. He planted seeds of distrust about strong association leaders and contributors. Dropping all ingratiating manners, he discounted or ignored anything done or said by the administrative officer. This contracted director of the society's central office was a professional colleague hired to revive and invigorate the association. She worked for five years as peer-collaborator with two previous presidents.

The administrative officer, who received a token salary and expenses that did not cover actual costs of operating the society, found the shift in leadership confusing, frustrating, and insulting. When the president asked for feedback on how things were going, the administrative officer naively and straightforwardly stated concerns and issues as a colleague. Subsequently, the president cut-off communication and circulated ambiguous rumors about the administrative officer's abusive supervision, self-serving motives, and even possible misappropriation of association funds.

This president, who wept openly in his first meeting with other elected officers because he had, at long last, wrested organizational power from his arch-rival in the discipline, permitted no discussion of differences in management philosophy. He believed himself, with some justification, to be an expert in his narrow specialty within this academic field. The problem arose when he expanded his expert role to mean he was also expert in management even though he had no formal training and minimal experience.

His overestimation of himself, or overcompensation for a prior sense of inadequacy, led him to indulge in practices where he could seem all-knowing and all-powerful. He left a wake of froth and fume. Over the next several years, two office managers were dismissed, private-club mentality revived, conference attendance went down, and one event went into debt in excess of $85,000.

Prior to events described above, the association contracted with a colleague with management background to turn around the shrinking, isolated, and out-of-date organization. That vision of an inclusive mission was dismissed by the anti-hero leader. Perhaps, it all happened because a president's dark-side took control. Perhaps, it was because the culture of the group was not ready for non-authoritarian relationships that allows several individuals to be equally, but differentially, influential. The result was a situation of no-growth with no viable merger or acquisition options.

Amazingly similar stories are told about power struggles in bureaucratic organizations. One such dark-side story comes from an article reporting the derailment of a government agency manager who accepted an assignment to straighten out and shape-up a sloppy work unit. In an interview a former CIA employee, given anonymity as "Jane Doe Thompson," explained how she took on a job assignment with specific instructions about disciplinary management of certain subordinates. These direct reports, soon submitted, fabricated accusations against her character. The subordinates' accusations were taken seriously by headquarters' staff who knew the charges came from persons suspected of misconduct. Nevertheless, agency officials proceeded with actions against Jane Doe Thompson, ending her career and, in the process, causing her husband to lose his job.

Disgruntled workers sabotaged organizational improvement efforts, culminating in an internal bureaucratic backfire. In the professional association, a subordinate not selected for promotion complained loudly that she had been unfairly treated by the administrator who was ripping-off the association. The direct report claimed she had not received certain paychecks, checks which she later acknowledged that she had "mislaid." As happened to turn-around manager Jane Doe Thompson, accusations against the association's hired change-agent were taken seriously. Unlike the pre-informed government headquarters staff, association board members were unfamiliar with the complainant's history of temper outbursts, vengeful retaliations against other co-workers, and under-the table income requests.

The president capitalized on the accusations and doted on the disgruntled employee as the victim of an unscrupulous administrator. Managers who find themselves in similar no-win, dark-side power conflicts, find refuge in gallows humor and reading office graffiti – *for every action there is an equal and opposite criticism; no good deed goes unpunished.* They take solace in studying Machiavelli, Dilbert, and self-help books like *How to Swim with the Sharks and Survive.* Those who step beyond the circle of disillusionment and sarcasm become wiser and less willing to be set-up as a miracle worker.

Assumptions and the Jackass Syndrome
Pygmalion Effects, Genesis Complex, Houdini Magic

Simply put, the quest for executive effectiveness can turn into a self-serving or image-defending power trip that is debilitating to the organization and abusive to co-workers. Hubris and sacrificial offerings of expendable managers are considered signs of an executive's failure to cope with anxiety emotions. These behaviors become a substitute for working out productive responses to surprise and change. Psychiatrist Karen Horney includes a *need-for-power* as one of several ways people deal with basic anxiety. She found that the several essential emotions, when unacknowledged and undisciplined, manifest in ways that can be described as a need for power, a need for prestige, or a need to exploit others. Each need can escalate into unhealthy or counterproductive resolutions of conflict. Some groups of therapists say efforts to exclude conflict from awareness evoke neurotic strategies, resulting in clinical conditions that have faint but recognizable echoes in normal states. "My way or the highway" is a workplace parallel in which the need for personal power influences the resolution of conflict.

Blatant use of one's job or organizational position in the service of one's inadequacies or deficiencies is not likely to contribute to corporate effectiveness in the long run. On the other hand, it is realistic for workers to expect to meet important normal personal needs as a consequence of employment in an organization. Conflicts can be expected to occasionally arise between individual needs and organizational needs, even in prospering ventures and especially in rapidly changing industries. Constructive resolution of such conflicts relies heavily on self-acceptance, satisfaction with life achievements, and experience in managing workplace dependencies, competition, and camaraderie. When leaders have not become skilled in ways of responding in the face of inevitable conflict, conditions are ripe for the *jackass syndrome* to emerge.

Some leaders, spiked by the grand assumption that power is an executive toy, miss the point of an often-told management-training joke. The instructor-humorist says, "Always remember, it's dangerous to assume you know what's right, or best, for anyone else. It's impossible to be sure what is going on in someone else's mind and heart. When I take for granted that I know best or that I am sure what you think or know, then I make an ass/u/me, an ass of u and me."

More than two decades ago Harry Levinson wrote *The Great Jackass Fallacy*. He continues to write about and consult with executives who fall into the trap of assuming that the "good employee is the willing-to-be-controlled-and-rewarded employee." And today's managers continue to report to me, as they did to Levinson, that they often feel themselves to be the jackasses caught between executives' carrot-and-stick strategies.

Jackass Case: Beware of Fast-Track "Carrots"

This is the story of a manager in a Tennessee-based corporate center who reports the consequences of accepting his superior's offer of an early career "opportunity for fast-track advancement." He was brought from the field into the corporate headquarters, given responsibility for administering the new corporate-wide performance motivation and quality improvement plan. He learned a hard lesson. After the program's introduction, full of high-intensity hype and full-court press, the superior moved on to higher, broader corporate realms.

The early-career "fast-tracker" remained, without a mentor, in the midst of peers and co-workers who were harboring resentments about abrupt, incomplete, and unwelcomed changes brought about as part of the quality improvement program. Peers saw the unwanted changes as caused by this outside enforcer, a hot-shot kid with no history as one-of-them. This fast-tracker acquired a "mole" stigma. He felt their distrust and skepticism on a daily basis. Other managers attending the seminar in which he described his experience, especially those also employed in quasi-governmental organizations, empathized. One said, "I felt like a 'jackass' after letting myself get carried-away with my 'leadership' role during a fever of management improvement." Two others quickly said, "Same here." "Me, too." Their once great expectations turned out to be figments of executives' grand assumptions and aggrandizements.

The executive causing the mangers' discomfort is the featured component in the jackass syndrome that is broken out into three especially troublesome varieties of coercion. These dark-side practices, *Pygmalion effects, the Genesis complex*, and *Houdini Magic*, illustrate how leaders who are without major-league flaws shift to over-controlling or egotistical manipulations.

Pygmalion Effects

Pygmalion is George Bernard Shaw's story of an uneducated, cockney-English girl, Eliza Doolittle, who was transformed into a cultured, British-lady by Professor Henry Higgins. The rags-to-riches tale won an enduring place in twentieth-century culture as the successful musical stage show and Hollywood film, *My Fair Lady*. In this Cinderella fable for grown-up city folk, the fairy godmother and the handsome prince are combined into one character who becomes the managing director of the poor but talented heroine, who must work hard to perfect her skills.

Less dramatically entertaining, but fundamentally similar, giant leaps in performance abilities are found in technical reports of coaching techniques and worker productivity. Improvements observed in controlled studies occurred most frequently when the coach and trainee were open and trusting with each other, when both accepted responsibilities fully, and when the trainee saw (a) the coach as a good model, and (b) the rewards for improvement as suitable.

Both Eliza Doolittle and Henry Higgins had great expectations, a vision of the goal plus a conviction that the necessary abilities were present in each of them. All that remained to be done involved arranging "conditions" and "contingencies" to set in motion a self-fulfilling prophecy. Training and rewards led to the achievement of what they expected to achieve. The fair-lady plot has variations in ancient lore and in scientific inquiries.

A workplace version is found in the frequently cited "Hawthorne studies" conducted at the Western Electric plant in Chicago during the 1930s. Some cite these earliest experimental investigations of influences on worker productivity as solid evidence that output improves if managers pay attention to the people doing the work. Improved statistics lent impetus to a management philosophy that *consideration* of workers' comforts, preferences, interests, and abilities leads to improved performance. Others, however, like Harry Levinson, point to the Hawthorne studies as one more example of the old "jackass between the carrot and stick" routine. The skeptics of *consideration* theory observed that, concurrent with the research program, impatient executives also motivated productivity by striking fear into the hearts of workers who didn't want to lose their jobs.

Radically different interpretations of the Hawthorne studies are possible because numerous studies were conducted at Western Electric. Results from individual projects or a small subset of the whole were reported periodically during the investigation. When reviewed all together, as a complete series or as a total collection, the comprehensive data do not provide a clear-cut, cohesive conclusion. For example, productivity went up when workers were placed in a more favorable setting, and also went up when the employees were placed in less comfortable circumstances. The human relations interpretation of these seemingly contradictory outcomes is that better work was a result of special attention, i.e., being selected to be part of a research study.

Nay-sayers to this argument hold a different assumption about motivation, and their point is well taken. It turns out that statistics indicating productivity improvement did not show up until after executives fired two dissident employees, who behaved as if they were independent from management. They were replaced by two employees who were more agreeable. Apparently countermanagement attitudes and project saboteurs needed to be weeded-out before a success story could be proved. Might this, then, qualify as an arranging of contingencies for a self-fulfilling prophecy?

Having the power to turn someone into an outstanding performer is a wish common among managers, as well as athletic coaches, Broadway play directors, and classroom teachers. An ability to influence another's behaviors or perceptions can be used to promote fulfillment of another's latent capability and life dreams, or it can be wielded to obtain employers' and supervisors' vested interests.

In effect, organizations assign managers to Pygmalion duty. The manager, besides being required to plan, organize, and control technical efficiency, is instructed to train, coach and mentor junior employees so that they attain performance excellence. This gives some managers cause to wonder: *Am I developing this person to serve the organization's ends—and, by the way, to make me look promotable; or, am I mentoring this person to bring out their own natural abilities? Am I an organizational henchman, or a human abilities facilitator?*

Most motivation experts agree that no motives are pure; and that organizational motives are *a priori* productivity-driven. Invitational executives and managers hear their inner dialogue and heed the fine line between exploitation and development. Task-focused or person-focused, managers agree that believing you can achieve a goal is a first requisite.

In R. Rosenthal and L. Jacobsen's widely publicized test of the self-fulfilling prophecy, circular influences were directly linked to positive gains in performance. In this study, classroom teachers were told that certain students' standard exam scores indicated they would have an academic spurt during the school year. In order to conduct a credible experiment, the investigators had randomly identified the spurt students. There were no facts to support their predictions. Nevertheless, testing at the end of the year showed the predicted students did improve academically more than their classmates. Researchers concluded the spurt occurred because the teachers were primed to look for potentials to manifest and gave extra attention to the spurters. Thus, the exceptional improvement by students who did not know they were predicted to have a burst of academic skill development was attributed to expectation-prompted behavior of the teacher-manager.

One of the first Pygmalion-type tales of Western civilization is a story of a mythical Greek, King Cyprus, who fell in love with a mythical goddess, Aphrodite. Early Roman lore speaks of a human-like god who carved a statue of the perfect woman and fell in love with it. In that romantic Italian version, the carving came to life as Venus. Undoubtedly, the carver of the Venus statue, like Henry Higgins, paid meticulous attention to minute details, and was relentless in task activities, e.g., Higgins insisted on Eliza's countless repetitions of "the rain in Spain falls mainly on the plain" until the enunciation was perfect.

A non-fictional twentieth-century psychologist, B. F. Skinner, was eloquently and unashamedly militant about arranging environments to elicit productive performances. Skinner, author of *Walden II,* writes in *Beyond Freedom and Dignity* that poet John Keats drank confusion to Newton for analyzing the rainbow, but the rainbow remained as beautiful as ever and became for many even more beautiful (p. 203). Skinner argued that when rainbows and humans are known accurately, effective management is possible. He used experimental analysis to show that rainbows and humans are controlled by the environment, which can be largely controlled by humans. "The evolution of a culture is a gigantic exercise in self-control" (p. 205).

In spite of poetic and scientific arguments about positive consequences of manipulation, the dark-side of humans brainwashing other humans remains a frightening prospect and perpetuates the apprehension associated with words like power and manipulation. When invitational expectation becomes grand assumption, talents used to excess turn strengths into flaws. Results can be perverse and degrading, as was discovered by families of youth attracted to "reshaping" programs of charismatic personalities like Sung Moon in Seattle during the 1970s.

Genesis Complex

The jackass syndrome prompted by a self-serving interest produces a drive to be first and best—a genesis complex. The Greek word "genesis" means origination, creation, formation. On the surface, the term represents a noble ambition that is admired and promoted in many U.S. households. Strong achievement striving is rarely considered a major flaw. Even so, in excess, this externally benchmarked and openly competitive motivation grows like the weed that takes over the garden.

The person who begins a company or initiates a project acquires a special importance. Being first within an organization, as a member of a group, or in a sequence of events, implies power. Holding first place gives status in most Western cultures. It even enters into gender issues. Certain religious groups advocate a Judeo-Christian theory that God created woman second by taking one of Adam's ribs, thus making the female subordinate to the male. Others prefer a biological explanation, based on the natural cycle of embryo development in birds and other living creatures. All are at first female, with the male of the species being formed as a secondary development—a consequence of changes to the basic pattern. The naturalist scenario makes the female first.

The drive to be number 1 is experienced to some degree by every sports fan, every marathon runner, every dedicated filmmaker. Those with the desire to be in first place, to come out ahead of others, to create an artwork better than the last one, comes face-to-face with the Genesis specter. Achievers can become obsessed by expectations that turn into demanding assumptions.

These demands are summed up as dangerous "more-thans" by physician Sanford Danzigler and Krista Daehler-Danzigler in their book *The Power Balance.* They are concerned about people who take the "power of positive thinking" to the extreme by saying to themselves: I am more objective. I am more sensitive. I am more intelligent. I am more organized. I'm unique. I'm faster. I'm more responsible. I'm more experienced. I'm more compassionate.

Those who take this inner self-talk too seriously can be caught in a trap. They feel an unrelenting pressure to be "more and more." According to the Danziglers, the achiever with a continuous improvement motto, who is thinking that "I am (or, must become) more-than . . .," tends to overshoot the mark. I notice that, while overdosing on positive self-accolades and targeted self-improvement goals may help to overcome shyness, anxiety, or skepticism, the process leaves little time for attention to others.

High expectations become assumptions when achievers think (a) that it is NOT OK that others are not as smart—or caring, or busy, or dedicated as I am; and (b) think that when someone else shows up with more experience, more speed, more persistence, then my ability is diminished; or, (c) when achievers believe that others should notice and appreciate me more than they do because of the fact that *I work harder, I am so fair and honest.* The Danziglers have examples from their practice to show connections between such thoughts and successful work, successful relationships, and good health. My emphasis is on how a genesis drive with subsequent entitlements subtly inhibits invitational power, and can subvert genuine expectations.

Being hailed as championship caliber, as a first-place trophy winner, as worthy to wear a golfing master's green jacket, is so important in college cultures and public sports that young executives easily transfer that emotional zeal to their corporate striving. It's easy to get caught up in a Fortune 500 rush, or to become possessed by a Baldridge Award competition. At the very least, the executive over-achiever wants, for the resume, solo credit for one original product that is now a household word in the industry, or for leading a major project credited with "more thans"—more revenues, more cost savings, completed more quickly. . . .

Public accolades feed the sense that I am the genius behind something *more than* anyone else. Being seen as prime-mover is a seductive, tasty portion of life. A widely touted maxim claims that everyone should have at least one standing ovation in their memory. The caveat here is that the tragic cost of wanting repeated and louder applause is recorded in biographies of authors, politicians, and stock market executives who preferred death to not being able to equal or better their last triumph.

A surprising aspect of the godlike genesis complex is guilt and self-blame. The manager who says *"the buck stops here"* implies personal power and liability. The words suggest that I am more able to handle mistakes or problems, and I am more in control of things and events than anyone else. Noble as these words spoken by Harry Truman ring, they are also words of self-indictment and culpability. Being responsible for making things right all the time is a heavy burden, not to mention a misconception of reality. Unlike Harry Truman, corporate executives seldom need to assume the blame for a world-class catastrophic event. The few notable exceptions like gigantic oil spills, the Three-Mile Island incident, Chernoble, and chemical plant disasters in India are as stigmatized as is Truman's decision to drop the atomic bomb on Hiroshima. That bomb, for all practical purposes, ended World War II, but also left a cloud of shame that even Harry's down-to-earth pragmatism could not dissipate.

Superheroic executive behavior is seen as charismatic, and can lead to achieving once-impossible dreams, but also can, like steroids, carry destructive side-effects. Steroids artificially enhance athletic strengths, producing spurts in physical capabilities. These short-lived gains, in worst-case scenarios, are acquired at a high price, and even premature death. In corporate arenas, private and public sectors, pumped-up executives' dreams and visions become delusional and paranoid. Consequences of radical leadership are felt in every part of the world—a mass suicide in a Swiss-Canadian cult in 1994; poison gases released in

Tokyo's subways in 1995; car bombs driven into embassy houses, the bombing of an Oklahoma federal building, Heaven's Gate cult group suicides, kidnappings and executions by Middle Eastern terrorists.

Less extreme radicalism can be spotted in the work place, especially in times of surging bull-markets or in endangered economies. An example comes from harshly captioned reports about "Chainsaw Al," a CEO who boasted that he "axed" 11,000 employees.

Hero Turned Antihero Tale. Chainsaw Al Dunlap.

The one-time Sunbeam CEO, tagged chainsaw by the press and some employees, was hired by an established, but struggling producer of household appliances because of his reputation for turning around a business, making it profitable by radical restructuring and regrouping, cutting costs and personnel. Hailed as Rambo-in-Pinstripes, Dunlap championed corporate shareholders in his best-seller book, *Mean Business: How I Save Bad Companies and Make Good Companies Great.*

This time things were different. Dunlap initially painted a glowing forecast of profits of $1 per share in 1998. His predicted corporate climb to success first seemed to be true as stock prices more than doubled to $51 per share. However, in June 1998, immediately after Dunlap's salary was doubled and his contract extended three years, shares plummeted to $11.2. This was lower than the $12.50 per share price when Dunlap was hired in August of 1996. Sunbeam shares went down 78 percent in the few months following Dunlap's decision to go forward with a $2 billion acquisition of three other companies, Mr. Coffee, First Alert, and Coleman. Dunlap, a published advocate of giving directors shares and not salaries, was fired by a Board made up of members who were major shareholders. They allowed Dunlap no severance package. The once-thought superheroic leader who made his living axing others was axed in kind.

The well-intentioned achievement quest is an emboldened form of the competitive spirit when it shifts into a dark-side genesis complex. Competitiveness has become highly regarded and is a vaunted business-culture status symbol. A superiority drive that demands self-promotion and requires the put-down of others is a dangerous arrogance. It may produce short-term "wins" but can quickly crash and burn.

Houdini Magic

Houdini, Siegfried and Roy, the Great Kreskin, and David Copperfield, like skilled magicians through the ages, captivate audiences using science, perceptual tricks, and attention management. They exert power over events, fascinating their incredulous admirers. Unable to comprehend wondrous feats performed in front of their eyes, audiences are happily entertained, and few pursue learning the mechanics of the tricks. Just as some of us are mesmerized by staged charisma—top hats, glittering capes, swishing wands, beautiful assistants, regal jungle tigers, and massive, intricate apparatus—others of us are intrigued by the workplace leader who "rallies the troops" with a compelling vision, speech, and promise. Employees who willingly do whatever a manager-magician instructs are not hypnotized. They are happy to see finished products and a paycheck and prefer not to bother with learning details of processes, or the science behind how it happened.

Charismatic leaders are noticeably influential during times of crisis and hardship. Such is the story of Antonio Conselheiro, a nineteenth-century Brazilian victim-hero. Conselheiro led an unsuccessful and catastrophic backlands rebellion. The thousands of disenfranchised poor and unhealthy whom he had gathered in a hard to access place called "wet-city" were boxed in by the national military and died miserably without gaining government support for the needy population. Only recollections of the revered leader, Conselheiro, are noted by historians.

Business and government executives who address crisis and hardship usually project an appealing charisma that differs from the charisma of self-sacrificing, social-cause zealots willing to be martyred. The invitational-style corporate leader promotes life and dialogue. And unlike the magician, the invitational executive is not reluctant to discuss secrets of strategies and mechanics. Inspirational business managers stand ready to describe the logic that informs corporate goals, priorities, and methods. They repeatedly invite others to evaluate, replicate, or improve procedures and products.

Incredible undertakings that are not submitted to scrutiny and reality testing will set in motion neurotic and irrational behaviors. Five distinguishing characteristics of counterproductive operations are noted by Uri Merry and George I. Brown. They report that neurotic organizational behavior can be defined as (1) repetitive patterns of (2) pathologic (3) seemingly unchangeable (4) organization behavior (5) involving distortion of reality.

Similar circumstances are mapped in anthropological histories of the rise and fall of civilizations. Historically, an individual with charisma who is also healthy and stable, not like an Adolph Hitler, is considered critical when old systems and actions fail to be productive for formulating new systems, for communicating the ideas, and for organizing, adapting, and transforming the group into a new routine.

Taking a deep look at repetitive patterns in organizational life, McGill University's Manfred Kets de Vries speculates how executives imprint organizational culture. He describes five ineffectual influences, suggesting each style is like black-magic, a spell cast by senior executives upon the workforce: *dramatic, depressive, paranoid, compulsive* and *schizoid.*

Anti-Hero Types

A *Dramatic* executive displays bold, ambitious, grandiose leadership, and the management group emulates this energetic, audacious pattern. Negative consequences of such hubris are predicted to occur as the firm continuously overextends its resources, until early burnout. Did this happen at Sunbeam?

The *Depressive* executive puts into play centralized decision-making, misplaced cost-cutting measures and public scoldings. Depressive-style is characterized by the appointment of a mouthpiece deputy who assigns tasks and carries out the face-to-face management, following the executive's directives to the letter. Depressive behaviors lead to stagnation, decreasing profitability, and, eventually, a depressed organization. Is this the fate of the professional association?

Paranoid executives and businesses are full of suspiciousness and hyper-alertness. Leaders are concerned with hidden motives and suspect corporate infiltration by enemies or incompetents, and waste employees' time and talent in witch-hunts. This differs from the *paranoia* Andy Grove discusses in his best-selling book, *Only the Paranoid Survive: How to Exploit the Crisis Points That Challenge Every Company.* Grove's attention-grabbing message is a red flag for saying that a leader, to stay a leader, needs to be vigilant in noticing changes in business fundamentals and in customers' needs and interests. Grove talks about *morphing* the business, i.e., *shaping* the company so that it keeps up with the *Zeitgeist,* the spirit of the times. He is not addressing the paranoia behind repeatedly locking onto a phantom enemy heat-missile that might be out to zap you.

Compulsive organizations reflect the perfectionist executive who is preoccupied with trivial details. In the wake of micromanagement comes a lack of spontaneity, ironclad dogmatism, and an over-reliance on regulations and conformity (i.e., as claimed in criticisms of legal systems; and, in federal regulations guiding preliminary testing for new medicine and drug therapies).

The *Schizoid* pattern is reflected in subordinates' detachment, similar to that of the fast-track manager hero who got hooked, dumped, and burned by joining a short-lived quality improvement band-wagon. Double-messages turn corporate reality into a zone of smoke-and-mirrors, an environment that can no longer be trusted. A schizoid-style executive may be hyperactive and excitable, or may be aloof and remote, but each demands action toward unrealistic or contradictory objectives.

Even without imminent crises, and with no neurotic tendencies, workplace shadows are generated when leaders accept credit for "pulling the rabbit out of the hat." Executives with eloquent and elegant logic make corporate priorities appear and disappear in the twinkling of an eye. Powerful speaking and writing abilities are rare and valued talents, ones known to be readily crafted into forked-tongues. For example, job application resumes were reported on National Public Radio as places of deceit. A Chicago search firm reported that 75% of the resumes that they receive contain major embellishments and one-third are flat-out fabrications. Moreover, and harder to combat, are the spins put into on-going business transactions. Clever, subtle, beguiling language deftly blames and absolves from blame, slicing information to save face and to ingratiate, especially where fresh power is rising. For example, an international leader selected a title for his major conference event using some words identical to those of a symposium title submitted by a smaller organization.

After reviewing a draft of the conference program schedule, the senior leader angrily asserted preeminent and exclusive right to reserve words used in the title. As requested /instructed, the subordinate leader changed wording for her group's event, even though that terminology (including the word "forum") was in established-usage in the smaller association for a number years.

A third leader, newly assuming office in the secondary organization, wrote to the senior leader for clarifications about the several roundtables she was to attend. A cordial explanation commented that it was no wonder that people got confused since a group tried to make use of the same wording reserved for use in the general program. Thus, blame was attributed to a lesser leader, while other leaders were absolved from contribution to any confusions.

In an historical how-to guide on the abuse of power by the powerful, Niccolo Machiavelli wrote his tour de force, *The Prince*. In an effort to prove himself after a change in political leadership, he filled the manual with vigorous imagery, the bluntness of which was taken too literally by contemporaries and by posterity. Machiavelli was a soldier without a job in 1512 after the Medici put down freedom fighters in Italy and the Pope returned to power. After a time in prison, he retreated to Florence where he penned his management wisdoms in hyperbole, which he hoped would convince the new powers to recognize his cleverness and then give him a job. Because of his ingratiating activities, his shifting allegiance, and his caustic management treatises, he did get small jobs as a historian. However, he was never able to regain his former stature as a man of integrity and promoter of rights for the common person.

Executives, advisors and consultants who proclaim their technique will stop inefficiencies and bring profits are playing Houdini. Ethically, forecasters are limited to making probability statements about the expected success of goals and strategies intended to reduce worry, work pressures, and anxiety. When present problems are solved, other problems will fill the void. Answering today's questions leads directly to tomorrow's questions. Managers, who assume a magician's aura, perform perceptual tricks as they present statistics or when they redirect attention. They leave intentional informational gaps, knowing others will fill in the blanks, giving the magician credit where credit isn't due. One consultant I admired and learned from in my early career astonished me while we were working on clarification of decision-making authorities given to managers in a medical center. He was asked by a staff member if he was a doctor. His response was "Yes, as a matter of fact, I am." I knew that he had not earned an M.D., a Ph.D., a J.D., or any other terminal graduate degree. He later explained to me that he once received an honorary doctorate from a small college in a remote country. That was the beginning of my moving away from this working alliance.

The Right Person, the Right Place, and the Right Time

We are wrong to think that human nature is the determinant of culture. It is quite the reverse, culture is the determinant of human nature. . . . Culture is the organization of phenomena—acts (patterns of behavior), objects (tools, things made with tools), ideas (belief, knowledge), and sentiments (attitudes, "values")—that is dependent upon the use of symbols. . . . Culture began when man as an articulate, symbol-using primate, began . . . it flows down through the ages from one generation to another and laterally from one people to another . . . culture is . . . a symbolic, continuous, cumulative, and progressive process . . . it is a system sui generis *[a force unto itself]. . . . We are convinced that the great man is best understood as an effect or manifestation rather than as a prime mover. p. 190*

Leslie White. *The Science of Culture.* 1949.

Powerful invitations convey great expectations. Invitational executives avoid the sand traps of grand assumptions by reducing personal blind spots and by steering clear of excessive or exaggerated strengths. At the same time, they *carpe diem,* seize the day. A sense of timing becomes acute, like that of a trained hunting dog whose keen sense of scent leads it to the quarry, and who then waits to move in response to the next movement. When the mission is to lead, the powerful invitations are extended in keeping with both the time and the place. *Zeitgeist* and *ortgeist,* the thinking of the times and the mind of the place, inform decisions and strategies that keep managers out of repetitive, defeating patterns like those described as dramatic, depressive, compulsive, paranoid, and schizoid styles.

In an era of business globalization and increasing exposure to the differences between managers who learned the ropes in group-centered (Eastern) societies and managers who were trained in individual-centered (Western) societies, the East-West debate about the greater good of collectivism or individualism continues. The arguments are reminiscent of statements made by Leslie White. He stood opposed to the popular great-person theories of his day and concluded that leadership is an effect of the social and cultural conditions more than a consequence of individual characteristics.

Do successful achievements and watershed innovations came about because of the presence of a person with exceptional talents, or are they determined by social-cultural ideas and sentiments, with the person but a pawn used by the flow of events? Does the collectivism - individualism difference have any connection to the day-to-day business world? Actually, it does.

For example, it is a significant consideration to specialists who assess "Western" managers for selection to work in the "Eastern" offices of an international company and must define the differences in generic strengths typical of Western and Eastern managers. Some boil it down to those with competencies in short-term action (Western) and those with competencies for long-range endurance (Eastern). Hard-driving, direct, goal-focused North Americans are believed to bring needed balance and enthusiasm to the calm, indirect, protocol-focused East Asian. The indirect, relationship-building, impeccably respectful collectivists ride unwaveringly through troubled waters, showing the way of continuous progress toward their destination. The attributes of both, as long as neither is assumed to be better, are envisioned as complementary and beneficial in a corporation.

I see a growing consensus among the geneticists and biobehaviorists that 80% of what an individual is or can be is "given" at birth. What a person can do with the remaining 20% is as impressive as the shifting of a compass setting by less than 20 degrees. A Los Angeles executive could wind up in Sydney rather than Hong Kong. In a ying-yang approach, one can respect the power of the culture, remain humble about individual power, and in no way dilute respect for those distinctive individuals with vision and a willingness to do what it takes to turn that vision inside out. Those with an invitational style will hesitate to force either-or decisions and avoid premature assumptions.

Background Reading

The great person versus the ripeness of the time, synchronicity, debates have subsided since the middle of the twentieth century. The leading contributor to theories supporting the coincidence of events and cultural beliefs as the primary selection of leaders was Leslie White. *The Science of Culture.* 1949 pp. 130-140. Others have continued the stream of thought, but in diverse ways, such as the work of scientist B. F. Skinner, author of *Beyond Freedom and Dignity.*

Psychoanalytic interpretations of organizational life / culture is found in numerous publications by Manfried F. Kets de Vries. *Power and the Corporate Mind; Organisational Paradoxes: Clinical Approaches to Management; The Neutrotic Organization: Diagnosing and Changing Counterproductive Styles of Management; Unstable at the Top.* Also, Kets de Vries and Sidney Perzow. *Handbook of Character Studies: Psychoanalytic Explorations.* 1991. Madison, Connecticut: International Universities Press.

Harry Levinson wrote *The Great Jackass Fallacy,* now a classic title, based on his work training managers and executives at the Levinson Institute in New England. His book, *The Executive,* is another popular guidebook. Levinson continues to produce articles and hone insights, and to consult with leading corporate figures.

Everett Shostrum's Descriptions of Manipulative Patterns.

Dark-side and Sunny-Side

What's important & how it comes across:		Dark side	Sunny side
Goals	Judge	Criticalness of others > > > Own Opinion Expresser	
	Protector	Over-Supportive of Others > > > Invitational Guide	
Affect	Bully	Aggression > > > > > > > > > > > > > > Assertion	
	Nice Guy	Phoney Warmth > > > > > > > > > > > > > Carer	
Methods	Calculator	Control > > > > > > > > > > > > > > > > > Respector	
	Clinging Vine	Dependent > > > > > > > > > > > > > > Appreciator	
Social image	Dictator	Dominator > > > > > > > > > > > > > > > > Leader	
	Weakling	Hypersensitive > > > > > > > > > > > Empathasizor	

Franke, R. H. & Kaul, J. D. (1978). The Hawthorne experiments: First statistical interpretation. *American Sociological Review*, 43, 5, 623-642.

French, J.R.P. & Raven, B. (1959). The bases of social power. In D. Cartwright (ed.), *Studies in Social Power.* Ann Arbor, MI: University of Michigan, Institute for Social Research.

Hogan, R., Raskin, R. & Fazzini, D. (1990). The dark side of charisma. In K.E. Clark and M. B. Clark (Eds.), *Measures of Leadership,* pp. 343-354. West Orange, NJ: Leadership Library of America.

Kets de Vries, M.F.R. (1989). *Prisoners of Leadership.* NY: Wiley.

Kets de Vries, M.F.R. (1989). Leaders who self destruct: the causes and cures. *Organizational Dynamics,* 17, 4-17.

Purkey, W.W. (1970). *Self Concept and Student Achievement.* Englewood Cliffs, NJ: Prentice-Hall. Purkey and Betty L. Siegel, President, Kennesaw State University, established the International Alliance for Invitational Education in 1982. "Human potential, though not always apparent, is there waiting to be discovered and invited forth." (Alliance brochure. 1997. School of Education. UNC-Greensboro, NC 27412.)

Chapter 10

"Who's the Boss?"

"Boss" comes from words that mean excellent, and/or, an area that is raised above the surface. Today, a boss is the one in control: calling the shots, setting expectations, giving out rewards and punishments, determining values and standards. Control is action or reaction by an executive in the interest of corporate survival, adequacy, growth, meaningfulness. Control-actions organize, administer, and allocate resources.

- Climbing the Wind is Standing Watch With Hand on the Tiller and Eye on the Sail
- Participatory Command, Control and Communication is Not an Oxymoron
- Charismatic Agenda Making and Rainmaking
- Benchmarking and Globalizing are Ways to Extend Powerful Invitations

John P. Kotter. THE LEADERSHIP FACTOR. 1989.
The effective leader, whether a mayor, a corporation president,
or a general manager, has two hallmarks: an intelligent agenda for change and
an energized network of appropriate resources.

Richard Bode. *First You Have to Row a Little Boat.* 1993.
What I had to do was stop steering with such a vengeance and pay attention
to what the sloop wanted to do. . . . I had to let the boat go, let her climb the wind
until the peak of the foresail fluttered ever so slightly, and then I had to steer off
the wind a fraction until the breeze filled the sail again
and the fluttering disappeared.
Then, as the wind picked up once more, I had to climb the wind, climb the wind—. . .
The sailor who refuses to abide by the wind sets his course by a mark on the land . . .
he holds rigidly to that mark, the way a king clings to his crown . . .
he sails his dogmas, and his dogmas deaden his senses . . . he is the . . . boss who is
less interested in the well-being of his workers than his short-term-profit goals.

Peter Drucker. *The Practice of Management.* 1954
Whether they like it or not, managers are not private, in the sense that what they do
does not matter. They are *visible . . . managers are on the stage,*
with the spotlight on them.

228

Climbing the Wind: Standing Watch

Invitational leadership begins when an executive gets realistic about "Who's the boss?" Responses that I receive from managers are often hastily-shaped *either-or* scenarios—while, in matrix reality, who's-the-boss is more a *both-and*. The executive at the helm who uses invitational power as a style of control steers a course toward alignment of organizational expectations and goals with management practices. That CEO knows how to capitalize on internal and external resources, and seize the moment, climbing the wind. Control is the rudder of organizational success.

The word "boss," currently somewhat out-of favor in workplace vernacular, identifies a person in authority over employees—an employer, a chairman of the board, a manager, a supervisor, a foreman, a director, a coordinator. Authoritarian and political-boss overtones overshadow the former slang use of boss to identify something as "excellent." Now-generations interpret boss in reverse, as ssob: stupid s.o.b. Boss, in other workplaces, reflects a French lineage from *bosse—an ornamental projecting piece, a bump on a flat plane*—more than it does a Dutch etymological connection to *baas,* which means master, expert, uncle, or mentor. In most work settings, boss continues to be a relational reference to the person who has the last word, the decision authority to hire or fire, to say "stop" or "go."

As a boss moves higher up on an organizational ladder, the internal control-span broadens. At the same time, and as a direct consequence of assigned responsibilities for greater numbers of people and more varieties of tasks, exposure to external controls increases. Hence, with more to control, there are more ways to be controlled. A leadership-effectiveness paradox is that the higher-status boss is *ipso facto* encumbered with greater dependence on direct reports. This irony becomes full-blown when a boss recognizes that being captain of the crew on-board is only one side of success in the job of shaping an effective management control system. Organizational momentum also requires skillful adjustment of corporate sails, such as reframing business objectives, regrouping structures and processes, and redistributing assets and liabilities.

Having your hand on the tiller of a sailboat or of a corporation means you are "standing the watch," constantly alert and responsive to both internal and external conditions. Information and feedback, the products of observation, accrue boss-power. Today's benchmarking-and-globalizing executives are busy reviewing statistical analyses of productivity and profitability, studying multi-rater evaluations of personnel, and, as well as digesting internal details, they scan the horizons of business innovations and social-economic conditions.

In the *Wall Street Journal (WSJ)*, a profile on the rising stardom of CEO's notes that these newest celebrities are still busy giving orders, identifying new markets, and approving products, even as they go, full-speed ahead, cultivating status as supershrinks, coaches to employees, and identifying with a managerial cause. Their actions and reactions in response to what they are seeing and hearing allow the company to climb the wind, to sail and tack, and keep moving forward. This multi-athalon marathon is not for the faint-hearted, nor do many choose to enter.

Weekly reports of executive failures and Hogan's estimated 50% to 75% base rate of incompetent managers imply that a lack of management control exists in many organizations. Recruitment specialists look for executives who have a track record of hiring talented, competent managers. Training and selection specialists look for essential-and-necessary competencies and absolute disqualifiers. And executives hope to select new staff that can give relief from stress overloads and deal with crisis situations.

Establishing the internal and external controls that make for a smooth-running organization is not as simple as controlling the cold water faucet with one hand and hot water spigot with the other. Corporate controls require navigating non-stop streams of task activity without losing sensitivity to personal and group dynamics. Actions and reactions of the executive hand on the tiller produce far-reaching, rippling wakes and waves that readjust workgroup potentials and priorities. They set in motion circumstances that are conducive to, or interfere with, individual performance.

Outstanding performers at all levels in an organization are those who give concentrated attention to the job at hand, and dedicate time to the acquisition of relevant experiences and competencies. Development and training programs will promote a manager's perseverance across time, strengthening the will to continue the quest, to maintain executive focus in spite of inevitable distractions. Authors James Kousner and Barry Posner found that firms that encouraged employees in their pursuit of competence have maintained their excellence-status across the years since they were selected as outstanding by Tom Peters and Robert Waterman in the 1980s. In these "boss/excellent" organizations, development programs received double-digit percentages of budgets. Internal bosses/decision-makers put their money where their need for competence was. Morgan McCall cites studies saying that acquisition of expertise can be speeded up by providing for individual exposure to a select set of opportunities. Critical learnings are emphasized in career ladders, through mentoring experiences, in corporate rewards and benefits, and from participation in professional associations.

Competency in any job, even given exceptional talent, takes effort and persistence. A classic anonymous quote tells it well: A woman went up to Jascha Hiefetz, the world famous violinist, following one of his extraordinary performances and gushed, "Maestro, I'd give my life to be able to play music like that." With great dignity, Hiefetz replied, "Madam, I did."

Strategies for motivating employees to excel in their work include an incongruous range of organizational tactics, materialistic to idealistic: Increased pay, stock in the company, extra health-care benefits, additional days-off, diplomas for framing, promotions, and social recognitions. Among the various reward techniques, social recognitions have the advantage of collective spin-off and halo side effects with comparatively low dollar-time investments. As noted earlier, it is recommended that every good worker be given at least one standing ovation in their career.

Generally speaking, social recognitions carry either a collaborative or a competitive bias. Collaborative rewards are those that permit association with important people, events, or places, such as top-drawer educational programs, national or international conferences, local community leadership gatherings. In contrast, recognitions are more often made when someone does more or better than someone else, a by-product of challenges and competitions.

Claiming to have a competitive edge is popular in blue-chip *WSJ* advertisements. Public boastings are, in one way or the other, bossy— evidence of something excellent or of a ssob: Full page ads dominated by white space; slick recruitment blurbs describing competitive-edge in every category—diversity to brilliance. The fine line between competition and collaboration reveals itself as a double-edged sword in the National Football League's legal wranglings to establish what the NFL is. The identity-crisis question is: Are we one company with a number of divisions whose job is to compete—sibling-like, yet by-the-rules of the game, fairly, and honorably? Or, is each NFL team an independent company without obligation to collaborate with the NFL as a parent organization? The answer becomes intensely contested as it impacts owner's pocketbooks, players' salary scales, and free agents' contracts.

Courtroom competition between the NFL and players' attorneys may inspire a trophy-worthy caricature of collaboration-competition. *Flash: Big-bucks sports organization, whose business is to provide public demonstrations of controlled physical competition with cheer-leader-led ventilation of spectator rivalries, settles in-house conflict through legally-refereed verbal competition with media-managed venti-lation of public-opinion and outrage about athletes' over-compensa-tion.* After the big-bucks baseball strike, that sport's popularity took a heavy drop, not lethal, but certainly noticeable enough to carry a message NFLers can surely hear.

Executives and football players who emphasize short-term, imme-diate pay-off are those who prefer that competitive motives dominate collaborative interests. Invitational power intentionally reverses that formula. Unless the organization is a sports league, the greater compe-tency-need will be for internal collaboration than for internal competi-tion. Unless a company is in a one-product, maxed-out market situation, the greater corporate-growth need will be for more external collabora-tions than competitions. In most cases, innovative thinking, talent devel-opment, and long-term progress are results of collaboration, not solo grandstand behaviors.

This is not news to many executives. An AMA survey of 100 executives conducted by a national management consulting firm shows that these executives expect more joint-ventures and alliances (69%), more mergers and acquisitions (64%), less elimination of management layers (58%), and less corporate control (48%). These executives expect CEOs will devote more time to strategy (71%) and to long-term finances (61%), and less time on operations (62%). Nevertheless, half of them predict they will keep the same level of time devoted to short-term results. They do not see themselves taking shorter watch-duty, or letting their hand off the tiller.

Participatory Command, Control, and Communications Is Not an Oxymoron

Final authority for short-term and long-range decisions traditionally comes from a command, control, and communications (3c) center. The 3c functions are initiated from the headquarters of a military operation and from the executive suite in private and publicly-owned organizations. As a noun, borrowing the French use of the *-ory* suffix, a *partici-patory* is a place for doing 3c work. As an adjective, from the Latin, participatory is a modifier, describing how the 3c activities are carried out. A leader can have a job in a participatory (n.)/laboratory where command, control, and communication activities are performed using participatory (adj.) methods rather than autocratic or *laissez-faire* methods.

Participatory command, control, and communications are a deployment of participative management practices that are different from employee and public-friendly bureaucracy. Communication style, credibility, and consequences are linked across the *input*, *through-put*, and *out-put* process. Participatory communication *inputs* are the hallmark of the careful transmitter, one who is open, frank, an active listener, and somewhat informal. Participatory *through-put* factors establish credibility by working in ways that are seen as trustworthy, informative, and dynamic.

Participatory *outputs* are management style consequences. There will be role clarity, effectiveness, and role satisfaction. Moreover, studies conducted by Bernard Bass at SUNY Binghamton showed that only open, two-way communication contributed directly to *satisfaction with the boss.* Two-way communication, careful listening, and informality contributed to *trustworthiness.* Two-way communication, frankness, and careful presentation contributed to *informativeness.* Two-way communication becomes a key characteristic of participatory behavior patterns because it contributes directly to trustworthiness, informativeness, and satisfaction with boss. Thus, the boss who is most satisfactory is not only trustworthy, but moreover, provides substantive information to workers.

Participatory actions reflect a hopeful approach to goals, plans, resources, and organizational structure, as well as demonstrating the welcoming attitude described above. Participatory bosses, whether working at production level, organization level, or systems level are problem solvers, continuously engaged in gathering information to reduce uncertainty about what to do. Elliot Jaques' research tells us that a detective mind-set is required at both junior and senior executive levels. The problem solving and thinking varies primarily in terms of time horizons and action latitude. Supervisors are looking ahead at three months with limited money and personnel. CEOs look ahead five, ten, or more years and have access to lines of credit with multiple zeros. Both depend on accurate, free-flowing communications.

The art of participatory communication is described in countless self-help books and programs. Executives learn how to mix public speaking with audience participation. They project participatory flair while presenting data with an instructor's precision.

Two-Way Communication: Internal and External Trust Building

Bank executive Edward Crutchfield, First Union, worked to keep his ever-enlarging organization from seeming too impersonal by meeting with small groups of employees who are new to the system. Focusing on internal issues, he loosens his necktie and says, "I bet no one here has the guts to ask me an insulting question." Meanwhile, Bill Gates, at Microsoft's helm, works on the external conditions by having the company organize a retreat for him and a group of reporters at his family residence. He planned to repeat this invitational, personalizing event with a different group of selected media guests. Even as Gates' internal associates wished for similar invitations, they quickly acknowledge the profitability payoff of Gates' time with the media. Employees know that their customers equate a meeting with Gates as the equivalent of shaking hands with Michael Jordan. Invitational leadership works inside and outside corporate perimeters. And, as Microsoft is discovering, too much success generates a widespread distrust of the corporate sense of responsibility. How the federal government and anti-trust regulators contain and disperse the giant technological business will revolve around issues of unfair competitiveness and equal opportunity for small businesses just as it did for AT&T.

Crutchfield and Gates demonstrated that structured but open two-way communication techniques are well received. Less is heard about unstructured executive communications. Yet, the importance of informal exchanges is a clear contributor to airline safety records. Evidence shows fewer accidents occur when cockpit crews talk to each other more frequently.

Crew members are not discussing the scenic views, according to reports by Foushee and Manos. Crewmates speak about flight conditions. They take as much time as necessary to talk through discrepant information. They take time to acknowledge hearing and concurring with other's comments. In contrast, the airline crew that crashed into the Colombian mountain, killing 106 passengers, might have realized that their plane had already passed the signal beacon if the pilot or the control tower contact—or anyone listening—had inquired about puzzling comments captured on black box recordings. First-language differences, English-Spanish, notwithstanding, that crash was determined avoidable.

Executives are busy exchanging how-things-look on business horizons during industry networking and professional conferencing. Senior executives report that they get the most insight and useful information from collegial activities, round-tables, or forums with experts. They work together to interpret and to impact complex information from the broader community. Junior executives are attending courses with peers from other corporations, on the alert for corporate acquisitions and ideas for new business. In this type of reconnoitering work, executives are choosing to be participatory. There can be no productive consequence without mutual respect and candid discussion of differences. The alternative is to retreat into corporate spying, cloak-and-dagger secrecy, and deception. Such cold-war gamesmanship ends in win-lose competition, winner take all, and zero-sum paranoia.

An unexpected fallout from failed mergers is that discussing business issues with a biggest and strongest competitor becomes a learning experience, according to Thomas Stemberg, chairman and CEO of Staples. The office supply superstore's proposed merger with Office Depot was halted when a federal judge ruled the combination was anticompetitive. The *WSJ* article (3/10/98) also describes how "big-six" accounting firm KPMG plans to revamp its internet web site based on what it learned in five-month negotiations with Ernst & Young. They conclude that whatever the risks of exchanging ideas, credible CEOs are convinced that considering a corporate merger requires open two-way communication, including discussions of strengths and blemishes, in order to know if the combination is workable. PhyCor and MedPartners called off their plan to merge after what they termed as *completely open* discussion showed major operational and strategic differences."

A "Participatory" Workplace

A successful bureaucratic *participatory,* as in *laboratory,* occurred in a government agency created in order to bring together communications equipment specialists from a variety of separate departments and organizations. All personnel in the new agency were on temporary-duty assignments and would return to work for their original employers. The focal communications problem for these ad-hoc co-workers was to resolve interface incompatibilities. Representatives of competitive groups were able to put aside historical differences and collaborate to eliminate design variances in radio and telephone speakers-and-receivers being produced by a variety of organizations. The resulting re-designs enable people standing on the ground to communicate with persons in an aircraft flying overhead. Likely, this so-called architectural enhancement prevents recurrence of military problems like those the U.S. experienced in the brief Grenada conflict, and spawned the commercial equipment we use to telephone home or office while flying to a meeting on a far coast.

Stepping back from official and technological aspects of two-way communications, there is a general consensus that informal participatory-communication, at its best, includes generous doses of humor. David Campbell, a master of executive-level humor, the author of *If I'm in Charge Around Here Why Is Everyone Laughing,* analyzed tasks and actions associated with executive leadership. For all his poking fun at himself as a CEO, Campbell believes that no matter how talented or motivated members of a group may be, they cannot be collectively effective without a central focus—a leader, a boss in the command, control, communications office.

Campbell reports that the focus-person has eight essential tasks: vision; management; empowerment; politics; feedback; entrepreneurship; personal style; and interrelationship of tasks. These tasks, for the most part, call for two-way communication and participatory management, e.g., empowerment. Campbell goes on to assess competence in these named tasks by asking questions about leadership actions. He surveys leaders about the things they do to focus resources to create desirable opportunities. These actions include planning, organizing, disciplining, compromising, confronting, writing, speaking, inspiring, and motivating.

While two-way communication between a boss and a subordinate is implicit in most actions that Campbell named, the word "control" is not mentioned once. Does this avoidance make *control* the proverbial elephant-in-the-corner, a huge presence that is not acknowledged on purpose or by accident?

Others do tackle control head-on. Control characteristics were found to influence the immune system. One personality-health risk assessment, as reported by Shapiro, considers control as a personality variable with four modes: positive assertive; positive yielding; negative assertive; and negative yielding. Each control characteristic had its own impact on the body; the mind; the interpersonal self; the work; and the environment. The most healthy were those who emphasized self-control and positive assertive modes. Based on this study it appears that control begins at home-base by taking control of the self and then by taking positive initiative—all in all, not a bad way to describe participatory.

Command and control approaches that are operationally realistic will include a range of decision-making methods. *Decision styles* are considered leadership styles by a number of management researchers, as seen in popular decision-tree models recommended by Meyer, Vroom, Yetton, Kepner and Trego, and the Center for Creative Leadership. Bass also connects decision-making methods with the core of leadership. He writes that studies of management effectiveness indicate that all managers need to be directive at times. At other times, managers will be negotiative. When working with subordinates, the consultative, participative, and delegative methods were found more productive. The one style that proved not to be beneficial in any circumstance was a *laissez-faire* approach, when the leader's approach is one of indifference with hands-off. The Bass studies show that bosses can increase employees' job satisfaction by using consultative methods and by increasing subordinates' clarity about the organization's goals.

Command, control, and communications functions can be delivered in a mandatory or an invitational tone. The objective is the same— delivery of information necessary to get the job done and to set the stage for the next scene. But, even the most efficient mandatory or invitational process will fall flat without substance. This means supplying a compelling agenda and the wherewithal to fulfill that agenda.

Charismatic Agenda Maker and Rainmaker

Controlling what gets talked about and what gets funded is power. Each time executives act on the prerogative to schedule discussion topics or to authorize the wherewithals, such as the money, people, or supplies, they are exercising primary boss-power. This manifestation of leadership becomes invitational power when charisma is introduced into the dynamic of agendas at all venues: meeting agendas, corporate agendas, or executive agendas. Charisma, as defined in the context of entrepreneurial leadership, is transmitted through seizing opportunities to provide vision, to give a sense of mission, to instill pride, to generate respect and trust. The executive choosing the invitational approach will be budgeting agenda time and corporate resources to give the lion's share and up-front place to topics and projects that show promise of innovative problem solving and information acquisition.

What's being recommended for corporate agendas? And what resources are to be mustered? Change is the essence of an executive's agenda. Fleshing-out change: new products, new markets, new facilities, regrouped operations, recycled supplies, retired products. Next place on the agenda of a rainmaker is getting-clear about what resources to track down. The one who can make resources available, in a timely way, gains respect and trust.

Old business is no longer the first item on the meeting agendas. Prime-time and attention goes to start-up thinking. Past events and ideas, the mop-ups, are assigned as interim activity, to be reported on tracking tables, not in brain-work sessions. Change agendas may have as few as three topical slots: *people, places,* and *things.* Under each, the change subtitles are: markets, technology, organization, managers, and workers. This means executives are stepping beyond being full-time controllers, planners, and inspectors. Paternalism is replaced with coach, facilitator, and mentor activity. Attention shifts from performance reviews that talk about job descriptions to discussion of how to introduce changes to create output that is of value to a customer and will move the business toward more global perspectives.

Can this be happening? Here are some supporting trends: Since the 1960s the percent of U.S. economy exposed to international competition increased from 7 to 80%. There were more than 7 million permanent lay-offs since 1987. 81% of the companies that downsized in a given year were profitable that year. They were downsizing because they decided to improve productivity; or to transfer to a new location, or to close an obsolete plant, or to change technology, or because they entered into a merger or made an acquisition.

Details of corporate strategy, structure, and culture vary according to industry or service, and the executives who survive are savvy business administrators, are grounded in industry knowledge, and stay informed about cutting-edge technical advances. What senior executives from radically diverse businesses will have in common will be a need to promote an agenda that creates motion for motion's sake, and to remember that they are thinkers more than knowers. The thinking is constantly toward corporate profitability, growth, and product or service quality. The executive paves the way for achieving corporate advantages, flexibility, value, reputation, and the contract-fit with employees. This is not an agenda to sneeze at, nor is it a mission impossible.

Corporate rainmakers, unlike water-finders, have little use for forked divining-sticks. They are instead actively out locating necessary information and resources—investors, talents, tools, buyers, suppliers, distribution systems. They recognize changes and bargains, and they make sure these items appear on agendas, rolodex records, and tickler files. They fill the change agendas with calls for strong advocacy and for strong inquiry.

Executives need to see the deals and, then, be able to grease the environment for change. They need to be able to make people feel safe enough to do something else, to buy into the change. It's more like being a conductor than being a dictator, and more like controlling attention by waving your agenda than your baton. As rainmakers, executives need to control and command resources through networking in much the same way as the internet links information across trails of menus and electronic sites. Consider the similarity to what's happening in the wake of industry-wide change in health care services and insurances: Physicians who deliver patient care from private office settings are aligning themselves into provider networks for centralized billing purposes. That way the solo practitioner, or small group office, can take part in health maintenance insurance programs that provide their client populations access to all specializations. These astute independent practice physicians prepared their own change-agenda and describe their billing coalitions as clinics-without-walls.

In a climate of strategic outreach, invitational control means cultivating core corporate capabilities simultaneous with increased reconnoitering. Reconnoitering prepares, not to map out enemy outposts, but for collaborative working with external dependencies. Reconnoitering, like cruising, means getting out and about, seeing how others go about doing things, and discovering what's happening down the road that causes local traffic jams. It's a matter of building bridges, canals and dams out there where the corporate work is heading. Quite literally, a dam constructed on the upper Nile in the Sudan initiated controls that dramatically reduced crisis management.

A dam in the Sudan regulates the amount of water that floods into the lower Nile valley and sets-up conditions necessary for regular harvests, economic stability, and healthier families. The dam was a radical improvement over long-standing leadership and management initiatives. Centuries ago temple priests learned to read the color of the Nile's waters in order to predict flooding or drought in the weeks ahead. The white, green, or murky waters are now known to be caused by weather trends in regions surrounding the Nile's three tributaries. White water meant there would be too little flooding in the Nile's downstream regions, for the waters were primarily coming from a drier region with a calmer tributary. Murky waters came from an area with frequent torrential rains and were forerunners of overflooding. A favorable blue-green color in the waters came from a tributary that traveled through a place of ideal rainfalls, just right for crops to ripen fully. Recent leaders in the Sudan, armed with extended climatic information and engineering technology, took actions to control distant water flows so that their country's workers would not face as many catastrophic events. (Adapted from Peter Schwartz, *The Art of the Long View, 1991.)*

Benchmarking and Globalizing Are Ways to Extend Powerful Invitations

Who's the boss? Information and feedback exert noticeable boss-power. Executives eyeball tangles of data, facts, and numbers about things that are directly measurable. They consider what must be indirectly assessed, such as opinions, interests, beliefs and intangible values. Reconnoitering brings back information and feedback for the change-agenda and innovative problem-solving. Detection of gold-mine opportunities for growth depends on micro and macro expertise, teasing some clues into smallest factors, while elaborating and embedding other clues within global constellations.

Tom Peters, corporate excellence specialist, said during a morning TV interview that it is crucial for executives to quick-shift attention between micro and macro perspectives. Smith-Richardson Foundation's founder was a master with that transition. Richardson reportedly unfolded his ten-year vision for his research center over lunch with the staff, and during dessert re-calculated the tip and the bill which proved, as he suspected, to be incorrect—by 10 cents.

Viewing with a microscope one minute and with a telescope the next is not a built-in, automatic reflex. Interest in both facts and opinions, in both details and ramifications is, usually, an acquired habit. Attention is driven by preference and personality. Carl Jung shed light on personality habits related to gathering information and feedback. In his view the second most important personality characteristic is how a person sorts perceptions. He noted that while some like their facts and opinions to be detail oriented, others like things big-pictured and overarching, somewhat of a default focus.

The good news is that both abilities are active to some degree, and both are trainable. Successful personality development is described as becoming excellent with one's favorite way of looking at things and becoming adequate with one's less preferred way. Contemporary authors of magic-eye picture books, who may not have heard about Carl Jung, also guarantee universal ability to look at things differently, and to find hidden big picture, three-dimensional scenes: *Do not despair*, they write, *the magic-eye talent . . . did not miss you.*

When attending to the fine points of development of individual abilities to strengthen corporate core-capabilities, specific targets can be identified using benchmarking methods. The 360-degree surveys are detail oriented, a factual-sensing approach. Traditionally, benchmarks are standards of behavioral adequacy or excellence that have been prescribed by a select set of experts. Applications of the technique have been expanded to provide measures of how well an employee is performing in terms of company-set behaviors. The comparison of ratings provided by self, peers, direct reports, and boss seldom fails to fascinate an employee. Good or bad, a 360 feedback profile is compelling. Proliferating as rapidly as the MBOs of the 1960s and the competencies of the 1950s, in-house benchmark items can be generated to address needed capabilities and targeted actions and impressions.

When the executive needs to attend to the development of the business as a whole and for the long haul, a strategic approach is more productive than the tactical 360 view. Strategic thinking about the big picture calls for invitational power. A broad range of information needs to be introduced. Macro level thinking aims to identify alternatives, options, best scenarios, fall-back and regrouping strategies. This wealth of global information and feedback on internal and external situations is what places an executive's change agenda on solid footing. This is when charismatic energy can work at its best.

The debate about open and closed systems becomes more and more of a mute point. Few companies or businesses are fully self-sufficient. An artist who makes paints from berries and shapes pictures on stones from the farm yard, may be almost independent—provided the stone artwork sells for a good price and the cows don't go dry or crazy. Margaret Wheatley considers our ability to notice the difference in open systems and closed systems to be our tool for sorting out the living from the dead.

What she means is that by using ourselves as benchmarks for the open system—a complex, changing collection of organs and electrochemical information that can collaborate to keep us going and growing—we can determine what things in the corporation are closed systems and best maintained in states of stable equilibrium, such as certain time-keeping devices, mechanical mass-production equipment, heating and refining processing systems. These types of things in the corporation can be controlled directly and autocratically, by the book.

Human parts of the corporation fall into a living, open system classification. These will thrive on autonomy when kept in motion through continuous dialogue that keeps focusing on a clear core of corporate values and vision. Wheatley advocates allowing individuals in the corporation to follow their own random, sometimes chaotic-looking paths toward their assigned corporate objective.

Even though few companies are ready for embracing the Wheatley random pattern of management control, certain chaos theory events are here to stay and require attention. Leaders in business, service, and government organizations face unavoidable and ever expanding external connections, dependencies and interdependencies. Executives move ever deeper into external politics as international competition looms larger and closer. One in five jobs is already tied, directly or indirectly, to international trade. The tide of free enterprise will not be slowed, not even by events like the tragic April 1996 airplane crash in Tuzla, Bosnia-Herzegovina. The deaths of a dozen entrepreneurial executives from telecommunications, banking, and construction industries traveling with U.S. Commerce Secretary Ron Brown shocked the business world. Their mission was to offer expertise, products and services to help the war-ravaged former Yugoslavia begin rebuilding. Even tragedy did not slow down the mission they launched.

Executives witnessing an increasingly diverse employee-pool and an energized assortment of world-wide marketers find it less and less practical to take an isolationist stand. Ayman, Kreiket and Maszta describe a pattern of corporate progression from nationalism to globalism as reflected in leadership style and management practices. When an organization takes a step into internationalism, the leaders typically begin with an ethnocentric attitude—my country comes first and our ways are best. This authoritarian style of thinking is carried out in a centralized approach to command, control, and communication. It's essentially being a seller or a buyer in a two-way exchange of goods or services for money.

As a company progresses beyond one-country exchanges, it moves from ethnocentric to polycentric internationalism. At stage two, offices or operations are located in at least two countries and a host country takes control of filling positions locally. Corporate headquarters keeps a hands-off attitude, as long as the bottom line looks good.

Phase three is regiocentric internationalism and allows for collaborative planning for business in multiple neighboring countries. The final phase, globalization, is geocentric (world-wide) and espouses top to bottom collaboration in decision making and policy setting. These corporations are often the result of a joint venture or a merger. They employ different nationals at all locations and all management levels, especially in board composition.

Cultural nuances require contextual attention beyond social etiquette and polite conversation. It involves rituals and assumptions about preliminaries necessary before doing business, about the nature of ethical and unethical business transactions, and about the form and content of evaluations of what happened.

A response I received from a management workshop participant in Taipei should have come as no shock—*oh no, we would not use anything like that* [the multi-rater evaluations of a person's performance]. *It would not fit with our way of working together.*

Cultural-political ramifications of individual and corporate actions are frequently the trump cards in the winning or losing of bids and contracts. David Campbell determined that one of the eight primary tasks of leadership is *politics*. Politics, without political-boss overtones, is defined as the science of government, the activities of those engaged in controlling an organized system of government. In corporate organizations, politics means the actions and reactions taken by an executive in the interest of corporate survival, adequacy, growth, and meaningfulness.

Big-picturing or fine-detailing, both are intended to reduce uncertainty about what to do. It is a matter of gaining information and feedback that permits greater control over movement and direction. Control can be packaged as executive leadership or participative management; it can be omitted from lists of tasks for leaders, and it can be parsed into subspecies. It will be, in the final analysis, a matter of decision-making style and who has the last word. There will be a focus and a focuser. There will be a boss. If successful, that boss is looking for information and feedback, is respecting the 3cs, is making an agenda, and is checking it twice.

Odds for success go up dramatically with both alpha and omega checks on significance. Alpha, a statistical probability of something being true, right, means the facts are adequate and accurate. Omega is a statistical analysis of how much of the variation in outcomes is caused by what matters most, thus is the practical significance of the information. When both alpha and omega tests are supportive, it means that the bosses have taken into account external threats and opportunities as well as internal strengths and weaknesses.

First and last, it takes repeated and multiple powerful invitations to assemble adequate and accurate data that has practical relevance to the job at hand. The invitational leader is seeking input from internal and external sources, is making collaboration more valued than competition, and is opening the change-agenda for macro and micro moments-of-truth. This is a charismatic-participatory way of demonstrating who is an excellent boss, one who is raised above the rest.

Background Reading

Background reading for the participatory and charismatic leadership definitions is available from Bernard M. Bass, Director of the Center for Leadership Studies, Binghamtom University, State University of New York, PO Box 6015, Binghamtom, NY 13902-6015. His award winning research produced the Transactional-Transformational Leadership Paradigm which transcends organizational and national boundaries. See also his articles in *Organizational Dynamics,* Vol 13, No. 3, and the February 1997 *American Psychologist,* Vol 52, No. 2, 130-139.

Details about the progression of executive competencies, the three-tiered, seven-layered model, were developed by Elliot Jaques and T.O. Jacobs. 1987. Leadership and complex systems. In J. Zeidner (Ed.) *Human Productivity Enhancement,* pp. 7-65. New York: Praeger.

The classic management wheel was published by Alex Mackenzie in 1969. *Harvard Business Review.*

Moments of truth in service organizations are described in *Service America* written by Karl Albrecht and Ron Zemke, 1990. New York: Warner Books.

Companies of excellence were named by Tom Peters and Robert H. Waterman in their 1982 book, *In Search of Excellence.* New York: Harper Row. Information about follow-up studies of what happened to those companies can be obtained by contacting the TPG/Learning Systems, Tom Peters Group trainers, or authors James Kousner and Barry Posner who developed "The Leadership Challenge Program."

Reports on the studies of leadership tasks and actions by David Campbell are found in the CCL newsletter, *Issues and Observations,* and details are provided in other publications offered by the Center for Creative Leadership, 5000 Lurlinda Drive, Greensboro, NC. 27438. *The Campbell Leadership Index,* 1982, 1991, is published by National Computer Systems, Minneapolis, MN.

Information about the changing roles of managers is available from Wayne Cascio, professor at the University of Colorado, Denver.

For more information about the assessment of *control* and health risk factors, contact Deane H. Shapiro, Jr., Department of Psychiatry and Human Behavior, California College of Medicine, University of California, Irvine.

The phases of international management development, *ethnocentric, polycentric, regiocentric,* and *globalization,* were mapped by R. Ayman, N.A. Kreiket, and J. J. Masztal. See "Defining Global Leadership in Business Environments," 1994, *Consulting Psychology Journal,* Winter, pp. 64-67.

Chapter 11

Pathfinders and Mapmakers

In the executive run for the roses, a horse named Hope finds the openings, never breaking stride, and carries the rider toward the finish line: survival, adequacy, growth, and meaningfulness. When the going gets tough, the hopeful are ready.

- Alternate Routes: Many Pathways
- Rethinking Goals: Re-mapping the Vision
- Learning and Teaching: New Ways and Means
- Fresh Players and Fresh Starts

Hope is not the loosey-goosey ethereal thing people have made it out to be.
It's about having goals.
C. Rick Synder, University of Kansas. 1991. *APA MONITOR*

If wishes were horses, then beggars would ride like Princes.
Old English Proverb

[#] 29. Retired CEO's report that leadership starts with vision, but the skill of a great leader is to give it the appearance of rationality, which provides people a chance to argue, refine the decision, gain commitment, and get it implemented.
[#] 93. A leader can stimulate good performance by 1) structuring work, 2) providing support for getting it done, 3) attending to the problems of the people who perform the tasks, 4) commending their good work, 5) helping them improve, 6) attending to them as individuals, and 7) settling disputes within the group.
Kenneth and Miriam Clark. *Choosing to Lead.* 1994

Management is, of all things considered, the most creative of all arts.
Because it is the organizer of talent.
Jean-Jaques Servan-Schreiber. *Pocket Calendar Quotes*

I sat in the corner of the dinghy, facing the stern, my destination somewhere behind me, a landfall I couldn't see. I had to judge where I was headed from where I had been, an acquired perception, which has served me well—. . . the goals of my life, and especially my work, haven't always been visible points of light on a shore that looms in front of me.

246

They are fixed in my imagination, shrouded and indistinct, and I detect them best when my eyes are closed. All too often I am forced to move toward them backwards, like a boy in a row boat, guiding myself by a cultivated inner sense of direction which tells me I'm on course, tending toward the place I want to be.

Richard Bode, *First You Have to Row a Little Boat.*

Alternate Routes: Many Pathways

Researcher C. Rick Snyder works in Kansas, a proper place to study hope—at least in the mind of anyone familiar with twentieth century children's literature and film classics. Kansas is "home" for Dorothy Gail, that place she hoped to get to with assistance from the Wizard of Oz. Dorothy and her dog, Toto, were blown into the land of Oz by a fierce tornado. The film chronicles, in unprecedented technicolor, Dorothy's quest. Her goal was to return to those that she loved the most, Aunt Em and Uncle Henry, who lived on a farm in black-and-white filmed Kansas. After meeting with good witches and bad witches, and making friends with a scarecrow, a tin man, and a lion, Dorothy learns that she always had the power to get back to Kansas—just as her traveling companions always had the wisdom, the courage and the caring they sought as gifts from Oz, the great fake wizard.

Snyder looks at hope objectively, moving as far beyond the power-of-positive-thinking and positive self-concept as Kansas is from Oz. When Snyder investigates hope, he talks to successful and not-successful people from the real world of business. He finds a clear difference between the two groups. Snyder calls those he interviewed who were successful the *high-hope* people, and those who were not successful the *low-hope* people. High-hope people consider goals as challenges, while low-hope people see them as threats. Moreover, high-hopers choose more difficult goals, yet do not cling to them when they become obviously unattainable. A second major distinction between the two groups is that those with high-hopes generate alternative pathways to their destination, and keep on going even when things are tough.

According to Snyder's findings, hope is quite different from optimism. People full of optimism do, indeed, look on the bright side, and are full of ideas for goals they'd like to pursue. However, the optimist can fail to figure out the "how-to" part necessary for reaching the goals. High-hope people don't stop at wishes and ideas; they get busy identifying ways to move toward those goals. The two principal success indicators are labeled *agency* and *pathways*. Agency means having a responsible, can-do attitude and trust-in-self. Pathways refer to working out action plans, and moving into action. Neither agency, nor pathways, shows dependence on past achievement, intelligence, affability, or optimism. High-hope stands on its own two distinctive merits and goes to work.

Strategies that foster high-hope range from reading autobiographies or books about successful people, to prescribing exercise programs and behavioral self-management programs. Sometimes reverse logic challenges a person. In this surprisingly effective method, the leader-coach begins by agreeing with a person's negative images of themselves or statements about the future: "Of course you haven't the smarts to figure a way to motivate those deadbeats who work for you." Victor Frankl, in his book, *Man's Search for Meaning,* calls this technique paradoxical intention. The purpose is to rekindle inner fires, sparking-the-fight, the will-to-growth, the survival instinct. Once enlivened by high-hope, whether vicariously reading biographical tales, or directly with behavior modification objectives, or with humorous de-reflection popularly called reverse-psychology, a mind turns to detailing options and possibilities.

This new definition of hope seems to echo folk-wisdoms of songs and maxims. A popular song in the 1940s claimed that busy ants with High Hopes moved mountains, and that people are nourished by apple-pie-in-the-sky-hopes. In the 1970s, a folk wisdom recorded in Richard Bach's small book, *Illusions,* is that *we are never given a wish without also being given the power to make it come true.* Bach's maxim comes with a warning: *You may, however, have to work for it.*

Such work, involving step-by-step plotting of a journey to a destination, is the work of mapmaking and pathfinding. Once a leader gets a mental map of the lay-of-the-land, as Ken and Miriam Clark remind us, the task is to develop enough structure so that the vision takes on rationality and clarity. At this juncture, participatory leadership can begin. As soon as others are able to see and hear the vision, they are invited to argue with, amend, and commit to the vision and goal.

Historically, land surveyors demonstrated that maps are improved when two or more are working at the charting and recording. Without Mason and Dixon's work in 1763-67, people might not remember where the north begins and the south ends. Without the 1880's mapping team Lewis and Clark, the Pacific northwest might have remained unpioneered decades longer. In the 1930s geography was proclaimed to be the most important thing to learn in school by the renowned educator-philosopher John Dewey. Today, in the surgence of global markets and international exchanges, it is wiser than ever that young students be trained first as mapmakers—to know where home is, to know where school and Kansas are, and to know where Oz is not.

Geography and traveling have long served as analogs for how to make strategic business plans, and as formats for systematic career planning. The questions were: Where are we? Where do we want to go? How do we want to get there? A multi-level "business school" format capturing this concept was mapped several decades ago by Edward J. Green in a 1970 American Management Association publication:

> *Where we are*
>   *1. Business/Activity. What are we doing?*
>   *1.1 Mission Statement*
>   *1.2 Statutes, Bylaws, Guidelines, Incorporation*
>   *2. Environment/Competition*
>   *3. Capabilities/Opportunities*
> *Where we want to go*
>   *4. Assumptions/Potentials*
>   *5. Goals/Objectives*
> *How we want to get there*
>   *6. Policies/Procedures*
>   *7. Programs/Strategies*
>   *8. Priorities/Schedules*
>   *9. Organization/Delegation*
>   *10. Budgets/Resources*

Another favorite business map-making formula was, and is, SWOT: the analysis of an organization's strengths (S), weaknesses (W), opportunities (O), and threats (T). When conducting SWOT analysis, an invitational leadership style is advantageous. Construction of the business plan comes after a cross-department work group collaboratively prepares two databases. The first one derives from assessment of internal strengths and weaknesses based on numbers and facts descriptive of corporate resources. Corporate resources are not limited to dollars, properties, equipment, and inventory, but also will include people—talents, accomplishments, and achievements. A second database comprises information and intelligence about external situations and is used to pinpoint opportunities and threats that complete the corporate SWOTs.

SWOT data can flesh out the business plan, giving new life to in-house three-ring notebooks, to spiral bound board reports and investor's slickpaper booklets. There's more payback for the investment of time and brainpower when leaders value operational continuity. Evaluation of progress reflects the wisdom of the boy who first learns to row a little boat. Biggest dividends come when periodic status checks produce fresh targets, measures, and methods. Thus, a company capitalizes on where they've been and what's behind them. Synchronizing learning from the past with preparations for innovative futures, assures business plans can have life-after-SWOTs.

For getting the odds close to eventual realities, evaluation is the operant word. At one time evaluation underscored accountability and served as a white-collar strong-arm technique. Equally self-defeating are *laissez-faire* approaches. Self-evaluations can result in managers jumping on their horses to ride off in all directions. This puts a business on a path leading nowhere, or worse yet, heading in terminal directions, going the wrong way. Participatory practices, a middle-ground approach to evaluations, replaces blame with shared responsibility, links practiced competencies with plans for rapid-transit into unfamiliar territory, and works proactively to head-off corporate wrong-turns.

The row-boater's view of the home-port of management practices shows a skyline that is distinguished by the classic-five: planning, organizing, staffing, directing, and controlling. Published in the *Harvard Business Review*, November-December 1969, R. Alec MacKenzie's heuristic is called *"The Management Process in 3-D."* This representation of the first theory of management functions is attributed to the work of Frenchman Henri Fayol and was first published in English post-WWII. some 33 years after Fayol wrote it. The 3-D model pulls together, sequences and overlaps everything you-ever-wanted-to-know-about-management. It's all there, the recurring management activities, elements, tasks, and functions performed by a typical manager.

At the center of the model are *people, things,* and *ideas.* These words reflect MacKenzie's assumption that people *need* leadership; things *need* administration; and ideas *need* conceptual thinking. Next, three activities are declared equally important in all functions of a managerial job: *problem analysis, decision making,* and *communications.* The nine-tiered wheel, constructed from elaborations on MacKenzie's assumptions, makes it appear that any simple explanation of managerial functioning is, at best, shallow. The 3-D management wheel is the quintessential management map of the twentieth century. Mechanical science, which measures everything with gauges, is the most likely inspiration behind Mackenzie's ratchet-wheel vision of management. This toothed and layered wheel unfortunately did not come with a "prawl" stick to keep activity going in a forward direction.

Einstein's science, quantum physics, influences turn-of-the-century management models. Emerging twenty-first century management practices are built on assumptions that information is nature's pristine building block, that organizations thrive with information exchange networks, and that work relationships are most productive when they are expanding, self-regulating, and non-permanent. Margaret Wheatley, a leading pioneer of management models, proposes bold, chaos-is-beautiful paradigms. She reframes the classic management wheel so it will never be seen in the same light again.

Quantum perspectives restructure the substance of both the executive role and management functions. Quantum science thinkers, like organizational re-engineers, offer hope of a simpler way. This new way calls for executives to take up roles in support of self-organizing and self-structuring. Corporate leaders are to assure resources and conditions that allow the business to flourish, while managers are urged to ask about the quality of relationships, about how much access we have to each other, about how much trust exists, and about who else needs to be in the room with us—be it office work room or computer chat room. In spite of these inspiring visions of what management may become, today's workworld seems to be in a time warp, caught up in habits of current beliefs and fixated on the efficiencies of old-methods.

Rethinking Goals: Re-Mapping the Vision

When the going gets rough, executives find little comfort in high energy optimism, libraries of management models, and meticulous plans "A," "B," and "C." Predictions from diverse sources, such as Kentucky consultant, Tom Brown, and Kansas researcher Snyder, are that successful, high-hope executives will, on many occasions, be called upon to let go of unrealizable goals, and will need to turn away from blocked pathways.

This is not news to managers who can flash back on two- and three-day planning retreats that wallpapered meeting rooms with chart pad notes on priorities and action plans. In *Leadership and the New Science,* Meg Wheatley poignantly recalls such experiences with managers as they struggled to develop alternative pathways, to plot fallback options, and to brainstorm new markets. Her first remedy was to put a tenth ring around MacKenzie's model that served as the missing prawl stick: continuous feedback.

Wheatley proclaims the manager's life-preserver is the constant gathering of feedback about what is going well, while also, and especially, showing zest for collecting feedback that causes disequilibrium. She advises managers to be avid collectors of data that suggests something is not going positively. She, like many consultants, claims gathering negative feedback prevents colossal mistakes. Unfortunately, Wheatley did not write a "how-to" book.

One critical disequilibrium loop is the one that recycles to goals and objectives. Corporate goal statements work as genetic building codes for organizational productivity and growth. They are the manifestation of an organization's identity, and Wheatley observes that "Every organization is an identity in motion, moving through the world, trying to make a difference." In both classic and futuristic maps of the domain of organizational management, rethinking goals and objectives means re-examining identity: what is the purpose and mission of the work in process. Goals, and their multi-tiered objectives, are the skeleton outlines of organizational purpose. They are the bare-bone structure that enables the business plan to walk around. Goals make explicit corporate answers to the ten items in Green's business plan: 1. What are we doing, why, and by what authority; 2. What's our work environment; 3. What's our in-house talent and capability; 4. What's our common ground: assumptions, potentials/beliefs values; 5. What are our goals, objectives, destinations; and what are our navigational tools: 6. Policies, procedures; 7. Programs, strategies; 8. Priorities, schedules; 9. Structure, delegation; 10. Budgets, resources.

Rethinking goals suddenly became mandatory as market shares, capital gains, returns on investment, and competitive edges assumed global dimensions. Ninety-day turn-around CEOs were in great demand as mega-mergers, hostile takeovers, and leveraging became soup *du jour.* Strategic business-thinking, in a quantum physics context of relativity-of-relationships-of-objects-in-motion, replaced the linear mentality of return-on-investment as shown in quarterly financial profits.

In a real sense, the executive in an organization works from a theory about the nature of the business, which serves as a mental map of the company's business territory. From that beginning point, hypotheses are developed about how to conduct corporate business to achieve maximal benefits and outcomes. The new breed CEOs are pioneers, leaders brave enough to test hypotheses, and to keep on exploring pathways until one works. As they discover which routes don't work, they demonstrate high hope: an optimism that selects challenging goals and sweats out the pathfinding, doing the arduous task of preparing plans using participatory methods.

The management-by-objectives era gave primary attention to exceptions, to mistakes. The attitude was "if it ain't broke, don't fix it." Action plans began with defining a problem and detailing what will be avoided if the prescribed actions are taken. As a result, a generation of managers, trained fault-finders and complainers, had to be retrained to express appreciation and give encouragement.

A contrasting approach to management-by-objectives begins by defining ideal outcomes. Proponents of this tactic encourage workers to dream boldly, to be innovative and creative. Their first objective is to cultivate shared vision and shared accountability, using brainstorming techniques to uncover similarities among values, hopes, and expectations held by the majority of the group. Then comes the construction of goals, objectives, and job descriptions aimed at attaining selected desired-outcomes.

This technique yields statements of collective purpose similar to one attributed to Steven Covey's family. The *Wall Street Journal* reports that Covey's family agreed on a statement of common goals after eight months of group thinking, undertaken at his request. Their collective purpose included responsibility, independence, interdependence, and service to society; as navigated by faith, order, truth, and love; with expected by-products of happiness and relaxation. This type of broad, intangibly specific declaration can, indeed, frame activities for a lifetime. Or it can prove impotent. Fancy words and apple-pie idealism become laughable, a joke among workers in highly-competitive, skeptical environments.

Managers and employees experienced in the school of hard knocks prefer for goal-setting and re-thinking to begin with solid, up-to-date facts and evidence. An empirical technique that is more elaborate than either SWOTs or Covey's principle-centered formula, yet is equally participatory, gained recognition by proving dramatically beneficial to the Dutch Oil /Shell Group. This megacorporation saved huge sums of money re-thinking and re-shaping their goals for off-shore oil-well drilling. Their decision called for accurate awareness and knowledge of complex global activities, events, and likely consequences. Peter Schwartz, Shell's re-thinking consultant, facilitates corporate workshops that rehearse the future.

Schwartz begins the process of getting ready to enact the future by posing a question about the corporation's business to the employees invited to participate in the workshop. Those selected to come to this planning event are chosen to represent a broad assortment of work units. Those who agree to attend the workshop will have to complete extensive "homework" assignments. They will be studying the future. Schwartz believes that making decisions that impact future business activities means reading about, inspecting, and evaluating the advances in relevant technologies, techniques, attitudes, and ideas. If business goals are to be adapted to new ways of doing and being in the future, workers must first be sent out on a proverbial hunting-and-gathering type of expedition. Re-thinking of goals begins by building wide-net bases of information about current conditions—describing what is, sniffing out what is shifting, and gathering evidence to indicate what trends are likely to take hold.

Employees given specific hunting-and-gathering assignments are to focus simultaneously on the question that matters to the organization's business and to keep a sharp eye out for the unexpected. According to another business forecaster, Faith Popcorn, the best way to predict the future is to pay special attention to changes in food and restaurants; new products; family structures; shifts in the workplace; the environment; the economy; and prevailing moods—anxious or hopeful.

She notes a trend toward protected and contained centers for leisure activities that could otherwise be dangerous, or canceled out by the weather. She expected someone to soon build an indoor rock climbing facility that isn't a training miniature. (Note: Las Vegas is building a shopping mall with a resized version of the Grand Canyon. No announcement is made of climbing opportunities or donkey rides.) Faith Popcorn forecasts that, if there is, indeed, a continuing social trend toward cocooning, increased business opportunities will emerge for all industries that work to avoid violence, accidents, and schedule delays.

Making a map of the future, which Schwartz calls scenario writing, illustrates a participatory way to think through positive and negative information. The impact on rethinking goals is easy to imagine in the following report of Schwartz' work with a publishing firm.

Following several months of preparation, the company's information hunters-and-gatherers met for the scenario writing workshop. At that time, they collectively generated a map of what things would be like for the organization's business given the best configuration of social conditions and trends. Scenarios are prepared also for the worst composite of likelihoods, and for two nothing-much-different situations. One scenario assumes there is not much different in social-economic conditions, and that there are major collaborative efforts among independent businesses. A second scenario assumes again that there is not much different, but that competition intensifies among independent businesses in the industry.

Instructions given to workshop participants for scenario writing include surprise twists of circumstances to challenge participants' rethinking and reshaping of possible goals. At various junctures in the progress of the workshop, undercurrents are introduced that are relevant to the question posed in the invitation to participants. Examples of possible unexpected instructions are for the planners to now assume (a) that conflict is inevitable, covert alliances evolve; or (b) that there becomes a necessity for sustainable development under depleting natural resources; or (c) that change will occur in an evolutionary manner— slowly toward growth (or decline), or (d) that there will be a revolutionary change.

According to Schwartz's example taken from his work with a publishing industry, in the best of all possible future worlds there would be a larger number of literate, well-educated people who spend some of their time reading. In a worst-case future, a larger number of people are watching television, listening to radio, and spending less time reading. In a not-much-new future where collaboration prevails, several kinds of media businesses merge (print publishing, television, radio, computer). Or, they form mutually supportive constellations with some common goal. Together they agree to promote quality of life through educational programs, by language translating assistance, and / or through shopping and marketing services. However, when competition prevails, rival media coalitions form, some appealing to the popular thirst for sensational information and others taking on a social service and education function. A third cluster of businesses would be half-and-half, appealing to targeted audiences such as children, seniors, sports fans, fashion fans, gourmet fans.

The workshop expects the hunting-and-gathering evidence to be converted into information that logically determines the company's best course of action under each type of condition. While rehearsing the future, the cast of hunter-and-gatherer employees talk out the possible future maps of their business territory. They can draw together goals and objectives pertaining to the initial question. Schwartz advises that warning signals and feedback disconfirming a *yes, let's-do-it* decision are to be given special attention.

Intriguing tales of corporate success and failure come from authors Schwartz, Popcorn, Peter Drucker and Tom Peters. Most likely they never met, even though they address a common audience—thinking executives who re-think the future of their organizations. All four writers encourage getting out and talking with knowledgeable people, especially those on the cutting edges of your industry. Moreover, each, an expert advisor on preparing for future success, acknowledges that after hunting-and-gathering and scenario workshoping, comes the cliff-hanger act—a bold declaration of new goals.

Employees who did not participate in working out the new goals need motivation. They do not automatically accept and support mandated changes. At this juncture, stimulating others to change becomes the white-water challenge. How to deal with natural resistance to revised goals, fresh objectives, and unfamiliar methods? The specter of change can sabotage the most creative, innovative, well-researched, thoroughly mapped plans.

A pioneer organizational development (OD) specialist, Gordon Lippitt, long based at George Washington University in Washington, D.C., and president of one of the first national and international psychological consulting firms, saw twelve reasons why people resist change in work organizations.

1. *When the rationale and goals for [change] are unclear*
2. *When the "appeal" . . . is based on personal rather than [work]-related reasons*
3. *When there is a lack of trust and respect in the person initiating the [change]*
4. *When the effort is introduced too rapidly or follows a previous change (or crisis) too closely*
5. *When the present situation seems "satisfactory" and people question "why start something new?"*
6. *When there is a fear of failure because of lack of skills in or knowledge of [the new undertaking]*
7. *When the "cost" . . . is too high or the benefits . . . seen as inadequate for the resources and effort which will be required*
8. *When there is a perceived loss of job security or status for the people involved*
9. *When excessive work pressure is involved*
10. *When the habitual patterns of the work group are ignored*
11. *When there is poor communication about the [change]*
12. *When people are not involved in planning the [change]*

Accumulated observations and conclusions about the hazards of making changes in organizations are put together by Joel DeLuca, a comparative newcomer in management technology, who argues that the resistance which is most difficult to overcome, and the most elusive, is behavioral resistance. He cautions that it is futile to attempt to implement a change strategy without first establishing agreement with those who must do the changing that there is a need for change. In the absence of understanding and commitment to new goals or methods, employees' behavioral changes will be minimal. Employees may go so far as to learn a few new words used in the revamped vision statement so they can manage to sound politically correct, while they remain closet saboteurs: "I told you it wouldn't work."

To avoid derailment of innovations, DeLuca proposes a participatory method. Executives who state the changed goals and methods simultaneously establish a change steering-team and several task-force groups. These groups are composed of representatives of each division or department in the company, a strategy similar to the one used to invite employees to participate in a SWOTS planning project or a future-scenario scripting workshop. The steering team, comprising senior management representatives, monitors the changes occurring in all departments and components of the organization.

The steering group establishes their own work agenda related to changes, supplemental to the executive mandate. The steering team, limited to less than ten members when possible, then gives a charter to each task force. The charter's topic may be specific or general, but each group is assigned to bring in regular feedback and input to the steering team about additional changes needed and particular spots of difficulty. Called a dual-cycle approach, the specially appointed change management groups provide a way of quickly sending feedback and information up and down the organizational chain. Executive decision-makers are encouraged to involve employees from the beginning of a change, in a manner that is visible, structured, productive, and efficient.

The dual-cycle organizational change process is reminiscent of quality circles, TQM self-managed teams, and Likkert's linking pin model. Moreover, it is comparatively easy to implement. It's a form of remapping and pathfinding that takes into account predictable resistance-to-change. DeLuca builds on knowledge about instinctive human reluctance that has been found to be expressed three ways—intellectually, emotionally, and behaviorally. As DeLuca says in sound-bite terms, in order to deflect negative responses of workers who are confronted with assignments that are novel or involve making skill adjustments, change implementers need to address the head, the heart, and the feet.

Typically, addressing resistance in that order proves effective. In particular, this concept expresses one rationale for the sequence of the three parts of this book: Part One, what's important—an intellectual foundation *(head)*; Part Two, surprise and change—emotional driver *(heart)*; and, Part Three, invitational power—productive behavior through charismatic-participatory leadership *(feet)*. When an organization's change agenda involves revision of the mission, goals, and activities, it is important that follow-up events quickly move to reduce intellectual defensiveness among employees. Reducing resistance is a matter of timely learning and teaching.

Learning and Teaching: New Ways and Means

A learning corporation, as promoted by Peter Senge in *The Fifth Discipline,* is one that keeps up with advances in industry knowledge, technology, and psychology. More pragmatic social consciousness is found in Latin America where management consultants report that businesses and industries recognize economic survival means educating adult employees who never learned to read and write. A similar need exists in the U.S. when new immigrants join a workforce and are unskilled at reading and writing in English.

Learning, at both basic and graduate levels, is increasingly important to corporate vitality, capability, and endurance. Following the example of the professions, businesses learn the value of taking responsibility for the continuing education of specialists and technicians, and for assisting employees who are making work or career transitions. Some organizations broaden educational interests to macro perspective, such as identification of individual potentials and encouragement of life-long learning. A positive side-effect of downsizing was that people whose primary talents were latent and undeveloped were faced with the forced opportunity to update, retool, and extend their knowledge and skills.

Executives serve more and more time in a teacher-motivator role. A decade before *The Fifth Discipline* became a bestseller, Harry Levinson's still popular book, *Executive,* championed the executive-as-teacher. He wrote that "There are no prescriptions that the executive can follow in acting as a teacher. In the organization, as in any classroom, teaching is a matter of doing what comes naturally, taking care to make opportunities for showing what it is one does, how, and why, and how these same strategies could be adapted and used by the students. . . . What can be made more explicit [by executives] is the act of teaching . . . it can happen, say, during one meeting a week. . . ."

Corporate success is directly linked with the teaching efforts of the executive in Bernard Bass' book *Leadership & Performance Beyond Expectations.* Empirical evidence supports his case for a Socratic role-model for executives. Furthermore, Bass proposes that a transformational leader with charismatic influence is universally successful, across national and cultural boundaries. Bass defines the transformational leader using his four decades of scholarly national and international research. Three of the four characteristics that distinguish outstanding performers involve guiding others' learning: providing employees with inspirational motivation, intellectual stimulation, and personal attention. The fourth transformational characteristic is vision.

Executives who have vision ability are those who are competent in scenario development and adept at developing plot variations and imagining feasible pathways. When working as an executive consultant, a good bit of my time is spent in closed-door sessions in the executive suite. I spend hours listening to a transformational thinker talk through a variety of ways to go about making changes and improvements in the business. With a bank president, it was planning to open two branch offices and how to go about staffing three separate operations, dispersing current resources and talents. With a steel corporation CFO, it was listening to options and consequences associated with an employee leveraged buy-out of family-owned stock, or accepting an acquisition offer from a foreign investor, or stepping up debt loads to acquire production plants owned by smaller companies in neighboring states. With a hospital VP, it was listening to the free-flowing, verbal-processing of a variety of restructurings of departments and services. They talked and I noted or sketched variables and variations on chart pad paper to capture their images and scenarios.

In each case, it was a matter of my being a safe but knowledgeable audience as ideas were floated, refined, and contrasted. Transformer executives chose to talk-it-out with me because their experience told them I was a source of ideas and a non-threatening questioner. They had learned that exploring change with subordinate staffers can result in unnecessary alarms and anxieties. Preliminary, first-draft vision-work is often best done in private consultation, or with a trusted peer.

The other three-fourths of a transformational leader's special talents, according to Bass, are devoted to influencing and inspiring those on the payroll. A teaching role is not likely to be difficult or unnatural for executives. They are usually persons who made the most of their own schooling and experience. Formally educated or not, they are typically bright, quicker-than-average learners. Fred Fiedler, an internationally recognized expert on characteristics of effective executives, selects intelligence as the cornerstone characteristic. He found that work groups performed best for a leader when that leader was slightly brighter and quicker than the average of the followers, but not so much quicker that others have trouble understanding and following instructions.

Intelligence, as reflected in speed of new learning, is not a static possession. This is a personal characteristic that fluctuates over time, depending on stimulation or inspiration plus exercise, sometimes referred to as old-fashioned perspiration and application. If mental exercise is neglected, boredom and depression flourish. These symptoms alert executives that it's time for learning something new. Executives who become intentional on-the-job learners and educators are acting as transformational leaders. By example and by transfer of learning, they work to motivate and intellectually develop employees at the same time they are keeping their own mental capacities sharp and active. This is the least expensive anecdote to depression.

Post-retirement adults who were once productive business managers are finding continuous rounds of tennis, golf, and bridge to lack meaningfulness. They eagerly flock to elder-hostels, studying everything from international policy to oil painting. Some relocate near colleges and universities where communities of alert seniors continue to study, share their experience and knowledge with students, and provide services in the local community. From building ultralight airplanes to surfing cyberspace, former executives are able to continue their teaching-learning role. These leaders enjoy the benefits of extended life and self-esteem. Their high-hope spirit is knocking the tops out of actuarial tables on longevity as they carry on as leaders, exploring the frontiers of productive, healthy endings to distinguished careers.

Long before they move into the role of "U.S. Executive, Retired," these leaders recognize that successful succession planning and role transitioning is not like a table game where knights, bishops, and castles are carefully arranged and re-arranged on a stationary field of squares in rows. It is more like the wise farmer who is continuously active, cultivating, tending, improving and protecting the crops.

This work is accomplished over long periods of time. Even then, as was the case for Coca-Cola, a successor turns out to have an unforeseen flaw. The *WSJ* (12/17/99, p. 1) described M. Douglas Ivester, long groomed by Coke's charismatic CEO, Roberto Goizueta, as tone deaf. Former accountant Ivester was considered to have all the skills of a CEO except the ear for political nuance. Ivester resigned at age 52 after serving at the helm of Coca-Cola for two years. After a half dozen or so small crises, he began losing popular support. The delayed handling of a contamination problem in Europe and a cavalier comment that the prices of the soft drink could be increased as the local weather temperatures increased left board members and customers feeling uncomfortable. Trust waned. Ivester, meanwhile, continued to pursue the international expansion plans envisioned by Goizueta. Times and issues changed.

The durable executive stays current and is busy hiring, developing, promoting, retraining, revitalizing, always looking for the new hybrids that improve corporate yields. Nor is there neglect of personal adaptation, including preparation for a transition to an emeritus advisor. The final quest includes more than rocking-chair conferences and golfing fundraisers. These elders are learning new tricks and revamping postcareer pathways.

Fresh Players and Fresh Starts

In addition to being inspirational teachers, encouragers, and motivators, high-hope pathfinders are indefatigable initiators and unrelenting recruiters. The executive understands the common-sense wisdom behind oft-quoted political slogans, such as "new brooms sweep clean," "the new deal," and "a contract with America." These and similar campaign slogans continuously fill the U.S. House and Senate seats with fresh players. The power of the new face, the different perspective, the untapped drive-to-the-goal rejuvenates energies and brings to light neglected or mismanaged programs.

Few non-fiction plots are more intriguing than political elections and new party take-overs. The 1995 Republican takeover of the legislature after forty years of Democratic dominance brought great attention to the new Speaker of the House, Newt Gingrich. When interviewed for the public broadcast station about his sudden prominence and ascension to public limelight, he was quick to note that Kentucky's Henry Clay became Speaker after a campaign based on equally important changes in legislative policy, but that Clay's breakthrough was in 1810, before television.

Gingrich went on to comment about his several highly visible, highly criticized goof-ups. He acknowledged his mistake in accepting a contract for millions of dollars to write a book about his political contemporaries, which, on second thought and after a public outcry, he turned down. He also confessed a mistake in selecting a woman with questionable credentials to serve as congressional historian. Keen knowledge of history pulled him through these first denouements.

Republican Gingrich chose to cite as his precedent the beloved Democratic president, Franklin Delano Rosevelt. FDR was widely admired for his ability to say, "OOPS, that was the wrong thing," and not lose a step in searching out the right thing. This contract-with-America Speaker of the House admitted errors of judgment, saying that the most important thing in effective leadership is to be able to admit that something was a bad move, and move on. It took several years before public opinion shifted against the speaker who continued a pattern of political and self-serving manipulations, ranging from holding legislative actions hostage to collecting speaking fees from a small college in Georgia. Glib historical rhetoric became impotent.

Gingrich's contemporary, the Democratic President, Bill Clinton, headed into his second term of leadership and was at times eclipsed by the speaker of the house. Soon Clinton needed to make his own dramatic declarations about being less than perfect. He made numerous public expressions of regret. Clinton's *mea culpa*s were of an intensely personal nature. He confessed to libidinal outbreaks and to withholding information. Clinton's esoteric and self-serving definitions of his sexual behaviors did not reap immediate, or enduring, public acceptance.

As citizens lost trust in the wheeler-dealer speaker-of-the-house, the president began receiving favorable public opinion polls. Citizens apparently appreciated that Clinton maintained a daily focus on national issues while the circus of legal actions leaked allegations of romantic peccadilloes to the media. Although taped telephone conversations and legal testimonies titillated media consumers, Clinton chose not to comment or to make historical comparisons. That editorial work was done with relish by historians glad for the opportunity to bring up their favorite amorous misadventures of Washington, Jefferson, Kennedy, and others.

What the president did do was make fresh news. He concentrated on international and national events and crisis situations. He initiated fresh starts in arenas that made improvements or authoritative postures of consequence to many people in many places.

The importance of fresh initiatives and players is illustrated routinely in most athletic events, like basketball, hockey, soccer. Coaches who send in fresh players from the bench have teams that play a stronger game to the finish. Even seasoned veterans get winded or begin to fumble frequently, and it's important to have others on the bench who can quickly move in to play on the court or field. A time-out or reprieve lets exhausted players catch their breath, gather their thoughts, and return to the game with renewed vigor and a fresh start with a new game plan.

Years ago, football found a way to minimize the wear-and-tear on individual players by working with two sets of players—offense and defense teams. Coaches have always protected the talents of the extra-point kicker from the constant rushing and tackling. These agile players are typically slight of frame and are only sent into the rough and tumble body contact game when it is time to put finishing touches on a touchdown with extra points, or to make field goal attempts when a touchdown seems out of reach.

In contrast, corporate executives have been heard to tackle the fresh players issue with a woe-is-me perspective. At conventions they trade ain't-it-awful tales about how hard it is to find any good workers and that, when they are hired, they don't stay long. Executives complain about a lack of loyalty and commitment from the young people these days, a weakness they see as similar to Clinton's transient affections.

However, these same bright young people are more likely acting on a practical observation. The only way to "fast-track," if you don't have a favored-nation status with the big boss, is to jump ship. Their technical knowledge and intellectual properties make it easy to climb aboard another corporate ship with broader responsibility at a higher pay level. Young managers become bored when they are stuck in a slow-moving or skewed procession up a promotion ladder. Some got caught in the undertow of the corporate push to achieve politically-correct personnel profiles. Corporate satirists derided promotion decisions based on rare-species attributes, such as being a female competent in a non-traditional skill who is a descendant of a Native American with a Spanish surname and is confined to a wheelchair.

Bright young organizational players who adopt a corporate-shift careerpath are viewed as side-effects of corporate decision failures by Frank Heller and his associates at the Tavistok Institute in England.

Their study of management decision making found that poor executive decisions were associated with corporate underutilization of mid-level managerial talents in Great Britain.

Leveraging and Compensating for Underutilization of Talent

A robotics engineer recently decided to make his third corporate shift, going with a fourth employer. The first change came shortly after a mega-firm that sent the young engineer to graduate school for specialization in robotics, aka automated industrial manufacturing, assigned him, to a position having nothing to do with robotics or automated manufacturing.

A small entrepreneurial firm, founded by a German and based in Canada, stole him away to design and install production lines for a new, fully automated plant. He thoroughly enjoyed seeing his ideas put into action. Interestingly, this mass production project was the result of interoperability solutions worked out by the government agency described earlier that used participatory methods for problem solving.

During the equipment purchasing phase of this installation, the young engineer collaborated with managers of a well known mid-sized U.S. corporation. Corporate shift number two came about when that more established organization offered him a substantial increase in salary to come design and install an unusual new product they were gearing up to produce for luxury automobiles.

Four years later the innovative product was still two years away from production. The robotics specialist was assigned to investigate what kinds of glue-gunk would be easiest to remove from increasingly miniature and complex computer mother-boards. This cleaning project was not exactly exciting, challenging, or innovative.

One day a sailing acquaintance said, "Hey, we need you." The fellow engineer reported that their not-yet-on-the-big-board company was going great guns, with more business than they could keep up with. Informal, sporadic communications continued with an offer of another noticeable salary increase, plus coverage of accumulated retirement benefits. The unfulfilled young man soon left the stalled project group, which remains caught in a *cul de sac* created by mergers and ancillary outsourcing contractors, but did not join the unsettled start-up firm.

First, he went on an extended sailing venture in the Caribbean. Then, he went for a new job. He found a specialty manufacturing company where he could use and extend his abilities to design and create and, importantly for the quest, become involved with management decision-making at an executive level. Will he become a next generation Lee Iacocca? Will he become the genius behind his industry's development of a "mustang" of switching systems? Hard to predict, but the smile is back in his eyes. He is glowing as he looks down from his office and across a neatly organized production floor.

The view from the glass windows across the back of his newly furnished office lets him see from start to finish what's happening in one of the two plants he supervises. This new Director of Operations is well on his way toward his quest.

Although the gifted engineer may move along in a career path leading to executive status in this British managed conglomerate that is less gigantic than Chrysler or GM, he would be an unlikely candidate for heir apparent in one of America's grand old companies. Many U.S. commercial ventures began, and continued, as family affairs. Exceptionally talented founders turned what began as a family business into professional corporations, but with an extended-family approach to their work. They maintained a personal respect for their managers as individual human beings, sometimes to the point of paternalism. Original executives were typically lauded as benevolent patriarchs, acclaimed for their innovative ability and drive. In this atmosphere and corporate culture, the family took care of its own first and promoted from within.

Successors to the founders of the corporate giants were considered first among equals in the eyes of their cohort group and former management peers. New CEOs would be committing fratricide if they fired or terminated those who grew up managerially with them. An attachment to corporate status, derived from widely acclaimed founders or charismatic predecessors as in the Coke situation, is seen behind efforts to sustain positive corporate self-concepts and to maintain family treasures such as organization structures and competitive edges. Harry Levinson was a harbinger of things to come.

"The attachment of one's professional skill and orientation . . . and its translation into a given set of products, into an organizational value system, into identifiable products, into a certain kind of relationship with one's customers—all these attachments become psychological anchors whose pull inhibits adaptive change. A major leadership task is to free people from their attachment to their established practices and favored products and to wrench them from modes of work and organizational structures that have become an intrinsic part of themselves."

Harry Levinson, 1997, pp. 154-155.

The plight of America's senior corporations has been described in terms of organizational narcissism. Massive mergers and realignments, such as the six billion dollar combination of the Burlington Northern

Santa Fe and the Canadian National Railway, can relieve some of the pressures of "family" history. Pressures remain to project an aggressive, top-dog, biggest corporation on the block image. Levinson diagnoses this drive as symptomatic of a business group that is in love with their own identity. Management leaders are soon acting out of internal dependency and conformity. In such organizations, the primary objective of a new executive is to avoid catastrophe during their tenure. Consequently, the main efforts are defensive. They take action against anything that rocks the boat, upsets the applecart, or loses market share. Their job is to maintain visible success, be trustee for corporate "attachments," and to work rationally through problems.

A problem faced by those second-in-command in a big-business enterprise or those who follow an inspiring chief executive is that change of any kind can be interpreted as a criticism of the predecessor. If the revered founder or leader lives to sit on the Board of Directors, the second CEO works in the shadow of a commanding, and often resistive, presence. A struggle to live up to the expectations and stature of the predecessor adds to the burden carried by the new senior executive. Those chosen to carry the corporate flag into the future are often endowed with a conscientious conscience. This very attribute qualified the individual as the best candidate for grooming in the first place and later weights down their effectiveness with worry and hesitation.

Some who are selected to succeed as corporate heads are executives who came up through technical ranks, such as finance or engineering. Many such specialists chose to work with numbers or machines to avoid direct contact with their own or others' emotions. Those who deny feelings, such as fear, may be seen as brave, but they can also stifle their ability to see what is happening around them. Repression and isolation is associated with an increased incidence of executive depression. Complex corporate difficulties arise when CEOs fail to recognize their own depression and their own limitations of conceptual thinking ability.

Management consultants recommend that corporations avoid loss of clear-headed management by filling vacancies in divisional vice-president positions with talented persons from outside the company. When senior executives wish to stimulate overall management competence, division-chief slots are particularly suited for seeding fresh-players. Hiring seasoned talent with fewer sharp edges to polish can shorten the learning curve factor.

In-house promotions, most often into positions that support a CEO, can also be a source of ideas and vigor. Those managers who cross over to the executive ranks from within an organization report sensing a shift in expectations and performance evaluation criteria. In order to succeed in the new role, they need clarity about how they are doing and when they are out of step. Those who worked with facts and equipment are not used to calculating the impact of personal emotions on business activity. Those whose background is marketing or sales find speaking up self-assertively to showcase one's own ideas and skills, recommended early-on as directly relevant to receiving promotions, receives the cold shoulder. Others from personnel and training are astonished to meet suspicious derision of behaviors that are advocated and work well for mid-level team building and consensus seeking. One time Surgeon General Joselyn Elder discovered in her seventeen months in office that the executive must curb public expression of personal opinion about sensitive social issues and sexual behaviors, or front-line tenure is brief. An advantage of calling in a seasoned division chief when hiring outside the corporation is that they have typically developed a sense of timing.

Gathering feedback about how others perceive what's going on helps the fresh player to adjust responses in unfamiliar territories. Feedback information is important for long-timers and new-hires alike, but for different reasons. The new-hire needs a quick course on people, processes, and problems, and an orientation to the history, heroes, and culture, which is the very advantage that the long-timers enjoy during their first months working beyond the glass ceiling.

Feedback has been promoted for several decades as a means to shape behavior and to modify attitudes or opinions. B. F. Skinner, psychologist-author of *Science and Human Behavior* (1953), demonstrated with pigeons and people how giving rewards like food and candies will increase desired behaviors. Some businesses found they didn't need to give sweets at the end of the day; they could just ask employees to record their own daily work totals on a large chart showing all employees output for each day of the week. Most people want to improve and like seeing information about how they are doing on the job. They find it rewarding to see the evidence of productivity and to publicly recognize each person's contribution to the effort, variable as they are.

Feedback, done in a structured manner as described in the output charting example above or in one-to-one discussion, is one of the surest ways to send in a fresh player. Watching a fast-paced basketball tournament game, it is easy to see even a brief time-out session make a difference. The coach gives team members information about what they are not seeing in the heat of the plays and about something that might work better for them. They slap hands, have close contact with their coworkers, catch their breath, and encourage each other to press on toward the win. They dash back onto court with increased determination.

For those of us who never played basketball, an example about a bowling game may bring this point closer to home. Think about how much fun a bowling game would be if you wore earplugs and there was a curtain placed between you and the ten pins you hoped to strike down. Although you are only being deprived of feedback—direct information about what happened when you rolled the ball down the alley—you are not likely to find the game as rewarding and satisfying as usual. It's much more fun when you can hear the ball connecting with the pins, see how many of the pins fall down, and immediately know what the score is. Not only is the game more enjoyable, you have gathered information about how to perform better the next time you roll the ball. You can change the spot where you stand, you can change the way your eye lines up the pins with the ball on the upswing, or you can angle the ball down the alley to slant across a different path.

Obviously, feedback is a powerful management tool. The usual feedback experience at work comes in conjunction with performance appraisals. A less well-known source of feedback is found in the executive training programs that I conducted for fifteen years. During the week-long courses, each participant receives feedback on their behavior and how it would be seen if that person had an executive position in the other participants' workplace. Each one is also coached in how to give feedback that, first, can be heard by the other person, and, then, in a way that is not judgmental or invasive. Participants typically report major insights about ways to improve their personal leadership style and that they returned to their workplace with renewed vitality.

Intel Corporation chief-executive Andy Grove promoted on-the-job feedback exchanges. He advised managers to be constantly on the lookout for what's working so they can continue it, and what's not working so they can stop, change or do differently. His direct-and-to-the-point formula for executive success stands tall in the test of time. He recommends one-to-one status discussions, leveling with personal caring, and adding value and zest.

An executive can extend a powerful invitation to managers and employees by simply asking information questions. *What is the most important thing that you will need from us in order for you to be an outstanding performer here?* A second powerful invitation is to ask for more personal feedback. *What is it I'm doing that is helping get our job done? What is it that I'm doing that prevents getting the job done as well as it could be? What is it I'm neglecting that needs attention?*

Feedback is an available, efficient method for assuring executives and players stay fresh. Feedback keeps those who are new, active ingredients in a situation from running into hidden land mines or unnecessary flak. It also works to freshen-up a long-time player. A number of individuals only receive feedback from one circle of admirers and detractors. They grow immune to that input. When these persons are put into feedback situations with significant superiors or strangers, they may be told the same information, but will listen for the first time.

Corporate pathfinders and mapmakers need to be looking for ever more sophisticated feedback loops. As an executive realizes ever more clearly that an organizational leader is necessary, but not sufficient, they learn how to be both important and humble. Rather than becoming bogged down by the multiple dependencies, a high-hope executive stays busy envisioning alternate routes and discovering new pathways. The charismatic-participatory leader will rethink the goals and re-state the vision. This executive is actively learning and teaching new ways and methods and assuring that there are fresh initiatives and players.

When an executive invites and appreciates information from every corner of the company, everybody can step forward to be an active stakeholder in the future success of the organization. That's the secret of Wizard of Oz magic and high-hopeful executive functioning. High hope stands in realities far from Oz and far from wishful fantasies. The old English proverb says: *if wishes were horses, beggars would be riders like princes.* A new world proverb says that when the going gets tough, the hopeful are ready.

Background Reading

Information about high hope and successful business managers:

Snyder, C. R., Harris, C., Anderson, J.R., Holleran, S.A., Irving, L.M., Sigmon, S.T., Yoshinobu, L., Gibb, J., Langelle, C. & Harney, P. (1991). The will and ways: Development and validation of an individual-differences measure of hope. *Journal of Personality and Social Psychology,* 60, 4, 570-585.

Snyder, C. R., Cheavens, J. & Sympson, S.C. (1997). Hope: An Individual Motive for Social Commerce. *Group Dynamics: Theory, Research and Practice.* 1, 2, 107-118.

An overview of the concepts developed by researcher C. Rick Snyder, U. Kansas, were prepared by Tori DeAngelis, "When the going gets tough, the hopeful keep going." *APA MONITOR,* July 1991, p. 18.

Anecdotes and parables:

Richard Bach's small book, *Illusions,* became almost as popular as *Johathan Livingston Seagull.* These two, quickly read tales are prime examples of the power of the parable to communicate complex ideas and wisdom that is confirmed by convolutions of scientific study. In fact, Warren Bennis recommends that the leader become a master of the metaphor and symbolic communications.

Richard Bode, 1993. *First You Have to Row a Little Boat.* New York: Time-Warner Books.

Andy Grove's 1989 book of advice to managers, *One on One with Andy Grove,* is a collection of anecdotes in a "Dear Abby" mode. It is easy to read with real-time "smarts." His managers report that he actually practiced what he preached. Grove's more recent books are more complex commentaries of what it takes to be successful.

General references:

Bass, B. M. (1985). *Transformational Leadership: Performance Beyond Expectation.* New York: Free Press.

Drath, W. H. & Palus, C.J. (1994) *Making common sense: Leadership as meaning making in communities of practice.* Greensboro, NC: Center for Creative Leadership.

Goodstein, L., Nolan, T. & Pfeiffer, J. W. (1993) *Applied Strategic Planning.* New York: McGraw-Hill.

Green, E. J. (1970), *Workbook for Corporate Planning.* New York: American Management Association Publications.

Heller, F. (1989). The underutilization of competence in British management. In B. J. Fallow, H.P. Pfister, J. Brebner (Eds.). *Advances in Industrial Organizational Psychology.* Amsterdam: North-Holland, pp. 47-52.

Levinson, H. (1968). *Executive.* Cambridge, MA: Harvard University Press.

Levinson, H. (1981). When executives burn out. *Harvard Business Review,* May-June.

Levinson, H. (1994). Why the behemoths fell. *The American Psychologist.* 49, 5, 428-436.

Harvard Business Review, November-December 1969, published *"The Management Process in 3-D."* R. Alec MacKenzie's elaboration of what management is all about remains basic to training in business and organizational operations.

O'Roark, A. M. *(1991)*. Organizational planning and systematic betterment: The case of the pilot planning project. *Consulting Psychology Bulletin,* 43, 2, 7-15, Summer 1991. (R)

Senge, P. (1990). *The Fifth Discipline.* New York: Doubleday.

Wheatley, M. J. (1992). *Leadership and the New Science. Learning about Organization from an Orderly Universe.* SF: Berrett-Koehler Publishers. Wheatley observes that "Every organization is an identity in motion, moving through the world, trying to make a difference" (p. 58). She makes a strong case for the value of discrepant feedback.

Chapter 12

Making a Difference

Every success has a beginning. From birth to death each self is an organized process directed toward four goals: survival, adequacy, growth, and meaningfulness. We can use our innate organizing capability to turn our visions inside-out.

Invitational leadership releases a collective capacity generated by relationships and produces an organization with a future.

- Alive and Well: Survival
- Wised-up and Re-sized: Adequacy
- Global & Local Input: Growth
- Making a Difference: Meaningfulness

Alive and Well: Survival

[#] 101. The ideal leader uses power to achieve goals, and solve problems, to gather information and make decisions. Thus described, power can be viewed as a positive, even an essential, force. . . . [#]30. Active corporate CEO's indicate they create an agenda for change that includes strategies for achieving their vision and building an implementation network strong enough to elicit cooperation, compliance, and teamwork.
Miriam and Kenneth Clark. 1994. *Choosing to Lead*

Goodby, Woolworth. Hello . . . Venator.
[Goodby, five and dimers . . . Hello, sports apparel wearers.]
Yumiko Ono. *Wall Street Journal.* April 2, 1998

In organizations with a future, *invitational leadership* bridges the individual-collective divide in order to assure that vision and power connect with trust and values. Charismatic-participatory management inspires and enables a corporate community. Once coworkers value the vision and trust that doing their best contributes to fulfilling the dream, senior executives have put in place the conditions that are conducive to survival, adequacy, growth, and meaningfulness. This is leadership that manifests core values, that stimulates high hope, and that commands respect for individual differences while demonstrating enthusiasm for synergistic cooperation.

In chapter 12, organizational power and executive effectiveness emerge as consequences of organized, directed processes. It is a process that begins with innermost perceptions about self, others, and tasks. These are the bare-bones behind Part One that guide how we go about putting things in order. Part Two traces the process of enlivening ideas and ventures by recognizing how the emotions curiosity, anxiety, and anger motivate and inspire action. And, Part Three arrives at a culmination of readiness for the executive quest through attainment of organizational savvy and charismatic-participatory leadership.

As we forge ahead in the new millennium, my confidence in the invitational approach is bolstered by what managers tell me about executives whom they admired and who taught them about the path to success. The following capsule summary of personal experiences was generated in an executive effectiveness course. The class was assigned the task of describing the characteristics of the ideal executive based on what they admired most about the manager or executive who had the greatest impact on their own management style. They were each given time for describing the manager they admired most and why. A time limit was given for discussion and the group was instructed to achieve a group consensus statement by the end of the time allocation. They determined that:

> *The executive that makes a difference is one that is a strategic visionary. [This person is] Fair, delegates to subordinates, allows them to perform and is interested in their development. [Moreover, the executive] Realizes that there is life beyond the job and stresses family values in it.*

This was an almost-perfect class. Yes, they left out words as they raced the clock to craft a mutually acceptable abstract of their evidence. But, the greater shortcoming, in my reflection on the week, was one felt by a hyper-competitive executive. In a class of twelve, he was the only participant who indicated in his course evaluation that he did not get the full measure of everything he expected to get from the class.

Why? What would have provided him with his full-measure of meaningfulness? The simple answer is: *vision, motivation, and action.*

This almost-but-not-quite-satisfied manger, an investment special-ist, revealed no vision of what he hoped to achieve in his management career, no image of his quest. He demonstrated no motivation to engage in emotionally honest discovery of what would let him be more effec-tive. During the week he gave little evidence of working hard to accomplish something for himself, for others, or for the tasks at hand.

His attention to the present was divided and half-hearted, except for occasional heroic-defensive reactions to someone else's problem situa-tion, as he rescued or protected his selected "best buddies." He avoided and abetted others in avoiding the hard questions posed by the group. He missed parts of several sessions, explaining that he had to talk on the phone with an adult-child who was in trouble as a result of being overdrawn at the bank. And, he missed the opportunity to receive the most important benefits of the course.

The illustration of "An Invitational Leadership Approach" (ILA) shows three domains of executive competence—enterprising vision [cognitive and perceptual], charismatic motivational ability [emotional and inspirational]; and, participatory action skill [understanding and applying the range of solo-to-total group decision making]. In the ILA figure, three competency cubes are anchored within a person who is living and maturing within a complex environment. That setting is an interactive network of interpersonal relationships that exist within a workplace with its own unique culture. The organization is, in turn, imbedded within a social-political community. The ILA illustration combines highlights of earlier chapters. It plots an effectiveness path-way through a zeitgeist-ortgeist [time-place] terrain.

The executive competence trio, *vision, motivation, and action,* provide a simple set of reasons why the manager in the almost-perfect class fell short of his goal. His lack of vision for what to get from the course is revealed in his lack of motivation to initiate action in the class. It is a cyclical escalation somewhat like the chicken and the egg puzzle—which came first, the chicken or the egg? For example, he may have had a prior lack of motivation for personal development which truncated his vision and objective.

In this ILA illustration, an executive initiates the organizational process and productive flow with a vision or an idea for an enterprise or collective venture. Then, the executive job shifts to an emphasis on motivating others to action.

The more complex answer to the manager's sense of dissatisfaction, like the story behind the short and the long chop sticks, lies deep within

An Invitational Leadership Approach

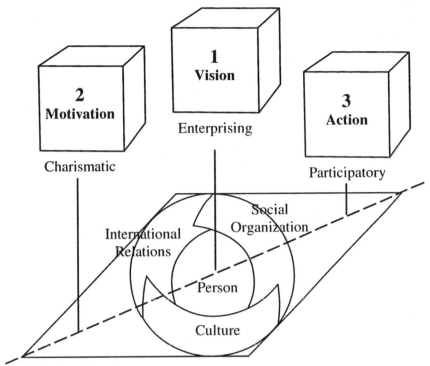

The EXECUTIVE within an ORGANIZATION within an ENVIROMENT

Charismatic-Participatory Style

national culture. In many workplaces unwritten norms attached to meaningful achievement call for Man of La Mancha tilting with each windmill that appears to be challenging, à la Don Quixote. In the case of the unfulfilled manager, he was taken aback when I suggested that his derailment danger was that he would be easy to "hook," to distract. His own "war-stories" revealed how cleverly he succeeded whenever the boss or his peers informally challenged his versatility and courage. They bet him that he couldn't drink as much as "Jack." They suggested that he wouldn't bid a deal as high as "Sally." He even boasted how he won a dare that surely deflated his credibility and eroded trust. A peer bet him that he couldn't lie convincingly to a superior. Such sidetracks lead to derailment.

I will never know if he chose to digest or discount my feedback about how he is easily sidetracked from what's important. Accepting this uncomfortable message, he can modify his windmill tactics and survive to become a senior executive in his warp-speed industry. Senior-level success depends more on proactive, trustworthy collaborations and less on spur-of-the moment joustings.

In class settings, as in the workplace, survival challenges and defensive interests get instant attention. For training purposes, there are dozens of survival exercises, with names like *Survival at Sea, Jungle Survival Exercise, Caribbean Island Survival Exercise, Desert Survival Problem.* Class members are challenged to think through what to do after being involved in an accident. The practical spin-off is that the debriefing provides technical knowledge about what experts say to do. The primary learning target, however, is how to take time to collaborate with others in emotional circumstances and to arrive at the surest plan for survival.

The simulations named above may give veteran managers flash-backs to on-the-job training in teamwork. Course objectives were communication skills and consensus decision-making. An estimated 60% of major US corporations provide in-house workshops in which supervisors are introduced to group problem solving methods. Human resources training manuals rely heavily on the ever-popular survival exercises. This statistic is a real head-shaker when thinking about the estimated 60 to 75% base-rate for managerial incompetence. Those shaking their heads will ask, is it a matter of ineffectual instructors and inadequate training? Or, are we not getting the incompetent managers into training?

Executives familiar with consensus outcomes are impressed that thinking out loud together in a workshop can come closer to producing the ideal survival plan whether the scenario is an airplane crash in the desert, a jeep accident in the frozen tundra, or a boating mishap in the South Seas. Again and again, negotiated rank-orderings of priority items and actions come closer to recommendations of survival experts than a ranking by a non-expert working alone.

Now and then, one or two individuals produce independent scores that match the experts more closely than the small group consensus does. This outcome is interpreted to mean a group did not achieve synergy. Synergy is considered to occur when the group makes the most effective use of resources of the individuals present. The group ideally recognizes and concurs with the most knowledgeable and/or logical person in the group. It is an objective rational merging of individual knowledge and thinking. The implication is that each individual's ideas are given attention and the better ideas are selected based on the reasoning behind the idea. The method avoids voting, which can quickly establish cliques within a group. Nevertheless, a lot depends on communication skills and emotional-motivational abilities of the individuals in the group.

Translating training room insights to the executive suite is always questionable and risky. One possible take-away message from the survival exercises is that success begins with a rank ordering of what's important. Such here-and-now priorities, no matter how expertly done, will be ineffectual unless they are acted upon as ranked. Ranking priorities is an everyday activity. In every organization, senior executives select how to spend time each day, their own and others' time. They determine what to do first and next. Their success depends on bringing together people so that strengths become productive and weaknesses become irrelevant. Leaders continually define objectives and review the thinking behind deciding what *not* to do. They evaluate the means being used to reach goals and assure that methods promote the values of the organization. They update the system of rewards and punishments and make explicit organizational aspirations. They exemplify the corporate spirit and its culture.

Executives facing an in-process crisis must assemble survival information and composite best-thinking for best-quality solutions. A leader's efforts to reduce threat and lessen fear will unfreeze the group's physical, mental, and emotional talents. A resulting problem-solving competence is an expansion of a quaint definition of general intelligence, crafted by Stern in 1946. Known as the "g" factor, it refers to the resonance of the interaction of the several thinking abilities of a person. Classroom consensus work suggests there is a "g" factor of organizational survival intelligence. It is the resonance of the interaction of the thinking capabilities of group members.

Managers who were not fired or outplaced during corporate retrenchments attributed their survival to one or more earlier experiences. The Center for Creative Leadership [CCL] researchers summarized these events in four statements. Survivors were persons who had taken on challenging job assignments. Survivors were those who had been mentored or influenced by significant people. Survivors had been exposed to and endured hardships. Survivors had been involved with coursework at the right time.

Executive survivors who participated in the CCL interviews thought that those who derailed either relied too much on one strong ability or did not attend to personality patterns that inhibited their learning of more effective approaches. These conclusions are similar to previous descriptions of executives' dark-side. Tragic flaws often emerged from excessive use of strengths or naive blind spots.

What would be the lessons-of-experience for executives with great expectations who are working in an opposite corporate climate, when the enterprise is expanding and things are snowballing? History may already have recorded that wisdom for us. It's our inheritance from a famous entrepreneur who, after he was sixty years old, brought us "the greatest show on earth." P.T. Barnum, grand style survivor who was once declared the most widely-known American who ever lived, gave ten business success rules.

Barnum's tips from the 1850s were elaborated by Joe Vitalle almost 150 years later, not into three ring circus tales, but into ten rings of business power.

There is a customer born every minute; use skyrockets to get people's attention; give people more than their money's worth; use publicity; use advertising; network to get results; treat employees with respect; persevere; believe in the power of the written word; believe in the power of public speaking.

Barnum's version of invitational power is decidedly charismatic and participatory, and directed to those who survive by becoming bigger and better.

Wised-Up and Re-Sized: Adequacy

. . . power in organizations is the capacity generated by relationships . . . pp 144-145
Margaret Wheatley. 1993. *Leadership and the New Science*

Political advisor Machiavelli and psychoanalytic visionary Freud saw power as intriguing, but more importantly, as critical to a sense of adequacy. With perspective on *who's the boss*, leaders are wised-up and resized. They are managing internal and external controls, never letting the rudder swing helplessly in multiple cross-currents. A great threat to that sense of adequacy is helplessness. The feeling of helplessness is a central factor in depression, which remains a closeted barrier to executive success.

A Dagwood-sandwich generation of executives is working between transitions from vertical to horizontal to matrix to virtual organizational structures. They are adjusting to twenty-first-century "brick-and-click" business, a phrase used to describe businesses that have both buildings for selling products and electronic websites for customer purchases. At the same time, companies yo-yo between downsizing and up-scaling while realigning. Reported incidents of depression increase when work complexities intensify.

Adding to the pressures of the internal and external management challenges, the self-driven initiative in conscientious junior executives may include being highly self-critical. These achievers must work hard to separate disappointment from defeat. In times of highly visible and widely felt corporate quakes and faultline shiftings, organizational decision-makers struggle to keep a distance from a rumor-hungry press. Inevitable business disappointments and fickleness of public opinion can leave well-intentioned executives vulnerable to anger and guilt. Typically, this emotional sequence includes feelings of depression intensified by a sense of helplessness and being inadequate to impact the immediate situation.

Swarms of self-help books recommend warding off unacceptable mental states by taming the sense of helplessness. They accomplish this sleight of hand by shifting attention to controllable details. Quick-read paperbacks and hardbacks tell us how to dress for success and how to emulate Attila the Hun, or Sonya Friedman's "smart-cookies" that don't crumble.

A number of less opportunistic writers agree with the helplessness-fixers that good manners and smiling win more friends than rudeness and frowning. But these authors advise against sublimation. They think fluff and store-bought suits and jeans cannot cover up lack of ability and character. Agreeing that assertive initiatives and porcupine exteriors may, indeed, back-off an enemy, they add caveats. Wise-up, they admonish. Excessive or obvious energy spent on costuming and posturing can be seen by others as manipulative, deceptive, and intimidating. Most importantly, it fails to address the most important issue of adequacy, the competence to do the job.

Accessories and mannerisms can reflect inner wishes and intentions, but the sense of adequacy to manage situations stems from competence and ethics. The hallmarks of the manager who has been wised-up and re-sized are twofold. They arrive with updated industrial and technological knowledge and a well-defined ethics-without-arrogance. Adequacy under high stress is the ability to apply skills and knowledge to problem solving while maintaining moral standards of conduct.

Executive behaviors under intense and pressured circumstances began to intrigue Henry Murray and his Harvard research associates more than half a century ago. They continued their studies in conjunction with the U.S. Office of Strategic Services throughout the winds-of-war decades. By systematically observing behaviors they were able to assess central motivating forces that organize perception, thinking, and action. They identified patterns that worked constructively to transform an unsatisfying situation. They could confidently select persons for irregular duty assignments who had strength and stamina to endure heavy stressors. Today, we think of these persons as the hardy executives or leaders who seem to thrive on stressors.

As early as 1939, leadership adequacy and social power was discussed in terms of autocratic, democratic, and *laissez-faire* practices. Later, in 1959, when focus turned to peacetime business activity, social power was studied according to two practices, authoritarian vs participative decision-making. These investigations, which were conducted within a democratic society, found democratic and participative methods to be the most productive.

Subsequent researchers encouraged executives to enlarge their participatory practices to become more-than carrot-and-stick contractors who lead by issuing rewards and criticisms, gifts and threats. Recent evidence shows that effective senior executives and leaders are emphasizing techniques proven to be more productive in the long haul. They are spending more time on transformational negotiations and goal settings than on the work of transactional contracting and finger pointing. Evidence collected at the Leadership Studies Institute at SUNY Binghamton shows greater entrepreneurial success for a transformational method. The approach is sometimes referred to as inspirational and sometimes called charismatic. Survey respondents use both words to describe a transformational leader's behaviors. This chain of discovery dates back to the 1940s Ohio State studies. Their research on task-and-consideration behaviors of managers provides a foundation for partnering charismatic consideration with participatory task-actions. The behavior pattern that is presented in the ILA model can be illustrated on a two-axis grid. The consideration or relationship behaviors are the vertical axis and the task behaviors are the horizontal axis.

Strengthening the chain of discovery, post-WWII Harvard scholars and their corporate collaborators found that persons who proved most adequate under high stress and who moved higher up corporate career ladders were persons with a strong desire for *achievement*. These individuals worked hard to excel according to externally benchmarked goals and their own internalized standards. Executives-in-training who attended Donald McClelland's programs and who later actually improved were those who took personal responsibility for finding solu-

CHARISMATIC- PARTICIPATORY LEADERSHIP

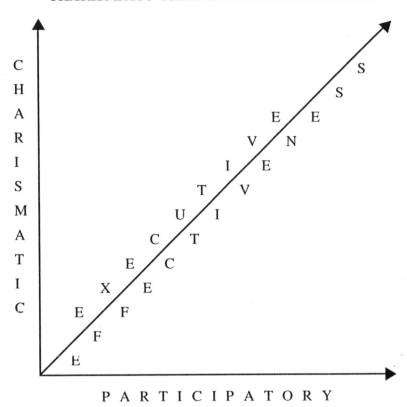

The Invitational Leadership Approach (ILA)

tions, who set goals that offered good potentials for success with moderate levels of risk, and who demonstrated genuine interest in getting concrete feedback on progress.

A keen desire to impact group productivity (task) was observed in those with a strong drive to influence groups (relationship). This indicator of power motivation connected with adequacy in management. Furthermore, these executives expressed a desire to be seen as strong and influential in the achievement of corporate prosperity. These power-motives were observed in a manager's on-going efforts to be given increased responsibility and frequent behaviors directed toward influencing outcomes.

The effective manager's power motive is labeled a *socialized* achievement motive. This workworld power motive is distinguished from two different power-objectives that are labeled *personal* and *affiliative*. *Personal* interest in power is considered by some specialists as self-serving and a reflection of unresolved early-life issues. Leaders with a strong *personal* power drive have been associated with psycho-analytic interpretations of a "narcissistic borderline personality with paranoid delusions of grandeur." *Personal* power motives are considered to be a dark-side characteristic by these interpreters. Even non-psychoanalytic observers forecast trouble for a work group led by someone whose sense of adequacy depends on accumulating personal power.

Others forecast positive potentials for *personal* power, when associated with careers in politics or those noted in I. A. Taylor's studies of the artist's "will to power" and transactualization. In the creative work of the gifted, whether they are craftspersons, technological specialists, or fine artists, personal power is directed toward mastery of the media to express inner images and ideas, i.e., musical instruments, paints, stone, wood, words, machines. While these individuals have a dominant *personal* power drive that enables creative, innovative, and important achievement, it is quite a different process from the typical work of the corporate manager and considered unlikely to lend itself to routine work group leadership.

Furthermore, poor prognosis for managerial adequacy is reported for those with a dominant *affiliative* motivation. This person primarily wants to be liked. Staying on good terms with everybody makes it impossible to be consistent in implementing organizational policies. They make frequent exceptions that create morale problems among those workers who see those exceptions to rules as unfair to themselves.

Power over situations can be expressed in one or several ways that command attention and respect. The classic set of five power tactics observed in democratic society begins with three economic and legal-based sources of influence that are labeled *legitimate, reward* and *coercive.* Two other ways to make an impact are referred to as *expert* and *referent.* Power that is called *legitimate* comes with the formal contract for the job. *Reward* power, also a function of a management position, is based on ability to administer extrinsic and intrinsic rewards that are valued by the target of influence. These "carrot" inducements sometimes infringe upon desires that are not work related. *Coercive* power is based on fear and is similar to, but the opposite of, reward power. These "stick" influences involve the giving of punishments or withholding of something desired. The latter two are transactional bases of power.

Expert power is based on extensive knowledge or analytical competence in a given area. *Referent* power is based on being liked and admired by others because of personality or shared interests, goals, priorities. These two bases of power are consistent with descriptions of behaviors of transformational and charismatic leaders.

Two additional sources of power available to executives were added to the original set, *information* and *connection*. *Information* power is similar to but different from knowledge. It refers to possession of or access to methods, facts and ideas considered valuable to others. *Connections* power is similar to *referent* power, but does not imply shared values. It is simply access to influential persons and higher executives.

In 1997 French and Bell's 1950s concepts were reaffirmed and reshaped into six ways of influencing: *coercive, formal, expert, moral, referent*, and *relationship*. An AMA excerpt from Brill and Worth recapitulates these bases of power in a newsletter for corporate leaders. Power tactics are separated into two camps. One set is associated with a legitimate position and includes only two of the six, *coercive* and *formal*.

In the second set are four types of subtle power. *Expert, moral, referent* and r*elationship* are methods that influence the hearts and minds of employees. They are recommended as the most effective for achieving corporate alignments. Alignment powers lend themselves to bringing about charismatic motivation and enterprising action. According to Brill and Worth's interpretation, legitimate powers represent participatory action and the subtle influences are associated with charismatic motivation in the ILA model.

A great deal of the sense of adequacy depends on the situation and on how others respond, immediately and in the long run. Power may be coercive or consentive, and it may appeal to higher or lower values and objectives. Invitational leaders cultivate ways of being directive that are more consentive than coercive.

It is easy for a superior in an instructive role to unintentionally present ideas and decisions in ways that are received by a subordinate as being forced to comply. This is the logic behind the legal codes that argue for stringent harassment interpretations of superiors' acts. There are, indeed, times to be instructive and to expect compliance based on work objectives that are not self-serving or harassing. Compliance becomes a consentive event when carried out in light of previously agreed upon conditions, i.e., prescribed standards and methods; predetermined time and consistency constraints; negotiated agreements for acquisition of alternative or innovative skills.

An invitational style means assessing realities at hand while maintaining visible respect for self, others, and tasks. The infamous Peter Principle says that managers will be promoted to one step beyond adequacy. A non-fatalistic, less waggish, opinion is that leadership adequacy is an equal opportunity ability. Situational adequacy will not be restricted to or guaranteed by age, gender, height, power position, career path, or training background.

Standing Tall. Mountainside Burials and Moments of Adequacy

The soft blue-grey mists that hover protectively in and among the blue-green hills and vales of eastern Kentucky were overpowered by the downpouring of mid-day sunlight. Only the striped tenting strung hastily across the tops of a dozen or so gleaming white poles shaded the small crowd of perhaps a hundred who gathered on that steep Appalachian mountainside. A much greater number had attended the service in the simple, but adequate country church some forty miles away. That humble place of worship was built from the contributions of the man who was being buried deep in the soil of the people he had cared for and doctored for over 70 years. Dr. Will Jones was 96 years old when he died as he lived, peacefully and gently.

Here was a man a whole state was honoring for the difference he had made in generations of lives. All seven of the elected state officers were in attendance, having flown from the capital to the far corner of the state to pay homage to an exceptional individual. Also among the guests were two past governors and a state icon, Col. Sanders. As the church service began the fried chicken entrepreneur was ushered into the small space open by the aisle in a family pew. He was breathless after having been driven in his white suit and trim white beard with his white cane in his white luxury stretch-car in great haste. The state trooper who stopped the car for speeding was obligated to write out a ticket before escorting him—at the same rate of speed—to the door of the church. More breathless was the astonished small boy that Kentucky Col. Sanders sat down beside.

Dr. Will's great nephew, attending his first funeral, sat especially close to his mother. This made the extra space in the family pew for the KFC originator. The boy spent the rest of the solemn event, eyes wide open, mouth agape, gazing at the nationally recognized entrepreneur. Harlan Sanders had opened his first restaurant a few miles from the country church. He was a lifelong acquaintance, sometimes patient, and great admirer of Dr. Will.

After the final prayers and hymns, the hearse and state flag-bearing cavalcade made the forty-mile trip to the cemetery for final liturgies while over 100 state troopers stood at attention, saluting the procession at every mile along the rural byways and interstate highways. When the dignitaries were past, the uniformed honor guard stood "at ease." None could have predicted the unexpected conclusion of the full-honors requiem at the burial grounds landscaped deep within wooded hills and above the river banks near Cumberland Falls.

After declaring the first words of the final paragraph in an impassioned rendition of the Masonic Order burial rites, the doctor's long-time friend and head of the local Masonic lodge pitched forward into the open pit, falling dead of a heart attack onto the casket. The undertaker-funeral director rose to attend to the fallen speaker and collapsed onto an artificial grass strip covering the dirt that would soon fill in the open grave.

The current governor who was seated less than ten feet away in the place of honor, on the first row and next to the doctor's State Treasurer-daughter, rose up, looked this way and that, saying words like, "I've got to get out of here, get me out of here, someone get me out of here." He rushed away from the open grave, pushing his way out of the tent and through the covey of state troopers helping him into his flag-flying long-car—the governor's wife scurried along behind as fast as she could.

Others who had seats under the awning began standing up quickly, knocking over their folding chairs which were precariously arranged on the steeply slanting mountainside. As mourners prepared to escape from frightening sights of death and dying surrounding the open grave, the grand and then very old first commissioner of baseball, also a former state governor, moved deliberately toward the grave, turned, steadied himself with his cane, and spoke loudly and clearly, telling the crowd, "There is no need for alarm. Please leave quietly in respect for the departed and those who are in need of care. Would a doctor please come forward."

A medical person came to aid the two graveside casualties. Others left the tent in a calm and orderly manner. When the guests were all gone, an ambulance arrived to transport the funeral director who suffered a non-fatal heart attack to a nearby hospital, which was also built with contributions from Dr. Will, his father-in-law, and three of his cousins. All were physicians who spent their lives attending to the birthing, healing and dying in the mountain communities. The hearse that delivered Dr. Will to this final resting place returned to the funeral home carrying the body of the eloquent Masonic Lodge leader.

As the last state trooper waited at attention on the uphill roadway, Dr. Will's daughter, brother-in-law, and niece stood together at the side of the grave and completed the ritual interment service. The brother-in-law knew the Masonic ceremony, the niece knew the Christian scriptures, and the daughter shed tears over the loss of her father.

The next day a new state law was drafted, one that prohibited elected officials from flying on the same airplane at the same time, en masse, for any official or unofficial business.

How many leaders demonstrate adequacy in this word picture? Which ones made a difference in the past? Which made a difference in the present? Which made a difference for the future? This roll call of leaders would come to at least 119. Representing diverse careers, training, and levels of status, the gathering included 5 physicians, 7 elected state officials, 2 former governors, 1 highly successful entrepreneur, 1 Masonic Lodge head, 1 funeral director, 1 brother-in-law who was a retired Army Colonel, 1 niece with a Ph.D. who was serving as Assistant State Treasurer, and over 100 state troopers. The numerous guests were neighbors and relatives of all walks of life. Their abilities ranged from farming to schooling. Their jobs were as diverse as car dealerships and railroading.

Each had made a difference in the past working to promote the health and safety of the citizens of the commonwealth. Several made a difference in the present: the former governor and baseball commissioner; the brother-in-law; the niece—each of whom took initiative to assure the dignified closure to the memorial. Many of the 119 influenced the future. The doctors and elected officials had provided for building churches, hospitals, and government offices and memorials. Others established wise policies about activities of the Governor, Lieutenant Governor, Secretary of State, Treasurer, Clerk of the Court of Appeals, Superintendent of Public Instruction, and State Auditor. The state is assured that in the event of a tragic travel accident the citizens will not lose the entire group elected to lead the commonwealth's government system.

Adequacy at any stage or phase of a leadership career, according to accumulated observations by social scientists, depends upon talking a lot, being a somewhat dramatic or entertaining communicator, and thinking somewhat quicker than the average of the group. It begins to sound like the Peter Principle is more a function of loss of zest, hope and vision than a lack of capability.

Ending the century, *fin-de-siècle* executives-in-waiting dealt with multiple diversities. They were solving problems that included everything from personnel, to work sites, to markets, to salary plans, to legal entities. Senior managers may be troubleshooters and corporate black belts or an expert with a hot skill. According to Hal Lancaster's *WSJ* interviews, new era middle management will add substantive value and will be positioned as interpreters, conduits, shapers, and drivers of corporate strategy. To be adequate they will need to be comfortable and competent at organizing complex subjects, solving problems, communicating ideas and making swift decisions. They will need to be able to bring order to traumatic situations as smoothly as Happy Chandler did at Dr. Will's funeral.

Searches for general managers, below the division head level, increased 58% in one year, 1997. Hiring agents did not consider it adequate for candidates to just be good at presiding over narrow departments, doling out task assignments, doing performance appraisals, and passing information up and down the organizational hierarchy. Adequacy mazeways for managers have gone multi-dimensional. Roots of adequacy are comparatively constant, but the maintenance of adequacy requires intentional and appropriate growth and continuing high hope.

The figure below illustrates the roles of perceptual and maintenance functions in the achievement of invitationally powerful executive behavior. Competence and ethics are shaped and informed through education and intentional reflection on the current relevance of assumptions and beliefs that comprise the perceptual foundation.

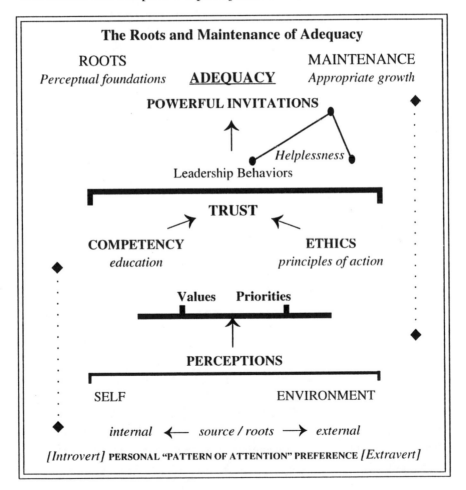

Global and Local Input: Growth

Contrary to common belief that innate talents are the critical factors for exceptional performance, investigators have found that acquired skills, knowledge, and physiological adaptations in response to intense practice are the primary mechanisms, mediating the highest levels of performance . . . experts optimize improvement in their performance and eventually attain excellence . . . elite performers are shown to have engaged in deliberate-practice activities specifically designed to improve their performance . . . the elements of deliberate practice [are] . . . specific goals to improve performance, successive refinement through repetition, feedback and instruction . . .

Anders Ericsson, 1998, *The Road to Excellence*

A need for lifelong learning is not a fresh awareness. Neither is it news that a significant amount of adult learning takes place on-the-job. The ancient Greeks referred to the never-ending transformation of the personality as *paideia*, which was education that is not limited to the classroom, or to parental adjusting of the young to the ways of the society, or even to an organized, conscious process. Paideia includes the structured and unstructured making-and-shaping of a person across the years that allows that individual to convert hopes and plans into consummation and realization.

Harvey Cox's book title, *On Not Leaving It to the Snake,* calls attention to taking on personal responsibility rather than adopting a helpless resignation to apocalyptic disaster or messianic rescue. A multiplying population of post-retirement adults intensifies the need for a comprehensive approach to lifelong learning and adjustment. Full blown, age relevant curricula and lesson-plans are making later years more productive and interesting, and fostering a major social sector industry.

It is increasingly incumbent upon management experts and corporate leaders to enlarge preretirement knowledge bases and skill repertoires in order to assure that their organizations have productive and interesting later years. Tomorrow belongs to collaborating organizations, whether they operate in private business and industry, in the public and government sectors, or in the non-profit social services. Peter Drucker has transformed his "organization man" into a vision of constellations of organizations, where private and public workforces are coordinated by the "social sector" organizations. This proliferating type of organization increased by 70% between the 1960s and 1990s. Social sector corporations and institutions will be recognized by their common purpose—the changing of human beings through healing, training, and developing. Drucker squarely places schools at society's center with the task of creating citizenship in workplaces, in communities, and in government.

Authentication of competence and knowledge assumes greater importance as corporations need wider ranges of expertise to comprehend and respond to world-wide inputs and diversification of technology and distribution systems. Businesses will rely on multiple delivery specialists for transfer of information, goods and services. Expediters with global capabilities will be essential to local productivity and prosperity. Business leaders inherit the job of preparing workers to understand, cope with, and take advantage of electronic communications and advanced infrastructures of commerce.

While employers cannot assume the full adult schooling responsibility, a senior executive has an unavoidable assignment as dean of a paracurriculum for corporate adequacy and growth. More and more management books devote considerable space to the duties of the executive as teacher, as role model, as mentor, as coach, as inspirer, as first among innovative learners and problem solvers.

Some executives also find themselves deans of basic education. Management specialists in Mexico and Columbia report that businesses are providing the 3-Rs to adult workers who missed out on their elementary schooling. Similarly, U.S. companies assume a basic education function when hiring emigrants or the long-unemployed who are attempting to re-enter the job market. At the advanced extreme, the medical industry is in a constant struggle to help employees keep pace with advances in health treatment procedures. High-tech computer firms are reported to find it quicker to bring in workers with the newest software skills than to retrain those skilled in the last generation of procedures.

Out-of-date workers often must take it upon themselves to go out and get retrained. Some will and some won't. A percent remain curious and eager to acquire the latest techniques. Others resist going through the awkward stages of acquiring a new skill. They prefer the familiar comfort of old methods. Fortunately, there are places where many earlier methods are still used and do the job adequately. Perhaps, one day these businesses will continue in compounds like the historic center of Williamsburg, VA. Workers and activities thrive on preservation and re-enactment of early American crafts and lifeways.

A number of mainstream companies already have "universities" that provide education and training for networks of franchises or field operations. The students range from new hires to mid-life workers and executive think-tankers. The SPRINT university is in Kansas City.

MacDonalds is proud of their hamburger university. The military services have a progressive schedule of learning events that often culminate for the highest ranks at the National Defense University in Arlington, VA. Academic colleges and universities are giving credit to adult students for work/life experience as they seek to complete traditional degree programs.

None of these growth-promoting activities comes without investment of time, effort, and money on the part of the company and the worker. One woman in the banking industry could have received her bachelor's degree in a year's time, if she had only been willing to complete the tedious, onerous task of putting down in words the details of what her life experiences taught her. She decided that she didn't need degree credentials enough to take the time to do the reflecting and writing work. She also rationalized that banking industry changes were up in the air to such a degree that she did not yet know what she would need to learn to advance in her organization.

For this young woman, as is predicted for any adult growth, learning will be most appealing, will be achieved more rapidly, and will have more lasting effects when it is connected to something personally meaningful and immediately useful. Problem solving and experiential methods advocated by educator John Dewey were proven by Kurt Lewin and experimental social psychologists to deliver durable lessons and to effect major attitude changes. The next generation educator-scholars, like Arthur Combs and Malcom Knowles, taught that human learning is a simple and natural event, IF threats are removed and there is here and now relevance. Even the most global information can be made locally relevant when put in terms that are down-to-earth and delivered in ways that are interesting to the learners.

Knowles called the science of adult teaching and learning *androgogy*. He wanted to make it stand out distinctly in the general science of education. For many generations schooling was considered to be something that elders provided for the children of a society. Thus, the art and science of teaching and learning became known as "pedagogy," a word related to pediatrics and the Greek word for small child. A distinction that goes beyond the words used to describe learning and growth is that adults are quickly given notice that they need to take responsibility for their own learning. In addition to this important transference of primary initiative, other conditions for productive adult learning are a climate of mutual respect, collaboration, mutual trust, authenticity, pleasure in the process, and physically comfortable surroundings. The first job of the teacher, trainer, facilitator, or executive leader is to assist a learner in becoming aware of a need to know relevant information. This is the insight that sets the stage for the learner to accept responsibility for learning.

Executive inspirers of adult learning can take heart in knowing that coexisting with pre-set genetic maturation and circadian hormonal patterns are vast realms of growth potentials. The potentials are adaptable to environmental influences and responsive to formal teaching. These human growth and development notions may seem unfamiliar to managers and executives but they can be trusted. The concepts have proven to be reliable. Lifelong learning is now promoted as a human agenda in schools and in bookstores. Scientist Eisley's *Grow or Die* and Deepak Chopra's *Ageless Body, Timeless Mind* continue to be nonfiction bestsellers.

As early as 1981, Harry Levinson wrote that executives who see themselves as leaders and teachers are those who recognize that the essence of their task is to enhance the capacities of their subordinates. The executive's job as educator is to support ways that will enable both themselves and their subordinates to accomplish their mutual goals and fulfill their joint needs. Levinson warned that there will be no "pat" recipes for an executive leader's teaching role. He envisions that every executive brings his or her own unique talents, skills, and personality to the task and will innovate ways to make the organization a learning, growing, curiosity-filled workplace.

When issuing calls to growth, corporate halls often echo with the words creativity and transformation. Even reengineering iconoclasts call for innovation when they suggest a total starting over. Hammer and Champy, before their statistical-controls "fishbone" model got stuck in their throats, cheered the reengineering of Ford company's North American accounts payable department. The situation before reengineering = 500 workers, after-reengineering =125 workers; before reengineering = 3 pieces of paper documentation, after-reengineering = no paper documentation. All work was entry into data bases. One piece of paper was generated—the payment check. Statistical Profile: Before-reengineering = 3 departments: accounts payable, purchasing, receiving; After-reengineering = 1 process: procurement. Smoothly modernized departments soon learned the lesson of the 3-Mile Island nuclear power plant. Only alert human observers of automated processes can prevent major problems, mistakes, or fraud and glitch fallout.

Discovery of ways to increase efficiency in work processes is certainly half of the corporate education goal. This shakes off slow-downs and backlogs from the yesteryears. The other half of the goal is thinking about future days and readiness to meet customer needs that don't yet exist. Applied imagination suddenly becomes more than a skunk-works luxury.

People enjoy brainstorming in focus groups and at owners' meetings. It's even proven to be an upbeat energizer for greybeards and the increasing number of wealthy older women, bluehairs, at stockholders meetings. *How can we adapt this product? What other uses could it be put to? How could it be modified . . . in shape, in color, in motion . . .? What could be added to it to make it stronger, higher, give extra value? What could we subtract, take away, condense, make lighter, quieter . . . ? How could we substitute an ingredient, revamp the work situation . . . ? What could be rearranged . . . resequenced? Can something be reversed, turned backward? Can it be combined with something, blended with an ensemble, made to address several appeals?*

Local and global learning and creative thinking will cross barriers of time and geography to keep us and our organizations growing throughout longer lifetimes.

Making A Difference: Meaningfulness

Human beings create meaning the way spiders create webs.
M.C. Bateson. *Calendar Pocketpal Quotes*

[#]48. The influence of the leader on a group is not merely in terms of the accomplishment of organizational objectives, but extends to standards of conduct as well. If the group does not hold to high standards, it may produce great damage within the larger community. Leaders must not ignore the responsibility for maintaining high standards. . . . [#] 53. Leaders must learn the use of language applied to values and must differentiate among moral values, ethical values, pragmatic values, absolute values, and universal values.
Miriam and Kenneth Clark. 1994. *Choosing to Lead*

20th Century Presidents
TIME magazine ranks America's Chief Executives

1.	Franklin D. Roosevelt	1933-45	10. Bill Clinton	1993-2001
2.	Theodore Roosevelt	1901-09	11. William Howard Taft	1909-13
3.	Woodrow Wilson	1913-21	12. Gerald Ford	1974-77
4.	Harry S. Truman	1945-53	13. Calvin Coolidge	1923-29
5.	Dwight D. Eisenhower	1953-61	14. Jimmy Carter	1977-81
6.	Ronald Reagan	1981-89	15. Richard Nixon	1969-74
7.	Lyndon B. Johnson	1963-69	16. Warren Harding	1921-23
8.	John F. Kennedy	1961-63	17. Herbert Hoover	1929-33
9.	George Bush	1989-93		

> *"Making the Break From Middle Manager To a Seat at the Top"*
> *What does it take to squeeze through that final, narrow bottleneck between middle
> management and the exalted ranks of senior executives?. . . delivering results . . .
> thinking strategically, being persuasive and politically adroit, and having a 'signifi-
> cantly' broader organizational awareness . . . use humor to soften tough messages
> and relieve stress . . . manage time . . . set priorities . . . sort through the noise and
> stay on target . . . earn respect for being exceptionally good at what you do . . .
> treating all people with respect . . . get results and not embarrass me . . . be fun to
> hang out with. . . consistency. . . risk taking. . . volunteering for the biggest tasks. . .
> broaden your knowledge . . . seek . . .*
> Hal Lancaster. *Wall Street Journal.* 7-7-98

How do you get into the executive hall of fame and become remembered as having made a meaningful difference? A paradox is that executive achievement starts out as an individual inspiration but is meaningless until it is transformed into collective motivation and action. The narrow passage of the execuquest is through trust.

My first nominee for an executive hall of fame is an ethics specialist. D.L. has had, so far, two distinctly different careers. In his second career, he became CEO of a niche company in a high stakes business, professional liability insurance for lawyers. As CEO, he mastered new knowledge, mapped strategic efforts, and implemented a financially successful venture. The enterprise was so effective that it got the attention of the big name companies, the mega-insurers. These highly competitive firms actually regrouped and reduced their policy fees to reasonable levels.

Ethical standards became the substantive foundation for the upstart insurance firm. It was the backbone of their insurance policy decisions and of their successful courtroom judgments. Continuing education for the insurees in the fine points of ethical practice became the niche firm's very effective "ounce of prevention" strategy. The CEO was soon recognized for his work. D.L. became the first recipient of the Spain Award for outstanding service in continuing legal education. His citation said:

> *Over the past five years, the number of . . . attorneys affected
> by [his] knowledge and contribution to our CLE [Continuing Legal
> Education] effort is staggering . . . not only has he donated his time
> and expertise selflessly, he remains among the highest ranking and
> most popular speakers throughout the state, often receiving perfect
> scores. Not only does the audience appreciate his skillful and
> entertaining teaching methods, program managers appreciate his
> thorough and timely submission of top-quality materials and his
> well-prepared presentations . . . his contribution to this program*

*was nothing short of incredible . . . he believes in what he is doing
and . . . he believes in the legal profession—and the finest tradition
of what our profession is. . . .*

A Long-Line of Flying Geese Continues.
A Lawyer General Teaches Ethics

If you want to get a round of jokes going in a group, just mention the
word *lawyer. The only good lawyer is the absent lawyer. You can count all
the honest lawyers on the head of a pin. . . .* The historically honorable legal
profession that includes attorneys, barristers, legal counselors, and judges
takes the blame for unfair court judgments, monumental costs for legal
service, and unresolvable social problems.

Next, mention brigadier *general* and you activate dramatic images of
fierce warrior-dictators. Yet, there is a *lawyer General*, now retired, who
writes about transformational leadership and teaching the JAG* elephant to
dance. [*Judge Advocate General Corps, U.S. Army]

D.L. is now the senior advisor to his successor as CEO of the thriving
legal liability firm. He periodically teaches ethics at state university law
schools. He travels the state providing continuing education courses on legal
ethics to practicing attorneys.

In his first career, D.L. spent 25+ years as an Army lawyer. One of his
mentors, a three-star Lt. General conceptualized and practiced *power-down
leadership*. D.L. served as his legal council while he was the commanding
officer in the heavy armored branch known as "tankers." These two generals
are leaders in a new breed of American military professionals. They are
proud-to-be-soldiers in a volunteer army committed to peace.

They strive to demonstrate role-model leadership and to advance democratic ideals. They function within a structured framework, rich with tradition and war stories. Moreover, in spite of the occasional headline exceptions
to the rule, most are bright, practical visionaries with impeccable character
and genuine caring. In my assessment work with sixty-some new brigadiers,
I met two who had shortfalls later in their careers. The overwhelming
majority were physically fit, responsible problem solvers and likeable.

My hall of fame candidate, D.L., stands in a long line of Irish Flying
Geese. This group of 17th-century leader-generals migrated to the far
corners of the earth rather than submit to the tyranny of occupation and
massacre in their native Ireland. The Flying Geese were known to have
traditions similar to those of the early Greek philosopher-poet-soldiers. Their
influence can be found in the literatures, governments, and practices of many
nations, from Russia and South Africa to the United States.

The code of the Flying Geese can be seen in the military resume of this
20th century descendant. That brief summary reports that D.L. reworked
repatriation laws to guide the fair and equitable return of properties used by

U.S. military forces on duty outside the United States. He supervised a major overhauling of the curriculum for the JAG graduate school while serving as a professor on the staff.

Some years later he became Dean of that master's program at the Army's law school on the grounds of the University of Virginia. When he earned his star, he was also "frocked" with a judicial robe. He then administered appeal activities as chief judge of the military court of review and commander of legal services. His medals are not for battlefield injuries or wartime deeds, but for scrupulous integrity. His ethical practices stood the tests of court martial and contracts assignments in Berlin to two tours of duty in Vietnam. He was the last legal advisor with U.S. forces as we were standing down from the Vietnam conflict.

D. L. is my number-one nomination for the Executive Hall of Fame because he defies stereotypes of lawyers, of generals and of high-bonus executives. He exemplifies a strength of moral character tested and tempered in the fires of public, professional, and personal challenges. Humor and anecdotal wit prove to be balancing factors that helped this champion executive to turn his visions inside-out.

Using the power of the chuckle and the grin, he gave feet to justice and innovative education. A small glass alligator sitting on his desk symbolizes the supportive foundation from which he critiqued and supervised subordinate lawyers, prosecutors and defenders alike. If he needed to "chew-out" one of his professional staff for their job performance in a trial or case, he would turn that alligator toward the lawyer and say, "This old gator is about to chew your tail a bit."

Never flinching from serious attention to flaws in logic or behavior, an unwavering expectation of high standards and excellence in thinking served to inspire fellow workers to do their best, to improve, and to follow in his footsteps. D.L.'s shadow side is darkened by a trait best called "continuous worry." A worry factor is prominent in the emotional motivator I call "the executive challenger." Constructive worry is one of the two components in the definition of anxiety. It is also evidence of caring. He cared about achieving the mission. He cared about the people working to do the job. He cared about fairness and application of ethical methods for reaching the objective.

His successor as chief judge of the court of military review, the first African-American to hold that post, named this Irish-heritage lawyer general as his mentor and role model. He admired D.L. not only for his intellect and visions of creative leadership for the corps, but also for his dedication to his family. That personal commitment, his successor remembered, was affirmed and typified when the general slept on a hospital floor in order to spend time near his mother during her last weeks.

Affirming that commitment to standards and values can result in increased organizational capability and effectiveness, McDonald and Gandz cite results of interviews with 45 senior executives. They found that 44 of these executives representing 32 organizations were enthusiastic about a resurgence of interest in values. These executives believe twenty-first century managers want, in addition to a pay check, a sense of meaning. "They expect to feel comfortable with the existing values and culture of the organization. They want a sense of psychological attachment."

McDonald and Gandz developed a management model that balances *tangibles* such as goals-and-controls with the *intangibles* like values-and-commitment. Their dual drive path for organizational success in the future led to their preparation of a list of 24 organizational values. The values were then linked to a model of organizational cultures. This path of success from a vision to the emergent reality is eloquently simple.

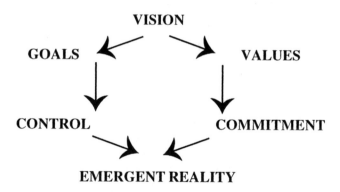

> An emergent reality is—*Pleasing progress toward fulfillment of stakeholder needs: customer needs, employee needs, shareholder needs, society needs.* McDonald, P., & Gandz, J. (1992). Getting value from shared values. An organization can turn shared values into competitive advantage. But we need to develop values-measurement profiles relevant to the modern corporation.
> *Organizational Dynamics,* Winter 1992, 64-77.

Based on their interviews, they came up with a list of values that answer questions that inquire about what corporate values are important in the organization. Building on the work described earlier by Milton Rokeach, they produced a list of 24 organizational values.

adaptability, aggressiveness, autonomy, broad-mindedness, cautiousness, consideration, cooperation, courtesy, creativity, development, diligence, economy, experimentation, fairness, forgiveness, formality, humor, initiative, logic, moral integrity, obedience, openness, orderliness, and social equality (p. 68).

Values are the cornerstone of the motivational track in the management model. Values and commitment balance and parallel the pragmatic goals and control processes of doing business. One application of value preferences is to use employees' preferences to analyze organizational culture. For this purpose, the 24 values are sorted to fit Quinn and McGrath's model of organizational cultures. This model is based on an organization's information processing methods and the resulting culture-types are labeled *market, clan, adhocracy,* and *hierarchy.*

Market driven organizations emphasize efficiency and productivity. A market culture strives to keep the focus on the task and pursuit of objectives. It would be reflected in the McDonald and Gandz values list by preferences for aggressiveness, diligence, and initiative.

Clan-oriented organizations emphasize morale and group cohesion. They spend time on relationships and promote care for all members of the group. The clan culture strives for group cohesion. The organization would be characterized by preferences for the values like broad-mindedness, consideration, cooperation, courtesy, fairness, forgiveness, moral integrity, and social equality

Adhocracy companies emphasize transformation and growth. They view change as an indication of progress that will lead to increased quality and productivity. This culture is in continual development and has broad purposes. The value preferences are adaptability, autonomy, creativity, development, and experimentation.

The hierarchy organizations are noted for their emphasis on stability and execution of regulations. These cultures protect the status quo and the hard won standards of living. A hierarchy culture is associated with values for cautiousness, economy, formality, logic, obedience, and orderliness.

Executives working to turn their vision into an emergent reality increase success potentials by attention to both the hard and the soft systems described by McDonald and Gandz. Leaders who consider values and the organization's culture are likely to have lasting impact. This CEO, president, or general is likely to become a candidate for an executive hall of fame. More and more corporate and military chiefs become recognized as celebrities. Gates, Turner, Trump, Colin Powell, Schwartzkopf. They appear on live TV network broadcasts and publish advice books. They take up managerial causes and hold open-mike call-in radio interviews.

Even in a rush of popularity, the practical bottom line for those who continue on with their executive quest is a reminder of the importance of time-outs. Standing in the spotlight did not contribute to Iacocca's career, nor is it getting compliments for Ted Turner as he makes critical remarks about his merger partners. Back in 1966, Peter Drucker wrote in *The Effective Executive* that any one executive is limited to twenty-four-hour days and forty-to-sixty high-gear working years. Time is a paramount element in success. This resource, if it is not managed, will lay waste to the most compelling vision, the finest tuned emotional intelligence, and the most astute organizational leadership approach. Each executive effectiveness course I taught began with a personal, bottom line commitment:

> The purpose of our time together is for each of you to increase your personal effectiveness as an executive by increasing
> 1. Self-awareness. Your impact on others.
> 2. Awareness and understanding of others. Other's impact on you.
> 3. Awareness of options and choices for your behaviors and perceptions.
>
> Development can't be done for you or to you. There are no vitamins or vaccinations available. You must concentrate on the task at hand and use your own strengths and knowledge. Stay constantly alert to what's working and continue, and to what's not working and stop.
> I pledge my full time and attention to you and this purpose from now until we say good-by on Friday.

In more routine circumstances, executives steadfastly consolidate discretionary time for attention to top-ranked actions and issues. Drucker advised that one-fourth of a day dedicated to one priority item is better than three-fourths of a day given to the item in scattered moments across the week. He also warns us not to get sidetracked by taking care of the secondary matters in order to get possible interruptions out-of-the-way, or to free the mind from nagging unfinished business.

The time-out habit recommended for the invitational leader goes beyond looking at a desktop checklist and beyond thinking in terms of one week and task items. Meaningful time-outs involve multiple hours, retreats, and reflections. Time was significant to Albert Einstein, acclaimed as the most important person of the twentieth century. Scientist-thinker Einstein was selected by *Time Magazine* after a year-long parade of special issues published on the top 100 in diverse categories of human endeavors—corporate titans, visionaries, government leaders, and artists, writers, and performers.

Einstein was said to be a dreamer, often walking alone, pondering and thinking. He acknowledged that nothing was more fundamental than time and once said his happiest moment was when he first conceived of relativity. Another time Einstein was asked about the importance of science as compared to that of politics, which had an indelible impact on his life and brought him to the U.S. from Nazi Germany. He replied that politics is for the moment and a formula is forever.

The formula for the invitational leadership approach is vision, motivation, and action that is charismatic and participatory. In time-outs that executives use to translate this formula into their own language and behavior, they begin by scrutinizing the innermost self and those apperceptions that are behind their on-the-spot decisions. Extended time-outs allow the leader to refocus what and how to best contribute to the development of those who give talent and time to the organization. It is important to make sure short-term and long-range targets are not set too low or aimed at the wrong things. From individual vision to collective motivation, from encounters with the surprise-change process, from power to impact and contribution, the executive is managing the individual and collective organizing processes. These natural functions assure energy for survival, adequacy, growth, and meaningfulness: executive *élan vital* and verve, the substance of organizational consciousness and nature.

Background Information

Wall Street Journal. Numerous articles in the *WSJ* have reported opinions of executives and managers consistent with what I have been hearing in the courses I've taught, as well as from those I meet in organizational consultations. I am especially indebted to Hal Lancaster and Thomas Petzinger who write columns often featured on page 1, Section B. Lancaster's *Managing Your Career* and Petzinger's *The Front Lines* capture the meat and the heart of the life and struggles of those who offer leadership in contemporary organizations. The initial idea for the executive hall of fame was almost tossed aside until I read the Wed. Sept. 3, 1997. "Corporate

Chiefs Have Become Celebrities" The quote is from Lancaster, Hal. (Tuesday July 17, 1998). Making the break from middle manager to a seat at the top. *Wall Street Journal.* B1.

Survival Exercises. The earliest survival exercises I recall were in J. William Pfeiffer and John E. Jones' series, *Handbook of Structured Experiences for Human Relations Training*, published by University Associates. "Lost on the Moon" was the first one in which I was a participant. I do not know its source. The American Management Association has a large publications division offering many training materials. The Association of Supervision and Training Development is another source for exercises. Bernard Bass and his associates at SUNY Binghamton, The Center for Leadership Studies, developed simulations which are published by Transnational. The exercises mentioned in this chapter are listed in the general References sections.

Miscellaneous, academic

French, J.R.P. & Raven, B. (1959). The bases of social power. In D. Cartwright (ed.), *Studies in Social Power.* Ann Arbor, MI: University of Michigan, Institute for Social Research.

McDonald, P. & Gandz, J. (1992). Getting value from shared values. An organization can turn shared values into competitive advantage. But we need to develop values-measurement profiles relevant to the modern corporation. *Organizational Dynamics,* Winter 1992, 64-77. The quote: "They expect to feel comfortable with the existing values and culture of the organization. They want a sense of psychological attachment." (p. 67)

O'Roark, D. L., Jr., (1994). The first annual Hugh J. Clausen leadership lecture: Transformational leadership. "Teaching the JAG elephant to dance." *Military Law Review, Vol. 146,* 224-233.

Schrof, J. M. (Nov. 28, 1994). Brain power. Your mind shouldn't disintegrate as you get older. New research debunks many myths we believe about what happens as the brain matures. U.S. *News & World Report,* pp. 89-97.

William Stern's "g" intelligence definition is in Stern, W. (1916). *The Psychological Method of Testing Intelligence.* Baltimore: Warwick & York. He also discusses it in an article he published in *ACTA,* 1946.

Management self-help books line the shelves at most bookstores. Since the popularity of management guru Blanchard's *One Minute Manager,* there was a backlash reaction that executive work is not something that can be reduced to sixty-second activity formulas. A notable heavier fare is *The Witch Doctors* by John Micklethwait and Adrian Wooldridge. These writers organize, review, and critique the mainstream self-help writers—as they place themselves in the queue with the best of them.

The P.T. Barnum ten rings of business power appear in Joe Vitalle's book, *There's a Customer Born Every Minute,* New York: AMACOM Publisher. An overview of the Barnum tips are given in *Leadership,* Vol. 1, No. 1, April 1998, pp. 4, 5, 8, an AMA newsletter.

Brill, P. L. & Worth, R. (1997). How to use power: [Excerpts from *The Four Levers of Corporate Change].* New York: *Leadership, A Member Newsletter of the American Management Association International,* pp. 5, 6.

Friedman, S. (1985). *Smart Cookies Don't Crumble.* New York: Pocket Books, Simon & Schuster, Inc.

Postlog

Open-Ended Closure

To Ithaca
"When you set out on your journey to Ithaca
Ask that your way be long,
Full of adventure,
Full of knowledge . . .
But do not hurry the voyage at all,
Better that it last for years."
Constantine Cadafy

In-Process

The intent of *The Quest for Executive Effectiveness* is to present a leadership model and a process of development for executives who choose an invitational style and leadership philosophy. It is a business strategy that can make a contribution to world culture. Why is that relevant or important to busy executives? Economics and commerce influence the behaviors of every constituency in every land. They can even make a difference in ending ongoing tribalistic, archaic atrocities and use of modern killing weapons to terrorize people. Economic role models and sanctions have greater impact than the staged diplomatic posturings that flood the media.

The *hopeful* press forward with efforts to extend methods and venues for constructive, creative problem solving. In the dawn of a millennium, management specialists highlight the importance of the quality of the executive-leader's perspective and character. *Management Review*, the American Management Association (AMA) magazine, published a cover story about "The CEO as Psychologist."

302

In this article G. William Dauphinais and Colin Price say, "Freudian disciples, they [CEOs] are not. But in their own common sense way, CEOs have turned their attention to issues of human behavior and psychology. . . . Liberated from the shackles of excessive hierarchy, contemporary CEOs have rolled up their sleeves and reconfigured their goals. They've become all-around activists with a more direct involvement in the determinants of corporate success, from brand management to human relations." (p. 10, Sept., 1998.)

The article included four priorities reported in a Price Waterhouse survey of 377 CEOs from the world's 2,000 largest companies. The corporate seniors believe they will be busy *setting vision and strategy, exploring mergers and acquisitions, reshaping corporate culture and employee behavior,* and *monitoring corporate financial information.* As interest in employee productivity increases, the American Psychological Association (APA) announces preparations for a "decade of behaviorism."

Coincidence? Synchronicity? Either way, this is a confluence of nascent potential. The AMA reviewers predict that managers will be made responsible for behavioral aspects of the work: What behavior do we seek? What are appropriate measures and feedback? How should my own behavior be reviewed, what are legitimate standards and what are off-limits to corporate scrutiny? And, what models exist that others can adopt to improve their behavioral performance.

The last question especially connects with a primary purpose for writing this book. The ILA *charismatic-participatory* model offers an aspirational baseline. It is a flexible way to incorporate a range of scientifically proven methods for establishing standards, defining limits, devising measurement and feedback systems, and describing techniques for influencing and developing others. The ILA recapitulates the essence of current thinking about executive leadership.

1. The Invitational Leadership Approach works to achieve the vision through motivation and action. The leader stays in touch with being a perceiving-thinking person within an organizational culture, within a social system, involved in an environment that is increasingly influenced by international relations.

2. The Charismtic~Participatory [C~P] behavioral patterns are intentionally an amalgamation, a pastiche. The bits and pieces formulate a synthesis and extension of recent practical and scholarly thinking, applied research, and behavioral health information that proved productive in my practice.

AN INVITATIONAL LEADERSHIP APPROACH [ILA]

Achieving Vision through
Motivation and Action

VISION – MOTIVATION – ACTION

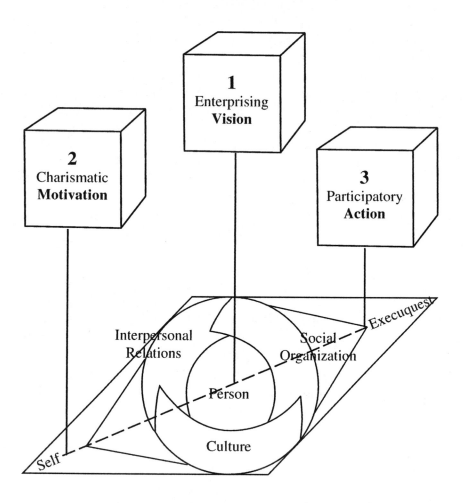

Synthesis and Extension of Current Behavioral Concepts
Charismatic ~ Participatory Behaviors [C~P]

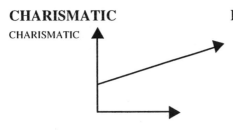

CHARISMATIC   **Inspirational, Educational, and**
                                   an Empowering Role Model
                                   The vertical connection

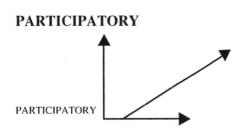

PARTICIPATORY   **Involving Others as Much as**
                                   Possible in Order to Turn
                                   the Vision Inside-out
                                   The horizontal connection

THE DEVELOPMENT OF EXECUTIVES WITH INVITATIONAL LEADERSHIP APPROACH [ILA]

1. **Vision.**   **What's Important?**
    Within the self

             Trust in Self, Others, Task
             Value-Basing: Shared Beliefs, Standards, Goals
             Enterprising Vision-Motivation-Action

2. **Motivation. Dealing with Surprise & Change**
    The vertical Momentum: Charismatic Leadership
             Emotional Zest & Vitality
             Curiosity, Anxiety, and Anger

3. **Action.   Invitational Power**
    The horizontal Momentum: Participatory Leadership
             Expectation: Control and Ethics
             High Hope: Function of Goals, Plans, Resources

My fascinations with the *execuquest* will continue to be a "work in-process." I see a daily *passing parade* of executive-arena activity that is marshaled by colorfully masked themes and variations. Effectiveness will remain an absorbing puzzle and an alluring challenge. It will prompt an unusual safari for those writers who are bold and brave enough to attempt to capture, to meld, and to conversationalize the sights and sounds of successful leadership.

Taking knowledge and psychology to work is where *the rubber meets the street,* where the wheels of research and theory meet executive suite carpets and hallways. We need ongoing translations of complex research. I attempted to show the wealth of underutilized knowledge in extrapolations from Sidney Blatt's thinking on perfectionism and sui-cide, and from Charles Spielberger's work on the emotional underpin-nings of depression.

Several matters remain to be highlighted in the postlog. An impor-tant banner-slogan for my consulting has been: *synergy, syntality, and serendipity*—the energy of the group, the personality of the group, and fortunate coincidence of the right blend of leader, others, and task. We know too much today to allow the productive, constructive, congenial blend of human activity to be left to serendipity alone. It does not need to be allowed to come about now and then by accident or by chance happenstance. Resurgence of attention to leadership is one way of becoming deliberate and intentional about achieving the effective worklife, without repeating dead-end methods of mankind's inhumanity to mankind.

Evidence of resilience is seen in the persistence of individual investments in commercial stocks. Though some thousands buy lottery tickets, more thousands invest in (gamble-on) enterprising ventures. From IPO stock purchases to charitable endowments, many persons who are interested in executive effectiveness invest or contribute money up-front. They do not wait for evolutionary, incremental serendipity. Com-mon sense tells them what Kansas researcher Rick Snyder verifies: more often than not, achievement comes from being intentional and rational.

There is mounting clarity that success, as demonstrated by survival, adequacy, growth, and meaningfulness, will be a matter of *vision, motivation, and action.*

Home-front HERO.

She sets priorities for where to spend her time; she serves on boards of organizations that improve quality of life; she takes responsibility for calling together diverse groups of individuals to talk about survival and progress; she maintains open lines of communications with key network members who are remote, troubled, or not functioning as well as usual. She takes courses to extend and re-direct skills that capitalize on her special talents. She attends to the status of health and stress in herself and in her immediate contacts. She keeps a kitchen radio turned to the community news and current music station. She is the advisor, counselor, action-planner, executive partner of the successful Kentucky banker described in chapter one. Yes, she is known as a homemaker, a dedicated manager of family business with considerable good taste, proven wisdom, and impressive financial success. Yes, she is a leader, a leader who gives us a micro-level view of the anatomy of a thriving corporate venture.

Thinking Smarter About the Quest for Executive Effectiveness

This is a last look at where we have been in this time together. Time is all that we have been given in equal amounts—24 hours in the day, 7 days in the week. This constant reminder is provided in the hourglass symbol where trust is the narrow passageway through which our joint venture-experiences must navigate. It is like the story of the naval officer who engaged in an unusual sea battle. He had his ship send a communication with instructions to those he was approaching to change their course 15 degrees north. A reply came, with all due respect, requesting that the admiral shift his ship's course 15 degrees south. The Admiral retorted, "I am an Admiral with a battleship and five escort vessels; change your course immediately."

The response was, "Aye-Aye, Sir. I stand at your service. I am a lighthouse. Your call."

We have looked at how to go about turning vision into collective success; allowing surprise to guide our changing, and applying power in ways that can lead to meaningful impact. One of my executive classes states this same message in everyday, manager-speak: "We believe leadership can be a positive impact by having confidence in yourself, building trust by addressing the needs of your employees, motivating others to do their best, encouraging risk taking, and treating people with compassion and respect." (Oct. 1996, Hilton Head, NC).

Thinking smarter is being advocated and advanced from pragmatic and theoretical perspectives. Dauphinais and Price suggest in their AMA report on CEO-psychologists that measuring the expression of values is important in reshaping corporate culture and employee behavior. They attempt to pair values with behaviors in order to be as free of subjectivity as possible. For example, their 360-degree questionnaire assesses a value for *PRIZING CREATIVITY by observing actions that encourage innovation, support new ideas, or express impatience with status quo.*

Another example of a 360-degree measurement tool, *The Effective Manager Questionnaire,* opens Chapter 1 and illustrates how executive behavior can be assessed against a spectrum of ideal management behavior. This assessment starts with behaviors reflective of innermost apperceptions. (See Part One References. A. The effective executive has a positive self-regard and purpose. B. The effective executive is aware of his/her own feelings, needs, motivations, and defenses.) Final items ask about actions that denote identification with the world community. Here values and trust are tracked across the range of interactions with others.

On the theoretical side, Tom Petzinger Jr., *Wall Street Journal* writer who is quoted frequently here, had a banner headline article in the February 26, 1999 Marketplace Section. "A New Model for the Nature of Business: It's Alive: Forget the Mechanical—Today's Leaders Embrace the Biological." In writing about *paradigms lost . . . and gained,* Petzinger illustrates the evolution of paradigms from Newtonian mechanical models to new era *natural* models—drawn from knowledge given to us by Einstein, quantum physics, and complexity theorists. Petzinger's book, *The New Pioneers: The Men and Women Who Are Transforming the Workplace and Marketplace* (Simon & Schuster, 1999), reviews paradigm shifts in terms of leadership implications, central metaphors, organizational structures, strategic objectives, cultural expressions, sources of value, sources of economic authority, and other dimensions.

In contrast, Anthony Vlamis' slender volume, a quick read, is called *Smart Leadership.* He interviewed a "select team" of eight, which included business executives, trainers, consultants, authors, and academics. His eleven questions included, What do you see as the five or so defining characteristics of good leaders and managers? How does a leader inspire leadership at every level of the organization? What are the main challenges/issues today's leaders face? Six of the eight of these "in-the-trenches" experts name *trust* as a primary factor, directly, or using terms like integrity and authenticity. On other topics there were differences of opinion, especially about the importance of quick-paced action vs. the importance of the ability to do nothing, to take no action.

When thinking smarter, decision making is, indeed, one of the sticky wickets. Which decision mode, when and where? Delegating means not interfering, and patiently trusting others to do what's needed. On the other hand, role-model leaders cannot be passive observers. Workers want the leader to lead. They want the manager to resolve conflicts, to stand tall, to make the hard calls. Even in the opinions of Vlamis' carefully selected group, including Champy of reengineering fame, involvement of the executive in motivational and technological advances was seen as a hallmark of the future.

I argue that the time is right for practicing *invitational leadership through charismatic and participatory behaviors,* and that the successful leader will progress from emphasis on vision, to emphasis on motivation, to emphasis on action. Yes, all three are at work simultaneously, however, to different degrees in different arenas. The book outline tells the story:

INDIVIDUAL
VISION

TRUST

COLLECTIVE
SUCCESS

PART ONE.   What's Important?
Vision, Motivation, and Action

Introduction.   Quest Priorities: Putting Things in Order
Chapter 1.   Every Success Has a Beginning *[self]*
Chapter 2.   The Truth Begins with Two *[others]*
Chapter 3.   Enterprise and Collective Investment *[task]*
Chapter 4.   The Critical Core *[trust and values]*

SURPRISE

TRUST

CHANGE

PART TWO.   Surprise and Change:
Emotion and Motivation

Introduction.   Zestful Living with *Curiosity, Anxiety,*
                and Anger
Chapter 5.   Curiosity and the Executive Edge
Chapter 6.   Anxiety: The Executive Challenger
Chapter 7.   Anger: Heroic Idealism in Action
Chapter 8.   Wholeheartedness and Passion for Life

INVITATIONAL
POWER

TRUST

LEADERSHIP
IMPACT

PART THREE.   Invitational Power:
Organizations with a Future

Introduction.   Charismatic-Participatory Leadership
Chapter 9.   Great Expectations and Grand Assumptions
Chapter 10.   "Who's the Boss?"
Chapter 11.   Pathfinders and Mapmakers
Chapter 12.   Making a Difference

Part One builds on the *perceptual psychology* foundations I established during graduate studies under the guidance of *Art Combs*, psychology, and *Hal Lewis*, sociology and education. *Part Two* blends the wealth of information I discovered in post-doctoral efforts to learn about behavioral neurobiology and *executive stress from the inside*. Charles Spielberger mentored and coached me in making logical connections and deductions and in how to give meticulous attention to wordsmithing. During that period, I took a sabbatical at the Jung Institute near Zurich, where I refreshed and extended concepts about *personality assessment* and lifelong *personality development* that I learned from Mary McCaulley and Isabell Myers in graduate school.

Part Three is a product of *organizational psychology*, which was a fascination at first sight. My first introduction was a short course at Princeton which inspired my application to attend graduate school. Organizational development and psychological consulting theories and models came alive in early on-the-job-coaching experiences. My appreciation goes to Gordon Lippitt, Bernard Bass, Harry Levinson, David Campbell, and numerous Center for Creative Leadership staffers.

I realize that I have broken psychological rules and norms as I composited my map of the quest for executive effectiveness. I acknowledge that I am rooted in humanistic psychology with a firm conviction that what's important are *individual differences* and an innate momentum toward self-fulfillment. Each can be respected and nurtured in ways that avoid the contamination of arrogance and its self-serving agenda.

Early feedback on *The Quest* included diametrically opposed comments. Some see the material as too academic, while others said it was too basic, a beginner's level. A few readers liked the mixing of theoretical schools and academic disciplines; others felt it could be taken as brazen border crossing, ignoring *accepted boundaries*. I hope I have done all of the above, so that a wide range of executives, managers and professionals will find this *executive time-out* to be a refresher and an extender.

Thanks. Sail on, and remember to enjoy and respect the lighthouses you encounter. My personal favorite lighthouse is Old Barney on Barnegat Bay, Long Beach Island, NJ. This beacon from childhood days continues to cast beams of light on visions that began on sunny sand dunes and were shaped and reshaped by the ever changing, ever fascinating Atlantic Ocean waves.

Ann Marie O'Roark, Ph.D.
December 29, 1999.

PART ONE
*Every success
has a beginning.
Comfortable Competence
and Confidence*

PART TWO
*Motivation.
No one would ever know:
this was the THIRD one
you had rolled over
the side!!*

PART THREE
*Executive Hall of Fame.
Recipient of the Spain Award
for Outstanding Service in
Continuing Legal Education.*

References

Albee, G.W. (1982). Preventing psychopathology and promoting human potential. *American Psychologist*, 37, 9, 1043-1050.

Aldefer, C.P. (1972). *Existence, Relatedness, and Growth: Human Needs in Organizations.* New York: The Free Press.

Alexander, J., Groller, R.B. & Morris, J. (1990). *The Warrior's Edge: Front-Line Strategies for the Victory on the Corporate Battlefield.* New York: William Morrow and Company, Inc.; Avon Books.

Argyris, C. (1964). *Integrating the Individual and the Organization.* New York: John Wiley & Sons.

Argyris, C. (1993). Education for leading-learning. *Organizational Dynamics,* Winter 1993, 21(3), 5-17.

Associated Press. (Tuesday June 30, 1998). Aviation Pioneer, 82, is killed in robbery. *St. Petersburg Times*, p. 6A.

Atkins, S. (1973). *LIFO Training and OD Analyst Guide.* Beverly Hills, CA: LIFO Associates, Inc. Pub.

Atlas, James. (Sunday May 26, 1996). An ongoing love affair with the lone genius. *St. Petersburg Times.* 5D. First appeared in *NY Times*©

Ausubel, D.P. & Schiff, H.M. (1955). Some intrapersonal and interpersonal determinants of individual differences in socioempathic ability among adolescents. *Journal of Social Psychology*, 4, 39-56

Ayman, R., Kreicker, N.A. & Masztal, J. (1994). Defining global leadership in business environments. *Consulting Psychology Journal,* Winter, 1994, pp. 64-77.

Azar, B. (1996). Influences from the mind's inner layers. Research unveils the power that the unconscious mind has on judgment and behavior. *The APA Monitor,* 27, 2, pp. 1 & 25.

Bach, R. (1970). *Jonathan Livingston Seagull.* New York: Avon Books, Macmillan Publishing Co.

Bach, R. (1977). *Illusions. The Adventures of a Reluctant Messiah.* New York: Dell Publishing Co., Inc.

Barnard, C. (1929). Griesinger, D. W. Review of *The Human Side of the Economics of the Organization*. *Academy of Management Review*, 15, 3, 478-499.

Barr, N. & Barr, N. (1989). *The Leadership Equation: Leadership, Management, and the Myers-Briggs*. Austin, TX: Eakin Press.

Bass, B. M. (1960). *Leadership, Psychology, and Organizations*. New York: Harper.

Bass, B. M. (1985). *Transformational Leadership: Performance Beyond Expectation*. New York: Free Press.

Bass, B. M. (1991). From transaction to transformation: Learning to share the vision. *Organization Dynamics*, 19-31.

Bass, B. M. (1997). Does the transactional-transformational leadership paradigm transcend organizational and national boundaries? *American Psychologist*, Feb. 1997, 52, 2, 130-139.

Bass, B.M. (1981). *Stogdill's Handbook of Leadership: A Survey of Theory and Research*. New York: The Free Press, a division of McMillan Publishing Company, Inc.

Bass, B.M. (1990). *Bass and Stogdill's Handbook of Leadership: Theory, Research, and Managerial Applications* (3rd Ed.). New York: Free Press.

Bechtell, M.L. (1995). *The Management Compass: Steering the Corporation Using Hoshin Planning*. New York: American Management Association Membership Publications Division, AMACOM.

Belasco, J. A. (1990). *Teaching the Elephant to Dance: The Manager's Guide to Empowering Change*. New York: Plume/Penguin Group.

Bennis, W. G. & Nanus, B. (1985). *Leaders: The Strategies of Taking Charge*. New York: Harper & Row.

Bennis, W. G. (1976). *The Unconscious Conspiracy: Why Leaders Can't Lead*. New York: AMACOM Publisher.

Bennis, W.G. (1990). *Why Leaders Can't Lead: The Conspiracy Continues*. New York: AMACOM.

Bennis, W.C. (1959). Leadership theory and administrative behavior: The problems of authority. *Admin. Science Quart.*, 4, 259-301.

Berton, Lee. (Thursday September 5, 1996). Downsize danger. Many firms cut staff in accounts payable and pay a steep price. They find their computers, unlike people, can't spot a lot of errors. *Wall Street Journal*, A1 & A6.

Bishop, J. E. (Thursday October 19, 1995). Life line. A gene gives a hint of how long a person might hope to live. Those with one form of it stay free of Alzheimer's and heart ills longer. Cost of sloppy housekeeping. *Wall Street Journal*, pp. A1 & A14.

Blake, R.R. & Mouton, J.S. (1964). *The Managerial Grid*. Houston: Gulf.

Blanchard, K. & Hershey, P. (1969). Life cycle theory of leadership. *Training and Development*, No. 23, 26-34.

Blanchard, K. & Hershey, P. (1977). *Management of Organizational Behavior*. Englewood Cliffs, NJ: Prentice-Hall.

Bode, R. (1993). *First You have to Row a Little Boat.* New York: Warner Books, Inc.

Bolt, J. F. (1993). Achieving the CEO's agenda: Education for executives. *Management Review,* May, pp. 44-48. New York: American Management Association.

Boston Globe report. (1998). 'Mo' Udall never met a woe he couldn't disarm with humor. *Tampa Tribune Times,* Sunday, December 20. Nation/World p. 17.

Brannigan, M. & Lublin, J. S. (Tuesday June 16, 1998). Dunlap faces a fight over his severance pay. *Wall Street Journal,* B1 & B3.

Bray, D. & Howard, A. (1998). *Managerial Lives in Transition: Advancing Age and Changing Times.* New York: Guilford.

Bray, D.W., Campbell, R.J. & Grant, D.L. (1974). *Formative Years in Business: A long-term AT&T Study of Managerial Lives.* New York: Wiley-Interscience.

Bray, D.W. (1982). Assessment centers and the study of lives. *American Psychologist,* February, 37-2, 180-189.

Brief, A.P. & Aldag, R.J. (1976). Correlates of role indices. *Journal of Applied Psychology,* 61, 404-409.

Brill, P.L. & Worth, R. (1997). How to use power: [Excerpts from *The Four Levers of Corporate Change].* New York: *Leadership, A Member Newsletter of the American Management Association International,* pp. 5, 6.

Brommelsick, R. (1982). *Truth.* Sculpture in Vinoy Park, St. Petersburg, FL.

Brown, T. (1996). Managing 'on a tightrope.' [Review of *Corporation on a Tightrope: Balancing Leadership, Governance and Technology in an Age of Complexity.* Goldberg, B. & Sifonis, J. G. Oxford: Oxford University Press.] *Management Review,* July 1996, pp. 6-7.

Brunner, J.S. (1963). *The Process of Education.* New York: Random House Inc.

Buffington, P.W. (1989). No problem. Type "C" individuals—those who thrive on resolving chaos—are receiving increased attention. Just what makes these people experts at problem solving? *Sky,* July 1989, pp. 93-97.

Burke, J. (1996). (Interview). The fine art of leadership. *Management Review,* October, pp. 13-16. New York: American Management Association.

Byham, W.C. with Cox, J. (1988). *Zapp! The Lightning of Empowerment.* New York: Fawcett Columbine Book, Ballantine Books, Random House, Inc.

Calmes, J. (Tuesday April 28, 1998). Low profile consultant smooths Gore's organization. *Wall Street Journal,* B1.

Campbell, D.P. (1991). *Campbell Leadership Index.* Greensboro, NC: Center for Creative Leadership Publication.

Campbell, D.P. (1991). *If I'm in Charge, Why Is Everybody Laughing?* NC: Center for Creative Leadership Publications.

Campbell, D.P. (1991). The challenge of assessing leadership characteristics. *Issues & Observations,* ii, 2.

Campbell, D.P. (1992). *Manual for the Campbell Interest and Skill Survey.* Minneapolis, MN: National Computer Systems, Inc. (NCS).

Capparell, S. (Thursday April 2, 1998). Get ready for Shakelton-mania. *Wall Street Journal,* B1 & B14.

Carey, J. & Bruno, M. (Sept. 10, 1984). Why cynicism can be fatal. *Newsweek,* p. 68.

Carneiro, R. L. (1970). *Leslie A. White. Totems and Teachers.* New York: Farrar, Strauss & Co.

Castaneda, C. (1968). *The Teaching of Don Juan: A Yaqui Way of Knowledge.* New York: Ballantine Books, Inc.

Castaneda, C. (1980). *A Separate Reality: Tales of Power.* New York: Pocket Books, Simon & Schuster.

Castaneda, C. (1984). *The Fire Within.* New York: Washington Square Press.

Chambers, N. (1998). The long view. *Management Review,* January, pp. 11-15. New York: American Management Association.

Chandler, A. (1962). *Strategy and Structure: Chapters in the History of American Industrial Enterprise.* Cambridge, MA: MIT Press.

Chopra, D. (1993). *Ageless Body, Timeless Mind.* New York: Crown Publishers, Inc.

Clancy, T. (1984). *The Hunt for Red October.* New York: Berkeley Book & Naval Institute Press.

Clark, K. & Clark, M. (1994). *Choosing to Lead: A Center for Creative Leadership Book.* Charlotte, NC: Northgate Press.

Combs, A.W., Avila, D.L. & Purkey, W.W. (1971). *Helping Relationships: Basic Concepts for the Helping Professions.* Boston: Allyn and Bacon.

Combs, A.W., Richards, A.C. & Richards, S. (1976). *Perceptual Psychology: A Humanistic Approach to the Study of Persons.* New York: Harper & Rowe, Publishers. Inc. (Revision of *Individual Behavior: A New Frame of Reference of Psychology,* 1949, Snygg, D. & Combs, A.W.; and *Individual Behavior: A Perceptual Approach to Behavior,* 1959, Combs, A.W. & Snygg, D.).

Combs, A.W., Miser, A.B. & Whitaker, K.S. (1999). *On Becoming a School Leader: A Person-Centered Challenge.* Alexandria, VA: Association for Supervision and Curriculum Development.

Congers, J.A. (1993). The brave new world of leadership training. *Organizational Dynamics,* Winter, 21, 3, 46-58.

Congers, J.A. (1992). *Learning to Lead.* San Francisco: Jossey-Bass.

Covey, S.R. (1989). *The 7-Habits of Highly Effective People.* New York: Fireside/Simon & Schuster.

Covey, S.R. (1990). *Principle Centered Leadership.* New York: Fireside/Simon & Schuster.

Cox, H. (1978). *On Not Leaving It to the Snake.* New York: Macmillan.

Craig, D.P. (1978). *Hip Pocket Guide to Planning and Evaluation.* San Diego, CA: University Associates Publisher.

Crossen, C. (Tuesday Dec. 3, 1996). Nervous breakdowns by any name, aren't what they used to be. *Wall Street Journal,* A1 &14.

Crum, T.F. (1987). *The Magic of Conflict: Turning a Life of Work into a Work of Art.* New York: Simon and Schuster.

Cuzort, R.P. (1969). Chapter 11: The Science of Culture: The Views of Leslie White. *Humanity and Modern Sociological Thought.* New York: Rinehart and Winston.

Danzlger, S. & Daehler-Danzlger, K. (1991). *The Power of Balance: A New Route to Successful Work, Relationships, and Health.* Walkertown, NC: Partners in Performance.

Dauphinais, G.W. & Price, C. (1998). The CEO as psychologist. *Management Review,* September, pp 10-15.

Davis, E. (1995). What's on American managers' minds? *Management Review,* April, pp. 14-20. New York: American Management Association.

De Saint-Exupéry, A. (1946). *The Little Prince. [Le Petit Prince].* Paris: Gallimard.

DeAngelis, T. (1991). When the going gets tough, 'the hopeful keep going.' *APA Monitor.* 22, 7, July 91, p. 18.

DeAngelis, T. (1992). Illness linked with repressive style of coping. *APA Monitor,* 23, 12, pp. 14-15.

Deogun, N. & Schellhardt, T.D. (Tues. June 23, 1998). Some lessons learned from two who felt the ax of Al Dunlap. *Wall Street Journal,* B1.

DeVries, D.L. (1992). Executive selection: Advances but no progress. *Issues & Observations,* 12, 1-5.

Dewey, J. (1916, 1964). *Democracy and Education.* New York: MacMillan.

Dokken, D.D., Chakiris, B.J., Rumley, J.A. & O'Roark, A.M. (1980). *People in Planning.* Washington, DC: National Endowment for the Arts.

Drucker, P. (1992). *Managing the Future: The 90s and Beyond.* New York: Truman-Talley Books, Dutton, Penguin Group

Drucker, P. (1966, 1967, 1985, 1993). *The Effective Executive.* New York: Harper-Collins Pub.

Drucker, P. F. (1994). The age of social transformation. *The Atlantic Monthly,* Vol. 274, No. 5, Nov. 1994, pp. 53-80.

Eiseley, L. (1946/1957) *The Immense Journey: An Imaginative Naturalist Explores the Mysteries of Man and Nature.* New York: Random House.

Encyclopaedia Britannica. (1988). *The New Encyclopaedia Britannica, 15th Edition.* Chicago: University of Chicago, Encyclopaedia Britannica, Inc. [Marie Curie; Egyptian history; Tielhard De Chardin; Confucius; Machiavelli.]

Ericsson, K.A. (Ed.) (1996). *The Road to Excellence. The Acquisition of Expert Performance in the Arts and Sciences, Sports and Games.* Mahwah, NJ: Lawrence Erlbaum Associates, Inc.

Ettorre, B. (1995). Reengineering tales from the front. *Management Review,* January , 13-18. New York: American Management Association

Ettorre, B. (1996). Making change. When a new CEO comes on board, people expect to see changes with far reaching consequences for the company. But how much change, and how fast should it come? *Management Review,* January 1996, 13-18. New York: American Management Association.

Ettorre, B. (1996). Employment contract? Empty promises. *Management Review,* July 1996, 16-23. New York: American Management Association.

Eysenck, H.J. (1994a). Synergistic interaction between psychosocial and physical factors in the causation of lung cancer. In C. Lewis, C. O'Sullivan & J. Barraclough (Eds.), *The Psychoimmunology of Cancer* (pp. 163-178). Oxford: Oxford University Press.

Eysenck, H.J. (1994b). Cancer, personality and stress: Prediction and prevention. *Advances in Behaviour Research and Therapy, 16,* 167-215.

Fenn, D. S. (1991). Bambi meets Godzilla: Psychological assessment in real-world settings. *Contemporary Psychology,* 36, 6, 515-516.

Fiedler, F. (1959). *Leaders Attitudes and Group Effectiveness.* Urbana, IL: U. Illinois Press.

Fiedler, F.E. & House, R.J. (1988). Leadership theory and research: A report of progress. In C.L. Cooper & I. Robertson (Eds.) *International Review of Industrial & Organizational Psychology* (pp. 73-92). London: Wiley.

Fiedler, F.E. & Leister, A.F. (1977). Leader intelligence and task performance: A test of a multiple screen model. *Organizational Behavior and Human Performance,* 20, 1-14.

Fiedler, F.E. (1992). The role and meaning of leadership experience. In K.E. Clark , M.B. Clark & D.P. Campbell (Eds.), *Impact of Leadership,* pp. 95-105. Greensboro, NC: Center for Creative Leadership.

Firstenberg, P. (1993) Downsizing: What's your game plan? *Management Review,* November, pp. 46-51. New York: American Management Association.

Fleishman, E.A. (1953). The measurement of leadership in industry. *Journal of Applied Psychology,* 37, 153-158.

Flowers, V.S. & Hughes, C.L. (1973). Why employees stay. Of two people in identical jobs, one may opt to become a turnover statistic; the other may continue as a dissatisfied employee. Why? *Harvard Business Review,* July-August, 1973, 49-60.

Foushee, H.C. & Manos, K.L. (1981). Information transfer within the cockpit: Problems in intra cockpit communications. In C. E. Billings and E. S. Cheaney (Eds.) *Information Transfer Problems in the Aviation System.* NASA Report No TP-1875, Moffett Field, CA: NASA-Ames Research Center.

Foushee, H.C. (1984). Dyads and triads at 35,000 feet: Factors affecting group process and aircrew performance. *American Psychologist,* 39, 8, 885-893.

Franke, R.H. & Kaul, J.D. (1978). The Hawthorne experiments: First statistical interpretation. *American Sociological Review,* 43, 5, 623-642.

Frankl, V.E. (1962). *Man's Search for Meaning: An Introduction to Logotherapy.* Boston: Beacon Press.

Frankl, V.E. (1978). *The Unheard Cry for Meaning.* New York: Touchstone, Simon and Schuster Publishers.

Freiberg, P. (1995). Pathological gambling turning into an epidemic. The expansion of legalized betting is fueling what many psychologists fear will become the nation's next major addiction. *APA Monitor,* December 1995, 16, 12, pp. 1 & 32.

French, J.R.P. & Raven, B. (1959). The bases of social power. In D. Cartwright (Ed.), *Studies in Social Power.* Ann Arbor, MI: University of Michigan, Institute for Social Research.

French, J.R.P., Jr., Caplan, R.D. & Van Harrison, R. (1982). *The Mechanisms of Job Stress and Strain.* Chichester, England: Wiley.

Friedman, M. & Rosenman, R.H. (1947). *Type A Behavior and Your Heart.* Greenwich, CT: Fawcett Publications, Inc.

Friedman, S. (1985). *Smart Cookies Don't Crumble.* New York: Pocket Books, Simon & Schuster, Inc.

Gailey, P. (Thurs. May 30, 1991). Ethics and "Arrogance of Integrity." *St. Petersburg Times.* p. 3A.

Gast, J. (1994). A definition and illustration of democratic leadership. *Human Relations,* 47, 8, 953-957.

Gibb, J. (1978). *Trust, A New View of Personal and Organizational Development.* LA: Guild of Tutors Press, International College.

Gibbs, N. (1995). The EQ factor, New brain research suggests the emotions, not IQ, may be the true measure of human intelligence. *Time,* Oct. 2, 1995, 60-68.

Goleman, D. (1995). *Emotional Intelligence: Why It Can Matter More than IQ.* New York: Bantam Books

Gordon, I. J. (1969). *Human Development from Birth Through Adolescence.* New York: Harper & Row Pub.

Green, E.J. (1970). *Workbook for Corporate Planning.* New York: American Management Association Publications.

Greenberg, E.R. (1998). (Director of Management Studies, Ed.) AMA global survey on key business issues. *Management Review,* December, pp 27-38. New York: American Management Association.

Greenberg, E.R. (1998). (Director of Management Studies, Ed.) 1998 senior management teams: Profiles and performance. *Management Review,* September pp. 37-44 New York: American Management Association.

Greisinger, D.W. (1990). The human side of economic organization. *Academy of Management Review,* 15(3), July, 478-499.

Groebel J. & Hinde, R. A. (1989). *Aggression and War: Their Biological and Social Bases.* Cambridge, England: Cambridge University Press. Reviewed in (1991) *Contemporary Psychology.* 36, 3, 207-8.

Groebel, J. & Hinde, R.A. (Eds.) (1991). *Cooperation & Prosocial Behavior.* Cambridge: Cambridge University Press.

Greenwald, J. (1999). Springing a leak at Coca-Cola. *Time,* December 20, pp. 80-84.

Grove, A. (1987). *One on One with Andy Grove.* New York: Putnam.

Grove, A. (1999). *Only the Paranoid Survive: How to Exploit the Crisis Points that Challenge Every Company.* New York: Bantam.

Gupta, N. & Beehr, T.A. (1979). Job stress and employee behaviors. *Organizational Behavior and Human Performance,* 23, 373-387.

Hall, J. (1973). *The Conflict Management Survey.* P.O. Box 314, The Woodlands, Texas: Teleometrics Int'l.

Hammer, M. & Champy, J. (1993). *Reengineering the Corporation: A Manifesto for Business Revolution.* New York: HarperBusiness.

Harari, O. (1993). Stop empowering your employees. *Management Review,* November 1993, pp. 26-29.

Harari, O. (1995). The successful manager in the new business world. *Management Review,* April 95, pp. 10-12.

Harari, O. (1996). Why did reengineering die? Reengineering went from a management fad to a $51 billion industry—practically overnight. Today it's slowly fading. Was business just over anxious for a miraculous cure? *Management Review,* June 1996, pp. 49-52.

Harris, J. (1995). *Getting Employees to Fall in Love with Your Company.* New York: AMACOM.

Hart-Davis, R. (Ed.) (1962). *The Letters of Oscar Wilde.* London. [Citation found in Skinner, B.F. (1971), *Beyond Freedom and Dignity.* New York: Bantam, Vintage, Random House.

Harwood, J. (Friday August 29, 1997). Find out how many politicians can fit on the head of a pin: As political scientists convene, many wonder if the field has gotten too arcane. *Wall Street Journal.* A1 & A12.

Haynes, S.G., Feinleib, M., Levine, S., Scotch, N. & Kannel, W.B. (1978). The relationship of psychological factors to coronary heart disease in the Framingham study II: Prevalence of heart disease. *Journal of Epidemiology,* 107, 384-402.

Hersch, G. (1988). *The Shared Vision Process: Strategic Planning for Organizational Excellence.* Cincinnati, OH: The Sierra Group, Inc.

Hersey, P. & Blanchard, K.H. (1969). Life-cycle theory of leadership. *Training and Devel. J.,* 1969, 23, 26-34.

Hersey, P. & Blanchard, K.H. (1977). *Management of Organizational Behavior: Utilizing Human Resources.* Englewood Cliffs, NJ: Prentiss Hall.

Herzberg, F., Mausner, B. & Snyderman, B.B. (1959). *The Motivation to Work.* New York: Wiley.

Hill, R.I., Harmon, V.M. & Stubbs, I.R. (1978). Caribbean Island Survival Exercise. Richmond, VA: Designs for Organizational Effectiveness. In consultation with U.S. Coast Guard Rescue Operations; Charter Skipper; and Park Ranger, St. Thomas, VI.

Hodge, K. (1998). The art of the post-deal. Some mergers create value and others destroy it. But which factor best predicts that outcome? *Management Review,* February, pp. 17-20. New York: American Management Association.

Hogan, R. 1994. Trouble at the top: Causes and consequences of managerial incompetence. *Consulting Psychology Journal.* Winter, 46, 1, 9-15.

Hogan, R., Curphy, G.J. & Hogan, J. (1994). What we know about leadership: Effectiveness and personality. *American Psychologist,* 49, 6, 493-504.

Hogan, R., Raskin, R. & Fazzini, D. (1990). The dark side of charisma. In K.E. Clark and M. B. Clark (Eds.), *Measures of Leadership,* pp. 343-354. West Orange, NJ: Leadership Library of America.

Hollander, E. P. & Offerman, L. R. (1990). Leadership in organizations: Relationships in transition. *American Psychologist,* 45, 2, 179-189.

Hollander, E.P. (1964). *Leaders, Groups, and Group Effectiveness.* New York: Oxford U. Press.

Hollander, E.P. (1978). *Leadership Dynamics: A Practical Guide to Effective Relationships.* New York: Free Press.

Holmes, T. & Rahe, R. (1967). The Social Readjustment Scale. *Journal of Psychosomatic Research,* 1967, 11, 213-218.

Horney, K. (1937). *Neurotic Personality of Our Times.* New York: Norton.

Horney, K. (1945). *Our Inner Conflicts.* New York: Norton.

Horney, K. (1950). *Neurosis and Human Growth.* New York: Norton.

Hosmer, L.T. (1995). Trust: The connecting link between organizational theory and philosophical ethics. *Academy of Management Review,* 1995, Apr, 20, 2, 379-403.

House, R.J. (1976). A 1976 theory of charismatic leadership. In J.G. Hunt & L.L. Larson (Eds.), *Leadership, The Cutting Edge,* pp. 189-207. Carbondale: Southern Illinois University Press.

House, R.J. & Howell, J.M. (1992). Personality and charismatic leadership. *Leadership Quarterly,* 3, 81.

Hughes, C.L. & Flowers, V.S. (1976). *Value Systems Analysis.* Dallas, TX: Center for Values Research

Human Synergetics. (1987). Jungle Survival Situation. Plymouth, MI: Human Synertistics. In consultation with H. Morgan Smith, former director of the Arctic, Desert, Tropic Information Center, a research and operations office supporting military and civilian aviation.

Human Synergistics. (1970). The Desert Survival Problem. Developed by Lafferty, J.C., Eady, P. M., Canfield, A. in consultation with Pond, A.W. of the Arctic, Desert, Tropic Information Center.

Hymowitz, C. (Tuesday April 16, 1997). Task of managing changes in workplace takes a careful hand. *Wall Street Journal,* B1.

Isaacson, W. (1998). ...driven by the passion of Intel's Andrew Grove. Man of the year. *Time*, January 5, pp 48-72.

Isenberg, D.J. (1984). How senior managers think. *Harvard Business Review*, Nov.-Dec. 1984, 81-91.

Jacobs, T. O. & Jaques, E. (1986). Leadership in complex systems: Critical dimensions of organizational leadership. In J.A. Zeidner, (Ed.), *Human Productivity Enhancement. Vol. 2: Organization and Personnel*, New York: Praeger Publisher.

James, W. (1890). *Principles of Psychology, Vol. I & Vol. II*. New York: Henry Holt Pub.

Jaques, E. & Clement, S.D. (1991). *Executive Leadership: A Practical Guide to Managing Complexity*. Arlington, VA: Carson Hall.

Johnson, S. (1984). *The Precious Present*. New York: Doubleday and Co.

Jones, M.B. (1974). Regressing group on individual effectiveness. *Organizational Behavior and Performance*, 11, 426-451.

Jones, J.E. & Pfeiffer, J.W. (1975). Lost at sea. *Annual Handbook for Group Facilitation*. Officers of the United States Merchant Marine ranked the fifteen items and provided the 'correct' solution to the task.

Jung, C.G. (1971/1921). *Psychological Types. Vol. 6*. (H.G. Baynes, Translator. Revised by R.F. C. Hull). Princeton, NJ: Princeton University Press.

Juran. J. M. (1994). Juran on quality. (AMA Interviewer, unidentified). *Management Review*. January, pp 10-13.

Kamm, T. & Copetas, A.C. (Thurs. Sept. 4, 1997). Bain is sued for millions over Club Med report. *Wall Street Journal*. B1 & B12.

Kanter, R.M. (1981). Power, leadership, and participatory management. *Theory into Practice*, 20, 219-224.

Kaufman, J. (Monday May 5, 1997). Gray expectations. A middle manager, 54, and insecure, struggles to adapt to the times: Young colleagues make fun of his computer skills; no one else wears a tie. 'I've peaked in my career.' *Wall Street Journal*. A1 & A6.

Kaufman, J. (Thursday Sept. 5, 1996). Mood swing. White men shake off that losing feeling on affirmative action. Angst gives way to reality: Gains by women, blacks don't look so daunting. Bias or 'level playing field'? *Wall Street Journal*. A1 & A6.

Keen, S. & Fox, A.V. (1973). *Telling Your Story. A Guide to Who You Are and Who You Can Be*. New York: Doubleday & Co./Signet Books.

Keirsey, D. & Batges, M. (1984). *Please Understand Me: Character and Temperament Types*. Del Mar, CA: Pometheus Nemesis Company.

Kets de Vries, M.F.R. (1989). *Prisoners of Leadership*. New York: Wiley.

Kets de Vries, M.F.R. (1989). Leaders who self destruct: The causes and cures. *Organizational Dynamics*, 17, 4-17.

Kets de Vries, M.F.R. (1993). *Leaders, Fools, and Impostors*. San Francisco: Jossey-Bass.

Kotter, J.P. (1988). *The Leadership Factor*. New York: Free Press.

Kouzes, J.M. & Posner, B.Z. (1987). *The Leadership Challenge.* San Francisco: Jossey Bass.

Kouzes, J.M. & Posner, B.Z. (1993). *Credibility. How Leaders Gain and Lose It, Why People Demand It.* San Francisco: Jossey-Bass.

Kuczmarski, T.D. (1996). Creating an innovative mind set. *Management Review,* November, pp. 47-51. New York: American Management Association.

Kushel, G. (1994). *Reaching the Peak Performance Zone: How to Motivate Yourself and Others to Excell.* New York: AMACOM Membership Edition.

Lagnado, L. (Friday May 30, 1997). Intensive care: Ex-manager describes the profit-driven life inside Columbia/ HCA. *Wall Street Journal,* A1 & A6.

Lancaster, H. (Tuesday Dec. 3, 1996). Don't let the bosses get you down: You get better after 50. *Wall Street Journal,* B1.

Lancaster, H. (Tuesday Oct. 14, 1997). Getting your goals for life and work down in writing. *Wall Street Journal,* B1.

Lancaster, H. (Tuesday March 2, 1997). Leading a turnaround can make your career, if you are up to the task. *Wall Street Journal,* B1.

Lancaster, H. (Tuesday June 10, 1997). It's time to stop promoting yourself and start listening. *Wall Street Journal,* B1.

Lancaster, H. (Tuesday May 12, 1998). Many merger victims can take their time to look for work. *Wall Street Journal,* B1.

Lancaster, H. (Tuesday April 7, 1998). When uncertainty is a constant, you can still plan for surprises. *Wall Street Journal,* B1.

Lancaster, H. (Tuesday April 14, 1998). Middle managers are back—but now they're 'high impact players'. *Wall Street Journal,* B1.

Lancaster, H. (Tuesday April 28, 1998). Hiring a full staff may be the next fad in management. *Wall Street Journal,* B1.

Lancaster, H. (Tuesday May 26, 1998). Learning some ways to make meetings slightly less awful. *Wall Street Journal,* B1.

Lancaster, H. (Tuesday June 9, 1998). Giving good service, never an easy task is getting a lot harder. *Wall Street Journal,* B1.

Lancaster, H. (Tuesday June 16, 1998). Life lessons: Learning from a long career that had lots of turns. *Wall Street Journal,* B1.

Lancaster, H. (Tuesday July 16, 1996). Managing your career. Readers give tips on procrastination and renewing skills. Training by metaphor. *Wall Street Journal,* B1.

Lancaster, H. (Tuesday July 17, 1998). Making the break from middle manager to a seat at the top. *Wall Street Journal,* B1.

Lancaster, H. (Tuesday Nov. 16, 1999). An ex-CEO reflects: H-P's Platt regrets he wasn't a rebel. *Wall Street Journal,* B1.

Lansing, A. (1959). *Endurance: Shackleton's Incredible Voyage.* New York: Carroll & Graff Publishers.

Latour, A. & Steinmetz, G. (Mon. May 18, 1998). Swedish giant. Barnevik sets about task of preserving Wallenberg empire: Investor A.B. Chairman tries balancing family's values with shareholder values. 'All and sundry' interests. *Wall Street Journal.* A1 & A12.

Lawrence, G.D. (1993). *People Types and Tiger Stripes.* Gainesville, FL: Center for Applications of Psychological Type, Inc.

Lazarus, R.S. (1991). Psychological stress in the workplace. In P.L. Perrewe, *Handbook on Job Stress* (pp. 1-13). Corde Madera, CA: Select Press.

Lederer, W.J. & Burdick, E. (1958). *The Ugly American.* New York: W.W. Norton & Co., Inc.

Lee, W.G. (1995). Face to face. Southwest Airlines' Herb Kelleher: Unorthodoxy at work. *Management Review,* Jan. 1995, p. 9-12.

Leo, J. (June 17, 1996). On society. Let's lower self-esteem. *U.S. News and World Report,* p. 25.

Levinson, H. (1994). Why the behemoths fell. *The American Psychologist.* 49, 5, 428-436.

Levinson, H. (1981). When executives burnout. *Harvard Business Review,* May-June.

Levinson, H. (1973). *The Great Jackass Fallacy.* Boston: Harvard Graduate School of Business.

Levinson, H. (1968). *Executive.* Cambridge, MA: Harvard University Press.

Levinson, H. (1962). A psychologist looks at executive development. *Harvard Bus. Review,* 40, 69-75.

Lewin, K. (1947). The frontiers in root dynamics: Concept, method and reality in social science, social equilibria and social change. *Human Relations,* 1, 5-41.

Lewin, K., Lippitt, R. & White, R.K. (1939). Patterns of aggressive behavior in experimentally created "social climates." *J. Social Psychol.,* 10, 271-99.

Likert, R. (1961). An emerging theory of organizations, leadership, and management. In, P. Petrullo and B. Bass (Eds.), *Leadership and Interpersonal Behavior.* New York: Holt.

Lippitt, G. (1969). *Organization Renewal.* New York: Appleton-Century-Crofts.

Lippitt, G. & Lippitt, R. (1978). *The Consulting Process in Action.* La Jolla, CA: University Associates.

Long, C. & Vicker-Koch, M. (1995). Using core capabilities to create competitive advantage. *Organizational Dynamics,* Summer 1995, p. 7-22.

Loohaus, J. (Sunday Feb. 4, 1996). Floridian. Ancient Egypt casts a spell on our nation. *St. Petersburg Times,* 8F.

Lowen, A. (1967). *The Betrayal of the Body.* Toronto: Collier Macmillan Canada, Ltd.

Lowman, R. (1991). *The Clinical Practice of Career Assessment: Interests, Abilities, and Personality.* Washington, DC: American Psychological Association Pub.

Lowman, R. (1993). *Counseling and Assessment of Work Dysfunctions.* Washington, DC: American Psychological Association Publications.

Lublin, J.S. (Mon. July 8, 1996). More corporate fiefdoms become chiefdoms. *Wall Street Journal,* B1 & B2.

Lublin, J.S. (Thurs. April 9, 1998). Executive pay. Pay for performance. *Wall Street Journal Reports,* R1 & R4.

Lublin, J.S. (Wed. June 18, 1997). Dear Boss, I'd rather not tell you my name, but . . . *Wall Street Journal,* B1.

Lublin, J.S. & MacDonald, E. (Tuesday March 10, 1998). In the debris of a filed merger: Trade secrets. *Wall Street Journal,* B1 & B6.

MacDonald, Jr., A.P., Kessel, V.S. & Fuller, J.B. (1972). Self-disclosure and two kinds of trust. *Psychological Reports,* 30, 143-148.

MacDonald, E. & Paltrow, S.J. (Aug. 10, 1999). Merry-GO-Round. Ernst & Young advised the client, but not about everything. It didn't reveal business ties alleged to pose conflict with its consulting job. Settlement for $185 million. *Wall Street Journal,* A1 & 12.

Mahoney, T.A. & Dekop, J. R. (1993). Y' gotta believe: Lessons from American vs Japanese-run US companies. *Organization Dynamics.* New York: AMACOM

Mahzarin, B. (1996). Unconscious mind influencing judgement. *APA Monitor,* Feb. 96, 27, 2, p. 1.

Mannuck, S.B., Morrison, R.L., Bellak, A.S. & Polefrone, J.M. (1985). Behavioral factors in hypertension: Cardiovascular responsibility, anger and social competence. In M.A. Chesney and R.H. Rosenman (Eds.), *Anger and Hostility in Cardiovascular and Behavioral Disorders,* pp. 149-172. Washington, DC: Hemisphere.

Marks, M.L. (1996). A call for empathic executives. *The APA Monitor,* May 1996, p. 39.

Masciarelli, J.P. (1998). Are you managing your relationships? If not, you may fail to sustain your competitive advantages, build long-term customer loyalty and get (and stay) on the fast track. *Management Review,* Ap. 1998, p. 41-45.

Maslow, A.H. (1954). *Motivation and Personality.* Hartford, New York, Greensboro, NC.

Maslow, A.H. (1965). *New Eupsychian Management: A Journal.* Homewood, IL: Dorsey Press.

Mason, J.C. (1992). Leading the way into the 21st century. *Management Review,* October, pp. 16-19.

McCall, M. (1994). Identifying leadership potential in future international executives. *Consulting Psychology Journal,* Winter, 1994, pp 49-63.

McCall, M.W. & Lombardo, M.M. (1979). *Looking Glass IMC: An Organizational Simulation. Technical Report No. 12.* Greensboro, NC: Center for Creative Leadership.

McCall, M.W. & Lombardo, M.M. (1983). *Off the Track: Why and How Successful Executives Get Derailed.* Greensboro, NC: Center for Creative Leadership.

McCall, M.W. (1981). *Leadership and the Professional.* Greensboro, NC: Center for Creative Leadership.

McClelland, C.D. (1965). Achievement motivation can be developed. *Harvard Business Rev.,* 43, 6-24, 178.

McClelland, D.C. & Boyatzis, R.E. (1982). Leadership, motive pattern, and long-term success in management. *Journal of Applied Psychology,* 67, 737-743.

McClelland, D.C. (1965). N achievement and entrepreneurship: A longitudinal study. *Journal of Personality and Social Psychology,* 1, 389-392.

McCurdy, M. (1998). *Trapped by the Ice.* New York: Walker & Co.

McDermott, J. (1983). Fractals will help make order out of chaos. Computer generated abstract patterns provide a new way to understand nature's irregular ones. *Smithsonian,* December 1983, pp. 110-119.

McDonald, P., & Gandz, J. (1992). Getting value from shared values. An organization can turn shared values into competitive advantage. But we need to develop values-measurement profiles relevant to the modern corporation. *Organizational Dynamics,* Winter 1992, 64-77.

McIntosh, H. (1996). Solitude provides an emotional tune-up. We all need solitude for rejuvenation and contemplation, but some people have a chronic need to be alone. *APA Monitor,* March 1996, pp. 1 & 10.

Mead, M. (1969). Research with human beings: A model derived from anthropological field practice. *Daedalus,* 98, Spring 1969, pp. 361-386.

Merry, U. & Brown, G.I. (1987). *The Neurotic Behavior of Organizations.* New York: Gardner Press.

Michner, J.A. (1965). *The Source.* New York: Random House.

Michner, J.A. (1989). *Caribbean.* New York: Random House.

Micklethwait, J. & Wooldridge, A. (1996). *The Witch Doctors: Making Sense of Management Gurus.* New York: Times Books, Random House Pub.

Mink, O., Mink, B. & Shultz, J. (1979/1998). *Developing and Managing Open Organizations.* Austin, TX: Learning Concepts.

Mintzberg, H. (1994). *The Rise and Fall of Strategic Planning.* New York: The Free Press.

Mitsumi, J. (1985). *The Behavioral Science of Leadership: An Interdisciplinary Japanese Research Program.* Ann Arbor: The University of Michigan Press.

Mollenkamp, C. (1999). Tone deaf. Ivester had all skills of a CEO but one: Ear for political nuance. *Wall Street Journal,* Friday, December 17, pp. A1 &6.

Morgan, A.P. (Ed.) (1996). *The Psychology of Concentration in Sport Performers.* Mahwah, NJ: Lawrence Erlbaum Associates, Inc.

Morgan, G. (1998). *Images of Organization—the Executive Edition.* San Francisco: Berrett-Koehler Pub. Inc. with Sage Publ.

Morrison, A.M., White, R.P. & Van Velsor, E. (1987). Executive women: Substance plus style. *Psychology Today,* 21, 8, 18-27.

Morrison, A.M., White, R. P. & Van Velsor, E. (1987). *Breaking the Glass Ceiling.* Reading, MA: Addison-Wesley.

Morrow, L. (May 27, 1996). A battle with no victors. Who could have anticipated the suicide of an overly decorated admiral? *Time,* May 27, 1996, p. 33.

Murray, H.A. (1938). *Explorations in Personality.* New York: Oxford U. Press.

Murray, H.A. (1963). Studies of stressful interpersonal disputations. *American Psychologist,* 18, 28-36.

Murray, H. A. & Kluckhohn, C. (1953). Outline of a conception of personality. In C. Kluckhohn, H. A. Murray, and D. Schneider (Eds.), *Personality in Nature, Society, and Culture,* pp. 3-52. 2nd Ed. New York: Knopf.

Myers, I.B. & Myers, P.B. (1980). *Gifts Differing.* Palo Alto, CA: Consulting Psychology Press.

Myers, I.B. & McCaulley, M.H. (1989). *Manual: A Guide to the Development and Use of the Myers-Briggs Type Indicator.* Palo Alto, CA: Consulting Psychology Press.

Nilsen, D. & Hernez-Broome, G. (1988). Integrity in leadership. *Leadership in Action.* Greensboro, NC: Jossey-Bass with the Center for Creative Leadership.

Northwestern National Life. (1991). *Employee Burnout: America's Newest Epidemic.* Minneapolis, MN: Northwestern National Life Insurance Company

Office of Strategic Services Assessment Staff. (1948). *Assessment of Men.* New York: Rinehart.

Ono, Y. (Friday May 30, 1997). Marketers seek the naked truth in consumer psyches. *Wall Street Journal.* B1 & 14.

Ono, Y. (Thursday April 2, 1998). At Woolworth, a new moniker flags a new era. *Wall Street Journal.* B1 & B6.

O'Roark, A.M. (1973). The human potential movement as cultural revitalization. *New Voices in Education,* John Dewey Society, University of Florida, Spring 1973, Vol 3, No. 1, p 12-15.

O'Roark, A.M. (1979). Comment. Humanistic psychology: The ultimate singularity in the behavioral science universe? *American Psychologist* 34:6, June.

O'Roark, A.M. (1982). A model for planning. *International Association of Applied Psychology Congress.* Edinburgh, Scotland: July 26.

O'Roark, A.M. (1986). Job stressors and psychological type: Can managers' stressors be anticipated? *International Council of Psychologists Conference.* Tel Aviv, Israel: July 12.

O'Roark, A.M. (1986). Bass-Valenzi decision modes and Myers-Briggs dominant functions: Management perspectives and preferences. *International Congress of Applied Psychology.* Jerusalem, Israel: July 13.

O'Roark, A.M. (1987). *Effects of MBTI Preferences on Managerial Leadership Practices*. Resources from CAPT. Gainesville, FL: Center for Applications of Psychological Type.

O'Roark, A.M. (1987). Executive distinction, managerial attrition and personality. *International Council of Psychologists*, Aug. 25.

O'Roark, A.M. (1987). Executive distinction, managerial turnover, and personality characteristics. *International Council of Psychologists Conference*. New York: August 25.

O'Roark, A.M. (1987). Stress, strain and coping: Responses from female I/O psychologists and health care managers. *International Council of Psychologists Conference*. New York: August 25.

O'Roark, A.M. (1988). The SPIRIT measures: A microbattery assessment for managers and executives. *Society for Personality Assessment Midwinter Meeting*. New Orleans, LA: March 11.

O'Roark, A.M. (1988). Research perspectives on methods of promoting individual well-being in the workplace: Toward a self-management/individual assessment intervention. *International Council of Psychologists Conference*. Singapore: August 23.

O'Roark, A.M. (1988). Using personality assessment as a development intervention with managerial populations. 24th Congress of the International Union of Psychology. Sydney, Australia: August 28. In B.J. Fallon, H.P. Pfister & J. Brebner (Eds.), *Advances in Industrial Organizational Psychology*.

O'Roark, A.M. (1988). Using personality assessment as a development intervention with managerial populations. 24th Congress of the International Union of Psychology. Sydney, Australia: August 28. In B.J. Fallon, H.P. Pfister & J. Brebner, (Eds.), *Advances in Industrial Organizational Psychology*, pp. 355-365.

O'Roark, A.M. (1989). Using assessment in leadership development. The sunny side of the street: Assessing strengths and positive dynamics. Organizer, Chair & Presenter. *Society for Personality Assessment Anniversary Meeting*. New York: April 15.

O'Roark, A.M. (1989). Workstress in het management: Effectief leiderschap en de preventre van burnout. In H.M. van der Ploeg & J. Vis (Eds.), *Burnout en Werkstress*. Amsterdam/Lisse: Swets & Zeitlinger, 66-86. [English translation: Job stress in management: Executive effectiveness and prevention of burnout.]

O'Roark, A.M. (1989). Organizational psychology: Preparation for organizational interventions. *47th International Council of Psychologists Convention*. Halifax, NS, Canada: June 5.

O'Roark, A.M. (1990). Is creativity forged from the heat of conflict? Conflict: A threat to peace and an invitation to creativity. Organizer and presenter. *22nd International Congress of Applied Psychology*, Kyoto, Japan: July 23.

O'Roark, A.M. (1990). Strength-stress paradox: Tragic Flaw Syndrome. On the sunny side: Assessment of personality strengths and positive dynamics. Organizer, chairperson and presenter. *Society for Personality Assessment Midwinter Meeting.* San Diego: March 24.

O'Roark, A.M. (1991). Organizational planning and systematic betterment: The case of the pilot planning project. *Consulting Psychology Bulletin,* 43, 2, 7-15, Summer.

O'Roark, A.M. (1991). Using feedback to evoke leadership potential: Self-management and role clarification. Sunny side III: Assessment data feedback, critical path and frequent gap. Organizer, chair and presenter. *Society for Personality Assessment Midwinter Meeting.* New Orleans, LA: March 8, 1991.

O'Roark, A.M. (1992). Assessing managers' social responsibility. Organizer, presenter and moderator. *Society for Psychologists in Management Conference.* Tampa, FL: February 22.

O'Roark, A.M. (1992). Leadership development and personality assessment as a goal setting intervention: Executive assessment, ortgeist and self-concept. Presenter and chair. *Regional Meeting of the International Council of Psychologists.* Padua, Italy: July 10.

O'Roark, A.M. (1992). Occupational stressors and burnout resistance: Comparison of judges, managers, and ministers. *Regional Meeting of the International Council of Psychologists.* Padua, Italy: July 9.

O'Roark, A.M. (1992). Personality, emotion, and occupational stressors. *International Council of Psychologists 50th Convention.* Amsterdam, The Netherlands: July 16.

O'Roark, A.M. (1992). Assessing hardy, creative professionals and leaders: curiosity with an edge. Transactualization as creativity: The will to power. *International Council of Psychologists 50th Convention.* Amsterdam, The Netherlands: July 17.

O'Roark, A.M. (1992). New issues in international organizational psychology. *International Council of Psychologists 50th Convention.* Amsterdam, The Netherlands: July 17.

O'Roark, A.M. (1992). Professional life change-points: stress and coping. Stresses, strains, and adaptive responses of female psychologists: cross-cultural perspectives. *International Union of Psychology 25th Congress.* Brussels: July 23.

O'Roark, A.M., Culbertson, F.M., Communian, A.L., Farence S., Fukuhara, M., Miao, E.F.O., Muhlbauer, V. & Thomas, A. (1992). Stresses, strains, and adaptive responses in professional women: Cross-cultural reports. In *Psychology in International Perspective.* Amsterdam: Swets and Zeitlinger.

O'Roark, A. M. (1993). Revisioning the future: Updating personality assessment norms for use in executive development programs. *International Council of Psychologists,* Annual Convention. Montreal, Canada: August 18.

O'Roark, A.M. (1994). Assessment of Traumatic Life Experience (TLE) reactions. *23rd Congress of the International Association of Applied Psychology*. Madrid, Spain: July 19.

O'Roark, A.M. (1994). Toward healthful worklife: Assessing critical factors in environment and personality. *23rd Congress of International Association of Applied Psychology*. Madrid, Spain: July 20.

O'Roark, A.M. (1995). Globalizing and benchmarking: The 360-degree trends of the 90's. *International Council of Psychologists, Annual Convention*. Taipei, Taiwan: August 4.

O'Roark, A.M. (1995). Creativity, personality, and job stress: Critical factors and interactive processes. *International Council of Psychologists Convention*. Taipei, Taiwan: August 6.

O'Roark, A.M. (1995). Organizational psychology: Models, trends, and readings. *The Psychological Association of the Philippines*. Manila, The Philippines: August 12.

O'Roark, A.M. (1995). Occupational stress and informed interventions. In Spielberger, Sarason, O'Roark, Greenglass, Laungani, & Brebner (Eds.), *Stress and Emotion, Volume 15*. Chapter 8, 122-136. Washington, DC: Taylor & Francis Publisher.

O'Roark, A.M. (1996). International consulting: Pathfinders and mapmakers. *The International Council of Psychologists Convention*. Banff, Alberta, Canada: July 26.

O'Roark, A.M. (1996) Invitational leadership. Chair & presenter. *American Psychological Association, Annual Convention*. Toronto, Ontario, Canada: August 12.

O'Roark, A.M. (1996). Guest Ed. in C. D. Spielberger, I.G. Sarason, J. M. T. Brebner, E. Greenglass, P. Laungani, A. M. O'Roark (Eds.), *Stress and Emotion: Anxiety, Anger, and Curiosity. Volume 16*. Washington, DC: Taylor & Francis Publishers.

O'Roark, A.M. (1997). International consulting: Critical incidents. Organizer and discussant. *The International Council of Psychologists, Annual Convention, Graz, Austria*: July 16.

O'Roark, A.M. (1997). Looking for optimal stress. Workplace trauma and hassle. Organizer and presenter. *The International Council of Psychologists Convention*. Graz, Austria: July 15.

O'Roark, A.M. (1997). Leadership: The next generation. Organizer and presenter. *The International Council of Psychologists, Regional Conference*, Padua, Italy: July 22.

O'Roark, A.M. (1998). Understanding organizational stress: A function of individual SPIRIT and corporate conditions. *International Congress of Applied Psychology*. San Francisco, Aug. 14.

O'Roark, A.M. (1998). Looking for optimal stress. In R. Roth (Ed.), *Psychologists Facing the Challenge of a Global Culture with Human Rights and Mental Health*. Graz, Austria: Pabst Science Publishers.

O'Roark, A.M. (1999, in process). *Optimal Challenge: Job Stress Survey Applications*. Odessa, FL: Psychological Assessment Resources.

O'Roark, A.M. (1999, in process). Stress in the workplace: Assessing stress judiciously. In. C.D. Spielberger & I. B. Sarasion (Eds.), *Stress and Emotion, Vol. 17*. Washington, DC: Taylor & Francis Publisher.

O'Roark, D.L., Jr. (1994). The first annual Hugh J. Clausen leadership lecture: Transformational leadership. "Teaching the JAG elephant to dance." *Military Law Review,* Vol. 146, 224-227.

Osipow, S.J. & Spokane, A.R. (1981). *Occupational Stress Inventory Manual, Research Version*. Odessa, FL: Psychological Assessment Resources, Inc.

Parasuraman, S. & Alutto, J.A. (1984). Sources and outcomes of stress in organizational settings: Toward the development of a structural model. *Academy of Management Journal*, 27, 330-350.

Parsons, T. (1967). Evaluation and objectivity in social science: An interpretation of Max Weber's contributions. In T. Parsons (Ed.), *Sociological Theory and Modern Society*. New York: Free Press.

Pellegrin, K.L. & Spielberger, C.D. (1995). Interpersonal trust, distrust, and cynical hostility. Graduate study report. Tampa, FL: Center for Research in Behavioral Medicine and Health Psychology, University of South Florida.

Penderghast, T.F. (1993). Management and organization development. Decision making by type. *Bulletin of Psychological Type*. 16:4, 28.

Perrottet, C.M. (1996). Scenarios for the future. *Management Review,* January, pp. 43-46. New York: American Management Association.

Peters, T.J. & Waterman, Jr., R.H. (1982). *In Search of Excellence*. New York: Harper & Row Pub. Inc.

Petzinger, T., Jr. (Friday April 10, 1998). A well stocked library of business reading includes "Moby Dick." *Wall Street Journal,* B1.

Petzinger, T., Jr. (Friday April 24, 1998). A Banc One executive credits his success to mastering dyslexia. *Wall Street Journal*, B1.

Petzinger, T., Jr. (Friday February 20, 1998). David Isenberg sees smart business model in stupid network. *Wall Street Journal,* B1.

Petzinger, T., Jr. (Friday May 1, 1998). A city executive learns to adapt to his workers' style. *Wall Street Journal,* B1.

Petzinger, T., Jr. (Friday Oct. 17, 1997). Forget empowerment. This job requires constant brainpower. *Wall Street Journal,* B1.

Popcorn, F. (1992). *The Popcorn Report: Faith Popcorn on the Future of Your Company, Your World, Your Life*. New York: HarperCollins Publishers.

Powell, C.L. with Persico, J.E. (1995). *My American Journey*. New York: Random House.

Purkey, W.W. (1970). *Self-Concept and School Achievement*. Englewood Cliffs, NJ: Prentice-Hall.

Quinn, R.E. (1992). *Beyond Rational Management: Mastering the Paradoxes and Competing Demands of High Performance*. San Francisco: Jossey-Bass.

Quintanilla, C. (Tuesday June 23, 1998). So, who's dull? Maytag's top officer, expected to do little, surprises his board: Company man Hadley shows that disparaged No. 2s can rise to the occasion. A big bet on a fancy washer. *Wall Street Journal.* A1 & A8.

Rand, A. (1943). *The Fountainhead.* New York: Signet Books, New American Library of World Literature.

Rand, A. (1949). *Atlas Shrugged.* New York: Signet.

Rand, A. (1964). *The Virtue of Selfishness: A New Concept of Egoism.* New York: Signet Books, New American Library of World Literature.

Ransdell, E. (1996). The man who sees the future. Doug Engelbart built the mouse; he may alter computing again. *U.S. News & World Report,* May 20, pp. 47-48.

Reynolds, L. (1996). *The Trust Effect: Creating the High Trust High Performance Organization.* Milwaukee: Nicholas Brealey/Schwartz Business Books.

Rogers, C.R. (1969). *Freedom to Learn.* Columbus, OH: Merrill.

Rokeach, M. (1983, Form G 1988). *Rokeach Scale of Values.* Palo Alto, CA: Consulting Psychology Press.

Rokeach, M. (1971) Long range experimental modification of values, attitudes and behavior. *American Psychologist,* 71, 26, 453-459.

Rosenthal, R. & Jacobson, L. (1968). *Pygmalion in the Classroom.* New York: Holt, Rinehart & Winston.

Rothenberg, A. (1979). Creative contradictions. Some of the most remarkable creative achievements begin with the awareness of a tension between opposites. The tension is resolved by a conscious process. *Psychology Today,* June 1997, 55-62.

Rotter, J.B. (1967). A new scale for the measurement of interpersonal trust. *Journal of Personality,* 35, 651-665.

Ruben, J.V. (1988). Some wise and mistaken assumptions about conflict and negotiations. Presidential address: Society for the Psychological Study of Social Issues (SPSSI). Atlanta, GA: *American Psychological Association Annual Convention,* August 12.

Ryan, K.D. & Oestreich, D.K. (1991). *Driving Fear out of the Workplace.* San Francisco: Jossey-Bass.

Schein, E. (1985). *Organizational Culture and Leadership.* San Francisco: Jossey-Bass.

Schein, E.H. & Bennis, W.G. (1965). *Personal and Organizational Change Through Groupmethods.* New York: Wiley.

Schmidt, W.H. & Posner, B.Z. (1970). *Managerial Values in Perspective: An AMA Survey Report.* New York: AMA Membership Publications Division, AMACOM.

Schmidt, W. H. & Posner, B. Z. (1982). *Managerial Values and Expectations: The Silent Power in Personal and Organizational Life. An AMA Report.* New York: AMA Membership Publications Division, AMACOM.

Schrof, J.M. (Nov. 28, 1994). Brain power. Your mind shouldn't disintegrate as you get older. New research debunks many myths we believe about what happens as the brain matures. U.S. *News & World Report*, pp. 89-97.

Schuler, R.S. (1991). Foreword. In P.L. Parrewe (Ed.), *Handbook on Job Stress*. Corte Madera, CA: Select Press.

Schwartz, P. (1991). *The Art of the Long View. Planning for the Future in an Uncertain World.* New York: Doubleday Publishers.

Schwartzkopf, N.H. (1992). Schwartzkopf on leadership. *Inc.* January, p. 9.

Selye, H. (1956). *Stress of Life.* New York: McGraw-Hill.

Selye, H. (1974). *Stress Without Distress.* Philadelphia: Lippincott Publishers.

Senge, P. (1990). *The Fifth Discipline.* New York: Doubleday.

Seppa, N. (1996). Downsizing: A new form of abandonment. *The APA Monitor,* May 1996, pp. 1 & 38.

Shapiro, J.P. with Loeb, P., Pollack, K., Ito, T.M. & Cohen, G. (1996). America's gambling fever. A nation's favorite pastime comes under fire from those who fear it won't help communities and families in the long run. *U.S. News & World Report,* Jan. 15, 53-61.

Shartle, C.L. (1949). Leadership and executive performance. *Personnel,* 25, 370-380.

Shea, G.F. (1984). *Building Trust in the Workplace.* AMA Management Briefing. New York: AMA Membership Publications Division.

Shostrom, E. (1967). *Man, the Manipulator.* Nashville, TN: Abington Press.

Siwolop, S. (1996). Outsourcing: Savings are just the start. If the fit is right, contractors can goose profits—and creative freedom. But that's a big "if." *Business Week/Enterprise,* Staples with McGraw-Hill, May, pp. 24-25.

Skinner, B.F. (1948). *Walden Two.* New York: Macmillan.

Skinner, B.F. (1956). *Freedom and the Control of Men.* New York: Appleton.

Skinner, B.F. (1971). *Beyond Freedom and Dignity.* New York: Random House.

Smith, D. (1998). Invigorating change initiatives. *Management Review,* May, pp. 45-48. New York: American Management Association.

Smith, E. (1988). Fighting cancerous feelings. Warning: Scientists haven't determined that repressed emotions are hazardous to your health—yet. *Psychology Today,* May 1988, 22, 5, pp. 22-23.

Snyder, C.R., Harris, C., Anderson, J.R., Holleran, S.A., Irving, L.M., Sigmon, S.T., Yoshinobu, L., Gibb, J., Langelle, C. & Harney, P. (1991). The will and ways: Development and validation of an individual-differences measure of hope. *Journal of Personality and Social Psychology,* 60, 4, 570-585.

Snyder, C. R., Cheavens, J. & Sympson, S.C. (1997). Hope: An individual motive for social commerce. *Group Dynamics: Theory, Research and Practice.* 1, 2, 107-118.

Spence, J.T., Helmreich, R.L. & Pred, R.S. (1987). Impatience vs. achievement striving in the Type A pattern: Differential effect on student's health and academic achievement. *The Journal of Applied Psychology*, Vol. 72(4), 522-528.

Spielberger, C.D. (1978). Anxiety, curiosity, creativity. *PSI CHI Newsletter*, Spring, 4/2, pp. 1 & 3.

Spielberger, C.D. (1987). *Understanding Stress and Anxiety*. London: Harper & Row Ltd.

Spielberger, C.D. (1997). *Lifestyle Defense Mechanisms Inventory: Preliminary Test Manual*. Tampa, FL: USF Center for Research in Behavioral Medicine and Health Psychology.

Spielberger, C.D., Gonzalez, H.P., & Fletcher, T. (1979). Test anxiety reduction, learning strategies, and academic performance. In H. F. O'Neil, Jr. & C. D. Spielberger (Eds.), *Cognitive and Affective Learning Strategies*. New York: Academic Press. Chapter 5, pp. 111-131.

Spielberger, C.D., Peters, R.A. & Frain, F. (1981). Curiosity and anxiety. In H.G. Voss & H. Keller (Eds.), *Curiosity Research: Basic Concepts and Results*. Weinheim, Federal Republic of Germany: Beltz. pp. 197-225.

Spielberger, C.D. & London, P. (1982). Rage boomerangs. A key to preventing coronaries is emerging: Learning to handle anger and avoid seven deadly responses. *American Health*, 1, 52-56.

Spielberger, C.D. with Vagg, P. (1982). *Preliminary Manual for the State-Trait Personality Inventory*. Tampa, FL: The Center for Research in Behavioral Medicine and Health Psychology, University of South Florida.

Spielberger, C.D. & London, P. (1983). Job stress, hassles and medical risk. *American Health*, 2, 58-63.

Spielberger, C.D., Jacobs, G., Russell, S. & Crane, R.S. (1983). Assessment of anger: The state-trait anger scale. In J. N. Butcher & C.D. Spielberger (Eds.), *Advances in Personality Assessment. (Vol. 2.)*. Hillsdale, NJ: Lawrence Erlbaum Associates. pp. 159-187.

Spielberger, C.D., Johnson, E.H., Russell, S., Crane, R.S., Jacobs, G. & Worden, T. J. (1985). In M. S. Chesney, S. E. Goldston & R. H. Rosenman (Eds.), *Anger and Hostility in Cardiovascular and Behavioral Studies*. New York: Hemisphere/McGraw-Hill, pp. 5-29.

Spielberger, C.D. & London, P. (1990). Blood pressure and injustice: Learning to control angry reactions to unfairness can help cut the danger of high blood pressure. *Psychology Today*, Jan-Feb., pp. 48, 50, 52.

Spielberger, C.D. & Reheiser, E.C. (1994a). Job stress in university, corporate and military personnel. *International Journal of Stress Management*, 1, 1, pp. 19-30.

Spielberger, C.D. & Reheiser, E.C. (1994b). The Job Stress Survey: Measuring gender differences in occupational stress. *Journal of Social Behavior and Personality*, 9:2, 199-218.

Spielberger, C.D. & Vagg, P. (1998). *Professional Manual for the Job Stress Survey (JSS)*. Odessa, FL: Psychological Assessment Resources.

Spielberger, C.D. & Starr, L.M. (1994). Curiosity and exploratory behavior. In H. F. O'Neil, Jr., & M. J. Drillings (Eds.), *Motivation: Theory and Research*. Hillsdale, NJ: Lawrence Erlbaum Associates. Chapter 12, pp. 221-243.

Spielberger, C.D. & Sydeman, S.J. (1995). Chapter 13. State-Trait Anxiety Inventory and State-Trait Anger Expression Inventory. In M.E. Maruish (Ed.), *The Use of Psychological Tests for Treatment Planning and Outcome Assessment*. Hillsdale, NJ: LEA. pp. 292-321.

Spielberger, C.D., Crane, R.S., Kearns, W.D., Pellegrin, K.L. & Rickman, R. (1991). Anger and anxiety in essential hypertension. In C.D. Spielberger, I.G. Sarason, Z. Kulcsar, G. L. Van Heck (Eds.), *Stress and Emotion: Anxiety, Anger and Curiosity*, Vol. 14. Washington, DC: Taylor & Francis Publishers. Chapter 19, pp. 265-283.

Spielberger, C.D., Reheiser, E.C. & Sydeman, S.J. (1995). Measuring the experience, expression and control of anger. In H. Kassinove (Ed.), *Anger Disorders: Definitions, Diagnosis, and Treatment*. Washington, DC: Taylor & Francis. pp. 49-67.

Spielberger, C.D., Ritterband, L.M., Sydeman, S.J., Reheiser, E.C. & Unger, K.K. (1995). Assessment of emotional state and personality traits: Measuring psychological vital signs. In J. N. Butcher (Ed.), *Clinical Personality Assessment: Practical Approaches*. New York: Oxford University Press. Pp. 42-58.

Spielberger, C.D. & Ritterband, L.M. (1997). *Construct Validity of the Beck Inventory as a Measure of State and Trait Depression in Non-clinical Populations*. Tampa, FL: USF Center for Research in Behavioral Medicine and Health Psychology

St. Petersburg Times. (Sunday Dec. 18, 1994). Health and Medicine. Almond-sized part of brain may control fear. 12A. NYTimes©

Stern, W. (1916). *The Psychological Method of Testing Intelligence*. Baltimore: Warwick & York.

Stetz, F.P. (1998). What Barnum [P.T.] can teach executives. *Leadership, A Member Newsletter of the American Management Association International*, pp. 4, 6, 8.

Stevens, T. (1994). Interview with W. Edwards Deming: Management today does not know what its job is, *Industry Week*, January 15, pp. 21-22, 24-25.

Stogdill, R.M. (1950). Leadership, membership, and organizations. *Psychol. Bull.*, 47, 1-14.

Stone, W.C. (1985). Guaranteed success. *Success*, 32, 4, p. 80.

Tam, P. & O'Brien, B. (Monday March 1, 1999). The luster of superstar manager fades. Funds find that low profile is quite preferable, thank you. *Wall Street Journal*, R1.

Tanouye, E. (Friday June 28, 1996). Heredity theory is 'like mother, like son'. *Wall Street Journal*, B1.

Tavris, C. (1982). *Anger: The Misunderstood Emotion.* New York: Simon & Schuster, Inc.

Taylor, F.W. (1911). *Scientific Management.* New York: Harper Brothers.

Thorndike, E.L. (1939). How may we improve the selection, training, and life work of leaders? *Teachers College Record,* 40, 593-605.

Thorndike, E.L. (1916). Education for initiative and originality. *Teachers College Record,* 17, 405-416.

Thornton, G.C. & Cleveland, J.N. (1990). Developing managerial talent through simulation. *American Psychologist,* 45, 2, pp. 190-199.

Time Magazine. (September 10, 1979). Science. To catch a fleeting gluon: Einstein's old dream of unity may yet come true.

Time Magazine. (August 6, 1979). Leadership in America: 50 faces for the future. New York: Time, Inc.

Time Magazine. (June 17, 1996). Special report: America's 25 most influential people. New York: Time, Inc.

Time Magazine. (March 9, 1998). 75th anniversary issue. New York: Time, Inc.

Time Magazine. (April 13,1998). Leaders & revolutionaries. New York: Time, Inc.

Time Magazine. (June 8, 1998). 100: Artists and entertainers of the century. New York: Time, Inc.

Time Magazine. (December 7,1998). 100: Builders & titans. New York: Time, Inc.

Tobin, D.R. (1998). Networking your knowledge. It's all in the knowing—and getting. A knowledge network allows your employees to access the company's collective information. *Management Review,* pp. 46-48.

Toufexis, A.W., Mattos, J. & Silver, E. (Jan. 15, 1996). What makes them do it? People who crave thrills, new evidence indicates, may be prompted at least partly by their genes. *Time,* p. 60.

Trigaux, R. (Sunday June 21, 1998). Innocence lost with chainsaw Al's fall. Charles Elson thinks owning stock makes you a better director. When he and other directors fired Sunbeam's CEO, they unhappily proved his point. *Wall Street Journal.* H1 & H2.

Tubb, W. (1975). Beyond Maslow. Saranac Lake, NY: *Lands End Newsletter,* Summer.

Turnage, J.J. & Spielberger, C.D. (1991). Job stress in managers, professionals, and clerical workers. *Work & Stress,* 5, 165-176.

Vlamis, A. (1999). *Smart Leadership: AMA Management Briefing.* New York: American Management Association, Int'l.

Vroom, V.H. & Jago, A.G. (1974). Decision making as a social process: Normative and descriptive models of leader behavior. *Decision Science,* 5, 743-769.

Vroom, V.H. & Jago, A.G. (1988). *The New Leadership: Managing Participation in Organizations.* Englewood Cliffs, NJ: Prentice Hall.

Vroom, V. H. (1974). Decision making and the leadership process. *J. Contemp. Bus.,* 3, 47- 64.3, 47- 64.

Wah, L. (1998). The alphabet soup of job titles. *Management Review,* June, pp. 40-43. New York: American Management Association.

Wah, L. (1999). Making knowledge stick. *Management Review,* May, pp. 24-29. New York: American Management Association.

Weathersby, G.W. (1998). Leadership at every level. *Management Review,* June, p. 5.

Websters New World Dictionary of the American Language. Second College Edition. Ed. D. B. Guralnik. New York: World Pub. Co.

Wheatley, M.J. (1992). *Leadership and the New Science. Learning about Organization from an Orderly Universe.* San Francisco: Berrett-Koehler Publishers.

White, J.B. (1996). 'Next big thing' Re-Engineering gurus take steps to remodel their stalling vehicles: Michael Hammer and others broaden their offerings, push growth strategies—two days for people issues. *Wall Street Journal,* A1 & A13.

White, L.A. (1949). *The Science of Culture: A Study of Man and Civilization.* New York: Farrar, Straus and Co.

Williams, R. & Williams, V. (1993). *Anger Kills.* New York: First Harper Perennial Publication.

Wilson, E.O. (1998). *Consilience: The Unity of Knowledge.* New York: Alfred A. Knopf.

Wozniak, L. (1996). Planning for bad news is important. Consultants say companies must be prepared for the deaths of their leaders. Ron Brown plane crash. Jet crash is worst corporate loss ever. *St. Petersburg Times,* April 4, 1996, 9A.

Wright, R. (1995). The evolution of despair. A new field of science examines the mismatch between our genetic makeup and the modern world, looking for the source of our pervasive sense of discontent. We are designed to seek trusting relationships. *Time,* August 28, 1995, pp. 50-57.

Wysocki, B., Jr. (Monday Sept. 8, 1997). The outlook. Retaining employees turns into a hot topic. *Wall Street Journal,* A1.

Wysocki, B., Jr. (Thursday April 30, 1998). Pulling the plug. Some firms, let down by costly computers, opt to 'de-engineer.' With it's software clashing, Chrysler chucks next and rediscovers phones. *Wall Street Journal,* B1.

Wysocki, B., Jr. (Tuesday Nov. 9, 1999). Defining the challenge. Corporate American confronts the meaning of a 'core' business. Is it a product, or a process, or even a role? Investors are forcing the question. *Wall Street Journal,* A1 & 12.

Zoglin, R. (May 27, 1996). A question of honor. The Navy's top admiral takes his own life rather than face queries about his right to a coveted award. For a "sailor's sailor," it seemed the only way out. *Time Magazine,* p. 30-32.

Zucker, L.G. (1986). Production of trust: Institutional sources of economic structure. 1840-1920. In B.M. Straw & L.L. Cummings (Eds.), *Research in Organizational Behavior.* Vol. 8: 53-111.

Zuckerman, M. (1979). *Sensation Seeking: Beyond the Optimal Level of Arousal.* NJ: Laurence Erlbaum & Assoc.

Zygmont, J. (1933). In command at Campbell. An impressive turnaround and a view towards unprecedented global expansion for the food giant, under the vigorous direction of CEO David W. Johnson. *Sky,* March 1993, pp. 52-61.

Leadership

US Psychologists and the Foundations of Leadership Knowledge

Peter Drucker
Leadership expert-opinion
Multi-disciplinary scholar
Multi-national training & background

USA PSYCHOLOGISTS Develop
Vision-Motivation-Action Thinking

FREDERICK TAYLOR   1911
    Structuralism—similar to Watson's BEHAVIORISM
        GOAL: WORK PRODUCTIVITY

HAWTHORNE STUDIES   1933
      ARGUED THAT PRODUCTIVITY INCREASED
      WITH ATTENTION TO WORKERS

LEWIN, LIPPITT, WHITE   1938
      Leadership in ONE DIMENSION:
    DEMOCRATIC STYLE VS AUTOCRATIC STYLE

OHIO STATE STUDIES   1945
      Leadership with TWO DIMENSIONS
      STRUCTURE & CONSIDERATION

FRED FIEDLER   Contingency Theory   1960s
      Effects of Personality and Situation
    Three Dimensional: Leader's Self in the situation

339

HERSEY & BLANCHARD   1960s & 70s
                    SITUATIONAL LEADERSHIP training
           Three Dimensional: Added Workers' ability & willingness

VROOM & YETTON   Rational-Cognitive theory   1970s
            Decision Making options: As determined by
               required commitment or compliance
         Range: Consensus to Participative to Solo Action

DOUG BRAY   1970s-1980s
                      Assessment Centers
             Behavioral Observations and ratings

Eduard Deming   1980s
              TOTAL QUALITY MANAGEMENT
       Statistical Control; Team / Worker Responsibility
         Continuous Improvement <<<< Re-engineering

BERNARD M. BASS   1990s
            Transformational-Charismatic Leadership
            vs Transactional Rewards Management

SYNTHESIS AND EXTENSION OF CURRENT MODELS

CHARISMATIC ┌─────────▶ INSPIRATIONAL, EDUCATIONAL, AND
            └─────────▶ AN EMPOWERING ROLE MODEL

PARTICIPATORY ┌──────▶ INVOLVING OTHERS AS MUCH AS POSSIBLE
              └─────▶ IN ORDER TO TURN THE VISION INSIDE-OUT

THE DEVELOPMENT OF LEADERS WITH
INVITATIONAL POWER

1. *Entrepreneurial* **VISION.**   **WHAT'S IMPORTANT?**
                                          Self, Others, Task
2. *Charismatic* **MOTIVATION.**   **Dealing with SURPRISE &**
                                          CHANGE: Vital Emotions
                                          Curiosity, Anxiety and Anger
3. *Participatory ACTION.*   **Goals, plans, resources**

CHARISMATIC- PARTICIPATORY LEADERSHIP
Turning Vision Inside Out

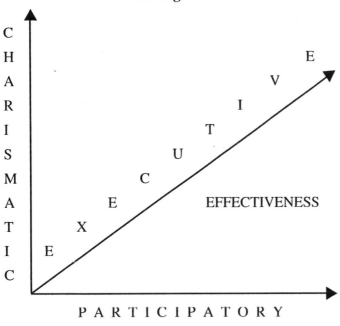

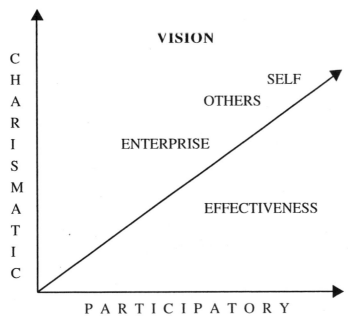

CHARISMATIC- PARTICIPATORY LEADERSHIP
Turning Vision Inside Out

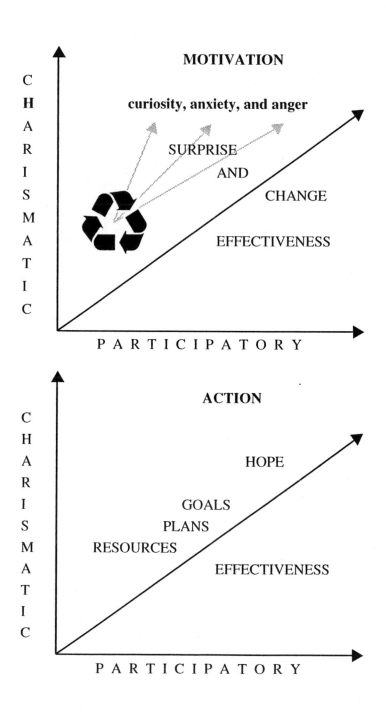

Index

343

Dedication

With love and appreciation for my grandsons and their potentials
And hope that words written here encourage readers to stretch for
Visions and possibilities that will lead to long lives rich in fulfillment.

Joshua Ryan Land, December 19, 1985

Lazarus Lauren Land, International Baccalaureate Candidate
June 6, 1983 – April 4, 1997

Ann M. O'Roark is a consulting psychologist who works with individuals and organizations interested in management and leadership development. Dr. O'Roark serves as on-call instructional faculty for the American Management Association's Executive Effectiveness Course and for the Center for Creative Leadership's Leadership Development Program. She is past President of the American Psychological Association's Division of Consulting Psychology and recently completed terms as Secretary of the International Council of Psychologists and as Consulting Psychology's Treasurer. Dr. O'Roark served on the Board of the Society for Psychologists in Management and the International Association of Applied Psychology Division of Psychological Assessment. She is a Fellow in the American Psychological Association and the Society for Personality Assessment, and a Diplomate of the American Board of Assessment Psychology. Dr. O'Roark serves as Regional Editor, USA and Canada, for *World Psychology* and on the editorial review board for the *Journal of Consulting Psychology.*

Dr. O'Roark received her Ph.D. from the University of Florida, 1974, an M.Ed. from the University of Florida in 1972, and her bachelor's degree from the University of Kentucky, 1955. She became a licensed psychologist in 1975, Kentucky Board of Examiners. She completed post-doctoral work in behavioral neurobiology at UF (1983) and independent studies at the C.G. Jung Institute in Zurich in 1992. Prior to becoming a private practice consultant, she was Deputy Secretary of the Education and the Arts Cabinet and Assistant State Treasurer in Kentucky. For five years, in addition to maintaining her private practice, Dr. O'Roark served in a part-time Administrative Officer position for the Society for Personalty Assessment. Clients include financial institutions, medical centers, state and federal agencies as well as enterprises and industrial firms. Before shifting from journalism, undertaking teaching and studies in Princeton, New Jersey, Dr. O'Roark was one of the first two women hired to work in the news office of the *Washington Post,* Washington, DC, 1955.